CONTEMPORARY SOCIETY: TRIBAL STUDIES

VOLUME SEVEN

IDENTITY, INTERVENTION AND IDEOLOGY IN TRIBAL INDIA AND BEYOND

CONTEMPORARY SOCIETY: TRIBAL STUDIES

Edited by

DEEPAK KUMAR BEHERA
and
GEORG PFEFFER

VOLUME ONE	—	STRUCTURE AND PROCESS
VOLUME TWO	—	DEVELOPMENTAL ISSUES, TRANSITION AND CHANGE
VOLUME THREE	—	SOCIAL CONCERN
VOLUME FOUR	—	SOCIAL REALITIES
VOLUME FIVE	—	THE CONCEPT OF TRIBAL SOCIETY
VOLUME SIX	—	TRIBAL SITUATION IN INDIA
VOLUME SEVEN	—	IDENTITY, INTERVENTION AND IDEOLOGY IN TRIBAL INDIA AND BEYOND

The Editors

Deepak Kumar Behera is Professor and Head of the Department of Anthropology, Sambalpur University, Sambalpur, Orissa (India).

Georg Pfeffer is Professor and Head of the Institute of Ethnology, Free University of Berlin (Germany).

CONTEMPORARY SOCIETY: TRIBAL STUDIES

VOLUME SEVEN

IDENTITY, INTERVENTION AND IDEOLOGY IN TRIBAL INDIA AND BEYOND

Edited by

DEEPAK KUMAR BEHERA
Department of Anthropology
Sambalpur University
Sambalpur-768 019
Orissa
India

GEORG PFEFFER
Freie Universität, Berlin
Institut für Ethnologie
Drosselweg 1-3
D-14195 Berlin
Germany

CONCEPT PUBLISHING COMPANY, NEW DELHI-110 059

Cataloging in Publication Data—DK
Courtesy: D.K. Agencies (P) Ltd. <docinfo@dkagencies.com>

Contemporary society : tribal studies / edited by Deepak Kumar Behera, Georg Pfeffer.
v. 7 cm.
Contributed articles.
Includes bibliographical references.
Includes index.
Contents: v. 7. Identity, intervention and ideology in tribal India and beyond.
ISBN 13: 9788170226406 (set)
ISBN 10: 8170226406 (set)
ISBN 13 9788180695346 (v. 7)
ISBN 10: 8180695344 (v. 7)

1. Tribes—India. 2. India—Scheduled tribes. 3. Ethnology—India. 4. India—Social conditions. I. Behera, Deepak Kumar, 1956-- II. Pfeffer, Georg, 1943-

DDC 307.772 095 4 21

Associate Editor
Dr. Nibedita Nath
Dr. Rashmi Pramanik

ISBN-13: 978-81-7022-640-6 (Series)
ISBN-10: 81-7022-640-6 (Series)
ISBN-13: 978-81-8069- 534-6 (Vol. VII)
ISBN-10: 81-8069- 534-4 (Vol. VII)

First Published 2008

Published and Printed by
Ashok Kumar Mittal
Concept Publishing Company
A/15-16, Commercial Block, Mohan Garden
New Delhi-110059 (India)

Phone: 25351460, 25351794
Fax: 091–(11)–25357103
E-mail: publishing@conceptpub.com

ACKNOWLEDGEMENTS

We are grateful to all the contributors for their academic generosity which has enabled us to complete this work successfully. The volume consists of some of the selected papers of the international conference "Tribal Societies in India and Beyond," organized jointly by the Department of Anthropology, Sambalpur University and Institute for Ethnology, Free University of Berlin at Jyoti-Vihar during December 17—19, 2004. The conference was organized as part of the Memorandum of Understanding signed by the two institutes for a long-term academic co-operation. We are grateful to German Research Council, Indian Council of Social Science Research, Anthropological Survey of India, Kolkata and Concept Publishing Company, New Delhi for providing us necessary support for the successful organization of the conference. The conference was attended by twenty Indian and equal number of overseas participants from twelve different countries. As organizers of the aforesaid conference, we take this opportunity to extend our heart-felt thanks to all those who presented their papers and finally contributed the revised version of the same to this volume. We thank all others who helped us directly or indirectly for bringing the volume to its present shape. We are also thankful to Concept Publishing Company, New Delhi for publishing this volume.

DEEPAK KUMAR BEHERA
GEORG PFEFFER

CONTENTS

SECTION III
DISPLACEMENT AND REHABILITATION

SECTION IV
ECOLOGICAL, ECONOMIC AND SOCIAL VALUES

SECTION V
RITUALS IN TRIBAL INDIA

SECTION I

TRIBAL IDENTITY

ONE

INTRODUCTION

DEEPAK KUMAR BEHERA and GEORG PFEFFER

1

The Background

Ever since Morton H. Fried (1975) denied "the existence" of tribes the concept of "tribal society" has gradually disappeared from the literature of socio-cultural anthropology. On the other hand, in India and other large countries with important minorities of "indigenous" peoples, the concept of "tribe" and "tribal society" is, under one name or the other, an administrative category of the state, even though Indian anthropologists usually fail to differentiate the bureaucratic usage and the anthropological category "tribe" as developed by Marshall Sahlins (1968). Innumerable Indian books may have been published on the "backwardness" or the "exploitation" of tribal people, but very few analyze tribal social structure as a result of long-term ethnographic fieldwork. As a result, theories on *tribal* India, in glaring contrast to theories on *caste* India, have, over the past 60 years, hardly been developed, even though some 68 million Indians are counted as members of the *Scheduled Tribes* in the Census of 2001 and perhaps many more could be associated with "tribal society" in anthropological terms. The vivid contemporary tribal value-ideas and institutions are hardly known or discussed beyond India.

In this volume an attempt has been made to present the most recent findings on tribal social structure as a result of long-term anthropological fieldwork. Special emphasis is given to the differences *within* the various tribal formations. A total number of 24 articles have been presented under five different sections, viz. (1) Tribal Identity, (2) State Intervention, (3) Displacement and Rehabilitation, (4) Ecological, Economic and Social Value, and (5) Ritual in Tribal India. The volume covering the contributions of 31 social scientists primarily discusses issues relating to tribal identity, state intervention and tribal ideology.

Tribal Identity

Identity, based on ethnicity, raises some points to ponder. First, identity has two dimensions, one connotes an outsider's perception of the tribal image and the other is a case of the self-image. The tribals create, and negotiate their social and linguistic identities in the face of emergent and continuous socio-economic differentiation and transformation.

Indigenousness, it needs to be said, is an attribute of personal and collective identity that emerges only when it is experienced. It is also a self-reflexive notion, which means that people have looked at themselves from the outside, identified the problems that face them, and understand why an assertion of their identity is a prerequisite for their survival. Invariably, therefore, indigenousness is an assertion by people directed against the power of outsiders, focusing primarily on the nation-state.

Ethnic self-affirmation is always related in one way or another to the defence of social or economic interests. In other words, people are willing to assert an ethnic identity only if they can gain by doing so. This is a common social phenomenon - for frequently those who have lost their culture, often become its most strident apostles. They now "identify" with their group, and may even do so in a highly vocal and exaggerated form.

Named *adivasis,* or aboriginals, or tribal - this group of people is facing tremendous pressure to *voluntarily* eject themselves to the realm of an anonymous nowhere. Besides, their history is in their resources hidden beneath their habitat. There are other distinguishing features that characterize the *adivasi* identity. However, for the moment, we identify them with the marked trait of high technological competence at the personal but not at the supra-individual level, the use of a *systematic* technology for the accumulation of surplus capital being the marked characteristic of the dominant economy. This restriction to individual technological competence - in marked contrast to the tribal socio-religious holism - has had to face an expansionist peasant and industrial economy responsible for the progressive marginalization of the tribes and their large-scale dispossession of the sources of livelihood. It has also made them experience a cultural shock and reduced their respective collective identity. But, wherever it occurred, this very threat to identity and livelihood has fed into their consciousness an awareness that identity assertion is an important tool of empowerment articulation (Ramagundam, 2002).

The colonial construction gave rise to an ethnocentric and isolated concept of tribe does not hold good today, given the impact of modernization as a consequence of globalization. Numerous tribals, confronted with the forces of change, are now experiencing conditions of transition. State-sponsored development programmes, the socio-economic influence of neighbouring caste-Hindu communities, and the ideological ambitions of Christian and Hindu organizations have led to issues of identity and ethnicity tribal consciousness. Contact and conflict have introduced dynamism in tribal society, a confrontation with strikingly new issues.

Given this external impact, traditional markers of identity are nonetheless conceived and retained in the tribal world. Just as Hindu or Muslim hairstyle, dress, and facial makeup of religious signification have, to a large degree, not given way to a universalist outfit, tribal people recognize one another, and can be identified by outsiders, on account of their specific dress and bodily markers. The Kuttia Kond, for example, cut the textiles - distributed by prudish government agencies - to the shape of their traditional dress, and each one of the many Chota Nagpur tribes is - for all who are able to read this "language" - easily identifiable by a small tattoo on forehead or arm. Similarly, insiders and those who take a serious view of the tribal world can distinguish the layout of a Kond village from that of a Gadaba settlement at a glance, or the shrines of the Sora from those of the Jhoria, even though similar rock material may have been used. Of all the ways that a culture distinguishes itself - through architecture, religion, ceremonies - ritual decoration is the most fascinating of all and the greatest exponent of ethnic identity. At first sight, each ethnic group displays its unique appearance. For all of their differences, they are ethnic markers to convey beauty, wealth, status, bravery as well as a general and visible or concrete and lasting exposition of the uniqueness of the given tribal constitution. The more neighbouring tribes are alike, the more they seem to stress distinctive signifiers and develop specific histories or variant rituals over time. Each one of the tribes - including the attached unit of craftsmen and petty traders of lower status - attaches the status of "humanity" to the own group and conceives mythical ancestors, often segmented according to clan, who were born by mother Earth or as celestial beings. Consequently, the descendents associated with the - endogamous - tribes of a region or the - exogamous - clans of a tribe, are well aware of their multiple status differences, recalled at every internal or inter-tribal ritual.

Who is a tribal and what constitutes tribal identity? Since the old techniques of shifting cultivation, practiced through millennia without any damage to the forests - have now mostly been abandoned, in a comparison to Hindu peasants, little difference is being noticed. Tribal languages are systematically disregarded by educational agencies and thus likely to vanish soon, but tribal religion has survived and is likely to remain for some time. In the latter context the emphasis on the integration of tribal culture with elements of nature - sky, earth, water and trees - is fascinating. In fact, a tribal person - just like a Hindu - regards each one of them as enlivened and bestowed with consciousness, but each form of tribal "animism" observes its own "grammar" or systematic patterning in accordance with the annual calendar and the life-crisis rituals when the time comes to communicate in this sacred context by the means, applied throughout the world of religion, i.e. specific songs and dances, narratives and rituals. The primordial or pristine vision of the world is recalled so that basic ethical ideas can be enhanced as constitutional framework. There are no written texts, no records and no documents, yet, knowledge is most precisely preserved and perpetuated. Many hours of verbal texts and multiple forms of expression that enfold the spoken words, visual images, and aural genres transmit the spirit of the whole. More importantly, all knowledge is experiential and enmeshed with the fabric of life as its warp and woof. Tribal cultures are rich repositories of mythical and historical past and yet provide significant and powerful models for contemporary social order, the core of tribal heritage.

Such a powerful heritage of social values has far-reaching implications in the context of planning the future of tribal cultures. Each contributor of the conference agreed that somewhere along the line, the tribal voices had not been heard. The issue of empowerment of the tribal, sharing discourses and domains were discussed at length. Tribal identity is not to be conceived as a unitary issue, though governmental agencies seem to assume a collective "other" to be developed. In fact, numerous cultural differences within this large minority are to be observed, the most obvious being the gatherer-hunter economy of some who have - voluntarily or not - taken to cultivation only very recently. However, their ritual activities and their socio-structural differentiation remain of the simple gatherer type, as observed and described in many other regions of the world.

Apart from the use of strictly administrative criteria, the problem of determining which groups and individuals are tribal is both subtle and complex. Because, it concerns economic interests and voting blocs, the question of who are members of *Scheduled Tribes* rather than *Other Backward Classes* or *Scheduled Castes* is often controversial.

Any of these criteria may not apply in specific instances. Language does not always give an accurate indicator of tribal or caste status. Especially in regions of mixed population, many tribal groups have lost their mother tongues and simply speak local or regional languages. Several regional segments of the great Gond tribe, for example, have "lost" their language and taken to Hindi, Bengali or Oriya, even though most Gond, i.e. several million people, still frequent the Gondi language. Self-identification and group loyalty do not provide unfailing markers of tribal identity either. In the case of stratified tribes, the loyalties of region, locality, phratry, clan, kin, and family may well predominate over those of the tribe, the least delimited unit in this context. In addition, tribes cannot always be viewed as people living apart; the degree of isolation of various tribes has varied tremendously. Gond, Santal, and Bhil have traditionally dominated the regions in which they lived, communicating closely with Baiga, Sora Paharia, or Kohli in their immediate neighbourhood. Moreover, tribal society is ideologically not more egalitarian than the rest of the rural populace; some of the larger tribes, such as the Gonds, being highly stratified, just as smaller units like the Gadaba, in spite of undifferentiated economic conditions, are keen to retain major status differences within each village. The apparently wide fluctuation in estimates of South Asia's tribal population through the twentieth century gives a sense of how unclear the distinction between tribals and non-tribals can be. India's 1931 census enumerated 22 million tribal people, in 1941 only 10 million were counted, but by 1961 some 30 million and in 1991 nearly 68 million tribal members were included. The differences among the figures reflect the changing census criteria and the economic incentives individuals have to maintain or reject classification as a tribal member.

These gyrations of census data serve to underline the complex relationship between caste and tribe. Although, in theory, these terms represent different ways of life and ideal types, in reality they stand for a structural continuum of society. In areas of substantial contact between tribes and castes, social and cultural pressures have often tended to move tribes in the direction of becoming castes over a period of years. Tribal peoples with ambitions for socio-political participation in Indian society at large have tried to gain the classification of *caste* for their units. Thus on occasion, an entire tribe or part of a tribe joined a Hindu sect and thus entered the caste system *en masse*.

State Intervention

Whichever word we may use, we can note certain common features to describe the tribal people. In most parts of India we can find the tribal people living closest to nature, in the hills and forests and remote interiors, away from the so-called high road of socio-economic development. Viewed from the other end, it means the penetration of the capitalist market economy is still quite limited in tribal societies, just as the bureaucracy appears in the shape of external agents, not as insiders. The familiar slogan of "bringing the tribal people into the mainstream of the country" describes the yet incomplete effort to control them by agencies of the state and the forces of the market, as utilized by the monopolists of the country.

Tribal methods of cultivation are considered "backward" because they do not yield surpluses for the market but rather represent an ecologically well adapted guaranty of survival, coupled with activities like collecting and processing forest produce, food-gathering and hunting. If, as has been observed frequently, tribal bands of workmen are cheated out of their wages, the penniless are still able to survive in their forest environment, because of their specialist knowledge of wild herbs and other eatables. What outsiders frequently view as a life of acute poverty and destitution for large sections of the tribal people may in fact amount to a simple disregard for the mode of dressing and eating, as practiced by urban observers, though a healthy diet of millet and a functionally applied loin cloth are most adequate for the climatic and work conditions. Accordingly, the myth of economic backwardness is accompanied with the myth of social destitution and the myth of a low quality of life. Wherever the tribal people have been left to themselves, their economy, their society and their recreational activities limited by the forces of nature only. Backwardness is the result rather than the cause of external interventions.

The process of class differentiation remains rather retarded in most tribal communities even though the system of reservation in education, employment and elections has given rise to some privileged sections. Many tribal representatives are furthermore constantly being co-opted by the ruling classes and their parties. Along with this emergence of a tribal petty bourgeoisie, some sections of tribal people have also found employment in modern industry and mining, while others have been deliberately excluded from the working force in industrial plants.

The pattern of inter-tribal diversity of large units (comprising, at times, millions of members) as well as local cultural cohesion has not changed much in the last decades. At the same time, eviction from the home territory continues though there is no "compensatory" employment to look for. The environment remains a major talking point in the new phase and once again, it is the tribal people who have to bear the brunt of environmental preservation and protection as though they, rather than the expanding industries or the timber trade, have been the cause of the environmental damages. The new forest laws and the government see tribals - living in their native regions - as "encroachers" who have to be evicted as soon as possible.

After independence, in its first phase, the policy of reservation had provided some employment opportunities to the tribal people. Now with the new policy of downsizing and privatization, jobs have started vanishing and reservation is fast becoming an empty phrase. The undermining of economic plans and the deliberate retreat of the state from the economy with an abdication of its social responsibilities - the social sector is being leased out to the network of NGOs - has left the tribal people at the mercy of the market and the giant corporations who are eyeing every natural resource within the tribal territory.

Under the pretext of preserving the natural forests, the Government of India is evicting tribal communities from their lands. These evictions cause loss of property and life, unemployment and utter poverty. They are coupled with police abuses, including torture and killing. The use of force against these groups has rapidly increased in recent years, as the International Decade of the World's Indigenous People draws to a close.

They have been steadily evicted from their lands by wealthy farmers and businessmen and forced into slavery and bonded labour. The illegal takeover of forest land by timber dealers has been regularized, and on several occasions encroachers have been issued purchase certificates for thousands of hectares.

It may be noted that different state-backed institutions seek to take control over vast natural resources including rich forests, and to seize and alienate the rights of thousands of tribal and other forest dwellers living in the mountains. It has led to the displacement of numerous tribal cultivators, alienation of their traditional rights of use and collection of forest produce, and the rights over their traditional, non-titled forest lands being used for cultivation.

Government policies on forest reserves have affected tribal peoples profoundly. Wherever the state has chosen to exploit forests, it has seriously undermined the tribes' way of life. Government efforts to reserve forests have precipitated armed (if futile) resistance on the part of the tribal peoples involved. Intensive exploitation of forests has often meant allowing outsiders to cut large areas of trees (while the original tribal inhabitants were restricted from cutting), and ultimately replacing mixed forests capable of sustaining tribal life with single-product plantations. Where forests are reserved, non-tribals have proved far more sophisticated than their forest counterparts at bribing the necessary local officials to secure effective use of forestlands. The system of bribing local officials charged with enforcing the reserves is so well-established that the rates of bribery are reasonably fixed (by the number of ploughs a farmer uses or the amount of grain harvested). Tribal people often end up doing unpaid work for non-tribals simply because a non-tribal, who has paid the requisite bribe, can at least ensure a tribal member that she/he will not be evicted from forestlands.

Most Indian tribes are concentrated in heavily forested areas that combine inaccessibility with formerly limited political or economic significance. Historically, the economy of most tribes was subsistence agriculture added by gathering and hunting. Lower status specialists in the tribal community traded with outsiders for the few necessities they lacked, such as salt and iron and operated as blacksmiths and weavers. The twentieth century, however, has seen far-reaching changes in the relationship between tribal in India and the larger society and, by extension, traditional tribal economies. Improved transportation and communications have brought ever deeper intrusions into tribal lands; merchants and a variety of government policies have involved tribal peoples more thoroughly in the cash economy, although by no means on the most favourable of terms. Large areas fell into the hands of non-tribals around 1900, when many regions were opened by the government to homestead-style settlement. Immigrants received free land in return for cultivating it. Tribal people, too, could apply for land titles, although even a title to the portion of land they happened to be planting that season could not guarantee their ability to continue shifting cultivation.

More important, the notion of permanent, individual ownership of land was foreign to most tribal communities. Land, if seen in terms of ownership at all, was viewed as a communal resource, controlled by the community that had cleared it and then probably given to relatives who needed it. By the time tribals accepted the necessity of obtaining formal land titles, they had lost the opportunity to lay claim to lands that might rightfully have been considered theirs. Generally, tribals were severely disadvantaged in dealing with government officials who granted land titles. The colonial regime, at times, realized the necessity of protecting the tribals of India from the predations of outsiders and prohibited the sale of tribal lands when of little mineral wealth. Although an important loophole in the form of land leases was left open, tribes made some gains in the mid-twentieth century. Despite considerable obstruction by local police and land officials, who were slow to delineate tribal holdings and slower still to offer police protection, some land was returned to tribal peoples.

In the 1970s, the gains tribal peoples had made in earlier decades were eroded in many regions, especially in central India. Migration into tribal lands increased dramatically, and the deadly combination of constabulary and revenue officers uninterested in tribal welfare along with sophisticated non-tribals willing and able to bribe local officials, was sufficient to deprive many tribals of their landholdings. The means of subverting protective legislation were legion: local officials could be persuaded to ignore land acquisition by non-tribal people, alter land registry records, lease plots of land for short periods and then simply refuse to relinquish them, or induce tribal members to become indebted and attach their lands. Whatever the means, the result was that many tribal members became landless labourers in the 1960s and 1970s, and regions that a few years earlier had been the exclusive domain of tribes had an increasingly heterogeneous population. Unlike previous eras, in which tribal people were shunted into more remote forests, by the 1960s relatively little unoccupied land was available. In a 1985 publication, anthropologist Christoph von Fürer-Haimendorf describes this process in Andhra Pradesh: on average only 25 to 33 per cent of the tribal families in such villages had managed to keep even a portion of their holdings. Outsiders had paid about 5 per cent of the market value for the lands they took.

Improved communications, roads with motorized traffic, i.e. what is known as development, and more frequent government intervention figured in the increased contact that tribal peoples had with outsiders. Tribes fared best where there was little to induce non-tribal to settle; cash crops and commercial highways frequently signalled the dismemberment of the tribes. Merchants have long been a link to the outside world, but in the past they were generally petty traders, and the contact they had with tribal people was transient. By the 1960s and 1970s, the resident non-tribal shopkeeper was a permanent feature of many villages. Shopkeepers often sold liquor on credit, enticing tribal members into debt and into mortgaging their land. In the past, tribes made up shortages before the harvest by foraging in the surrounding forest. More recently shopkeepers have offered ready credit with the proviso that loans be repaid in kind with 50 to 100 per cent interest after harvest. Repaying one bag of millet with two bags has set up a cycle of indebtedness from which many have been unable to break loose.

The possibility of cultivators growing a profitable cash crop, such as cotton or castor-oil plants, continues to draw merchants into tribal areas.

Non-tribal traders frequently establish an extensive network of relatives and associates as shopkeepers to serve as agents in a number of villages. Cultivators who grow a cash crop often sell to the same merchants, who provide consumption credit throughout the year. The credit carries a high-interest price tag, whereas the tribal peoples' crops are bought at a fraction of the market rate. Cash crops offer a further disadvantage in that they decrease the supply of available foodstuffs and increase tribal dependence on economic forces beyond their control. This transformation has meant a decline in both the tribes' security and their standard of living.

The final blow for some tribes has come when non-tribals, through political jockeying, have managed to gain legal tribal status, that is, to be listed as a *Scheduled Tribe*. It would truly be impossible for anyone to say that all the diverse communities listed as *Scheduled Tribes* conform to the notion of a tribal in its classical sense. At the same time, it would be impossible for anyone to say that all communities that can primarily be regarded as tribal are included in the schedule of tribes. The Gond of Andhra Pradesh effectively lost their only advantage in trying to protect their lands when the Banjara, a group that had been settling in Gond territory, were classified as a *Scheduled Tribe* in 1977. Their newly acquired tribal status made the Banjara eligible to acquire Gond land "legally" and to compete with Gond for reserved political seats, places in educational institutions, and other benefits. Because the Banjara are not scheduled in neighbouring Maharashtra, there has been an influx of Banjara emigrants from that state into Andhra Pradesh in search of better opportunities.

Extending the system of primary education into tribal areas and reserving places for tribal children in middle and high schools and higher education institutions are central to government policy, but efforts to improve a tribe's educational status have had mixed results. Recruitment of qualified teachers and determination of the appropriate language of instruction also remain troublesome. Commission after commission on the "language question" has called for instruction, at least at the primary level, in the students' native tongue. In some regions, tribal children entering school must begin by learning the official regional language, often one completely unrelated to their tribal tongue.

The commitment of tribes to acquiring a formal education for their children varies considerably. Tribes differ in the extent to which they view education positively. The effectiveness of educational policy likewise varies by region. In those parts of the northeast where tribes have generally been spared the wholesale onslaught of outsiders, schooling has helped tribal people to secure political and economic benefits. The education system there has provided a corps of highly trained tribal members in the professions and high-ranking administrative posts. Many tribal schools are plagued by high dropout rates. Children attend for the first three to four years of primary school and gain a smattering of knowledge, only to lapse into illiteracy later. Few who enter continue up to the tenth grade; of those who do, few manage to finish high school. Therefore, very few are eligible to attend institutions of higher education, where the high rate of attrition continues.

Tribal Ideology

Cultural/Spiritual Value

One of the purposes of the volume is to illustrate, by way of example, the practices, ideologies and governance structures that gave rise to conservation practices devoted to community interest. To address that question, we need not only to define what qualifies as conservation but to investigate the ideological underpinnings of such definitions and the practices that derive from them.

To some extent, investigating a history of conservation relies on defining just what we mean by the term. Definitions abound. According to the IUCN/WWF/UNEP World Conservation Strategy Definition, conservation is "the maintenance of essential ecological processes and life-support systems, the preservation of genetic diversity, and the sustainable utilization of species and ecosystems" (Talbot, 1980).

Conservation can be seen as embedded in the knowledge, practices, and institutions that contribute to social reproduction and community sustainability - defined as the maintenance of political viability, social vitality, economic viability and ecological integrity (Butz et al., 1991; MacDonald, 2002). Areas that have spiritual relevance for communities are a common feature of many societies - past and present - and such spaces are likely the closest historical precedent for contemporary community-conserved areas. Anthropologists and geographers have labelled such areas as sacred space; zones in which the concept of sacredness is invoked to mark a distinction between the divine and the profane. In many places these are recognized as marking a distinction between spaces imbued with spirituality and the spaces of everyday life.

While areas described as sacred are often demarcated according to myth, the application of spirituality to landscape or to individual species is often used as a means of bounding space. More than that, it is often a material representation of the symbolic connection between humanity and the forces that drive "nature". In effect sacred spaces amount to community managed reserves, and are likely the closest historical precedent to contemporary conservation reserves. Sacred space, for example, assumes numerous forms, from landscapes and the physical features they contain to individual trees seen to be the resting place of ancestral spirits. What seems clear is that the sanctioning power of religious authorities combined with the fear of divine retribution has and, in some cases, continues to enhance *in situ* conservation of biodiversity. The literature on sacred groves, for example, describes the processes through which both individual species and extensive areas of forest fell under regimes of prohibited or restricted use. The tradition of sacred groves is an ancient one that spans centuries and cultures.

A sacred space was an enclosure "set aside and often walled to mark the boundary between holy and ordinary space" (Hughes, 1984: 169). Rules protecting sacred land were strict and numerous and followed a consistent pattern though they varied over space and through time.

In other regions, areas designated as sacred groves derive their sacredness from a variety of cultural sources: sites linked to specific events; sites surrounding temples; burial grounds or cemeteries housing the spirits of ancestors; the homes of protective spirits; the homes of deities from which priests derive their healing powers; homes to a powerful animal or plant species; forest areas that surround mythically or spiritually significant natural features such as rivers, rocks, caves and 'bottomless' water holes; and sites of initiation or ritual (Posey, 1998; Gadgil, 1998). Motivations for protection, however, vary. While myth and spiritual belief underlie justifications of protection, the attitudes that derive from these narratives are not uniform. In some cases, myth may be the cultural expression of ecosystem dynamics. While there is little doubt that sacred groves have contributed to the conservation of biodiversity, it is important to recognize the complex history and traditions that have created and maintain these areas in individual locales, rather than treating them as a universal and equitable category.

While sacred spaces are manifestations of a range of traditions and cultural values of 'nature,' they share many similar features with conservationist value, including the containment and protection of species with important ecosystem functions. The regular presence of keystone species such as *ficus* in sacred groves and as individually sanctified species, for example, is suggestive of some appreciation of the ecological importance of such species by the groups assigning such protection. Regardless, they are human artifacts and have as much historical, symbolic, and socio-political significance as they do ecological significance. Chouin (2002: 39), for example, argues that "sacred groves were devices created to maintain social order by managing conflict and protecting society from a range of threats." In many cases, the profane events that have given rise to the creation of sacred space are forgotten, but the ritual activities, common to them persist. It is these rituals that are rich sources of history, as they serve as conservatories of the past. They also provide some insight into the role of sacred space in the maintenance of social order, for "whichever groups control the groves and their rituals, also have control over the production of truth and, ultimately, over power" (Chouin, 2002).

One of the principal means of securing the practical sanctity of sacred space is through the assignment of taboo to the species or areas concerned. Some argue that taboo is of little value in biodiversity conservation (Alvard 1993, 1994). Others describe taboo as a social restraint that leads to biological conservation (McDonald 1977, Berkes et al., 1994). Taboos, however, are not solely applied to sacred space but are used to effect regulation beyond the realm of the sacred. At the same time, species specific taboos - beliefs and accordant practices that totally avoid or prohibit any use of particular species and their populations - are not necessarily enacted because a species is endangered or threatened. Rather, species are avoided for a variety of reasons.

Shamans often take the role of initiating taboo by prohibiting the killing of certain animals in restricted areas whenever he thinks that a species is suffering significant population decline. Shamans also play a role in regulating extraction activities by directing harvesting activities in particular ways.

The degree to which communities have been able to maintain control over ecological resources, and engage in conservationist practice, in the past has been a function of their interaction with other political and economic systems. In the few studies that deal with the relationship between ecological practice, conservation and institutional authority, histories of social change in indigenous and small-scale communities reveal a decline in conservationist practice in relation to a number of factors including altered ideologies of nature, loss of secure tenure over lands and resources, and centralized authority. These are not mutually exclusive effects and often work together to undermine community sustainability and human-environment relations.

Concern for a focus on women in tribal studies has been very recent. It emerged out of general interest and concern with women's issues the world over. The value system governing larger Indian society has been in the process of change. With this there has been a shift in the image of tribal women who are thus invariably portrayed as enjoying a better social status than their counterparts in the larger Indian society. Tribal society in the post-Independence era has been witness to unprecedented change, which has been most marked in respect of culture, modes of making a living and social differentiation. Their bearing on women's status in society and gender relations has been far-reaching.

In 1978, the Indian Anthropological Society brought out a region-wise survey of tribal women. It points out that studies of women have either been ignored or, when discussed, such discussions have been brief and sketchy. Except in some works by Elwin, Furer-Haimendorf and a few others, there has been no explicit discussion on the status of women in tribal society. Even in these, the assessment of the status of women has been far from uniform. While some say that tribal societies generally assigned high status to women, others opine that women's position in tribal society is the same as in other societies.

Writing about the Nagas, Elwin, for example remarks, the tribal woman is in herself exactly the same as any other women, with the same position, love and fears, the same devotion to the home, to husband and children, the same faults and the same virtues (cited in Zehol 1998: 1). Yet elsewhere, he refers to Naga women as holding a high and honourable position. They work on equal terms with men in the fields and make their presence felt in the tribal council (Elwin 1961: 104). Elwin makes a similar observation with regard to the Baiga when he says that the women enjoy an excellent position in society. They enjoy freedom and authority, play a leading part in marriage ceremonials, and have a reputation for practicing witchcraft. Among the Baiga, there is no clear division of labour between men and women (Elwin 1986: 235-36). Furer-Haimendorf on the other hand, referring to the Nagas, writes, many women in most civilized parts of India may well envy the women of the Naga Hills, their high status and their free happy life and if you measure the cultural level of the people by the social position and personal freedom of its women you will think twice before looking down on the Nagas as savages (Furer-Haimendorf, 1933: 101).

Women continue to be governed by customary laws and norms. The data available on gender in tribal societies is sketchy, especially in the context of transformations that have been taking place. Given such heterogeneity, it is rather difficult to generalize on the position of women as a whole across tribal groups in India. What has been observed can at best be described as being illustrative and heuristic. Despite such heterogeneity, they seem to share one point in common, that they are different from the dominant community of the region.

Traditional Institution

Weekly markets (*haats*) in tribal areas are an important socio-economic institution. A *haat* caters for local needs and provides a forum where villagers can buy and sell their local produce. Tribal bring products of different species to these markets for sale. Traders from towns come to these markets to purchase forest produce; others set up small shops for selling consumer goods such as ready-made clothes, toiletries, utensils, stationery, some plastic goods, match boxes, and some cereals and tobacco. The most significant forum for interaction between tribal and caste Hindu has been at weekly village markets.

Artisan castes have traditionally produced and marketed their wares at these *haats* and consequently moulded them to suit the tastes and needs of their local tribal clientele. In Orissa, Bihar and Madhya Pradesh where the tribal population is considerable there are also a preponderance of village *haats*. In the north-east too there are large and small marketplaces where tribal women sell their handloom textiles, medicinal herbs, foodstuff and various types of forest produce. Handicrafts combs, mud pots, bamboo, baskets, musical instruments and wooden cooking implements are among the items that may be termed as tribal products.

While it may be stated that any hand-made item for decorative, ritualistic or utilitarian purpose within their cultures can be termed as tribal craft, it may not necessarily be true that all such items are made by the tribal themselves. In areas where the population is largely caste Hindu in composition, the crafts made for tribal are often actually fashioned by Scheduled Caste artisans and mistaken for tribal crafts in urban minds.

Ritual Performance

All human cultures appear to include faith in supernatural power, and it seems that this tradition has played an active and essential role in influencing how our ancestors perceived and adapted to their environment. This relationship between human belief and adaptive behaviour may have played a critical role in shaping cultural evolution.

The history of any society can demonstrate how sacred beliefs change over time, how they are created or borrowed, consciously or unconsciously, and how they may be subsequently abandoned. Beliefs about the natural environment and the supernatural environment are part of a larger system of learned ideas and customs that comprise a culture.

Ritual, particular type of formal performance in which the participants carry out a series of relatively stereotyped actions and make a series of relatively standardized statements largely prescribed by custom and sanctioned by precedent. Historical evidence suggests that rituals tend to be much more stable and invariable than most human customary activity. The capacity of the participants to modify the form and content of ritual activities is usually much less than would be the case if the activities were primarily focused on political, economic, or recreational concerns.

Rituals are not primarily recreational. For their congregations they are serious affairs, which do not merely communicate but also, through the intervention of a god or spirits or other invisible beings or forces, accomplish something. Rituals sanctify, define, and legitimize transfers of power and authority. Life-cycle rituals bless, mark out, and sanction significant transitions in the lives of individuals. Calendrical rituals provide an established, ordered, and meaningful pattern for the changing seasons, and the productive and other activities associated with them.

Rituals of initiation consistently impose an ordered framework on the often unruly transition from childhood through adolescence into adulthood. In these rituals the initiates are first dramatically separated from their mothers, from the households and symbolically from their childhood. They enter a liminal or threshold phase of the ritual in which their joint equality, their separation from normal society, and their lack of status are stressed.

Rituals require people to carry them out - special people who have done this routine before, experts who have been taught the secrets, initiates with a link to the spirit world. There can hardly be religion without priests. In tribal societies the priests are the medicine men/astrologers, known also as shamans. Their ability to communicate with the spirits is evident from the way they fall into trances - achieved usually either by self-hypnosis or by consumption of liquor.

Ritual also requires explanation, and explanation involves one of the most basic human talents, that of story telling. The spell-binding riches and infinite variety of the world's mythologies go back to such basic questions as how it all began, or why things happen as they do.

The gods of importance to tribal societies vary with the circumstances of the tribe, though nearly all give precedence to the sky. The sky is the largest fact of nature. With its ever-changing face, its resident sun and moon, it is clearly a force to be reckoned with. In most tribal mythologies a sky god is involved in the creation of the world.

Tribal ritual frequently involves sacrifice. The life destroyed is offered to the god. If an animal's throat is cut, the blood on the altar carries the life force to the deity. If ritual ingredients are consumed in flames, as a burnt offering, the smoke achieves the same purpose.

The rituals of agriculture are attached to specific moments in the year, such as the times of sowing or of harvest. The year itself also has moments of crisis which require the attention of the priests. New year is the prime example, just after the shortest day, when the sun must be congratulated and encouraged in its recovery.

The rhythm of human life demands similar care. In all religions there are rites of passage, marking some or all of the great events of birth, puberty, marriage and death. Life beyond death is important too. Everything necessary must be done for the spirit of the departed ancestor, who can in turn be relied on to help his living descendants.

Kinship ties, which require peacefulness and cooperation among people, are important in the customary ordering of social interaction. However, in many tribal societies, spirit-related persons are perceived as more closely linked than blood-related persons. This deeply affects the way that community is understood. In particular, the meaning most often given to the concept of community in traditional tribal cultures is those who are of a similar clan and spirit; those who are encompassed by a particular spirit-being. There is no separation between the social and the spiritual in such a worldview. Spirits are understood as directing individual action (through dreams, visions, direct encounter, or possession of power objects such as stones, shells, masks, or fetishes). Therefore, marital, family, and clan relationships are based on spiritual connections and spiritual guidance rather than purely civil, sexual, or genealogical concerns.

II

A total number of eight chapters are included under the **first section** titled **"Tribal Identity"**. First chapter is 'Introduction' by *Deepak Kumar Behera* and *Georg Pfeffer*. The second chapter by *Marine Carrin's* on Santal religious discourse covers everyday rhetoric, oral literature and the esoteric knowledge of the *ojha* priests. It deals with the relation between symbolism and oral literature. Carrin argues that religious discourse has played a major role in developing original forms of resistance expressing Santal identity through cultural activities. *R.E.S. Tanner* discusses about Sukuma identity. At the neighbourhood level Sukuma identity has shown considerable adaptive resilience. At the individual level it would seem that having a Sukuma identity is not very important as it is not a help in getting and retaining jobs or protecting them in an uncertain modern world should they leave their homeland. Tanner feels that under the conditions of modern life, tribal identity has to pay off pragmatically both psychologically and socially in order to survive. *Lawrence F. Van Horn's* makes an interesting comparison of two cases. The first case relates to a tribal government of Micmac Indians, an indigenous North American Indian people. The second case is part of a modern United States federal agency. In the first case, the supplicant's plan appeared to be initially successful, but ultimately did not work because it was not sustainable in the end. In the second case, the desired outcome of the supplicant was ultimately achieved, and the result turned out to be satisfactory for all concerned. *Christian Strümpell* points out that changes brought about by industrialization are barely investigated by social anthropologists. It is a pity to note that most of the privileged people in an industrial setting are the immigrants from other parts of India, whereas the majority of the locals have to maintain their livelihood as marginalized workers in the private sector economy. *Arima Mishra* discusses as to how the Kutia Kandha identity, traced through their association with Mother Earth, moves beyond village boundaries and excludes the "outsiders" (particularly the caste groups of Damba and Sundhi) referring to them as "vagrants" or "impure". Her analysis shows how the tribal worldview shifts between tribe and village as focus of identification. *Bhowmick* and *Jana* highlight the varying patterns of Santal identity under changing circumstances. They explain as to how the process of Hinduization in the form of various Bhakti-cults and the philanthropic work of the Christian Missionaries brought about new patterns of identity among the Santal. *Pujari* and *Mishra* write about the process of growing up in Juang community. The authors critically examine the passage of a Juang child into adulthood in a changing scenario.

The **second section** dealing with "**State Intervention**" covers as many as eight chapters. *Sita Venkateswar* in her chapter states that the final years of the last century resulted in some unprecedented changes in the lives of the Jarawa of the Andaman Islands. This paper traces some of the crucial events that shaped the lives of the Jarawa over the past few years as they became the focus of international attention. *Manzurul Mannan* writes about Santal in the Northern districts of Bangladesh. The existence of Santal community and their religio-political system is not given proper recognition by the Bangladesh state. State's relation to various ethnic and tribal groups in many ways is dysfunctional in the sense that state is unable to create space to accommodate ethnic groups in its development policies. *Jayanta Sarkar* seeks to unfold the impact of State intervention on the endangered small tribes like the Great Andamanese, the Onges, the Jarawas and the Sentinelese.of Andaman and Nicobar Islands. The chapter by *Tripathy* and *Nath* documents the changing land relations in tribal areas due to state interventions through land laws and forest laws on resource base of the people. *Md. Basar Ali* through a genealogical analysis of the Santal and the Malpaharia of Bengal presents a case study of their occupational displacement and further marginalization. The author makes some useful suggestions to policy makers for safeguarding the interests of the tribal *bargadars* of West Bengal. The chapter by *Ashis Kumar Das* deals with the different features of tribal unrest. It analyzes the Kolhan movement and the Forest *Andolon* of East and West Shingbhum districts of Jharkhand state from a socio-historical perspective. *Abhijit Guha* presents an ethnographic account of the dynamics of university-locality interaction on the basis of his 15 years experience. *Sinha* and *Banerjee* argue that traditional established ways are no longer capable of providing satisfactory solutions to various problems now being encountered by detribalized Kawars of Bilaspur district of the newly constituted Chhattisgarh state. This process of change has dislocated their life style and left them in a transitory state with dual value system.

The **third section** of the book consisting of three chapters deals with **"Displacement and Rehabilitation".** *Erasmus* and *Serekoane* in their joint chapter present an overview on the origin and early functioning of the Riemvasmaak community. It elucidates the impact of the move of the tribal community from their original tribal land on the units of their social structures. *Das* and *Behera* highlights the changes that have taken place in the economic organization of the tribal due to the advent of a mega project. The chapter focuses on the socio-economic status of the womenfolk of the tribal communities in a changing context. *Padhi* and *Lal* analyze the changing roles of Sabara tribal women in a post-displacement situation. The authors argue that the traditional roles of Sabara women have undergone profound changes in the post-displacement era resulting in their lowering status in economic and cultural spheres of community life.

The **fourth section** of the book deals with **"Ecological, Economic and Social Values"** in tribal societies. The first chapter in this section by *Binay Kumar Pattnaik* drives home certain points of environmental wisdom embedded in some of the folk and tribal cultures of India. In support of his argument, the author provides ethnographic account of several cases of folk cultural elements, tribal worldviews and traditional knowledge systems. *Hari Charan Behera* discusses about different socio-economic dimensions of the weekly market in tribal predominated Kondhmal district of Orissa. The author primarily focuses on the nature and functioning of weekly market, role of participants, business practices and mode of exchanges. The chapter also highlights some of the changes in the cultural tradition of weekly market due to the penetration of various market forces into tribal areas in recent time. *Debendra Biswal* examines the appropriateness of the use of European philosophical discourse on nature/culture dichotomy, concept of subordination and exploitation and oppression in the context of Kutia Kondh women of Orissa. The study explores the status of women in relation to economy, political institutions, religion, and division of labour, family organization, youth dormitory, etc.

The **last section** of the book on **"Rituals in Tribal India"** includes four chapters. In the first chapter *Lidia Guzy* highlights the interrelationship between local music and dance traditions of the Boro Sombar region of Western Orissa. She also explores the importance of local social structure and value system in musical tradition. The author highlights the socio-cultural specificity through musical patterns. The chapter by *Nibedita Nath* describes *Mangeri Sanpa,* a puja observed by the Kondh in village Robadi of Rayagada district in the state of Orissa. The chapter provides an account of religiousness of the Kondh community covering dimensions such as the invitation and propitiation of supreme beings with incarnations, music and dance, supernatural being with welfare and illness. *Rashmi Pramanik* primarily deals with the Paraja's perceptions on childbirth. She analyses various social categories and processes linked to childbirth. The whole analysis revolves around the concept of purity and pollution. It deals with categories of persons and objects that stand in opposition/affinity in the everyday life of the Paraja. *A.K. Haldar* analyzes the changing cultural patterns in the frame of "Nature-Man-Sprit Complex" and presents the perceptions of the community members on the ongoing interventions in the name of so-called development.

In a nutshell, the volume addresses to the central question "who are indigenous peoples"? The question has become highly contentious in India today, where eighty million peoples belonging to the state category of "Scheduled Tribes" are attempting to gain international recognition as indigenous people, as part of their struggle for recognition and rights in land and resources. Opponents argue that the term "indigenous people" is a misnomer that will lead to further division and ethnic animosity in a country already suffering from community divisions, and social conflict. This volume interrogates the politics surrounding the category of peoples in India known as "tribal" or adivasis and more recently as "indigenous peoples". It analyzes the way in which this category is being constituted and labelled, and examines the rights and present predicament of communities designated as such.

REFERENCES

Alvard, M. 1994. "Conservation by Native Peoples: Prey Choice in a Depleted Habitat," *Human Nature,* 5: 127-154

____. 1995. "Intra-specific Prey Choice by Amazonian Hunters," *Current Anthropology,* 36: 789-818.

Berkes, F., C. Folke, and M. Gadgil. 1994. "Traditional Ecological Knowledge, Biodiversity, Resilience, and Sustainability," (pp.269-287) in *Biodiversity Conservation.* The Netherlands: Kluwer Academic Publishing Company.

Butz, D., S. Lonergan and B. Smit. 1991. "Why International Development Neglects Indigenous Social Reality," *Canadian Journal of Development Studies,* 12 (1): 143-58.

Chouin, G. 2002. "Sacred Groves in History: Pathways to the Social Shaping of Forest Landscapes in Coastal Ghana," *IDS Bulletin,* 33 (1): 39-46.

Elwin, Verrier. 1961. *Nagaland.* Shillong: The Research Dept., Adviserís Secretariat.

____. 1986. *Baigas.* Delhi: Gyan Publications.

Fried, Morton H. 1975. *The Notion of Tribe.* Menlo Park: Cummings.

Furer-Haimendorf, Christoph von. 1933. *Naked Nagas.* Calcutta: Thacker, Spink and Co.

Gadgil, M. 1998. "Traditional Resource Management," in B. Saraswati (ed.), *Lifestyle and Ecology.* New Delhi: IGNCA and D. K. Printworld Pvt. Ltd.

Hughes, J.D. 1984. "Sacred Groves: The Gods, Forest Protection and Sustained Yield in the Ancient World," in H.K. Steen (ed.), *History of Sustained Yield Forestry.* Durham: Forest History Society.

McDonald, D. 1977. "Food Taboos: A Primitive Environmental Protection Agency (South America)," *Anthropos,* 72: 734-48.

MacDonald, K.I. 2002. "Human-use Management to Diminish the Impact of Visitation on Traditional Lifestyles," (pp. 259-70) in L. Taylor and A. Ryall (eds.), *Human Use Management in Mountain Areas.* Banff: The Banff Centre/Parks, Canada.

Posey, D.A. (ed.). 1998. *Cultural and Spiritual Values of Biodiversity.* London: Intermediate Technology Publications.

Ramagundam, R. 2002. "Control and Conflict: a Grassroots Perspective on Adivasi Rights Over Natural Livelihood Resources," paper presented at the Indigenous Rights in the Commonwealth Project, South & South East Asia Regional Expert Meeting, Indian Confederation of Indigenous and Tribal Peoples (ICITP) India, held at India International Centre, New Delhi during March 11-13, 2002.

Talbot, L.M. 1980. "The World's Conservation Strategy," *Environmental Conservation,* 7: 259-68.

TWO

SANTAL RELIGIOUS DISCOURSE AND THE ASSERTION OF ADIVASI IDENTITY

MARINE CARRIN

My study of Santal discourse relates patterns of speaking to other dimensions of interaction such as symbolism, ritual and assertion of identity. I am concerned here with relations between speech events and activities among Santals[1]. To study Santal discourse is to grapple with the interprenetration of different codes and genres such as myths, narratives, riddles, folk-tales and omens which all show some variation from one region to another. Despite these differences, Santal oral forms constitute a universe of discourse. The Santals have developed a particular conception of veiled language, "twisted speech", used both in daily life and in ritual discourse (Carrin, 2003). To interpret veiled utterances, they must refer, consciously or unconsciously, to a shared typology of speech events[2], such as exchanging riddles, consulting omens or questioning an *ojha* (priest and diviner)[3]. In these contexts, to make or not to make an uttrance becomes a matter of shared knowledge and labels the key social actor. Formal language is particularly rich, but everybody does not master religious discourse or political oratory. The knowledge of riddles, proverbs and prohibitions is unequally shared. They have their roots in everyday life but their elaboration depends on tradition known to chiefs, priests, and elders but beyond common knowledge. Still, ritual discourse allows us to explore the semantic universe of the Santals.

Forms of Speech

Today, traditional speech events become infrequent but mark important events or commemorations as well as private occasions such as a naming ceremony. Santal informants agree that there is a continuum from the most traditional forms of discourse to daily verbal exchanges.The creation myth is held as the most venerable form of discourse and is often sung during the cattle festival (Sohrae); then follows the Baha seren — invocations sung in praise of the *bongas* (deities) of the sacred grove — *da gama* the prayers for rain and *bakhen* invocations dedicated to the hill spirits, *buru bongas*. From then on, opinions vary : while some informants hold that the songs of Sohrae sung during the cattle festival are the next on the list, others stress the importance of the *karam binti*, a recitation to honour the memory of a prestigious deceased. In fact, the *binti* is a religious recitation which include other myths and which is sung during a festival which can also mark the election of a chief or a priest.

All Santals agree that *mantar* or invocations adressed to *bongas* during healing rituals are crucial, but some argue that they do not trust the *ojhas* (diviners) who are suspected to invent new *mantar* to get more money fom their patients. In fact, village rumour tells us that nowadays *ojhas* cure diseases with words as they are too lazy to go to the forest to gather medicinal plants. This accusation makes us feel that the inflation of religious discourse is criticized though everybody knows that nowadays the forest has deteriorated. Despite these criticisms eveybody enjoys stories of *bongas* and witches and some informants take them as serious testimony of real experience. If I compare the stories about *bongas* that I have heard to-day to similar stories which were written around 1900 by infomants who were sometimes more than eighty years old, I can see that there is a continuum of content (Andersen,Carrin, Soren forthcoming). The themes are still the same but we also find new additions : customary speech is becoming an object of prestige, it is preserved and reinvented through revivalist movements. Customary speech has become a metaphor for resistance[4] to pan-indian hegemony.

Definition of Traditional Speech

All these forms of speech have ritual value and contribute to the dynamics of knowledge. To characterize these dynamics, we need to understand what ritual communication is. Is it the transmission of a content? Barth, in "Cosmologies in the Making" (1987) objects to the idea that a discursive content is transmitted. He stresses that among the Ok of New Guinea, the ritual communication is expressed through analogical codes. Santals defend ritual speech as tradition, and the most traditional texts are seen as transmitted by the ancestors. On the other hand, symbolic utterances like omens or riddles form a tacit knowledge that is not consciously memorized. This tacit knowledge is cast in images or metaphors which stress analogies between humans and animals, humans and plants, and humans and deities. Traditional speech include religious invocations, stories about deities, and political oratory. Political oratory, used at the *kulhi durup* (to sit in the village street), allows good orators some degree of fame. They should know how to use euphemisms to avoid conflicts. Santals value political oratory as discourse of negotiation and they like to imagine how their ancestors used to discuss and negotiate, consulting omens whenever they were hesitating to make a decision.

Ritual Communication and *Bentha Katha*

In Santal language, good speech is straight as the village street, as when chiefs take the right decisions without hesitating. But ancestors often talked a veiled language using *bentha katha*, twisted like branches, since truth is never simple. The image of a branch makes us aware that Santals conceptualize their discourse as a living kind. The most important metaphors imply a relation of predication between natural species and categories of people: men, women, infants, youngsters and so on. More generally, trees allude to mythical times when ancestors used to rest in the forest under *sal (Shorea Robusta, L.) and mohua (Bassia Latifolia, Gartn.)* trees, both valued in ritual and evoking body substances. Bone is compared to the branch and the flower to the uterus (Carrin, 1986, 1997). Some metaphors[5] linking bone and grain occur as twisted speech during the funerals. The mourner takes the bones of the deceased and puts a flower on them, "to make them flourish again" in order to allow the continuation of the patriline. In myths, the branch is a metonymy of the person, thus bid dare to lift the branch alludes to the gesture of the chied during the hunt. The expression *karam dar* "branch of karam" alludes to a ceremonial friend and saplings evoke grandchildren. Similarly, the animal world is omnipresent in oral literature where animal species are attached to particular genres; thus insects, water snails and crabs are found in riddles, while jackals and hen are found in folk-tales. But tigers and leopards, the vehicles of the *bongas*, are taboo in oral genres and cannot be evoked in twisted language.

Santals use *bentha katha* in ceremonial speech or in ritual. For example, during the divorce ritual, the husband tears a *sal* leaf (symbol of ancestors) apart, but keeps silent: the metaphor is enough. I have shown elsewhere (Carrin, 2003) that two kinds of knowledge are at work in Santal society: the knowledge of ordinary people, relating to the tradition as transmitted by the ancestors, and the secret knowledge of the *ojha,* which belongs to a broader tradition, mixed with popular Hinduism tinged with tantric and shaktist elements.

Santals reflect on their own linguistic activity and stress that in ritual dicourse utterances transfer moral attributes to objects that frame specific kinds of interaction, such as "a fowl promised" *sim agom* which denotes a leaf, wrapping a few feathers of a fowl. In case of illness, a kinsman of the sick person dedicates the materialized promise to the *bongas*.

Santals distinguish different kinds of speech which relate to the mind. For example, heavy speech *(hambal)* conceals the intentions of the speaker and is often related to witchcraft.

Santals conceptualize the good knowledge of the *ojha (bidia)* as a language to appease malevolent *bongas,* while witches have stolen the *bidia* and made witchcraft out of it. This conception of knowledge enables us to evaluate how metaphors shape a model of knowledge production and transmission. The field covered by metaphors includes both daily communication and ritual discourse, two modes of speech which are parallel, as can be seen from words having a double meaning such as *gurgu*, the stone used to crush the roots of turmeric *(Curcuma longa, L.)* in the kitchen, which also alludes to possession as the *ojha's* disciple sits on such a stone to get possessed.

The Conceptual Structure of the *Ojha's* Knowledge

Some figures of speech, however, are shared by everybody: they are the "little talks" that everyone exchanges during rituals or on social occasions such as drinking rice-beer or smoking tobacco together. The conceptual structure of the *ojha's* knowledge is different, since he is used to confronting the knowledge of his colleagues — who may belong to different traditions. In opposing the knowledge of the *ojha* to that of the common man, I have tried to show how several branches of knowledge coexist, stressing the metaphoric base of both. But the *ojha's* metaphors seem superfluous to ordinary people, since they do not relate to ordinary knowledge. And though metaphors shape a tacit knowledge, the *ojha's* knowledge produces interpretations *(bheda)* that he consciously stores in his memory and transmits to his best disciples.

For the *ojha,* ritual discourse shapes another world where *bongas* and Hindu deities interact with the image they cast in rituals. The *ojha's* ritual discourse is framed on *mantars* (invocations) and *jharni* exorcism formulae transmitted from master to disciple during a ritual wandering which evokes the shamanistic voyage. Though he is generally possessed when uttering or chanting *mantras,* the *ojha* is able to interpret the content of the formulae.

Moreover, when performing healing rituals, he may add new invocations to his repertoire. Differences between *ojhas* reflect their religious inclinations; while tantric *ojhas* mostly worship the goddess Kali, destructive and powerful, others are deeply influenced by devotional religion *(bhakti)*.

Santal Discourse in an Historical Perspective

To become a discourse these oral forms are subjected to another transformation: the shift from memory to written records. When the Protestant missionaries, who established themselves in Ebenezer in 1867, invented a roman transcription of Santali they taught it to a few collaborators who were charged to collect stories to inform the missionaries' linguistic work (Carrin and Tambs-Lyche, in press). Skrefsrud, the Norwegian founder of the mission, wanted to found a national Church among the Santals. The national identity he aims to define is, above all, a matter of language. Skrefsrud wanted to store tribal knowledge by transforming heathen beliefs and ritual into a folklore of the past that children might learn at school, desacralizing the *bonga* to allow Santals to embrace Christianity. By the same token, precolonial history becomes prehistory. The "orientalism" of the Scandinavian missionaries was oriented towards the noble savage and probably contributed to reinforce Santal identity, especially through the literary activity resulting from the introduction of roman script among the converts (Carrin and Tambs-Lyche, 1998).

The richness of language makes up for the poverty of history in granting real culture to the Santals in the missionary mind. The Santals are fond of their language and love to play with words. This clearly impressed Skrefsrud and Bodding. But far from being static the Santal semantic universe is informed by historical changes, reflecting how they were obliged to migrate in search of land or forced to engage in labour. Encroachment on tribal territory, where migrants of Hindu origin came to develop new markets, intensified when the State started to exploit forests in Chotanagpur as well as in Santal Parganas.

Forms of resistance run from everyday reluctance to comply with the demands of dominant groups, to open rebellion in 1855-56. But the missionaries' interest opens a new venture for the Santal collaborators who start to write oral testimonies. Through this process, the Santal writers become interpreters of their culture. The idea to archive the Tradition leads our authors to create a model of narrative which includes village stories, narratives regarding custom, stories about bongas and witches and descriptions of rituals. But the development of these narratives reflects on Santal identity from 1867 onwards, and into the modern engagement in Jharkhandi politics from around 1920.

The Fascination of the Written Word

During the rebellion the Santals realized their inability to write, and had to ask Hindu sympathizers to do so on their behalf (Guha, 1983). Thakur, we remember, appeared to Sidhu and Kanhu brandishing a book, perhaps the Bible. Curiously, one text from the Santal archives *(Hul reak' katha)* tells us the brothers were taught reading and writing by a Brahman, as their stepfather Bhogon Manjhi was rich. Later, says the text, they went to mission school. On the way to school, they had a vision of a *sadhu* or *yogi* who blessed them, and told them to petition the government about the heavy rent. "If the raj does not listen to you, you make yourselves kings. I shall help you". He warns them not to be greedy and to stay pure. Anxiously, the two boys answer: "how we can make ourselve kings ? We do not know how to read and write". They ask the apparition to teach them. The narrator continues: "Somehow they wrote a letter". The fascination with writing is clear (Andersen, forthcoming). But the story also shows a consciousness of knowledge as a relation, one has to learn from somebody. Writing comes from without, whether its origin is colonial or supernatural. One parallel would be the supernatural origin of goods in the cargo cults. In both cases, introducing a supernatural agent to found knowledge otherwise colonial, effectively constitutes a counter-cultural claim. These observations also apply to the several later inventions, based on revelation, of a specifically Santal script (Carrin, 2002). The emergence of narrative stresses the rise of Santal opinion which opposes chiefs and priests to laymen and men to women. The written account allows narrators to construct the idea of a Santal society *(samaj)* founded on egalitarian values and different from caste society. This discourse stressses how the word of the ancestors becomes questionable, and how it is necessary to defend tribal values from hinduization or christianization. Santal narrators strongly defend attachment to the *bongas* as part of themselves and show that they have a religion which is not mere superstition. In other words they start to resist assimilation and conversion.

From 1905 to 1920 missionary education develops considerably and the idea of a Christian justice influences the Adivasi elites who feel they have lost the egalitarian values of their ancestors. From 1915 the Mundas take the initiative to found the Adivasi Mahasabha which later influences tribal activism. Meanwhile, the development of mines led to the proletarization of the tribals who worked in them. Later, these factors led to the formation of the Jharkhand party, founded in 1952 by Jaipal Singh, a Munda educated in Oxford. By the eighties the Jharkhand party had matured and knew many feats and failures until the creation of the Jharkhand state in 2000 (Ghosh, 1999; Prakash, 2001).

In the thirtees equally, Ragunath Murmu, reacting against the idea of writing Santali in different Indian scripts, invents a new alphabet. The characters of ol *chiki* are arranged alphabetically but motivated by ideogrammatical symbols and evoke, as Murmu told me much later, "the traditional language of branches". Very soon, the raja of Mayurbhanj supports the new script and industrialists of Jamshedpur finance the making of fonts to print the first newspaper in *ol chiki,* "Sagun Sakam" (lit. The divinatory leaf)[6] . This newspaper is very successful and leads to contacts with other Santals living in other States, who start to learn *ol chiki*. The government of Orissa acknowledges the script and sponsors the preparation of school-books printed in ol *chiki* characters[7]. The government also favours recruitment of Santal teachers for the tribal zones[8]. Nevertheless, most of the schools using *ol chiki* have volunteer teachers. In 1967 the association patronized by Ragunath Murmu for the diffusion of *ol chiki* establishes a college where members of the Santal elite teach in English.

The Village Theatre

In the seventees, I attend a Santal play written by Ragunath Murmu in Danbosh near Mayurbhanj. The plot stages Sidhu and Kanhu, the heroes of the Santal rebellion. In the second act of the play, two other characters appear. They are Santal local heroes killed in 1949, when the Santals wanted to stay under the authority of the raja of Mayurbhanj refusing the merger with Orissa. A few days later, I attend the ritual commemoration of a bloody encounter which took place in Marankindom village. This impressive ceremony is called *sahid bonga,* the bonga of martyrdom. The term *sahid* here alludes to solidarity with the Muslims, another suffering minority. Thousands of Santals sing Jharkhand slogans and beat the big drums while village priests wearing green gandhian caps inaugurate a new ritual, piercing the soil of a giant sacred grove with arrows, to commemorate the wounded body of Adivasi consciousness. The chiefs of more than fifty villages do a *puja*, pouring rice-beer libations on the arrows in order to commemorate the suffering of the rebels of 1855 as well as the memory of the insurgents of 1949. One day earlier, Jharkhandi leaders organised huge processions in

Baripada and adivasis leaders spoke at the stadium, in the presence of the *raja* of Mayurbhanj, a businessman from Calcutta who has come for the occasion. In Marankindom as in Baripada, thousands of Santal and Ho brandish banners with slogans written in *ol chiki*. In both places guest orators speak about the need for education and development of literacy.[9] "We should have a Santal Tagore", claims an old man and I am asked to say a few words about my working on the Santal archives in Oslo. When I stress the historical importance of these texts, people applaud and ask me to sing a short Santali song. We sing a few verses of a song in honour of Sidhu and Kanhu, then I am garlanded and made to sit close to the raja.

The orators do not content themselves with cultural claims. They also want a decent standard of living for everybody. Then comes Sitakant Mahapatra[10] , then Home Secretary, a poet who acknowledges the importance of ol chiki and takes an interest in Ragunath Murmu and the Santals.[11]

About that time, tensions arise due to smuggling of rice from Bihar to Orissa. Many tribals get arrested though big smugglers bribe the police. In 1972, the Government of Orissa fearing that the Santal newspapers sustain separatist claims, stops sponsoring education in ol chiki. But in 1977 the adivasis organize a conference in Jhagram (Bengal) which is attended by more than ten thousand Santals coming from Bihar and Madhya Pradesh. *Ol chiki* is strongly supported. Much earlier, in 1942 and 1948, Ragunath Murmu writes plays where *raskau*, the "pleasure of life", is made to express true adivasi sensitivity. He teaches a hedonistic way of life, not leading to selfish goals, but oriented towards the harmonious development of the communuty.

The Ideology of the Script

The supporters of the script do not take into account that a script needs a milieu to serve as a media of communiction. The santals who know *ol chiki* also know Oriya, Bengali, and Devanangari scipts. Jobs require the knowledge of these scripts and sometimes the knowledge of English. To serve as a medium the script needs to be supported by the speakers of the language, and such support has been wanting. The Santals have two other revealed scripts,[12] but only *ol chiki* has benefited from official support as it was found phonetically relevant. I cannot enter that discussion here, but I want to stress that *ol chiki* was probably able to function because reading and writing skills were first distributed among a limited number of specialists positioned in key social roles throughout the community. Ragunath Murmu does not claim a divine inspiration , he is a reformer who dreams of another age when the

Santals were not corrupted by drinking and led a spartiate life. He argues that the Santals had a glorious past and that their decline was due to the negative influence of neighbouring caste society. His puritanism shows how the Santals — like other *Adivasis* — have interiorized a stigma. Murmu had hoped that Hos, Mundas, Mahalis and Birhors who share an understanding of Santali might adopt *ol chiki*. In the seventies, among Hos, a neighbouring group living in Singhbhum, Lako Bodra has a revelation of another script. He claims to have found the graphs written in bright letters on a megalith stone, a *sasan diri*. According to Bodra, a Ho shaman had composed a lot of texts during the twelfth century, which Bodra thus rediscovered. As is claimed for Raghunath Murmu, this discovery is due to his "pure nature": he is the reformer who will save the Hos from decadence. Bodra writes in Kaji, the secret language of the Ho shamans. In 1954, Bodra founds the Adi Samaj, a movement to diffuse the alphabet, but also social reform, organizing cooperatives. But while Ragunath Murmu and his son Sidalal (who becomes a Congress MP) are secularists, Lako Bodra develops the profile of a religious chief. For him, the *bongas*, the tribal deities caution the Sari Dhorom, the religion of the truth. Meanwhile, Bodra reinvents the history of the Hos, arguing that they never forgot their vedic culture. They are *adi samskriti*; he criticizes the caste system and wants to promote a progressive model of adivasi consciousness where literacy would provide a window about language, knowledge, communication and relationships with the dominant society. Like Ragunath Murmu, he feels that literacy provides a special opportunity to build a better self-representation of the adivasi community.

In the sixties, Bodra's influence allows the Hos to refuse assimilation. Finally, during a Conference organized in 1977 in Jamshedpur, it is decided that the different revealed scripts should be used to develop social and cultural reforms. The Munda tribes, it is said, share a common religion, the cult of the bongas, and the sacred grove evokes the forest origin of the different Munda groups. Though different script are used, the common message rests on the idea of the sacred grove.

Meanwhile, in 1963, a Santal guru, Hopna Besnao, is founding a religious movement, the Sarna Dhorom, the religion of the Sacred Grove. It unites thousands of devotees from Bihar and Orissa. The term Sarna Dhorom, says Besnao, was first used by Birsa Munda, the leader of the Munda insurrection of 1895, who had declared that the Sarna would one day become the symbol of Adivasi identity. In 1970 the guru founded an ashram and created a repertory of invocations dedicated to the bonga of the sacred grove of Marankindom village. Guru Besnao's disciples criticize traditional priests and exorcists who are accused of exploiting their customers. Like Birsa, Guru Besnao obtains therapeutic powers. But he refuses to identify with previous leaders of reformist movements such as the Kherwars. He demands a non-vegetarian diet and stresses old Santal symbols, such as the system of greetings. In Singhbhum and Mayurbhanj, in the early eighties, his followers and those of similar gurus organize cooperatives and teaching centers, trying to play a social role. These different gurus try to act as voices of Adivasi consciousness and recruit disciples who pay them respect on the model of Hindu religious gurus.

We see here how the invention of a script weaves links between heroes of the past, present personalities and theatre characters. In some of his plays, Ragunath Murmu stages the script itself as a character. In one play, two human characters, Bidu and Chandan have been sent to the earth by Maran Buru, to teach men ritual dances in honour of the *bongas*. As an orphan, Bidu wants to take shelter in a small kingdom: the daughter of the chief falls in love with him but then he is banished. They run away together and see on the road *ol chiki* signs which puzzle them. They succeed, however, in deciphering the characters and understand that the neighbhouring chief is pondering an attack. They conciliate the chiefs of the two kingdoms, and the script becomes a symbol of peace and harmony. The heroes then declare that by mastering writing tribal people will suppress their stigma; or, as Ragunath Murmu writes, the adivasi culture has liberated itself.

In 1981, Gulia Hassdak, the young guru of the Sarna Dhorom of Mayurbhanj is possessed by the Jaher Bonga from Maṛankindom village. Suddenly, he speaks in three languages: Santali, Munda and Sadani, while fifty disciples throw themselves on the ground before him. Gulia decides to write plays about his visions which are to be staged in the villages. Chotrae Soren, one of his disciples, who is in charge of printing the *ol chiki* newspaper, affirms that the deities themselves have dictated the first of Gulia's plays, called "The deities of the sacred grove". The play stages the formation of the Sarna Dhorom Movement which, it is said, was inspired by the deities themselves when their cult was neglected.

Gulia's possession indicates the need to revive the cult. He criticises the urban Jharkhand elite, accusing them of using the Jharkhand symbols to serve their own interests. These accusations reflect the deception of militants who feel trapped when Hindu patrons control Jharkhand committees. The characters of the play share the militants' experience. They retreat to the forest till they see on a rock in bright letters a message of hope that they, pure as they are, decipher in order to serve their community.

Reinterpretation of Tradition: A Historic Process

For the Santals, the reinterpretation of tradition had already started by 1870 when the first writers start to legitimate Santal identity in their written narratives. Contrary to Haynes and Prakash (1991: 3) who hold that subaltern resistance is lacking in consciousness, the return to the sacred grove shows how subalterns have the resources to create their own values. The values of the dominant are not the only ingredients of Jharkhand culture. True, the prestige of writing comes from the outside and has borrowed from Christian ideas of scripture as introduced by the missionaries. But no outsiders were needed to invent the new scripts.

The idea of resistance implies the mobilisation of a collective consciousness able to produce an alternative culture. The situation I have described is no more the postcolonial situation that Sammaddar (1998) describes when he speaks of tribals who have been deprived of their identity and who feel uncertain about some of their cultural values. I do not deny that subalterns have been muted by colonial and postcolonial forces but I feel we should acknowledge the positive aspects of adivasi resistance. Despite the dissensions which have followed the invention of different revealed scripts, the idea of a script which has been forgotten and rediscovered by a shaman or a dramatist has produced a very conscious process of reinvention of tradition (Ranger, 1993). By asserting a model of literacy, the missionaries were overtly claiming a dominant role, promoting religious values and their idea of a Christian history. Goody (1968) has argued that the advent of literacy creates a new distinction between myth and history, where "history" refers to "true" accounts of the past. What the Santal example shows, is that myth and history are both embedded within particular social conventions: the difference does not necessarily correlate with a distinction between true and false, or between orality and history. *Ol chiki* epitomizes the idea of a common past shared by the *adivasis*. As Street (1995: 34) puts it: "The development of literacy in itself did not alter the traditional bases of knowledge". I have described how *ol chiki* implied a ritualized model of literacy developed by reference to religious practices. To many Jharkhandis, the adoption of *ol chiki* would not necessary lead to Santal nationalism at the cost of other communities but could and should stimulate an intellectual renaissance. For others who reject *ol chiki,* it is necessary to develop a common model of literacy to transcend language difference and express common aspirations. As B. Anderson (1983) has pointed out, in its printed form, writing has been seen by many communities of speakers as having the capacity to transform minor languages into a "language of power". Anderson also theorized that print allows for the creation of "imagined communities": group of readers who imagine themselves as sharing experiences with others, contributing to the growth of what we call nationalism. We may assume that the development of a model of literacy integrates different identity claims and contributes to the coherence of a community.

The theatre of the Sarna Dhorom movement glorifies a mythical past—where Santals or Hos were in contact with ancient written civilizations like Sumer or Harappa — to allow the past to effectuate a transformation of the present. The importance of *ol chiki*, and of the return to the sacred grove, grows and penetrates cities like Ranchi or Dhanbad in the 1990s, as noted by Damodaran (2000). Then Santal ethnicity is replaced by a common cultural sensitivity of the Munda peoples expressed through the common religion of the sacred grove in Jharkhand.

Though Santal identity develops throughout the period and takes on new forms, there is a continuity in identity affirmation which belies the idea that tribal identity was a colonial invention. Yet the changes throughout our period shows that Santal identity was never a constant : there is no "zero point" except that posed by the available sources. Santals would seem to have been migrating from well before colonial times, and these migrations, we may assume, brought them constantly new challenges. We do not thereby subscribe to an "essentialist" position, for we assume, precisely, that Santal identity has always been constructed. And there is nothing ahistorical about our view, since what we try to do is exactly to sketch the history of such constructions. The immediate agents of this process of construction are themselves Santals, which is not to deny that others, such as missionaries, colonial authorities and the modern state influence the process. We take for granted that the primary agents of the process are individuals, not in the sense of the Western philosophical construction of that concept, but as reflective actors, acting in the context of their time and the conceptual limits of their intellectual milieu. In the case of *ol chiki*, it would be interesting to analyze how reading and writing, considered as embodied practices, contribute to the constitution of multiple subjects—what we may call "readers", "writers", "journalists", "producers of drama". The circulation and consumption of *ol chiki* literature might reduce the asymmetry of knowledge which has often stigmatized adivasi communities and allow them to dialogue on a more equal basis with other Indian communities.

NOTES

1. Cf. Carrin, M. *Le Parmer des Dieux, formes et argument du dsicours rituel santal* (à paraître).
2. For the concept of speech event, see Duranti (1994). In Jharkhand, like in Samoa, speech events often refer to a political context.
3. Cf. Carrin-Bouez (1986: chap.V).
4. For the concept of resistance in the context of Jharkhans, see Carrin (*forthcoming*).
5. In my analysis of twisted speech, I refer to an interactional theory of metaphor which includes pragmatics. See Fernandez (1974).
6. In 1967, the Bihar ASECA registered in 1967, started a journal Samlet Sakwa printed in *ol* script.
7. The rairangpur Adivasi Socio-Educational and Cultural association took up the task of promoting the Santali language and literature and ol script.
8. R. Murmu realized that the Santals should be educated in their own language and script at least up to the primary level. So, he decided to write school-books to propagate the script.
9. The ASECA of Calcutta, Rairangpur and Chakulia have organized Santali literacy camps at different places. Santal teachers attended these camps developing a methodology of quick teaching in Ol chiki and Santali.
10. Cf. Mahapatra (1986).
11. Let us stress that the Santal leadership is divided on the question of the Ol script. There is a group in Bengal and in Bihar who want the roman script to be retained.
12. One is attributed to Ramadas Tudu of Ghatsila, the second to Ramachandra Murmu of Silda.

REFERENCES

Andersen, P., M. Carrin and S. Soren. (forthcoming). *From Firerain to Insurrection sengel dak'khon hul dhabic' Reasserting Identity through Narrative.*

Anderson, B. 1983. *Imagined Communities.* London : Verso.

Barth, F. 1969. "Introduction," in F. Barth (ed.), Ethnic Groups and Boundaries. London and Oslo: Universitetsforlaget.

____. 1987. Cosmologies in the Making. Cambridge: Cambridge University Press.

Bodding, P.0. 1932-1936. *A Santal Dictionary.* Oslo: i kommisjon hos Jacob Dybwad, 5 vols.

Carrin-Bouez, M. 1985. "L'inégalité bien partagée ou l'impureté comme mythe chez les Santal," *Cahiers de littérature orale,* 17: 71-104.

____. 1986. La fleur et l'os : Symbolisme et Rituel Chez les Santal. Paris: EHESS.

Carrin, M. 1997. *Enfants de la déesse : dévotion et prêtrise féminine au Bengale.* Paris: Editions du CNRS et Maison des Sciences de l'Homme.

____. 2002. "Le retour du bosquet sacré. Réflexions sur la reinvention d'une culture Adivasi," in M. Carrin and C. Jaffrelot (eds.), *Résistance et autonomie dans la société indienne,* Purusartha 23.

Carrin, M. and H. Tambs-Lyche. 1998. "Une église nationale pour les Santal: du romantisme scandinave à l'orthodoxie luthérienne," *Archives des Sciences Sociales des Religions,* 103: 99-127.

_____. (forthcoming). *Peripheral Encounters Santals, Missionaries and their Changing Worlds,* 1867-1900. Delhi: Manohar.

Corbridge, S. 1988. "The Ideology of Tribal Economy and Society," *Modern Asian Studies,* 22 (1): 1-42.

Duranti, A. 1994. *From Grammar to Politics, Linguistic Anthropology in a Western Samoan Village.* Berkeley: University of California Press.

Fernandez, J. 1974. *Beyond Metaphors: The Theory of Tropes in Anthropology*. Palo Alto: Stanford University Press.

Ghosh, 1999. *Jharkhand Movement: A Study in the Politics of Regionalism*. Calcutta.

Guha, Ranajit. 1983. *Elementary Aspects of Peasant Insurgency in Colonial India.* Delhi: Oxford University Press.

Haynes, D. and G. Prakash. 1991. *Contesting Power: Resistance and Everyday Social Relations in South Asia.* Delhi: Oxford University Press.

Mahapatra, S. 1986. *Modernization and Ritual Identity and Change in Santal Society*. Calcutta: Oxford University Press.

O'Hanlon, R. 1993. "Recovering the Subject: Subaltern Studies and Histories of Resistance in Colonial South Asia," *Modern Asian Studies,* 22: 189-224.

Ranger, T. 1993. "The Invention of Tradition Revisited: The case of Colonial Africa," T. Ranger and M. Vaugham (eds.), *Legitimacy and the State in Twentieth Century Africa.* London.

Samoddar, R. 1998. *Memory, Identity, Power: Politics in the Jungle Mahals, 1890-1950.* London: Sangam Books.

Soren, S. 1999. *Santalia Catalogue of Santali manuscripts in Oslo.* Copenhagen: NIAS.

Street, B. 1984. *Literacy in Theory and Practice.* Cambridge Studies in Oral and Literate Culture, Cambrige: Cambridge University Press.

Santali Sources:

Stories about bongas. 1469. sm Santal manuscript, University Library Oslo.

Murmu, Ragunath. 1942. *Bidu-Chandan,* Play, Rairangpur.

____. 1948. *Kharwal-Bir,* Rairangpur.

THREE

SUKUMA TRIBAL IDENTITY: A New Concept and Contemporary Change

R.E.S. TANNER

The Artificiality of the Concept of Tribe

How can we theorize that any particular tribe has acquired a new identity when the classification of being a member of a particular tribe is both undefined and variably interpreted by individuals and bureaucrats? The administrative and political boundaries put onto maps are for the convenience of bureaucrats, and members of a tribe may live inside and outside their defined area and indeed migrate over these boundaries as daily or seasonal commuters.

If we take the five million people in the north-western area of Tanzania who are officially classified as Sukuma, it is in practical terms somewhat foolish to think of them as tribally united with characteristics which are not those of the people in surrounding areas who are classified differently. It seems likely that individually they will refer to themselves as Sukuma when there is a political, social or economic reason to do so or when they are required to state their tribe for a bureaucratic reason.

The ecology of their environment has appeared to have made them create a pattern of living in widely separated hamlets suited to the low fertility of the soils and irregular dispersed low rainfall. This minimizes the effort to farm had they lived in villages.

At one time before the imposed peace of colonial rule when the population would have been much smaller, they may have lived in small concentrations round the holdings of their leaders. Although this arid region borders on Lake

Victoria there has been no pastoral concentration of population along its edge either now or in the past perhaps because they would have been exposed to water-borne attacks.

The Necessary Approach to Considering Tribal Identity

The current identity of these five million Sukuma starts with the logical difficulty over the word "identity" which is defined as the quality or condition of being the same, individuality, condition of being identified in feeling, interest, etc. and that which serves to identify the holder as an identity card of which the last definition dates from 1900 (*Oxford English Dictionary,* 1956: 1, 951). So we have first to consider to what extent to which these millions can have a common identity.

As a question of logic it would seem that every single Sukuma would have a separate identity and that might be shared to some extent with identical twins but as the numbers who are compared increases, the extent of hypothetically similar characteristics must become no more than the minimalist lowest common denominator.

In addition to this problem they are distinguished demographically by age and sex factors as well as geographically by their neighbourhood loyalties since they certainly see themselves as different individually and collectively to those in their own hamlet and the others who live next door in terms of social distance. Although there is a quite distinct Sukuma language (Batibo, 1985), there will be variations in how it is spoken within all the above categories; grammatically it is a tonal language with eighteen tenses but how many of the contemporary Sukuma can use these correctly.

In general the levels at which we must consider Sukuma identity are firstly the overall large scale block known administratively as Sukuma land for which data is available in the form of published customary law (Cory, 1953), then the neighbourhood—the so-called relationships within the geographical and social sky-line—and finally how they see themselves individually.

Then under each of these headings we have to consider the known historical aspects of Sukuma life starting with the explorer Stanley's comments in the 1880s (Stanley, 1878, 1890) and which was written up quite extensively in the colonial period perhaps to a larger extent than any other Tanzanian tribal community (H. Cory, D.W. Malcolm, H. Senior, R.E.S. Tanner, A.C.A Wright, etc) and then to see what has happened to their ideas and practices since then (F. Wijsen, J.W. Drangert, P. Brandstrom, C.M. Varkevisser, etc.)[1]

Modernity and Tribal Identit(y)ies

Firstly the boundaries within which a tribal identity can be identified are usually defined by the authorities and in most cases were originally defined by the colonial government as a start to the orderly processes of government as shown in the European model. Lines on the map which may have had little regard for the relationships of the people on the ground. The boundaries of Sukumaland were originally in uninhabited areas up to which the growing Sukuma population has moved and then passed over.

Identity in this context is a legal definition. For the Sukuma it does not coincide with tribal identity as in the Indian Reservations in the United States so residence within or without these boundaries defined by the central government does not necessarily coincide with tribal membership. To the west the boundary used to be that of Smith Sound, a branch of Lake Victoria with the Zinza living on the other side but steady migration has meant that the Zinza have been pushed back or absorbed.

Whether an individual is a Sukuma depends on whether he or she claims to be one; there is no documentary system which would substantiate such a claim except baptismal certificates for the Christian minority which states that a child came for baptism in a parish within Sukumaland in which the parents claimed residence or that individuals have tax certificates to the same effect. It is largely a personal matter whether an individual identifies with being a Sukuma enough to claim to be one or has some more immediate need to be accepted as one.

Sukumaland certainly contains a large majority of Sukuma but also large numbers of people with other tribal backgrounds as well as some who have created fictive Sukuma backgrounds for themselves or who have long-term relationships with Sukuma partners. There are no legal restrictions on movement within this country except some periodic mass expulsions of the seemingly unattached from the capital Dar es Salaam. With an exogamous marital system and no villages based on kinship it is not too difficult to claim agnatic or affinal relationships through a grandparent.

So it is initially a question of who are distinguishably Sukuma by their behaviour or do we just accept that saying they are a Sukuma when asked by an outsider for whatever economic, social or political reasons which either party have in their minds at that time.

Other than language the Sukuma have not had in the past or in the immediate present social behaviour patterns which would distinguish them from other tribal groups. No age grade system, no initiation rites for boys or girls, no circumcision, no identifying tattoos or hair styles, even their religious practices are not all that different to every other tribal group in Tanzania and particularly in those societies surrounding Lake Victoria. Nothing at all in any specific sense that would enable them to state categorically that "we Sukuma do this and you do not and we feel all the better for this distinction".

The Sukuma Expansion from Tribes to Tribe

Historically the present Sukuma were a number of dispersed "tribes" or groups of people who considered themselves distinct by their association with one particular ancestor who "opened" that piece of uninhabited forest. As a whole they were separated by vacant land and their own distinct traditions and were named collectively as "the people to the north" of the caravan routes from the coast to the Great Lakes whose identity depended on their "constitutional" leaders' ability to provide them with social and ecological stability.

These separate chiefdoms suffered under colonialism as it was assumed that these chiefs had power whereas these powers were no more than the ability to organize compromises and to provide rain which itself depended on relatively small populations. Each group looked inwards on its own ritual needs and subsistence concerns within a system of ancestor propitiation and over the last century few have converted to either Christianity or Islam.

Now the chiefs have been abolished and there is a system of district and parish councils depending on majority voting rather than compromise and without this overall consent such decision making does not necessarily lead to action and which often leaves a discontented outvoted minority

Certainly these particular groups have become much more clearly differentiated collectively as a Tribe from when they were no more than a number of petty chiefdoms/tribes. In a sense this has been forced on them by a relentless bureaucratic need for each individual to be classified and identified, but this has become outdated. In the Tanzanian context, there has been the political down-playing of tribalism as part of their political process caused by the disasters in other African countries of tribalism dominating politics. They have had the national good fortune to have had an imposed national language — Swahili, from the earliest days of German colonialism which is now the language of administration, education and business. This same language is now used in the rituals of Christianity and only Islam with its basic holy book written in Arabic remains outside this nationalising process which comes with the use of a single language by a very disparate tribal population.

This has resulted in Sukuma and other tribal languages being judged irrelevant as a handicap to the processes of development or not given any prominence in their overt political and bureaucratic processes. One suspects that there would always have to be a Sukuma holding a prominent departmental portfolio such as Paul Bomani who was the Finance Minister for many years.

Further the Sukuma identity has been progressively infiltrated by immigration and emigration, primary education in the national language Swahili, the emergence of occupations which have no origins in their past for which being a Sukuma is no particular advantage and familial instability caused by the innumerable pressures of modernity, the need to earn money from institutions which have no direct tribal connections except the federation of cooperatives based on cotton, the mass media, the dissatisfactions with economic and political progress, the failure of development hopes for a marked improvement in their standard of living and ecological change. The Sukuma have no isolatable characteristics other than language

The Expansion in Scale of Sukuma Life

In almost every aspect of their lives the Sukuma have been affected directly by outsiders and indirectly by factors from outside their borders. Firstly there were external expatriates whether administrators, missionaries and doctors and with political independence these have been replaced by internal expatriates. Their knowledge of the outside world in the past came from the thousands of Sukuma who visited outside communities as porters in the great trading caravans which passed through to the south on their way between the coast and the Great Lakes and currently from those who work elsewhere. They might well think that they are no more independent than they were a hundred years before and perhaps even less so with the abolition of the system of local government based on their own vaguely hereditary chiefs and the need for rain-making rituals.

Colonial rule was an influence but not a particularly active force in making them change since it worked within budget balancing limitations and small numbers of senior expatriate administrative staff which probably averaged out at not more than one per hundred thousand adult Tanganyikans. The political agitation for independence and the creation of a nation centred elsewhere forced them to recognize that whatever power they might have would always be controlled from elsewhere and even that was controlled by non-national international political and economic forces.

Change has also been forced on them by their own growth in numbers from the control of mass diseases, the progressive deforestation of their environment which has become significantly more arid, the individualism of education as a necessity for economic progress at the expense of communalism and even the imposition on them of real rather than social time by broadcasting.

Importance of an Identifying Language

Their own language is grammatically complicated but it is in the Bantu group of languages and therefore not all that different in its basic constructions to other Bantu ones and particularly it is not clearly distinguishable from that of the several million Nyamwezi to their immediate south. In fact they are surrounded by other Bantu speakers except for the cattle keeping pastoral Nilo-Hamitic Maasai to the east with whose language they have nothing in common, which is at least a contributing factor in their self-perpetuating intermittent mutual violent hostility

However to have their own language used particularly by women and religious practitioners in their divining and in their "talking in tongues" glossolalia which uses Sukuma phonemes, as well as in Christian ancillary prayers is internally important. It is used as a defensive mechanism against the intrusions of outsiders since it often can require the use of interpreters although most of those involved understand Swahili well enough. It has its own specialist vocabularies for plants, diseases and soils, in fact almost everything which distinguishes them from other tribal groups must lie in these specialized vocabularies, but of course even in this there is no clear dividing line between the languages and social practices of the Zinza to the west, Nyamwezi to the south and the Shashi to the east.

Retrospective Concept of Happiness

It is perhaps a common human illusion that the past was better than the present and to some extent this may have been true for the Sukuma whose environment has been progressively down graded by over-grazing and intensive cultivation particularly for cotton as a cash crop. The explorer Stanley in passing through Sukumaland after the annual rains had fallen and before the Rindepest epidemic described it in almost idyllic terms.

The past is seen as a period in which they were relatively independent in their domestic and local affairs. Their own customs predominated by popular agreement since other than expulsion which was always a failure of communalism, they did not have the means to impose decisions on people who did not agree to the decisions of arbitrators until the importation into East Africa of large numbers of muzzle loading muskets after the end of the Napoleonic European war in 1815.

This system of arbitration was replaced by democratic elections and voting on issues which meant that decisions were no longer taken by the prolonged working out of passive consent. The long period of one party government following the euphoria of gaining political independence did not lead to much local popularity for the achievements of the new central government which is probably much more locally intrusive than the colonial government which it succeeded. The contemporary cynicism of the new political processes has to be seen against the folk memories of a better past.

They would probably see themselves as less locally independent than they were even under colonial rule and would certainly see this is so now after the disastrous compulsory villagization programme which abolished their ecologically sound dispersed pattern of farming. This destroyed their traditional pattern of social organization which could not be recreated after the programme was cancelled and substantially reduced their agricultural output.

Their own military skills kept the Maasai at bay by counter raiding and such misfortunes as they had such as the Rindepest epidemic of the 1880s and contemporary AIDS epidemic, came from outside and was not the direct result of any Sukuma failings.

The Impositions of Modernity

They were probably better off in the past and the success of the cotton cooperatives in replacing the domination of Indians in the cotton industry was prior to Independence and was largely under the leadership of morally constrained Seventh Day Adventist minority who did not drink or dance. This was progressively eroded by inefficiency, corruption and the economic disadvantages of Tanzania internationally. The pay of government employees has been diminished by inflation so that it is not so attractive except as a source of corruption and prestige titles.

The growth of the population has led to widespread underemployment and limited urban opportunities have not provided much of an alternative to subsistence farming since people from other tribes have had equal opportunities there. Education has not paid off except in the first years of independence when the expansion of the state as a bureaucracy provided opportunities. Now upward mobility, as a way out of subsistence farming, has been severely limited by the cost of secondary education. It was popularly thought that the removal of expatriates from government service would provide job opportunities for those with limited education.

Whereas in other tribal societies large scale conversion to Christianity among the Chagga, Angoni and Haya has been a major influence towards change, this has not happened to the Sukuma. It is not so much that the major external religions have not provided alternative opportunities for worship and the relief from misfortunes as only a few purely Sukuma Christian sects have developed but that they are not more efficient than the Sukuma's quasi-traditional faith(s) in dealing with their problems. Their system of religious belief and practice and its easy availability in every locality related to payment by results, is not a modern adjustment mirroring what has occurred in developed states but a pre-existing one fitting into their exogamous dispersed social structure.

New Forms of Identity Imposed by Lowered Mortality Rates

The control of earlier prevalent mass diseases and the work of maternity clinics has led to a rapid expansion of the number of Sukuma so that the population pyramid has become distorted by the enormous increase in the young who are no longer successfully integrated into a system of traditional neighbourhood government controlled by middle aged men.

In the past the high rates of infant morality meant that it was usually possible to divide up the land quite equitably between sons who any way would have tended to segment and move to new areas since they had married exogamously; neighbourhoods contained people who at the most were only tenuously related.

The survival of women into adulthood may have lost to their families of having a scarce resource to profitably marry off and may have led to more young men and women making their own arrangements for partnerships.

New Forms of Identity from Imposed Peace

The colonial government imposed peace as far as it could on inter-tribal tensions and the successor government has continued this policy of trying to prevent cattle raiding between the Maasai and the Sukuma. This laudable policy had overlooked the fact that the threat of violence and its intermittent practice was a solution to existing social tensions; changes in relative population power and the unequal ownership of cattle caused by drought and disease. If moveable cattle are a principle means of gaining status and money, then moved they will be as their very visible presence is a temptation to theft and for young men a way of gorging on animal protein for a few days.

For law and order to become a reality requires not only the expenditure of considerable sums on maintaining staff and equipment by the central government but the active cooperation of the people to whom it is being applied, rather than the intermittent raids by armed police to seize and destroy bows and arrows. It is in this that the Sukuma have developed a modern form of their traditional identity

Traditionally the young men "basumba batale" under the direction of the elders kept the peace, controlled theft and kept a watchful eye on strangers, but theft increased without the police being able or indeed even being prepared to see that it was their legal responsibility to attempt to do so based as they were in the towns. For people who have very little property theft is very serious and thieves if caught are often killed regardless of the stolen properties value. So the Sukuma reorganized or rather revitalized their own traditional security system by creating local vigilantes the "*sungu sungu*" which quickly reduced theft but whom the police tried to arrest as usurping their legal powers It was only after the intervention of the President Julius Nyerere that they came to be accepted as local auxiliary police and became a matter for which they were congratulated and other communities were encouraged to copy their example.

Between 1970 and 1984, there were 3692 killings of suspected witches in Tanzania of which 2120 (1869 were mainly post-menopausal women) occurred in Sukumaland and these may be minimal figures. The killings were carried out by hired young men and the deaths were greeted with a local sense of relief.

What may have contributed to this characteristic of the contemporary Sukuma identity. Firstly the traumatic effects of the villagization programme expressed in disillusionment, frustration and annoyance (Mesaki, 1994), the abolition of the chiefs who had ritual rather than administrative roles and the decline of the ancestor cult because of the enforced rather than voluntary movement of the whole tribal population into locations which for most of them had no kinship or environmental connections.

The streamlining of the administration into a bureaucratic hierarchy centred on the capital hundreds of miles away and the development of a centralized system of local courts staffed by appointees who would not necessarily be Sukuma or who could not understand their language, made the administration even less popular than in colonial times. This left them psychologically unprotected for the coming together of multiple stresses.

Witchcraft has no definitions which could relate to specific events and behaviour. It is an idea which can be applied and in fact has been applied by the Sukuma to a wide variety of behaviour which is not otherwise explicable and controllable by the more traditional understandings of ancestor propitiation. The Sukuma have come to correlate it in some subliminal way with the misfortunes of illness such as AIDS and the deaths of children, material lack of success and the loss of jobs and promotion and even the politically supported advancement of women into positions of authority.

Whatever the reality of relationships with the spirit world, it is a field of opportunity for material advancement and even in colonial times there were more diviners or practitioners of quasi-traditional religious ideas in Mwanza town, the main urban area in Sukumaland which has now grown into a substantial city, than in the rural areas. There has now been a substantial expansion and commercialization of divination aided by the issuing of permits by district representatives of the Ministry of Culture which became increasingly devoted to the anti-witchcraft activities.

The Slow Rate of Cognitive Change

To travel and work in Sukumaland is to see people and overt practise which are no different to that of people anywhere else in Tanzania except for the cattle keeping Maasai or indeed in neighbouring countries. It is easy to think that since they are modern in appearance and in the carrying of watches, radios, shoes, ball-point pens and bicycles that they have become modern. This can be no more than an assumption but all these changes have concerned very few generations of Sukuma and their pattern of understandings will have originated long before these short-term accelerated changes have taken place.

Above all the Sukuma are pragmatists in all their relations with each other and the spirit world which are dominated by short-term as well as long ranging reciprocities; they were perhaps modern before modernity came into Sukumaland in their ideas of the own and tribal identities. Certainly, they have new ideas but they are within their existing cognitive patterning (Tanner, 1997).

There is always at the back of their minds that the spirit world is a major influence on what they can or have not been able to achieve and this pattern has shown considerable ability to adjust. Whether or not they are more credulous than other tribal people would be impossible to prove but the fact that they know that impostors exist now as much as in the past does not seem to affect their understanding that some cure and some do not just as modern Westerners know that their own system of "scientific" medicine must ultimately fail; in this sense those who might use "scientific" medicine have their own "tribal" credulities.

Their religious belief system has adjusted very well to the control of various forms of anti-social behaviour which are quite beyond any legal or political system based on literacy to control. It justifies and explains migration and crop successes and failure, personal and livestock fertility as well as a justification for inter and intra group hostilities. Above all this religion based morality is based on pragmatism, that it pays since it is not based on any abstract concepts of morality but one that is almost entirely circumstantial; theft or whatever is of course wrong and the elders consulted by Cory were happy enough to produce an overall system of Sukuma customary law but it is not theft to steal cattle from the Maasai or indeed to kill them in the process just as it is not wrong to kill thieves and witches if it leads to local peace of mind.

Some Tentative Conclusions about Sukuma Identity

In the sense of their major identity there has been a steady move from a situation in which they created and maintained their own identity before the era of Western influence towards the current situation in which their Sukumaness will only be activated by political changes which would seem to apply to them alone; they did not see villagization as a threat to them alone since it applied to the whole country. There would have to be threats to activate this dormant tribal identity which may be unlikely to happen as the national political framework of thinking is to avoid tribalism. Even the Bujora Sukuma Cultural Centre, the focus of their contemporary tribal identity has "discos".

At the neighbourhood level Sukuma identity has shown considerable adaptive resilience in developing a traditional idea of self-protection into neighbourhood policing with its hands-on immediate violence replicating the system which kept them and their property safe in the past. Similarly their religious system has changed with the times to provide a readily available local service for those who are in difficulties which is explicable within their own cognitive ways of thinking. The Sukuma identity in these two areas is very much alive even if it overlaps to the ideas and practices in other neighbouring societies.

At the individual level it would seem that having a Sukuma identity is not very important as it is not a help in getting and retaining jobs or protecting them in an uncertain modern world should they leave their homeland.

Under the conditions of modern life in which boundaries are not of much significance against the spread of ideas and practices as well as good and bad fortune, tribal identity at whatever level has to pay off pragmatically both psychologically and socially in order to survive.

NOTES

1. The bibliography of the Sukuma is too large to append to an illustrative chapter about tribal identity. Their ostensible uniformity, the ease of access, their lack of radically distinct practices. their resistance to conversion and the ways that they have moved themselves into modernity seems to have to have attracted and continue to attract social scientists.

REFERRNCES

Batibo, H.1985. *Le Kesukuma (langue Bantu de Tanzania)*. Paris: Editions Recherche sur les civilsations.

Cory, H. 1953. *Sukuma Law and Custom. London*: Oxford University Press.

Mesaki, S. 1994. "Witch-killing in Sukumaland," in R. Abrahams (ed.), Witchcraft in *Contemporary Tanzania*. University of Cambridge: African Studies Centre.

Stanley, H.M. 1878. *Through the Dark Continent*. London: Sampson Low.

____. 1890. *In Darkest Africa*. London: Sampson Low.

Tanner, R.E.S. 1997. "Cognitive Development, Socialisation and Cognitive Mutations. A Critique and Elaboration of Boyer's Naturalness of Religion," *Journal of Social Sciences*, 1 (2): 91-98.

FOUR

THE POLITICS OF IDENTITY: A Comparison of Two Cases

LAWRENCE F. VAN HORN

The term politics of identity in the title of this article is borrowed from Adrian Peace, an anthropologist at the University of Adelaide in Australia, who employs it analyzing "When the Salmon Come: The Politics of Summer Fishing in an Irish Community" (Peace, 1996: 85-106). Peace (1996: 85) notes that collective identity in general invokes "the ethos of the community as a whole" versus "the heterogeneity of its constituent parts." At certain times, unity of opinion is achieved; at others opposition or competition reigns from within and there is no unity. From a supplicant's point of view, is there a relationship between unity of opinion and the successful application of power? Such a posited relationship is intended to fit in with the theme of case studies of power in tribal communities, which is one of the themes of this volume.

I relate two cases that I personally observed. The concept of tribal community definitely applies in the first case because it relates to a tribal government of Micmac Indians, an indigenous North American Indian people. The second case is part of a modern United States federal agency, so tribal community only loosely applies to the "tribal" ways of European American players in the case. Nonetheless, the *politics-of-identity* concept does apply as with the first case. Within the *politics-of-identity,* I suggest that the process of psychological identification with the supplicant is a crucial step leading to empathy that the decision maker who holds and exercises power must take if the supplicant's request is to be accommodated and unity of opinion achieved. In each case, people with power made a decision. In the first case, the supplicant's plan appeared to be initially successful, but ultimately did not work because it was not sustainable in the end. The people with power decided not to allow it. In the second case, the desired outcome of the supplicant was ultimately achieved, and the result turned out to be satisfactory for all concerned. In this case, a person exercised dormant power that he at first had not appreciated he had. The two cases are compared for their similarities and differences involving the *politics-of-identity.*

The first case concerns a tribal government of a North American Indian people of Canada in which a leader introduced an economic change but could not make it prevail because the powers-that-be came to disagree with it. The second case concerns a unit of a federal agency of the United States Government in which an employee as a disabled person had difficulty prevailing but ultimately her need was met after a group's opposition was recognized and by-passed.

In two previous publications (Van Horn, 1983 and 2002), I describe and analyze the group ethic among the Micmac Indians of Canada and place it in an ethno-historical context. Data are presented therein to show that the so-called Micmac group ethic or response—people working together in groups for particular purposes—is an important cultural value that is congruent with Micmac egalitarianism. The source of the data is the village of Burnt Church in the Province of New Brunswick in eastern Canada. The data include classroom and business situations, incidents of behaviour in the wider community, Micmac versus English bilingual language choices among fellow bilinguals, and material taken from the life histories of many community members, including an older woman known as a *puuoin* or witch and a chief, who happens to be the subject of my first case. The data illustrate both positive and negative models of behaviour from Micmac perspectives.

Some years ago the Micmac chief mentioned above attempted to improve housing in his community by asking the heads of several households to turn over ownership of that family's house to the tribal government—the Burnt Church Band of Micmac Indians. The Burnt Church Band Council approved this plan according to their usual procedure by passing a legislative resolution. The plan was then to seek funds from the Canadian Bureau of Indian Affairs of the federal Ministry of Indian Affairs and Northern Development as monthly rent for that family to occupy the house. The former prime minister of Canada, Jean Chretien, was Minister of Indian Affairs and Northern Development at the time, having served in that capacity from 1968 to1974.

Federal funds coming into the community could be obtained to build a new house, but funds were lacking as a category for major home repairs including rewiring a house for new appliances such as electric stoves that were being introduced at Burnt Church. The leader will simply be referred to as The Chief as I continue. The Chief's position was an elected one, as are all of the other offices of the Burnt Church Band, such as the welfare officer and the several members of the band council. The Chief saw a need, and he thought he saw a way to meet that need and to save the federal government money in the bargain. In addition to new electrical wiring, new siding sometimes was needed for the wooden frame houses, as well as the addition of a new room when a family expanded by having more children. Why not seek band-administered rent money from the federal government for these needs? It would preserve existing homes and upgrade them at much less cost than building a new house.

Needless to say that in modern times, the traditional Micmac subsistence economy has not been in place, although it still exists to some extent—hunting, fishing, and gathering with limited horticulture—to supplement small-scale jobs making crafts with traditional themes for sale to tourists, cutting and collecting fire wood for sale locally and regionally for use in domestic wood-burning stoves, and the sale of fish in the same manner caught locally and distributed by way of the Burnt Church Cooperative Association, which includes craft-making, fishing, and wood-cutting and is known in short as the Burnt Church Cooperative.

Since this major-improvement need was not being met by any existing category of funding, The Chief attempted to meet it by implementing his plan. At first it worked well. Gradually, he had different household heads deed over their home ownership to the band council. The household heads then requested and received rent to continue occupying the house, since the band, that is, the tribal government now owned the house. The band's welfare officer initiated the rent requests, and the welfare-officer counterparts in the regional office of the Canadian Bureau of Indian Affairs (CBIA) approved the rent requests. This process worked so well that The Chief told other Micmac chiefs in other New Brunswick Micmac communities about his idea. He even mentioned it in the presence of officials of the Canadian Bureau of Indian Affairs. After all, they had been approving these requests for rent month after month for some time.

Suddenly The Chief was told by CBIA Officials to stop this practice. These federal Officials said that there was no provision for it in the regulations, so therefore it could not legally be done. How does the politics of identity help us understand this situation? I defer analysis until after presenting the second case.

In the second case, a United States Government employee, who is physically disabled, sought a better, more convenient spot to park her electric scooter overnight inside the building where she works. She needed to be closer to the door designated as the entry/exit for handicapped persons because it was becoming more and more difficult for her to walk the distance from her current scooter-parking spot to that entry/exit, which is level with the parking lot with no incline and no steps to negotiate. Such a request was within the purview of the Americans with Disabilities Act of 1990 (ADA). This is a wide-ranging federal law mandating accommodations in employment, transportation, building accessibility, and other areas. Henceforth-the woman supplicant in this case is called "The Employee".

The Employee has multiple sclerosis (MS) and walks with two canes when she does walk. She normally rides on an electric scooter that she drives up and down the main corridor of each floor to reach other office spaces when she has to leave her desk on the second floor and go elsewhere on business in the four-story building. She uses the elevator to accommodate her scooter to travel between floors. She had been parking her scooter overnight along a wall inside the office complex on the first floor that is occupied by a regional director of the agency, henceforth called "The Regional Director. The Employee" works for a nationwide planning office of the agency, housed primarily on the second floor. The Regional Director and her staff constitute a different unit of the same agency.

Some staff members of The Regional Director objected to The Employee's scooter being parked closer to the handicapped entry/exit alleging interference with the many visitors who come for appointments with "The Regional Director". This was not entirely logical because "The Employee's" scooter would not be there during the day, only in the evening starting at about six o'clock with removal in the morning at about eight-thirty.

Another location closer to the entry/exit was found across the hall corridor in the office complex of "The Regional Director's" financial officer, henceforth referred to as The Financial Officer. He observed that appropriate space was more readily convenient and available in The Regional Director's office complex. This was true physically but not politically.

During negotiations by a Union Steward on behalf of The Employee as a member of the American Federation of Government Employees (AFGE), The Financial Officer revealed that a cousin of his suffers from MS, and he then said, as if he had experienced an epiphany, that he understood the situation. Nevertheless, this case, which occurred a few years ago, took three months to resolve. What led to the resolution was the cooperation of "The Financial Officer" who apparently because of his personal experience with his cousin was able to identify with "The Employee" and not with the immediate staff of "The Regional Director." Once that happened, "The Financial Officer" used his power to make a workable arrangement with "The Employee" to park her electric scooter overnight within the office space that he controlled.

How does the *politics of identity* help us to understand not only the first case but also the second case? Both cases start out similarly in that each had a supplicant who needed help but who lacked the power to directly change the situation. Both supplicants enlisted additional help. The Chief secured the endorsement of the Burnt Church Band Council, which empowered the band's welfare officer to carry out the deed transfers of the homes of cooperating heads of household to the band and then request monthly rent monies for ongoing occupancy from CBIA Officials. The Employee asked a Union Steward to negotiate on her behalf. Both cases had people in power whose positions did not change. When the CBIA Officer realized that there was no existing funding category for the major home repairs they were inadvertently approving, they stopped the practice. Since the staff of The Regional Director never accepted The Employees as a member of their group, it was seemingly easy to deny the specific request because of a lack of identification with the supplicant. Consequently, there was a lack of interest in learning the facts surrounding the case. Resolution only materialized when The Financial Officer decided to use what power he had. He could have gone along with rejecting the request, but was persuaded reevaluate the situation by The Steward. That in turn led to his identifying with and achieving empathy with The Employee because of the similar infirmity of one of his relatives.

In the case of The Chief, no personal identification occurred. The CBIA Officials felt they simply could not identify with The Chief because his innovative plan had no precedent and no existing approved budgeting category for legal federal funding. Even though these officials had signed off on the monthly home rental payments under the deed transfers of The Chief's plan, they felt they had been deceived. However, The Chief was trying to deceive no one. He believed that he had found a legitimate bureaucratic way to meet an unmet community need, and he was willing to share his solution with other Micmac chiefs and with federal officials. The latter did not permit the establishment of his plan. Unity of opinion was not achieved; there was no unity.

The Chief did not have the aid of another source of power as The Employee did in the person of The Financial Officer who was prompted to identify with The Employee by the Union Steward. In the final analysis, The Union Steward acted as a culture broker (van Willigen, 1993) between The Financial Officer and The Employee by suggesting creative ways that The Employee could be helped under the auspices of the Americans with Disabilities Act. From the politics-of-identity perspective, the personal identification of The Financial Officer with The Employee was essential, causing him to invoke his power and use it to help her, thus accommodating her and her request. Although The Employee's request never actually reached The Regional Director herself and although her immediate staff never agreed to the request, effective unity of opinion was still achieved through the cooperation of The Financial Officer.

REFERENCES

Peace, Adrian. 1996. "When the Salmon Come: The Politics of Summer Fishing in an Irish Community." *Journal of Anthropological Research* 52 (1) 85-106.

Van Horn, Lawrence F. 1983. "The Group Ethic among Micmac Indians: Implications for Education and Work," (pp.99-107) in Kathryn T. Molohon (ed.), *Challenge for Change: Education and Modern Society,* Sudbury, Ontario, Canada: Laurentian University Review 15 (2, February 1983): 1-137.

—— 2002. "The Group Ethic versus Individualism among North American Micmacs," (pp.341-354) in Georg Pfeffer and Deepak Kumar Behera (eds.), *Contemporary Society: Tribal Studies* (Vol. V) *Concept of Tribal Society.* New Delhi: Concept Publishing Company.

Van Willigen, John. 1986 [1993]. *Applied Anthropology: An Introduction.* (Revised edition) Westport, Connecticut, USA: Greenwood Publishing Group. First published in 1986, South Hadley, Massachusetts, USA: Bergin and Garvey Publishers of the Greenwood Publishing Group.

FIVE

FORTS AND CAMPS IN TRIBAL ORISSA: Kshatriyaization and Industrialization Compared

CHRISTIAN STRÜMPELL

Introduction

The present paper deals with social relationships in a small industrial settlement in Orissa's Koraput District. It is attached to a hydro-electric power project, a public sector undertaking established fifty years ago and is situated in the hilly and until recently hardly accessible tribal belt between South Orissa and Northern Andhra Pradesh. The workforce of the industrial project is neither local nor tribal, but consists of migrant labourers. In this regard it is not at all unique, but follows a more general trend. Industrial enterprises in all parts of the country employ mostly migrant workers and not locals (Rothermund, 1978; Breman, 1994; Parry, 1999b,c, 2003; Meher, 2004).

The majority of the roughly 350 workers and their families originate from the coastal plains of the two adjacent states and perceive their small-scale industrial society to be distinctively different from both the tribal one in its vicinity and the caste society in their native villages left behind decades ago. The difference between migrants and tribals is locally not given much thought, it is simply explained with the latter's general "backwardness" and specific lack of "education". In contrast to that the difference between the migrants' industrial society and the caste society of their native villages is said to derive from an equality dominating almost all aspects of social life, an equality supposed to be proper for a modern, industrialised India. It shall be shown that this concept of equality cannot be equated with the Western concept of equality. It is not based on the idea of *Homo Aequalis,* i.e. an ontological equality between all individuals, but is a temporary deviation from the practice of *Homo Hierarchicus* accessible only to a few. This indigenous concept of equality, however, differentiates the industrial migration to the hinterland from earlier migration waves that led to the establishment of caste societies. It is the aim of this paper to highlight this contrast.

In the first section, I will briefly summarize the historical model of pre-independent, pre-industrial migration to peripheral Orissa followed by an ethnographic account giving evidence of its present day importance. In the second section, I will introduce the ethnographic setting in South Orissa and analyze the kind of equality among the migrant workers as manifested in contemporary social practise and in oral histories about the settlement's foundation. The findings will then be related to basic features of the local ritual arena. At the end, I will offer the tentative conclusion that the indigenous concept of equality or of a modern, industrial society led to a much more severe marginalization of the tribal population than earlier migrations from the lowlands to the hills.

Kshatriyaization or the Establishment of Forts

The central region of Orissa around the cities Bhubaneswar, Cuttack and Puri is encircled by a number of feudatory states called *Garhjat* or *gadajata* in Oriya literally meaning "born from the fort" (Kulke 1993a, b). The forts served as capitals for small chiefs and petty kings representing on this local level the Gajapati kings at the centre. Before the Pax Britannica began to spread to the hinterlands of Orissa in the late 19th century it was of crucial importance for these local kings to secure the loyalty of the tribal population surrounding the fort. Warfare between local kingdoms[1] was not uncommon and in such an atmosphere of instability, they needed the tribes' manpower to secure their political survival. They did so by inviting Brahmins to settle in their vicinity with the intention to spread Hindu law and therefore creating a process of "inner colonization". An important medium for that was the sponsoring of tribal deities. The local kings established these as their tutelary deities, their *kula devata* (ibid.). The tribal deities were Hinduized during this process, i.e. temples proper for a Hindu deity were constructed and Brahmins and other service castes were invited to settle in the chiefdom. Notwithstanding, this type of Hinduization did not imply an exclusion of the local tribal population. They were integrated into the newly emerging caste society as they were to perform specific roles during the worship of their former tribal deity.

Tanabe (1996) demonstrates that these goddesses continue to play a major role until today and he does so by referring to the context of local rituals as well as frequently told oral histories in a chiefdom situated south of Puri. According to the latter an ancestor of the present chief of Garh Manatir was given the permission to conquer and to rule over the region by the king of Khurda in whose vicinity the fort lics. The advise to seek permission from the king and the subsequent blessings for the undertaking he received from a goddess called *Ramachandi*. Hence, Tanabe concludes that legitimacy from royal authorities alone is not sufficient to gain rule over a territory, but first and foremost a legitimating relationship with the local earth goddess has to be established. After he achieved to conquer the territory, he Hinduized the cult of the goddess Ramachandi. He installed her as his *istadevi*, constructed a temple for her within his fort and attracted Brahmins by giving them tax free land in his chiefdom. By similar means also other castes such as washermen and barbers, scribesmen and swordsmen were attracted to render their caste specific services. This migration forced many of the Saora, the tribe inhabiting the conquered area around Garh Manatir, to leave towards the hilly hinterland, but nevertheless, they were also integrated to some extent. Their priest, the *jani*[2], continued to serve at the old tribal shrine of the goddess Ramachandi situated outside the fort and was given tax free land for his service just like all the other specialists. Thus, not only was a caste society established in Garh Manatir, but the local tribal population was made part of it and this integration lasts until the present day.

That comes clearly to the fore in the context of what Tanabe calls the present day ritual arena. In the month of *Asvina,* the major ritual for the tutelary deity Ramachandi is conducted. It starts with the performance of rituals by a tribal priest or *jani* in the sacred grove of Ramachandi situated outside the fort. There the goddess takes possession of him and enters the fort followed by the attendants of the festival. Inside the fort the chief awaits the goddess holding as a symbol of his royal authority a sword. The goddess takes the sword from him and lifts it, so that the chief as all other attendants get convinced that she possesses the body of the *jani*. The chief then bows down in front of her and washes her feet, a sequence unambiguously marking his dependence on the acceptance and protection of the goddess. The procession then leads towards the palace where the goddess is offered cooked food in the name of the chief. After that a process of unification of the indigenous power of the goddess and the royal dominance of the chief starts, which culminates after the sacrifice of a goat in the symbolic union of the two within the royal sword. This union is mediated by the Brahmin priest. Before the sacrifice takes place he enters the scene, separates the goddess from the sword and purifies the goat by chanting a mantra into its ear. The ritual concludes with a large procession inside the fort headed by the chief and followed by all other attendants, a procession whose order is a direct expression of the order within the chiefdom (*ibid.*).

The whole ritual is interpreted by Tanabe following Marglin as an expression of a circular hierarchy where the different participants change their hierarchical position vis-à-vis each other according to the ritual context. Initially the royal chief and Brahmin bow down in front of the tribal goddess and her priest, afterwards the Brahmin by the sake of his ritual status is able to pacify the dangerous aspects of the tutelary goddess and to unite the benevolent aspects with the chief, who then puts this power with his rule into effect. It was mainly by establishing a relationship with the local goddess that the fort emerged as a ritual centre and that it formed a social *holos* integrating migrants of all castes as well as the indigenous population into the wider framework of the newly emerging caste society.

Industrialization or the Establishment of Camps

The Setting

The establishment of the Sananadi Hydro Electric (Joint) Project, in short SHE(J)P, stands in a stark contrast to the model of kshatriyaization. But before turning to oral histories and the ritual arena a few more general data on the project and its setting shall be given. The project exploits the resources of a river called Sananadi[3] forming partially the border between the two Union States Orissa and Andhra Pradesh. The three project settlements are also situated along the border and shelter the 350 employees and their nuclear families. They are for the most part Telugu or Oriya from different provinces of the respective states, but might also come from Tamil Nadu, Kerala and Nepal. They belong to either of more than 60 castes and fill the different ranks from "engineer" to "helper" or "attender" in several departments distributed among three settlements. Generally, the number of high caste employees holding high ranking posts is disproportionately high, but also lower castes and Harijan can be found among the engineers as well as Brahmins may serve as peons. The order of the industrial project thus does not rest on caste, the notable exception being the "sanitary mazdoor", i.e. the employees cleaning latrines and drainages. They all belong to a caste of Telugu scavengers, the Pakhi.[4]

The two main project institutions are the dam and the powerhouse situated alongside the river in Jallaham and Chatamput respectively, 40 km apart from each other. Attached to these two massive buildings are a number of offices, small hospitals, clubs and filter and pump houses for producing potable water and finally the government quarters for the employees. In addition to these government-owned project facilities a private market has come up in all settlements engaging an increasing, but still marginal portion of its inhabitants. The public sector undertaking and its related institutions dominate life in the settlements. The surrounding land is nationalized and thus agriculture illegal and the market almost saturated. Livelihood can only be gained in the project and access to it is barely possible without the help of project officers or local trade unions.

The settlements all belong to Orissa's Koraput District one of the state's poorest districts having a large proportion of Scheduled Tribes, Scheduled Castes and Other Backward Classes. These are locally all referred to as Desia, literally meaning the "country people". As Pfeffer (1997, 2002), Berger (2002) and Otten (2001) have shown in recent publications the different Desia communities should be regarded as parts of a single society irrespective of their administrative classification. Their basic argument is that all the Desia share certain cultural traits that are typical for tribal societies and thus differentiate them from the caste societies of the lowlands. In addition to a common annual ritual cycle, a common kinship and marriage system these cultural traits are a generalized social structure, the principles of seniority and territoriality and a lack of a centralized political organization[5].

The Desia might all be engaged in shifting cultivation, even the client communities (see below) and those local lineages from where the bearer of sacral offices derive. The typical functional separation of caste society as it is expressed in the model of the four *varna* is lacking, so that one can speak of a generalized structure, i.e. a structure not differentiating between a political, economic and religious social domain as such. That does not render the Desia equals, but the hierarchy prevailing between them differs sharply from the one known from caste society. The different Desia communities might also refuse to interdine or intermarry, but do generally not avoid each other as strict as high and low castes. The Desia are always "senior" or "junior" to others and not more or less ritually pure. The centrality of the concept of territory is expressed in the specific relation the founding clan of a village maintains with the earth goddess. Even if nowadays land is bought and sold as a commodity it is only them who can offer her sacrifices, who can "communicate with the divine" (Pfeffer, 1997). The last point, the lack of a centralized political organization leads to another important value of Desia society, i.e. autonomy. The Desia communities classified as Scheduled Tribes, but also some of the Other Backward Classes regard themselves as autonomous "mountain kings". That this autonomy is first and foremost a value-idea becomes obvious when considering the relationship between them and the clients, i.e. petty traders and craftsmen. The tribal hills were economically never self sufficient and thus factually always depended on trade with the caste societies of the lowlands. Those dealing with the "foreigners" from the lowlands are junior in relation to other Desia communities, thus expressing the comparatively low status trade—like all other types of non-agricultural work—enjoys (*ibid.*).[6]

These basic aspects of Desia society formerly also held true for the settlement near the project's powerhouse, where I spent most of my time in the field. This spot, called Chatamput henceforth, was a small Desia village founded by a specific clan of the Gadaba community before it turned into an industrial settlement almost sixty years ago. They thus were the local "communicators with the divine" and recruited the ritually most important individuals, the *pujari* or sacrificer and the *randari* or cook of ritual food, among themselves. The Gadaba village Chatamput formed not only a ritual unit in itself, but was also integrated in the little kingdom of Jeypore. Chatamput belonged to a number of villages from which a *muttadar* collected revenue for the king. The *muttadar*, normally an outstanding person of the Rona, the Desia community serving as a kind of royal militia, in addition to the regular tax collected once a year an extra tax for the performance of the *Durga* and *Dasahara puja* in Jeypore. He attended the *puja* together with others of his village and revenue villages and he was ascribed a special position in the procession of the *puja* expressing his relationship towards the king and thus within the kingdom. The ethnographic details available for these *puja* do not allow an extended interpretation, but they unmistakably show that the Jeypore kingdom formed an integrated whole comparable to the one Tanabe presents concerning Khurda (Schnepel, 1997). Thus, I conclude the little kingdom of Jeypore did not substantially deviate from the model of kshatriyaization presented above. It formed an integrated *holos*.

Oral Histories

The conducted research had no historical ambitions and therefore no research has been done in archives, but as the scope of this article is limited to an evaluation of oral histories, this lack of data is barely significant. According to the few "hard" historical facts available in a booklet printed on the occasion of a project anniversary, the idea for the construction of a hydro-project came up in the beginning of the 20th century and was supported by the last king of Jeypore, Vikrama Deo Varma IV. A survey in the valley was conducted as early as 1931 and it was only due to the Second World War that the construction of the project was not taken up until 1946. It was completed and commissioned in 1955 and inaugurated by the first President of the Indian Republic Dr. Rajendra Prasad in the same year.

The decision to generate electricity in the Eastern Ghats was based on technical considerations. The rivers there have the advantage to carry sufficient water also in the hot season, so that the production of power can be guaranteed throughout the year. Although no data are available it seems also probable that the planning authorities might have had socio-economic intentions in mind. It is a well known fact that a central goal of state led industrialization in India was the socio-economic "uplift" of regions that were perceived to be "backward". That was the case with the huge public sector steel plants in Bhilai, Rourkela and elsewhere and might also have influenced the planning of the SHE(J)P.

The decision was taken by institutions of the modern Indian Republic, i.e. initially the Governments of Orissa and Andhra Pradesh,[7] then after the Electricity Boards of Andhra and since their privatisation the Andhra Pradesh Generation Corporation (APGENCO). These institutions are locally referred to simply as "the authorities". They did not ask for any divine support to legitimate their undertaking before setting up the project. Neither did they bother about local deities. The sacred abode of Chatamput's village goddess had to give way to the planned Inspection Bungalow, a spacious lodge for government officials. The Desia were left with no choice than to shift it together with their hamlets a few kilometres away from their old village.

The only reference to rituals in the oral histories related to the plant's set-up are widespread rumours that human sacrifices occurred at certain critical moments during the construction process. They were to appease the goddess in such moments[8], but these acts—if they have taken place at all - can neither be interpreted as a sponsoring of local deities nor as an incorporation into a local pantheon and as such do not conform to the model of kshatriyaization. They have to be regarded as unrelated individual incidents and not an expression of a social *holos*. According to local oral histories such sacrifices were ordered by a few contractors or in one case also by an engineer whenever a major accident on one of the construction sites had taken place. None of the informants themselves saw the sacrifices, it was always the "other" work groups on "other" sites that performed such type of worship, never the own. Furthermore, nobody mentioned that tribal priests were involved in the worship of these deities unlike in Tanabe's ethnographic example where their presence is of crucial importance.

After the authorities finally decided to construct the power project in the valley the land required for the project was nationalized and people from all over India attracted to work on the construction sites. Nowadays most of Chatamput's inhabitants come from Andhra Pradesh and Orissa and only a small minority from Nepal, Kerala and Tamil Nadu, but it is said that during the first years also Bengali, Gujarati and Punjabi as well as Indians from all other parts of the country were found among the workers. These assertions can of course not be confirmed, but it is important to note that the migrants perceive Chatamput and all other construction sites in the Sananadi Valley to have united individuals from all parts of the country. This perception resembles the idea of a "Mini-India", an expression commonly used to denote other industrial set-ups like the huge steel city Bhilai in Chattisgarh when referring to their cosmopolitan composition (Parry, 1999b). The workforce was not only made up of Indians from all provinces, but also from all confessions and castes. The elder migrants who were present already during that time regard it as an outstanding aspect of social life on the construction sites and in the barracks that all these distinctions were rather meaningless. They neither influenced the work process nor leisure time activities. They worked, stayed, cooked, ate and drank together irrespective of caste, religious confession and ethnicity. Life in the "camps" as the sites are frequently referred to was harmonious and it was all in all a time of "true religion" (*dharma samaya*[9]). The workers always state that they all did the same kind of work and were therefore equals.

It is important to note that the equality among the workers was not only a lip service, but social practice. The commensal restrictions characteristic for caste society lost their validity. Workers could eat in canteens or prepare their own meals, the raw foodstuff being provided by a "maintenance store" or the Desia of the surrounding villages. Some informants guessed that the cooks in the canteens might have been Brahmins, but nobody actually knew and neither did anybody care. Similarly, when the workers preferred to prepare their food themselves they normally did so in smaller groups and even then they did not bother about caste affiliations.

Another conspicuous feature of life in Chatamput as well as the other "camps" was the relative absence of the Desia. In contrast to the present day situation the migrants during the construction time did not mind to interact with the Desia, but they themselves were not too keen to intermingle with the "outsiders". The Desia formed a substantial part of the work-force on the construction sites, but retreated after working hours to their nearby villages. Apart from the context of work interaction between Desia and migrants was rather limited. Some of the migrants visited the villages from time to time in search for alcohol and women and some stayed with their Desia lovers in the "camps". These affairs are said to have occasionally lead to conflicts. The relatives of the Desia usually considered the relationship to be a marriage outside their jati and thus demanded a gift for the bride they have given to the migrant. If he refused to follow their demands a quarrel was sure to arise so that he either paid or quickly left the "camp" towards his native village.[10]

After construction completed around 1955, the authorities intended to send home the migrant workers and employ others for regular and well paid service in the plant. A massive strike uniting all migrants arose and it succeeded in hindering the authorities to fulfil their aims and forced them to employ those having built up the enterprise with their sweat and tears through all the years. After they obtained regular employment the migrant labourers went back to their respective native villages to marry and to bring their wives or families—if they were married already—to Chatamput. As regular employees they also abandoned the barracks. By simple architectonical tricks these were turned into quarters meant to shelter only a single nuclear family. Furthermore, also the canteens lost their importance. The employees now ate their wives' home-made meals and visited canteens only for a snack in the afternoon or if the wife was absent. All the migrants unequivocally state that the arrival of their wives and the subsequent foundation of families resulted in a sharp rise of caste consciousness or *jati phati* as it is called locally. The wives are said to have been keen seeing their husbands follow their caste specific commensal rules and were not appreciating their friendships with low caste colleagues too much. This *jati phati* still was limited, because the commensal rules were constantly broken again while the workers were on shift. Furthermore, the caste conscious wives to some extent also started neglecting the rules after a while. They maintained close relationships with neighbours of all different castes so that the feeling of an overall equality remained largely intact. Hence, I conclude this time as migrants from the plains reached the tribal hills a caste society was not established.

The Convivial Work-force

The basic aspect of these stories, the equality regardless of all social differences, might be seen as a confirmation of the general expectations the process of industrialization evokes. It was widely believed that "if industrialization proceeds rapidly [in India] ... the caste system will have essentially disappeared by the end of this century" (Davis, 1951: 176). As Parry (1999a) works out these expectations rest on the assumption that industrialization or the industrial mode of production in general has an intrinsic power to shape all societies in the same way it supposedly did in the West. He thus calls this assumption an "evolutionary teleology" and makes it a point that it was and is shared by laymen, academics and policy-makers in East and West alike (see also Breman, 1999). Following this assumption, the Government of India laid special emphasis on large scale industrialization after independence. The industrial projects were supposed to serve as melting pots and produce in addition to steel, electricity and other goods a worker able to form the avant-garde of a new, caste- and classless Indian society (Parry, 1999c: 147).

As I have argued elsewhere (in print and n.d.) the workers themselves evaluate the neglect of caste on the construction sites as only a temporal deviation from the norms of caste society. In contrast to the claims of the "evolutionary teleology" this deviation should not be regarded as a step towards a "historical", but as a "situational" change to use concepts introduced by Mitchell (1966). The workers neglect their caste identities in the settlement, but reconstitute them when returning to their native villages to whom they maintain vivid links. In contrast to Mitchell's proposition these "situations" or contexts are not only separate, but are perceived by the actors themselves to stand in an unambiguous relation to each other. For them the settlement is *bahar* or "outside", a term generally denoting ritual impurity, and the native village "inside" or ritually pure. The opposition between settlement and native village or "modern" and "traditional" compartment as Singer (1972) and Gould [1988 (1963)] would call the two contexts respectively is thus hierarchic in Dumont's sense.

Using a concept developed by Heidemann,[11] I described settlement and native village as social spaces dominated by conviviality and commensality respectively (*ibid.*). The concept of commensality is well-known and a central manifestation of the ritual hierarchy of caste society. As such commensality is regarded by the actors as an expression of a given, eternal and sacral, in short the *dharmic* order. According to Heidemann conviviality stands in a relationship of hierarchic opposition to commensality as it generates a created, temporal and secular order. Conviviality conceptually turns individuals of different ritual status, i.e. those of different castes, into equals and it does so interactionally by the same means as commensality. Convivials occasionally eat together and thus break with the traditional commensal rules. This breach of norms also manifests itself in other deviant behaviour that might occur on such occasions as the consumption of liquor or — if vegetarians are present— meat.

The obvious contradictions resulting from a coexistence of commensality and conviviality are suppressed by the temporal seclusion of both the commensal as well as the convivial groups. The former meet indoors or at temple feasts which are clearly marked events in time and space and convivials withdraw similarly from public view while transgressing against the proclaimed rules of the given order. It is important to note that the motivations behind these seclusions differ. Commensal groups seclude for the sake of securing a specific degree of ritual purity, whereas convivials hide because a public deviation from the norms of caste society would have to lead to an out-casting of the actors or otherwise would tackle the legitimacy of the caste system as such. Convivial interaction is only to occur in unmistakeably marked secluded social spaces and additionally by the adoption of a new "caste-less" identity.

These marked spaces and identities are most often provided by supposedly modern institutions such as political parties, trade unions and sport clubs, but as Heidemann emphasizes, should nevertheless not at all be regarded as a purely modern phenomenon. Neither should it be equated with the Western concept of equality among individuals. Convivials are not equals in an ontological sense, but only in regard to a certain identity. They are equals as sportsmen during a volleyball tournament or as students of a hostel. These identities overshadow caste identities temporally, but do not replace them and from this proposition it follows logically that all those unable to get access to convivial identities also have to remain outside the temporal convivial order of equality.

Heidemann adds that apart from those not able to adopt such identities also certain other relationships are excluded not from conviviality as such, but from stronger forms of conviviality and especially those involving consumption of liquor. Thus persons of different generations, different sex as well as siblings should never interact in an unduly convivial manner, because the asymmetries between them should never become ambiguous. Even more strictly excluded from conviviality are relationships with the divine. Although convivials sometimes withdraw in private households while engaging in their deviant behaviour they should under no circumstances enter the respective room where gods and goddesses are worshipped.

Heidemann's methodological concept of conviviality helps to grasp all basic features of life in the initial years of Chatamput's industrialization as well as the present situation. The migration to the construction site enabled the migrants to separate convivial identities and relationships from commensal ones. They were also able to adopt a new identity. On the construction site they were "workers" and not Brahmins or washermen. This convivial identity remained when the regular work-force was recruited, but when the wives entered the scene a commensal sphere was established subsequently in Chatamput. Nevertheless, conviviality still dominates all aspects of life in the "camps". That becomes manifest not only during lunch breaks in the plant where workers from all different castes frequently exchange their home-made curries, but also during regularly held staff and trade union parties. The central part of these gatherings is a common meal and that might be prepared and distributed by all members alike irrespective of their caste affiliation. In these contexts conviviality is also frequently increased by the consumption of liquor.

Furthermore, even the commensal context contains elements of conviviality. It is regarded as proper among neighbours and colleagues to exchange sweets in the course of rituals of the life and annual cycle and it is similarly almost obligatory to invite neighbours and colleagues to the feasts accompanying life cycle ceremonies. These exchanges would not count as a convivial interaction in the villages the immigrants originate from, because there neighbourhoods are still segregated according to caste. In the settlement neighbourhoods unite employees with a similar rank within the project and these ranks are not caste bound. It is thus not uncommon for Brahmin employees to reside next to their Harijan colleagues so that these symmetric exchanges ignore not only slight differences of ritual status, but even the "pollution line".

The ongoing ubiquity of conviviality in the "camps" rests on one basic precondition and that is the migrants continuing links to their native villages. Only there can they reconstitute their caste identities which are still essential to them. They return to the native villages for arranging and conducting marriages, for initiation rites and certain festivals of the annual ritual cycle. In the "camp" the workers stay *bahar*, in an impure place and in such a place especially the relationships to the divine cannot be properly maintained. Therefore, the migrant labourers do not install themselves ritually in Chatamput. They do not perform a *ghruha pratistha* when they move into the quarters provided to them by the authorities and thus their deities are not fully present there. The workers maintain separate rooms for worship (*puja ghar*), but there they keep only pictures of the deities, not the deities themselves as it was generally expressed.[12] The presence of the divine is crucial for all major rituals of life and annual cycle and it is therefore that the workers have to return to their villages on all major ritual occasions. Would they give up their links they would be left with no other choice than to settle also ritually in Chatamput. They would be forced to maintain their ritual purity also in the industrial settlement and to follow their caste specific rules concerning inter-caste contact. That would be incompatible with their convivial life style and so they prefer to stay *bahar*.

This, however, holds true only for Chatamput's public sector. The private sector is much more caste conscious. It is made up of priests of two local temples and a few high caste traders and low caste washermen, barbers, latrine cleaners and butchers. Apart from their apparent differences they all have in common that they settled ritually in Chatamput and conform to their caste specific rules of commensality. The maintenance of their caste specific purity goes along with the lack of a convivial identity. They do not hold employment in the project, they are not "workers" and are therefore unable to conceal their caste identity and hence remain trapped in it.[13]

The lack of a convivial identity also excludes the Desia residing in and around the "camps". During the time the project was under construction they formed a substantial proportion of the work force, but from the beginning onwards they never interacted convivially with the migrants. Neither did they reside in the "camps" nor did they eat in canteens or elsewhere together with them and kept them generally at a certain distance. Furthermore, although it was the explicit intention of the project authorities to make especially the local Desia part of the permanent work-force, they refused. Regular employment was offered to them first to compensate them for their nationalized land.[14] Only when the Desia refused, they were given either cash or land somewhere else. The elder Desia still living in Chatamput as well as their descendents state that they then had not much interest to join the industrial enterprise, because it would have resulted in a loss of autarchy. They would have to obey to a strict industrial time table and—what made things worse-that order would be supervised by "outsiders" from the plains (Strümpell, 2001). Therefore they, preferred to either take the money and spend it with the help of dubious traders or to settle on the compensatory land. Most of the latter returned after a few years because as they said on the new land they were struck by diseases. During my interviews the Desia generally expressed interest to work in the plant, but nowadays have no chance to obtain regular employment. The project constantly reduces its manpower and factually only recruits descendants of former employees. So-called rehabilitation schemes guarantee every nuclear family that lost an employee due to death or invalidity compensatory employment for one of its members and since the late 1960s these schemes are the only possibility to obtain employment. As access to employment is virtually ruled out, so is access to the convivial identity of a "worker" and to the group of convivials dominating Chatamput.

The Ritual Arena

The dominance of conviviality has also implications for the ritual arena of the "camp". As relationships with the divine require a rather high degree of ritual purity, it does not come as a surprise that those ritually active are also to a lesser degree involved in convivial interaction. The agents on the local ritual arena are the priests of a Ram and a Shiva temple, the traders and the Desia. No one of the employees plays a prominent role in this context, the notable exceptions being the wives of some of them. Generally also the attendants of the different religious activities are almost exclusively female, because the men have no time for engaging into ritual activities as they are busy with their shift duty or have other important work to do. Whether these are the true motivations for their absence shall not be questioned here, it shall only be stated that it is also in accordance with Heidemann's thesis of conviviality. The crucial point is that in Chatamput as well as in the other "camps" the relationships between the different agents range from competition to ignorance, but never form an integrated *holos* or local pantheon.

One of Chatamput's old village shrines did not get in the way of the plant and is visited by both the Desia remaining in the settlement and some migrants. The worship at a common shrine, however, does not result in common worship and an integration of tribal and migrant societies, but rather the contrary. Among the Desia at the outskirts of the settlement are also the descendants of the village founders and they still communicate with the divine on behalf of the whole local Desia community. The migrants performing *puja* at the same shrine are nowadays very few in number. On their part the priestly functions are fulfilled by a migrant family from Kerala as much prominent in local politics as in the trade of the local varieties of country liquor. In contrast to Tanabe's ethnographic example of kshatriyaization the migrants from Kerala do neither attend the Desia rituals nor do they call them for mediating between themselves and the goddess on the occasion of their worships. The relationship between migrants and Desia is for the most part one of mutual ignorance. Only once during my eighteen months of field work did both parties perform a ritual on the same day. In the early morning hours the Kerali accompanied by a handful of followers—for the most part regular customers of their country liquor shop—conducted a puja for the goddess *satha mangala*. However, all signs of their worship were washed off or thrown away by the Desia arriving there just one hour later. Only after they cleaned the place of all remnants left by the migrants did they start their own worship.

The worship at the common shrine has over the years led to an even more severe conflict that turned into an official case at the Jeypore Municipal Court recently. The reason is thc heightened efforts of the migrants to erect a proper stone temple right on the spot of the deities' old abode. Such a construction is incompatible with Desia concepts of the divine (Berger, forthcoming) and also stands in a stark contrast to the process of kshatriyaization as outlined above. As Tanabe has shown, the agents of kshatriyaization in the fort of Manatir did not demolish the tribal shrine, but constructed an additional temple for the deity. Thus, I conclude, also on the ritual arena integration is not taking place.

In contrast to the social fabric described in the preceding paragraph in the context of rituals also the relationships among migrants are marked by competition, conflict and disintegration. This is true for almost all rituals conducted in the settlement, but shall be exemplified here in the context of rituals for the village goddess.

The goddess manifests herself in a variety of places, but only a few attract attention from a wider range of inhabitants. Asked for their refusal to visit other manifestations of the goddess they stated that these are only "duplicate" shrines and that the goddess is not really present there. The crucial point is that what is and what is not a "duplicate" shrine is in a constant flux. Since I first travelled to Chatamput four years have passed and in three of those a *yatra* was performed, but each time it was performed at a different shrine and for a different goddess. In the year 2000, the *yatra* that was attended by the majority of villagers took place at a *Thakurani* temple in the month of *Chait*, in the following year no *yatra* was hold at all, 2002 a *Sambram*, a festival for *Mankadiamma* was performed in *Vaisakam* and in 2003 *Kondamakalamma* turned into the "real" or "veritable" goddess (*Prakruta Devi*) of the settlement.

The shift from one abode to another is matched by a shifting engagement of those fulfilling priestly functions. They come from a variety of castes and are both Telugu and Oriya, but since a few years some outstanding ladies from a Telugu caste of fishermen, the Vadabalija, dominate the rituals for what is generally supposed to be the village goddess. In the beginning it is said that the Vadabalija worshipped one of their goddesses called *Mankadiamma* along with other migrants nearby a tree, where some years later in the mid-seventies a temple for *Thakurani* was build. Soon after that conflict arose between those worshipping *Thakurani* and those worshipping the goddess *Mankadiamma* with the result that most of the Vadabalija and other migrants from the region around Kasibugga (Palasa) in the Srikakulam District left the temple and stopped performing *puja* for her.

After a few years have passed some Vadabalija women started to perform the *Mankadiamma puja* again at a different place on a nearby hillside. This puja started to attract more and more mostly female residents, so that one of the Vadabalija women, among whom a fierce rivalry has arisen by then, decided to collect money for the construction of a proper temple. Her undertaking proved to be successful and thus in late 2001 Chatamput had a new temple. The following year the *yatra* hold for *Mankadiamma* centred around that temple and was attended by a majority of migrants most of whom also had made a monetary donation for the performance. These villagers then all claimed that *Mankadiamma* was the "real" goddess of Chatamput and that they therefore should attend her *yatra*.

In the course of the year 2002, however, the Vadabalija woman at whose initiative the building of the temple started, more or less turned the temple into her private property as the other inhabitants said. She wrote her name on the temple and placed an idol of her deceased husband inside. The key for the temple was kept by her and she refused to give it to the other Vadabalija women acting as priests on request of the migrants. These women, who never maintained relationships of amity, decided to build another temple next to the one for *Mankadiamma*. The temple finished just a few weeks later and is said to shelter *Kondamakalamma*, a sister of *Mankadiamma*. At the inauguration of this temple a yatra for her was performed attracting again a big part of Chatamput's mostly female inhabitants, who all claimed that *Kondamakalamma* now is the "real" goddess of the village.

Furthermore, there are indices that this conflict was nothing new to the short history of the industrial settlement. As elder informants told, the *puja* for the tutelary goddess was in the initial years conducted at the Desia shrine mentioned above and then later shifted to the place where nowadays lies the *Thakurani* temple. These informants did not mention in detail why the shift occurred, but vaguely stated that conflicts among worshippers were the reason. Another crucial feature of the ritual arena in Chatamput is that after conflicts have arisen and are solved as described above the shrine of the former "real" goddess afterwards will be almost completely ignored by the majority of inhabitants. That leads to the situation that at the time a *yatra* for the "real" goddess is performed no additional *puja* will be conducted at the shrine of the other ones. This pattern contrasts sharply with the performance of comparable rituals in other parts of India and also the native villages of the migrants. In the contexts of the *yatra* conducted there all goddesses present in the village are given tokens of respect by minor worshipping (Mayer, 1966 [1960]: 101).

The interactional pattern revealed on the ritual arena in my opinion indicate that the worship of deities in the settlement does not form a structured whole and can thus not be regarded as a pantheon. To regard some shrines as "duplicate" manifestations and to neglect them can be seen as a denial of any relationships between the different goddesses. A relationship only seems to exist between the goddesses *Mankadiamma* and *Kondamakalamma*. They are said to be sisters, but there is no agreement as to who is elder to whom, so that also their relationship remains unclear to some extent.

These conflicts and their solutions, however, fit well into the patterns of relationships and interaction prevailing within the settlement. As Galey (1990) demonstrates for another part of India relations between gods and goddesses within a local pantheon are hierarchical and correlate with hierarchical relations of a local society. The non-relation between the different goddesses in Chatamput is therefore just another manifestation of its non-hierarchical, egalitarian social order. Hierarchy on a ritual level comes to the fore when individuals of a scavenging caste beat the drums and when washermen clean the sacred grove or act as sacrificer, but there is no hierarchy structuring the settlement as a whole.

This lack of relationships between the different goddesses in Chatamput stands in a stark contrast to the emphasis in the relationships of these goddesses with the worshippers' native village. The names of the goddesses worshipped in Chatamput are the same as those the goddesses carry in their native villages. The name *Thakurani* is frequently found to be the name of village goddesses in the region around the small town of Asika in the Ganjam District where many of the Oriya migrants originate from. Similarly, the village goddesses in Palasa in Andhra's Srikakulam District are often called *Kondamakalamma* or *Mankadiamma*. Furthermore, the date for the different *yatra* in Chatamput are fixed only after the worshippers received a message that similar *yatra* have taken place in their native villages. Thus, the *yatra* for *Thakurani* two years ago was conducted after the *yatra* for the same goddess has been performed in some of the villages around Asika and the same holds true for the recent festivals for *Mankadiamma* and *Kondamakalamma*. At last, most worshippers confess that they could spend much more money as a donation for the *yatra* in Chatamput as they all earn a quite substantial salary. However, they are not willing to spend more than necessary as they prefer to donate money to the *yatra* committees in their native villages instead. Many migrants told that every morning during their daily *puja* they put some money near the picture of their family's goddess, the *isthadevi*, and that they either send or personally bring the money to their native village so that it is used there for the yatra of the village's tutelary goddess.

These aspects, the names of the deities, the dates for their yatra and the donations of the worshippers lead me to the conclusion that the deities worshipped in Chatamput are not at all local ones. They originate from the coastal villages of Orissa and Andhra like the migrants and resemble them in some regard. But whereas the migrant workers from a variety of different local caste systems found a way to interact with each other rather harmoniously, they did not succeed to relate their deities to each other.

This difference between the ritual domain and the secular, industrial one again refers to the different quality of social relationships pertaining in them. The ritual domain builds on caste identities and they are under a constant threat in a milieu like Chatamput. The threat derives not only from the overall "modern" convivial interaction of workers, trade unionists and neighbours in the labour colonies. The migrants in Chatamput and also in the other settlements come from a variety of different local or empirical caste systems to use an expression introduced by Dumont (1980) and as the project does not take note of these primordial identities the migrants lack intimate knowledge of caste affiliations of colleagues, comrades and neighbours. People may say that they are priests, swordsmen or carpenters by caste, but nobody actually can confirm these claims reliably. A reliable, intimate knowledge of the caste affiliations of others is but the basic precondition for all interaction based caste. Without such knowledge purity is endangered per se, because those with whom one interacts might have a lower ritual status. That does not matter as long as the migrants only interact as "workers" in the plant, but becomes essential when their caste identity is at stake and that is the case in the contexts of rituals of the life as well as annual cycle. The crucial point is that relationships in these contexts bind the actors not only temporally, but permanently. Parry (1986, 1989) has shown that the gift of *dan* to a Brahmin, but in the form of a *kanya dan* (the "gift of a virgin") also to wife-takers establishes a relationship between giver and receiver that can never be dissolved and has severe consequences for the *karma* of those involved. Therefore, an intimate knowledge of those with whom one establishes relationships of such a quality is very necessary and as such knowledge is impossible to obtain in such a milieu the migrants do not trust the way the other migrants act out relationships in the ritual domain.[15]

Conclusion

Coming to my conclusion, I want to describe the situation in Chatamput using the concepts of exchange cycles as developed by Parry and Bloch (1989). In the settlement the migrant workers maintain only a short-term cycle of exchange, the cycle of self-interest, profane every day profits and losses or to express it in Indian terms, the domain of *artha*. They fight with their unions for an increase of their salaries and bargain as good as they can on the weekly market for vegetables, rice and meat, but in the settlement they do not invest their gains into a long-term cycle of exchange, the cycle that is to maintain the socio-cosmic order. The long-term cycle of exchange is of a different quality, it relates to *dharma* and remains oriented towards the well-known world in the native villages, because only there can ritual status be secured to a sufficient degree.

The ritual orientation of the migrants towards their native villages prevents the settlements from developing an own distinct ritual identity and from becoming a ritual centre in itself. Even after three generations it does not have a "real" village goddess and is in the words of the migrants all in all not a "real" village, but a "camp" and it remains *bahar* ("outside"), i.e. it is a conceptually impure place, capable only to create a temporal order and suitable only for temporary residence. As a consequence it renders local deities as superfluous as the mediation of local ritual specialists. The local tribal population being deprived of their land and lacking access to the well paid convivial work culture in the project thus face an even more severe marginalization in the wake of modern industrialization than they did during pre-industrial kshatriyaization.

NOTES

1. The term "little kingdom" and "little king" was coined by Cohn, but denotes here a kingdom whose king is able to pursue an almost independent regime, but needs the benevolence of an overlord to legitimise his rule (Berkemer, 1993).
2. For the sake of legibility indigenous terms will be given without diacritical marks.
3. Wherever possible, I use pseudonyms for places and persons.

4. As shall be shown below the equality rests upon the capacity to conceal one's caste identity and that is not possible for the Pakhi as they follow their caste specific profession also in the modern industrial project.
5. These four mentioned traits have been worked out as characteristics for tribal societies worldwide by Sahlins (1968).
6. The client-patron relationship between the Desia does not contradict the thesis of their generalized structures. Also the clients might be farmers just like the other Desia and as recent research by Hardenberg has made clear also they can "communicate with the divine" (*ibid.* forthcoming).
7. The project was already under construction before the independent union state Andhra Pradesh came into being. Initially it was a joint enterprise of Orissa and the Madras Presidency.
8. That the construction of massive buildings such as dams and plants, but formerly also forts, etc., require the support of deities that can only be secured by such sacrifices is a widespread belief (Gait, 1907: 489; Parry, 1999b: 113). Although such rumours cannot be confirmed, they have to be regarded as part of a social reality. Thus, Parry (*ibid.*) e.g. reports that they were one of the main reasons that kept the local population away from the construction site of the steel plant in Bhilai.
9. For the sake of brevity, I will restrict myself to only mention indigenous terms in Oriya and omit the Telugu ones.
10. For a more detailed discussion of social relationships during the time the project was constructed see Strümpell in print.
11. Frank Heidemann is Professor at the Institut für Völkerkunde und Afrikanistik at the Ludwig Maximilian Universität München, Germany. He developed the thesis presented here in a lecture given at the Institut für Ethnologie at the Freie Universität Berlin, Germany in 2000, but has not published anything on the topic yet. I am therefore very grateful for his suggestions regarding my research.
12. On my visits in the migrants' native villages it came to the fore that the *puja ghar* there do not differ very much in outlook from those in the settlement. The former generally just seem to be a little bit more lavish than the latter. The difference between them thus lies only in the performance of the *puja* for the installation of the deities and does not manifest itself physically.
13. The convivial identity to be a "worker" is not the only one prevailing in Chatamput as well as the other settlements. Convivial interaction also occurs among those who are "educated" (s. Strümpell, n.d.). It seems to be a new convivial identity, because the term is frequently used in contemporary discourse on social relationships, but never in the oral histories on the construction period. However, as this identity is not relevant for the argument presented in this paper it will not be discussed here.
14. This policy was and still is rather common in India, but has almost nowhere and due to the same reasons been successful (Parry, 1999b, c, 2003).
15. Another example of contested ritual is the *Dasahara puja* conducted in the project's powerhouse. There every year in the month of *Asvina* almost the complete staff working in the powerhouse gathers to attend the *puja*. I could observe it only once and at first it did not seem to be a contested ritual.

However, interviews with the workers revealed that the priests conducting the *puja* change frequently. Sometimes a Telugu priest from the Ram temple, sometimes an Oriya from the Shiva temple is engaged by the mixed Oriya and Telugu staff. In the same interviews it came to the fore that the Oriya generally do not appreciate the way the Telugu priest performs the *puja* and the Telugu vice versa are convinced that the Oriya does not conduct it in a proper way. Similarly, also the music played in the context of the *dasahara puja* has been a matter of conflict between Oriya and Telugu workers until it was decided a few years ago not to play any music at all. The Telugu demanded the engagement of musicians from a Telugu caste of scavengers (Pakhi), whereas the Oriya preferred Dombo musicians, a Scheduled Caste very prominent all over Orissa. Thus, it is in Geertz' [1997(1987)] words the differing symbolic systems that cause conflicts between Oriya and Telugu.

REFERENCES

Berger, Peter. 2002. "The Gadaba and the 'non-ST' Desia of Koraput, Orissa. Some Observations on their Interrelations," (pp.57-90) in Georg Pfeffer and Deepak Kumar Behera (eds.), *Contemporary Society Tribal Studies,* Vol. V. New Delhi: Concept Publishing Company.

____. (forthcoming) *Füttern, Speisen und Verschlingen. Ritual und Gesellschaft im Hochland von Orissa, Indien.*

Berkemer, Georg. 1993. *Little Kingdoms in Kalinga: Ideologie, Legitimation und Politikregionaler Eliten.* Stuttgart: Franz Steiner Verlag.

Breman, Jan. 1994. *Wage Hunters and Gatherers: Search for Work in the Urban and Rural Economy of South Gujarat.* Delhi: Oxford University Press.

____. 1999. "The Formal Sector: An Introductory Review," (pp.1-40) in Jonathan Parry, Jan Breman und Karin Kapadia (eds.), *The Worlds of Indian Industrial Labour.* New Delhi: Sage Publications.

Davis, Kingsley. 1951. *The Population of India and Pakistan.* Princeton: Princeton University Press.

Dumont, Louis. 1980. *Homo Hierarchicus: The Caste System and its Implications.* Chicago: University of Chicago Press.

Gait, E.A. 1907. "Human Sacrifice (Indian)," (pp.849-53) in James Hastings (ed.), *Encyclopaedia of Religion and Ethics.* Vol. VI. Edinburgh: T. & T. Clark.

Galey, Jean Claude. 1990. "Reconsidering Kingship in India: An Ethnological Perspective," (pp.123-87) in Jean Claude Galey (ed.), *Kingship and the Kings.* Paris, New York: Harwood Academic Publishers.

Geertz, Clifford. 1997 [1987]. *Dichte Beschreibung. Beiträge zum Verstehen kultureller Systeme.* Frankfurt: Suhrkamp Taschenbuch Wissenschaft.

Gould, Harold. 1988 [1963]. "Lucknow *Rickshawallas:* The Social Organization of an Occupational Category," (pp.59-89) in Harold A. Gould (ed.), *Caste Adaptation in Modernizing/Indian Society.* Delhi: Chanakya Publications..

Hardenberg, Roland. (forthcoming) Children of the Earth Goddess: Society, Marriage and Sacrifice in the Highlands of Orissa. Münster: Lit Verlag.

Holmström, Marc. 1984. *Industry and Inequality: The Social Anthropology of Indian Labour.* Cambridge. Cambridge University Press

Kulke, Hermann. 1993a. "Legitimation and Town Planning in the Feudatory States of Central Orissa," in Hermann Kulke (ed.), *Kings and Cults: State Formation and Legitimation in India and Southeast Asia.* Delhi: Manohar.

____. 1993b. "Tribal Deities at Princely Courts: The Feudatory Rajas of Central Orissa and their Tutelary Deities (istadevatas)," (pp.114-136) in Hermann Kulke (ed.), *Kings and Cults. State Formation and Legitimation in India and Southeast Asia.* Delhi: Manohar.

Mayer, Adrian. 1966 [1960]. *Caste and Kinship in Central India: A Village and its Region.* Berkeley: University of California Press.

Meher, Rajkishor. 2004. *Stealing the Environment. Social and Ecological Effects of Industrialization in Rourkela.* Delhi: Manohar.

Mitchell, Clyde. 1966. "Theoretical Orientations in African Urban Studies," (pp.37-68) in Michael Banton (ed.), *The Social Anthropology of Complex Societies.* ASA Monograph, 4. London: Tavistock.

Otten, Tina. 2001. "Changing Annual Hunting Festival, Chaitra Parba: An Outsiders View," *Adibasi,* 40/41: 82-91.

Parry, Jonathan. 1986. "The Gift, the Indian Gift, and the 'Indian Gift'," *Man* (n.s.), 21: 453-73.

____. 1989. "On the Moral Perils of Exchange," (pp.64-93) in Jonathan Parry und Maurice Bloch (eds.), *Money and the Morality of Exchange.* Cambridge: Cambridge University Press.

____. 1999a. "Introduction," (pp.ix-xxxvi) in Jonathan Parry, Jan Breman, Karin Kapadia (eds.), *The Worlds of Indian Industrial Labour.* New Delhi: Sage Publications.

____. 1999b. "Lords of Labour: Working and Shirking in Bhilai," (pp.107-40) in Jonathan Parry, Jan Breman, Karin Kapadia (eds.), *The Worlds of Indian Industrial Labour.* New Delhi: Sage Publications.

____. 1999c. "Two Cheers for Reservation: The Satnamis and the Steel Plant," (pp.128-69) in Jonathan Parry and Ramachandra Guha (eds), *Institutions and Inequalities Essays in Honour of André Béteille.* New Delhi: Oxford University Press.

____. 2003. "Nehru's Dream and the Village 'Waiting Room': Long-distance Labour Migrants to a Central Indian Steel Town," *Contributions to Indian Sociology* (n.s.), 37: 217-249.

Parry, Jonathan und Maurice Bloch. 1989. "Introduction," (pp.1-32) in Jonathan Parry und Maurice Bloch (eds.), *Money and the Morality of Exchange.* Cambridge: Cambridge University Press.

Pfeffer, Georg. 1997. "The Scheduled Tribes of Middle India as a Unit: Problems of Internal and External Comparison," (pp.3-27) in Georg Pfeffer and Deepak Kumar Behera (eds.), *Contemporary Society: Tribal Studies,* Vol. I. Structure and Process. New Delhi: Concept Publishing Company..

____. (in print). "Tribal Society of Highland Orissa, Highland Burma, and Elsewhere," in Johannes Beltz, Heiko Frese, Angelika Malinar (eds.), *Text and Context in the History: Literature and Religion of Orissa.* Delhi: Manohar.

Rothermund, Dietmar. 1978. "The Coalfield - An Enclave in a Backward Region," (pp.1-20) in Dietmar Rothermund and D.C. Wadhwa (eds.), *Zamindars, Mines and Peasants: Studies in the History of an Indian Coalfield*. New Delhi: Manohar.

Sahlins, Marshall. 1968. *Tribesmen*. Englewood Cliffs: Prentice Hall.

Schnepel, Burkhard. 1997. *Die Dschungelkönige. Ethnohistorische Aspekte von Politik und Ritual in Südorissa/ Indien*. Beiträge zur Südasienforschung Bd. 177. Stuttgart, Franz Steiner Verlag.

Singer, Milton. 1972. "Industrial Leadership, the Hindu Ethic and the Spirit of Socialism," (pp.272-380) in Milton Singer (ed.), *When a Great Tradition Modernizes: An Anthropological Approach to Indian Civilization*. Delhi/ Bombay: Vikas Publishing House.

Strümpell, Christian. 2001. "Industrialization in a 'Tribal Zone': The Desia of Koraput and a Hydro-Electric Power Plant," *Adibasi,* 40/41: 71-81

____. (in print). "Chatamput. An Industrial 'Camp' in the Tribal Zone," in Georg Pfeffer (ed.), *Periphery and Centre: Groups, Categories and Values*. Delhi: Manohar.

____. n.d. *The Limits of Homo Hierarchicus: An Ethnological Approach to Orissa's Industrial Society*.

Tanabe, Akio. 1996. "Indigenous Power, Hierarchy and Dominance: State Formation in Orissa, India," (pp.205-219) in Henri J. Claessen und Jarich G. Oosten (eds.), *Ideology and the Formation of Early States*. Leiden, New York: Köln, E.J. Brill.

SIX

INSIDERS AND OUTSIDERS: Studying Tribal Kandha Villages

ARIMA MISHRA

The paper focuses on the study of "tribal villages," which in the tradition of sociological or anthropological village studies is mostly concerned with multi-caste/tribe villages. Barring a few, (i.e. Jay, 1968; Roy Burman, 1973b; Sachidananda, 1968) studies of "tribal villages" as such are rare, in spite of a rich anthropological heritage of ethnographies of different tribes. Anthropologists, be they from the same or from other communities, tend to focus on the distinctive aspects of the tribe: the "tribal character", "tribal attitudes", "tribal value systems", "tribal identity", "the tribal way of life" etc. The reference point in most of these studies has always been a particular tribe (or a section of the tribe) such as Kandha, Maria, Naga, Lepcha or others. In the same vein, anthropologists have, particularly since 1970s, been interested in studying inter-tribal and tribal-non-tribal interactions (including those with the state) and the consequences of such interactions accounting for the changes in tribal organization and tribal life as a whole. The study of such interactions has resulted in the rather popular debate on the tribe-caste dichotomy, continuum, or even assimilation of tribes within the caste system. In this context the present paper raises a set of questions: how does one study a "tribal village"? What is a tribal village? How significant is the relationship/transaction between the tribal and the non-tribal in tribal villages in order to understand the tribal life as a whole? How do the tribal people place themselves in relation to the minority of thc non-tribal residents of the same village? What is the nature of this relationship and what significance does it have for the tribal people? These questions bear relevance not merely from the technical point of view regarding the definition of the unit of study but also for the tribal people themselves.

A tribal village is traditionally understood as the homogenous settlement inhabited by members of one single tribe with certain functional castes (Sachidanada, 1968: 9). Since, at the same time, the tribal inhabitants form the majority of the village the role of the minority is usually neglected in the research efforts. The relationship between the two status categories of a village is simply looked at as being functional in the sense that the tribal people depend on goods and services not produced by them on their own but typically supplied by other status groups. Alternatively, as Jay (1968) has explored concepts of "activity fields" and "networks" in his study of tribal villages in Middle India, the relationship between tribal and other groups can be looked upon as belonging to the "outside world" being characterized by friendship and contrasted with the intra-tribal relationship based on kinship.

My paper on a tribal village in Orissa will discuss, how at one level the Kutia Kandha identity, traced through their association with Mother Earth, moves beyond village boundaries and excludes the "outsiders" (particularly the caste groups of Damba and Sundhi) referring to them as "vagrants" or "impure". At another level, the Kandha include the minority groups into the village community by entering into a series of socio-economic transactions with them. In this regard, the physical village boundary includes all its residents as opposed to all outsiders.

The paper explores these shifting references between tribe and village in the context of, on the one hand, rituals like the festival of seeds (*Vihan Porba*), buffalo sacrifice (*Podh Puja*), and *Bali Yatra*, worshipping Goddess Ma Baulani that reassert the Kandha's exclusive identity with Goddess Earth and refer beyond the village boundary, while on the other hand, the nuances of the mutual recognition by Kandha and Sundhi are confined to the village. The relationship between these two communities cannot be understood in anthropological stereotypes such as, assimilation, integration, co-operation, rebellion, or even withdrawal. A detailed analysis of the intricacies of their interaction rather reveals elements of humor, secrecy, dependence, distrust and exploitation.

The above mentioned issues emerged from my doctoral research on the problems of chronic starvation in Kalahandi for which I did fieldwork in a tribal and a non-tribal village in 1997. Like any other anthropologist, I had sought to capture the 'tribal' view and experience of starvation to compare them, if given, with similar suffering in the non-tribal village. Even when I began to explore the particular phrases applied in cases of starvation, the process of economic decline in the context of relations of production, and the consumption of specific famine food among the tribal Kandha, the frequent reference to the Sundhi in various contexts made me realize the significant role of this non-tribal minority in the socio-economic life of the majority. I came across institutions and terminological usages that have emerged from a whole network of transactions between Kandha and Sundhi of the village. The mode of observed interaction was not a unique situational feature but rooted in a long history of the rights and privileges enjoyed by the Kandha in the course of an increasing process of attenuation of rights over land and forest on behalf of their counterparts. This paper is borne out of this anxiety of problematizing the study of tribal villages. After the research in the Kalahandi District, I probed this question further during my visit to two Kandha villages in Rayagada district of Orissa in October 2004, and the results are also reflected here. (see dots for districts on Fig. 6.1 of Orissa).

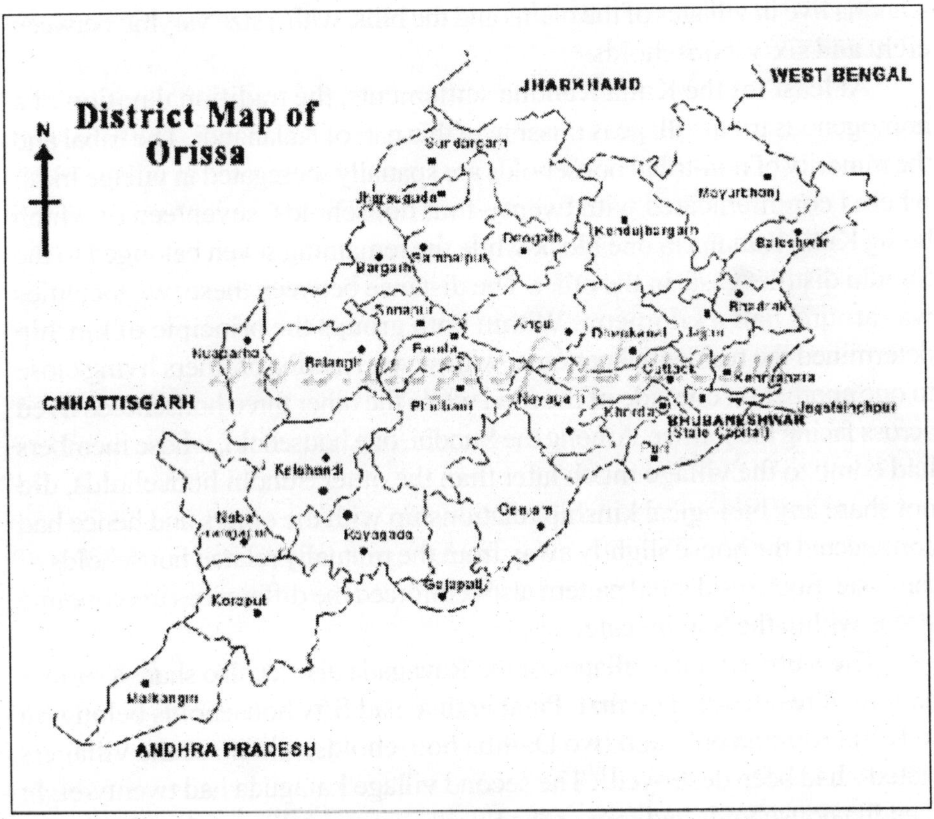

Fig. 6.1

The paper is divided into four sections. The first briefly reflects on the composition of tribal villages in Kalahandi. The second section dwells on the Kandha's self-identity and their notion of "outsiders," the third examines the intricacies of the relationships between the Kandha and Sundhi/Damba while the last section deliberates on the problematic issues of studying "tribal villages".

I

Social Composition of Tribal Villages in Kalahandi

Due to an increasing process of detribalization, the tribal people (mostly Kandha) are concentrated only in two blocks of Kalahandi, i.e. Lanjigarh and Thuamul Rampur. The Dongria Kandha usually live on the hill tops and have very little interaction with the plains. They come down only during *Bali Yatra* or occasionally during the weekly market days. The dominantly Kutia Kandha live in villages of the plains and the hills, with a size varying between eight and sixty households.

At least for the Kutia Kandha settlements, the traditional notion of a homogenous tribal village is missing in this part of Kalahandi. The tribal and the minority of non-tribal households are spatially segregated in village Irkuli where I communicated with twenty-four households; seventeen of which being Kutia Kandha in one block while the remaining seven belonged to the Sundhi distiller caste in the other. The distance between these two localities was around half a kilometre. Within both groups the principle of kinship determined the residential patterns, with seven Kandha brothers living close to one another on one side of the road while the other three households lived across facing the former. Among the Sundhi, one household, whose members had come to the village much later than the other Sundhi households, did not share any biological kinship relationship with the others and hence had constructed the house slightly away from the mutually related households of the caste. Such residential pattern also reinforced the differences in economic status within the Sundhi category.

The Kutia Kandha villages of the Rayagada district also share a similar pattern of residence. The first, Patabandha, had fifty households belonging to Kutia Kandha only and two Damba households, which, as the villagers stated, 'had been destroyed'. The second village Lataguda had twenty-eight Kandha households and four of the Sundhi category. Figs. 6.1 and 6.2 offer a physical description of village layouts.

Fig. 6.2: Village Patabandha

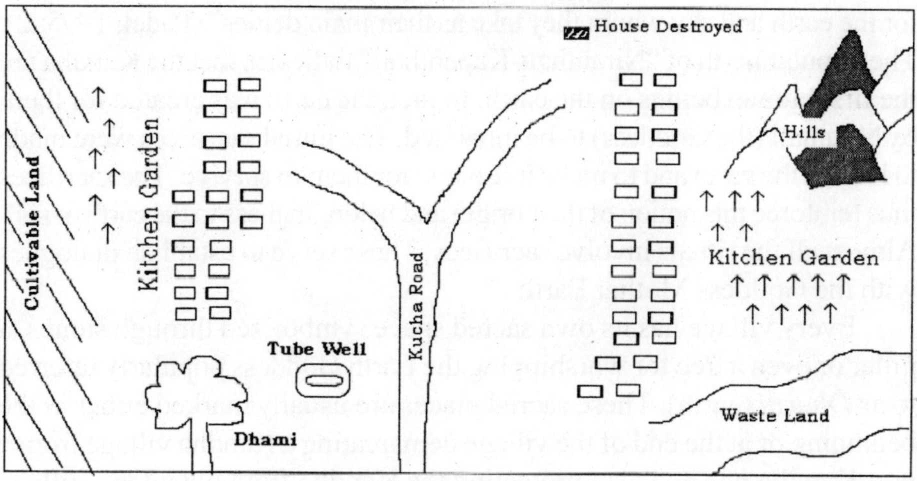

Fig. 6.3: Village Lataguda

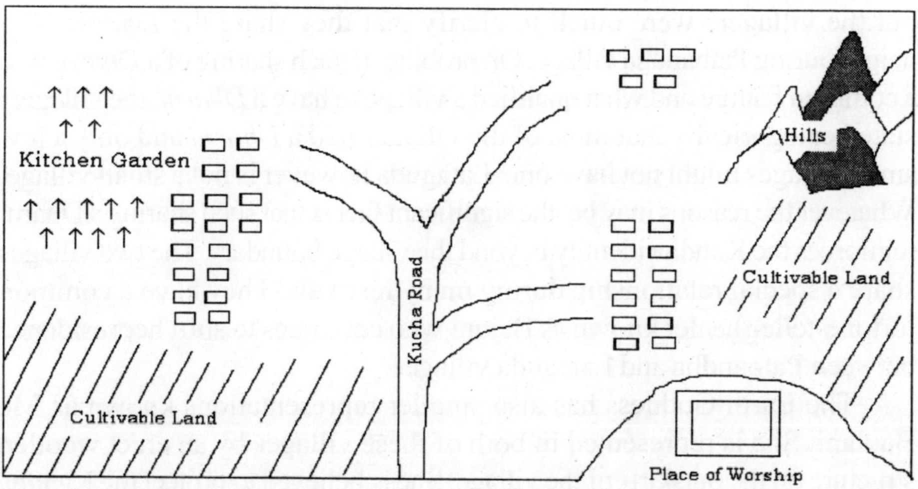

II

Kandha's Self Identification and Exclusion of "Outsiders"

The general scarcity of ethnographic literature on Kutia Kandhas is well known. Due to this fact, the many sections of this tribe are not really differentiated and no literature at all refers to the section I have visited. Notions of self-identity among Kutia Kandhas can, however, be reconstructed through myths and rituals. The different versions of the Kandha myths have been powerful media of reflecting Kandha identity. They are centring around the relationship between the Kandha and the Earth Goddess (Padel, 1995: 2) but the essence of these myths indicates "....in particular, the Kond's honour for the earth and sky whom they take as their main deities" (Padel, 1995: 2). The popular myth of "Niranthali-Kapanthali" indicates that the Kandha are the first human beings on the earth. In fact, the earth was created for them by Nirantali (the Goddess) to be inhabited. The initial sacrifices were made to harden the earth and to make it feasible for them to survive. The sacrifices thus reinforce this notion of their origin and belongingness to the earth or soil. Almost all the rituals involve sacrifices. These serve to establish dialogues with the Goddess Mother Earth.

Every village has its own sacred space symbolized through stones, a pillar or even a tree for worshipping the Earth Goddess popularly referred to as *Dharni* (earth). These sacred places are usually marked either in the beginning or at the end of the village demarcating a Kandha village from a non-Kandha one and also protecting the Kandha from outsiders. Village Lataguda in the Rayagada district surprisingly did not have the scared space but the villagers were quick to clarify that they share the *Dharni* with neighbouring Patbandha village. On probing, if such sharing of a *Dharni* was a common feature and what qualified a village to have a *Dharni*, the villagers stated categorically that most of the villages had a *Dharni* and only a few small villages might not have one. Lataguda however is not a small village. Whatever the reasons may be, the significant fact is that such sharing a Dharni reinforces the Kandha identity beyond the village boundary. The two villages share a special relationship during many festivals. They have a common fortune-teller/healer known as Bejuni who continues to shift her residence between Patbandha and Lataguda villages.

The Earth Goddess has also smaller representations known as Ma Baulani. She is represented in both of these villages by an erect wooden structure on the outskirts of the village. She is believed to protect the Kandha from deadly diseases like small pox, cholera and others. She is usually worshipped during December-January. The village *Disari* (astrologer) fixes a day and all the Kandha of the village assemble for the sacrifices of goats, sheep, and pigeons that are symbolically offered to the deity.

In the same spirit, the festival of seeds (Vihan Parba), popular among the Kutia Kandha in Kalahandi before the sowing period, is meant to symbolically offer seeds to the earth goddess. It is more of a household affair where some amount of rice is taken out and spread in front of the Goddess Dharni. A hen, goat (whatever is available in the household) is made to eat the rice and is subsequently sacrificed. A feast with the sacrifices of chicken and goats marks the festival. Sowing is considered inauspicious without this festival.

The *Podh Puja* or the sacrifice of buffalo is the major event among Kandha in terms of its scale, intensity, meaning and significance. While the buffalo sacrifice is practised with the same fervour among some of the different sections of the Kandha, there are also significant variations[1]. *Podh Puja* perhaps signifies Kandha identity par excellence. This is the single most ritual event, which brings together Kandha from different villages. Usually, two or three neighbouring villages as a cluster shoulder the responsibility of celebrating the event. However each of these villages alternatively gets its turn to host the event. All the villagers belonging to the particular village cluster and also their agnates and affine from nearby villages are invited to share the feast. The event in some villages also witnesses competing claims in sharing the feast among different groups of Kandha particularly where other sections of the Kandha (Dongria for instance) show up in the event. The celebration and the festive spirit start months before the *Puja*. All the male and female members smear oil on their bodies and wear new cloths. They celebrate the choral singing and group dancing separated by gender throughout the night of the sacrifice. The dance and the music serve to ward of evil and unwanted spirits. The priest (*Jani*) in Irkuli village narrated the essence of the festival, which lasted for days:

> We call our ancestors and gods, particularly Dharni Mata (the Earth Goddess), and tell them we are offering this sacrifice (buffalo) to them. We request them to give us a bountiful harvest and protect us from disease.

People of Patabandha village who hosted *Podh Puja* in the year of my visit (2004) added that a formal invitation goes only to agnates and affine in other villages while unofficially all Kutia Kandha of the area are allowed to participate. Only the Dongria priests, to whom a special invitation goes, do the actual *Puja* (worship). All of them reiterated that they could never understand what these Dongria priests actually chant even while they are aware of the larger message that the *Puja* conveys. They however lamented the fact that other Dongria Kandha, apart from the invited priests, come to know about the event and forcibly involve themselves in the sacrifice. These Dongria Kandha claim their right as the first to kill the buffalo and have a share of it. The Kutia Kandha consider the Dongria as the wild ones claiming the *Podh Puja* to be theirs originally.

The festival of *Bali Yatra* further brings together different sections of the Kandha even from villages from neighbouring districts to witness the power of the Earth Goddess symbolized by a human being in a state of trance, walking on fire or even sitting on a swing of thorns, i.e. involved in extraordinary acts.

I wish to emphasize that none of these rituals are timeless having witnessed no change but despite variations and changes over a period of time, the essence and significance of these rituals remain constant. The Kandha, through these rituals, identify themselves as the original residents and permanent owners of the soil. Even while some of these rituals are not inter-village affairs, their emphasis as unique Kandha events remains central.

I wish to add here that when I asked the Kutia Kandha in the two villages of the Rayagada district about the Kandha in neighbouring district, they did say that they are all the same with only minor differences in manners of speaking the Kui language. This is despite the fact that the Kutia Kandha in Rayagada district referred to themselves by the general label of adivasi ("aboriginals") in the first instance, an image that is used to introduce themselves to non-locals like researchers and Government officials while the specific identity of Kutia Kandha was usually meant for neighbours and people belonging to the area. Such use of different designations according to the context of interaction is a common practice among many tribes (Sahay, 1977: 8-57).

The intra-tribal identity beyond villages and districts is important and is reinforced through the rituals. Thus the Kandha rituals create and recreate the Kandha society by asserting the Kandha identity on the one hand and excluding the "outsiders" on the other. The Kutia Kandha consider the Damba and the Sundhi as outsiders in the sense of being vagrants. While almost all tribes have a notion of outsiders differentiating them from the non-tribal people, I wish to emphasize that the term outsider here has a derogatory meaning. For instance, the other higher Oriya castes (not living in the village, the Government officers and the researchers are considered outsiders in a technical sense but the outsider status of the Damba and Sundhi unavoidably has a derogatory connotation. They are called vagrants or impure ones who have a fleeting presence, drawing sustenance from Kutia land. The cultivation of land is for the Sundhi and Dambas, as the Kandha see it, merely a source of economic activity while for the Kandha themselves, it is their most important marker of identity guaranteeing and reassuring their belongingness to the soil. In village Irkuli, one of the Kandha females told me: the Sundhi have migrated from some place, we don't know. They never had any land. In Patabandha village, Kandha males were explicit about their relationship with the Damba:

> The Damba cannot live in our village. Our *Dharni* does not allow such outsiders to live with us in the village. One Damba household was living in our village and one day the house was destroyed. The Damba do not dare to live in our village, since they know that a tiger would devour them in such a case. We do not accept water from them or give them any. We do not even let them enter our house.

The story of the destroyed house signifies and reinforces the fact that Damba are a particular category of outsiders and the concept of the tiger's interference symbolizes the power of Earth Goddess.

Neither the Damba nor the Sundhi have assumed such an outsider status recently. The relationship between these groups can be explicable through reference to fragmentary but important historical evidence on these two castes. Sundhi are a traditionally a distiller caste (distilling country liquor, made out of the *Mahua* flower). Their role as merchants and in large commercial dealings in Phulbani district in Orissa has been discussed by Bailey (1957 and 1960). They have emerged as *saukars* (money lenders) in most parts of western and southern Orissa. Sundhi are infamous for their exorbitant credit rates, which is usually invested into agriculture. Popular notions view them as shrewd and cunning with a great potential of manipulating the interest rates. The Sundhi in Lanjigarh are known as the Dakhnia or those who originally belong to the south but were the earlier immigrants compared to the Garjatia found in other parts of Kalahandi. They have been settled in the Kondhmals since long and the latter belonged to the princely states of western Orissa, i.e. the Gharjats. In spite of the prohibition to distill liquor, the Sundhi continue to practice this profession though not on a large scale but for own consumption and for selling it to their Kandha neighbours.

The Damba are like the Pano of Phulbani district who as Niggemeyer (1964: 245) describes as tradesmen mediating between the Kutia Kandha and the outside world. The colonial administrative documents including the district Gazetteers refer to the category of Damba in an extremely derogatory fashion though needless to mention such documents need to be treated with caution[2]. The few remarks in anthropological studies also conform to a stereotype negative image of the Damba (Führer-Haimendorf, 1943; Elwin, 1950). While such derogatory image might not be the generalized pattern in the contemporary context as some of the studies have shown (Berger, 2003), at least in the villages I visited in Kalahandi and Rayagada districts, the negative attitudes towards the Damba by the other Oriya castes and the Kandha continue. Popular notions in these villages associate the Dambas with being cunning, manipulative, exploitative and low caste. Most of the Dambas in these villages are economically much better off than the Kandha. They are involved in agriculture, trading of cows and buffaloes, making and selling of country liquor made of *mahuwa* flowers and rice. Apart from their economic roles, the Damba continue to play their traditional role of drummers, who play drums on occasions of death and wedding rituals. However this service is utilized by other Oriya castes and never by the Kandha, who take pride in their own musical traditions.

III

Socio-economic Transactions and Inclusion of "Outsiders"

While at one level, Sundhi and Damba are excluded and treated as outsiders, at another level, they are included through a series of socio-economic transactions. In village Irkuli, I found it difficult to understand the tribal life, the nature of landholding, relations of production, and consumption without placing these in the context of the transactions between the Kandha and Sundhi within the village. These transactions include the buying of liquor, the borrowing of bullocks and rice or the mortgaging of land and the pawning of jewellery. These transactions are not sporadic but continuous and have existed since long. While the Kandha stated that they had little knowledge of how the Sundhi had moved to Irkuli (they seemed disinterested in this) the Sundhi were very clear about their migration history. Thus a senior Sundhi said:

> My father had owned a large estate of land in village Ishanala which he abandoned fearing tiger attacks. The Sundhi household who had been in Irkuli had died out and the land owned by the latter was given to my father by the King of that time essentially in order to pay land tax. Since then we have been here cultivating this land.

What needs to be emphasized is that the Sundhi have been living with the Kandha for three generations and many of the business transactions have evolved over these years. An analysis of the nature of landholding during the last three generations shows a process of significant land transfers from the

Kandha to Sundhi through a transaction called Kado Bikri, which is nowhere reflected in the official records. The details of the working of this institution have been discussed elsewhere (Mishra, 2005). In spite of the several credit schemes offered by the Government, the Kandha rely to more than 75 per cent on such informal credit sources, supplied mostly by the Sundhi and to a limited extent by the Damba of a nearby village. The transactions are never simple one to one sale or mortgage of land but they derive their complexity from the fact that such land transactions are interwoven with others like the borrowing of bullocks, buying of liquor for daily consumption, the borrowing of rice during hunger months and other contingencies. The complexity of these varied transactions could be captured only by exploring the nexus between land-cultivation-credit transactions. Thus the relationship is not only about the purchase of liquor or the borrowing for immediate contingencies but due to the changing relations of production and the attenuation of the Kandha rights over land and forest through such informal transactions.

The Kandha and Sundhi do not really share a relationship of occupational inter-dependence because both these groups are involved in agriculture, despite the fact that the Sundhi's involvement in agriculture is looked upon with sarcasm by the Kandhas saying "when did they have land to cultivate? They were never *raeet* (landholders). They are taking our land and cultivating". The Sundhi on the other hand identify themselves as essentially agriculturists with a passing mention of their making country liquor as a secondary activity. They look down upon the Kandha and consider them to be primitive because of their practice of shifting agriculture.

Drinking being the principal form of leisure activity for Kandha males and females, the tribal people of Patabandha and Lataguda buy liquor from the Damba who come to the Kandha villages to provide the drinks and carry out the transaction of buying cattle, buffaloes and other animals. The Damba are engaged in all trading activities and act as middlemen between Oriya castes and Kandha (Dongria and Kutia Kandha). The Damba usually buy a whole series of products like fruits, vegetables and lentils from the upper Oriya castes and also from the Dongria and sell these goods at the local market. The Damba are necessary partners in Kutia daily life while, at the same time, they are not allowed to live in a Kutia village. Such transactions bear significance for the understanding of the tribal life.

The intricacies of the transactions show that these are not based on institutionalised friendship nor kinship. The terms of reference between both of these communities are personal names while terms of addresses are vague. In village Irkuli, while the Sundhi address the Kutia Kandha in public by their names, I did not come across any Kutia Kandha doing the same. In Lataguda and Patabandha, Damba are either called by their personal names or by their village name. In Lataguda village the terms of relationship with the Sundhi are more cordial where the trust level is high simply because the Sundhi are economically very poor and do not own any land. Even the Kutia Kandha in this village do not own any land and work as tenants of Brahmins.

Most of the land transactions between Kandha and Sundhis are oral leaving a much desired scope for negotiations which always tilts towards the Sundhi. These vary in different contexts with different individual households. The transactions have a binding nature which significantly shows a high level of dependence of the Kandha on the Sundhi. Such binding nature is reflected in expressions like "moneylenders are always moneylenders and debtors are always debtors". Despite the binding nature of the transaction, the trust is neither assured nor guaranteed. In several instances the Kandha were not sure of availing credit in the approaching cultivating season. The Kandha clarified that trust is linked to creditworthiness of the households "If we go and request rice before the harvesting months, why should they give in, but if we prostate ourselves and beg, old rice will be given at double the interest rate," said a senior Kandha. The relationship does not witness any fictive kinship, which characterises many such transactions in other non-tribal villages[3].

All transactions are shrouded by secrecy and confined to the village. Despite frequent references to the Sundhi in several contexts the Kandha were reluctant to share information on the technical details of many of these transactions and even when they did share their knowledge, they would discuss these in a whispering tone. The relations had elements of fear with the tribal debtors fearing a termination of the transaction. I was constantly requested not to divulge any of this information either to the Sundhi households or to anybody outside of the village. Hence the knowledge of these transactions remained within the boundaries of the village. In this context the village boundary is demarcating a real social unit.

Thus many Government officials and the residents of the block headquarters had never heard about Kado Bikri while the relationship between Kandha and Sundhi is well known. To many of these administrators, this relationship is believed to be transparent and observable and always referred to in a humorous tone. One block level officer told me:

> Oh ! you are talking about the Kandha and Sundhi. It is so funny to see how the Sundhi cleverly induce the Kandhas to buy liquor from them and trap them in a long-term debt. Kandha are fools

> and get swayed by the Sundhi on whom they depend for their daily share of liquor. You know, Kandha are lazy while the Sundhi are enterprising. Everybody knows about this.

To an outsider, the relationship begins and ends with the buying or selling liquor. However, the transactions in these tribal villages go much beyond liquor deals involving many others. The long-term interaction, however, has not resulted either in assimilation or cooperation or even withdrawal. The co-existence contains elements of dependence, distrust and exploitation. Elements of rebellion are reflected in the negative Kutia attitude towards the Sundhi and the Damba. The inclusion of these outsiders is not a voluntary one. If the Kandha have excluded these caste groups, treating them as outsiders in a historical context of the belief in their origin and identity, it is again in the historical context of the changes in relations of production, attention of the rights of the Kandhas over land and forest that such transactions with the "outsider" castes living in these villages have emerged and continued.

IV

Studying Tribal Villages

The evidence thus shows how the tribal worldview shifts between tribe (Kutia Kandha) and village as focus of identification. It shows how the Kutia Kandha's identity as the permanent owners of the soil goes beyond village boundaries. The rituals of the Kandha serve to reinforce this identity bringing together Kandha from many villages or even neighbouring districts. At another level, the Kandha engage themselves in a series of transactions with the so-called outsider castes of Damba and Sundhi. Many of these transactions are marked by secrecy, distrust, dependence and exploitation that are deliberately confined to the village boundary. The analysis hence problematizes the study of tribal villages particularly when the researcher is interested in capturing the "tribal" character and assumes the numerical dominance underplaying the role of non-tribal influence. In tribal village studies, one thus needs to go beyond traditional questions of tribal distinctiveness *vs*. interactions between tribal and non-tribal people resulting in assimilation or integration. As the evidence has shown, the myths and the rituals are as important to understand the Kandha as are the socio-economic transactions. These rituals are at one time economic, social and religious. The content and timing of these are all related to the agricultural calendar. Hence I wish to abstain from the convenient argument of cultural distinctiveness *vs*. economic assimilation. The shifting boundaries between the tribe and the village are a reality and the roles of the non-tribal outsiders as well as those of insiders need to be examined in the study of the tribal Kandha villages. The social composition of tribal villages is different in different places but what I wish to emphasize is that neither the dominance of the tribal people in a village nor the functional/symbiotic nature of relations with non-tribal people can be taken for granted.

NOTES

1. The villagers did mention some of these changes in ways Buffalo sacrifice is being practiced currently in these two districts.
2. Macpherson, 1865; Senapati and Sahu, 1966; Fawcett, 1901 to cite a few references.
3. I came across evidence on fictive kinship between the Sabar tribal group and the Gouda caste in the non-tribal village in Kesinga block of Kalahandi district.

REFERENCES

Bailey, F.G. 1957 *Caste and the Economic Frontier.* Manchester : Manchester University Press.

Bailey, F.G. 1960. "An Oriya Hill Village-II," in M.N. Srinivas (ed.) *India's Villages.* Bombay: Asia Publishing House, pp.131-146.

Berger, Peter. 2003 "The Gadaba and the 'Non-ST' Desia of Koraput, Orissa," in George Pfeffer and Deepak Kumar Behera (eds.), *Contemporary Society: Tribal Studies* Series Vol. V, New Delhi: Concept Publishing House.

Elwin, V. 1950. *Bondo Highlander*. Bombay: Oxford University Press.

Fawcett, F. 1901. "The Dombs of Jeypore, Vizagapatnam District, Madras," *Man* 1: 34-38. London: JAI.

Jay, Edward. 1968. *A Tribal Village of Middle India.* Calcutta: Anthropological Survey of India.

Macpherson, S.C. 1865. Memorials of service in India from the correspondence of the late Samuel Charters Macpherson, C.B. Political Agent at Gwalior during the mutiny and formerly employed in the suppression of Human sacrifice in Orissa. Edited by his brother. London: John Murray.

Mishra, Arima. 2005 "Kado Bikri: Informal Process of Land Transfer among Kutia Kandhs," (pp.136-157) in Deeepak Kumar Behera and Georg Pfeffer (eds.), *Contemporary Society: Tribal Studies.* Vol. 6. New Delhi: Concept Publishing Company.

Niggemeyer, H. 1964. *Kuttia Kond.* Munich: Klaus Renner Verlag.

Padel, Felix. 1995. The Sacrifice of Human being: British Rule and the Konds of Orissa. Delhi: Oxford University Press.

Sachidananda, 1968. *The Tribal Village of Bihar.* Delhi: Munshiram Manoharlal.

Sahay, K.N. 1977. "Tribal Self-Image and Identity," in S.C. Dube (ed.), *Tribal Heritage of India.* Vol. 1, Delhi: Vikas Publishing House.

Magin Senapati, N. and N. Sahu. 1966. Gazetteer of India, District Koraput. Cuttack: Government Press

Roy Burman, B.K. 1973b. Rupa: A Sherdukpen Village in Arunachal Pradesh. Census of India, Village Monograph Series. New Delhi: Office of Registrar General of India.

SEVEN

COMMUNITY IN SEARCH OF A NEW IDENTITY: The Santal of West Bengal

PRADIP KUMAR BHOWMICK and SHYAMAL KUMAR JANA

Concept of Tribe, Tribal Identity and Ethnicity

Still today we do not find any criterion in the Constitution of India to identify a community as a Scheduled Tribe. There is also no uniform opinion among the anthropologists as to what makes a group of people a "tribe". There is a lot of ambiguity in the term "tribe". Perhaps the best way to categorize them is to see them in a continuum with other groups living in India (Beteille, 1977) or to recognize the continuum of political organizations with hierarchical dependent relations (Bailey, 1960).

The problem of identity arises from one's feeling of insecurity. It is a feeling of losing identity in the larger outer world. A society may be defined in terms of narrower criteria like language or religion, or in terms of broader criteria like region and culture. If culture simply means "a distinctive way of life", the tribal of West Bengal are definitely not without it. How far it is possible for a group to lead a "distinctive way of life" is a matter to be examined. However, there is still a distinctive focus on culture as a manifestation of group identity. All the tribes in India now confront with the important question of identity at a regional level. Now identity can operate as a broad cultural symbol or as an indicator of the pragmatic aspect of a people's behaviour. As David (1977) states that "identity is a cultural sign that operates both as a symbol, with semantic meanings, and as an index, with pragmatic meanings".

Geertz (1963) defines identity on the collective level as a "corporate sentiment of oneness". The point is why it has become necessary for the tribal of West Bengal to probe and assert their identities. No doubt, it is one of the proximal problems of today and the problem is not limited to the tribal of West Bengal alone. The problem of identity has become a more or less worldwide phenomenon and almost all the communities, irrespective of whether they are tribes or not, are involved with it in some way or the other. Identity here refers to "ethnic identity". To the tribes, it means "tribal identity".

"Ethnicity" is regarded as to a shared cultural identity that has a range of distinctive behavioural and possibly linguistic features passed on through socialization from one generation to another. According to Cohen (1978), "ethnicity is first and foremost situational". Within "situational" he prefers to include "the interactive situation" as a "major determinant of the level of inclusiveness employed in labelling self and others". Situation may vary depending on the "core" aspect of culture. In one situation the emphasis may be on occupation, in another it may be religion, yet another it may be region.

Cohen's (1978) concept of "situational ethnicity" provides a means for managing multiple identities, for understanding that an individual has layers of personalities, each one activates according to purpose. The concept of situational identity, to be truly useful, must account for cultural, political and social boundaries. Moreover, it must always leave room for the strategizing individual who can and often does move from one identity to another, changing "mask of identity" in the process. A true concept of situational ethnicity requires appropriate attention to political, social, economic, cultural-symbolic, and ecological and other aspects of the interactive network in which people find themselves. The main thrust in the present study is religion.

Tribal Society: Situational Analysis

The tribal society today no longer gives an impression of a society based upon kinship, where social stratification of any form is absent. By and large, the Indian tribal situation today gives an altogether different picture. If one neglects the economic aspect of the phenomenon, one would make a mistake. There has been a need to define the social situation in the context of development. One has to take a total view of the social, economic, ecological, political and technological factors — a system approach to the situation. Undoubtedly, there have been significant changes in the forms of demographic growth, adoption of urban elements and modern education, marginalization of traditional economic activities (farming and artisan production). The effect of coercion, conversion and the willing adoption to new ways of life has brought in tremendous changes in their traditional way of life. Cultural values and norms, which are communicable only through traditional linguistic symbols, are dying out leaving the tribal in a state of vacuum. In the absence of their complete assimilation with the alien values, which is seldom possible in the context of new time-space and natural-social environmental, they have practically turned into a new society struggling hard to establish their identity. Further there has been significant impact of mass communication, especially through radio and television, in their life. Non-participation of tribal in modern democratic political culture has been gradually replaced by their participation. Here one would like to know whether efforts at building a national identity by using the mass media, modern political and school systems could narrow tribal lines of affiliation.

No doubt, the tribal remains at the periphery of the mainstream culture, associating them with their own myths, symbols and codes as a reaction to the policy of exclusion maintained of the state. Probably the national policies are not culturally acceptable to the tribal. This involves examining the cultural values of the people and an understanding of their survival strategies. After all, for the tribal, a human being becomes whole only when he lives within his culture.

The primary sector is incapable of employing the ever increasing tribal labour force. As a result, there has been an increasing dependence of the tribal on the urban centres; particularly the markets. Growing involvement of the tribal with the national level politics is yet another new feature. Besides these, the emergent consciousness of the tribal as a marginalized group is a recent phenomenon. Pan-tribal movements should no longer be dismissed as defensive gesture in the form of innocent protests. These are the positive assertions claiming the rights of the tribal. These may even mean a nostalgic desire to return to a happy past showing aversion to their continual exploitation by the non-tribal and the interference of the State with their traditional way of living. Also implicit is a desire by the tribal to determine their own future.

Generally speaking, there has been an accelerated pace of change implicit in the development process that shakes up the age-old traditional structure of tribal societies in varying degrees. This accelerated change brings discontinuities and does not always allow for the evolution of existing perception to cope with and internalize change. Sometimes, the individuals experience the drift, anomie and the self-depreciation associated with ultimate adoption of negative images of self and society, and the consequent problems. The question of identity must start with an analysis of the social relation at its base.

But what is social may to some extent be explained in economic terms, because the specific features of any economy are mainly socially determined.

All these lead us to the important question of the validity of tribe as a social category in the contemporary world. It is not a new question, but it is an unresolved one and a vital one too, particularly from the development point of view. The growing manifestation of tribal identity has to be seen in the total context. It must take into consideration all facets of life, which are, in other words, expressions of culture — the way a person defines himself or herself. There is no scope for a simplistic explanation of the persistence of tribal affiliation and tribal ideology even in situations of diverse sets of social relations.

Tribal Society: Search for a New Identity

Tribes and low castes in India are no longer eager to be "sanskritized". Rather a process diametrically opposite to "sanskritization" is also operating in tribal India where there is conscious attempt to revive the age old tribal traditions for gaining momentum for political movements. In most of these cases after a period of initial contact with the dominant culture, the tribal try to revitalize their culture and this ultimately culminates in political movements (Oraons, 1965). Thus, it may be said that not through "sanskritization", rather through "de-sanskritization" or "re-tribalization", the tribal try to get themselves scheduled as "tribe" for receiving special treatment and privileges. M.K. Gautam described this aspect of Santal life in Bengal-Bihar border, an aspect of "Santalization", where "the cultural phenomenon works as mechanism for self-restraint. Revivalism is based on local ethnic traditions and ideals of golden age, a happy period in remote past, and provides internal unity by conforming or relating to the Santal standard behaviour" (Bhowmick, 1980).

The tribal groups and/or low caste groups are now eager to establish and maintain their separate cultural identity in order to avail of the economic and other opportunities ensured to them under the Constitution of India. The growing political consciousness and the leftist political parties have led the tribal people and the low castes to oppose the privileged and the high caste Hindus. Thus there is no longer a desire to shake off the tribal markers and assimilate the features of the high caste Hindus. Rather, the tribes and low castes are now engaged in a bitter struggle to establish their identities as separate socio-cultural-linguistic groups.

The present study is not a study on the process of tribal transformation as such. Evolving a set of indicators of tribal transformation is not the primary objective of the study. It only seeks to take a look at the Santal of West Bengal in different situations in the light of their own identity crisis.

Field Observations

It has been observed from the field that the status of Santal life in Paschim Medinipur and Bankura districts of West Bengal reveals a very clear picture of oscillation from one place to another. A gradual process of Hinduization of Santal in the form of various *Bhakti-cults,* in which *Vaishnavite* tendencies are reflected as part of Bengali-Hindu peasant culture. There has been also a line of development in some contact situations where the Santal, including other tribal converted to Christianity, get the opportunities of better education and economic improvement provided by many Christian missionaries. This has, to a great extent, awakened of a sense of collective consciousness among the tribal about the risk of losing their traditional identity. Along with this, a new type of retribalization movement can be found in some places in recent times. This is known as *Sari dharam,* a religion based on "truth" (*Sari* means truth).

Aiming at providing a traditional religious identity to the Santal in a region dominated by widespread Hinduism and conversion to Christianity, Sari dharam (a religion based on *Bonga-hor* and "truth") distinguishes itself from *Safa-hor and Um-hor*.

- *Safa-hor*: Followers of Saiva cult or local Hinduism represented by the *Deswali Majhi* community.
- *Um-hor*: Christian Santal.
- *Bonga-hor*: Followers of *Sari-dharam,* believers of traditional Santal gods.

The first group represents a case of "re-tribalization". The second group is an example of "de-tribalization" and last group presents a good picture of "contra-acculturation" or "santalization".

The Deswali Majhis: A Case of Re-tribalization

The prevailing theological and cultural differences between the two types of the Santal and its consequent attitudes, as discussed below, go a long way in determining their social interrelations and interactions. Their attitudes have affected their mutual social relations in a number of ways and it would be worthwhile to examine them here. The Deswali Majhis of Chilagara village in Ranibandh C.D. Block under Bankura district of West Bengal represent a good example of Re-tribalization.

The Deswali Majhis are the one of the group of the Santal community. Prior to Indian independence, in all Government records they have been treated as the Santal. But to uplift their social status they imitated or followed thc lifcstylc of thc local Hindus. As a result, they discarded to use the twelve patrilineal totemic clans of the Santal, e.g. Soren, Baskey, Murmu, Hansda, Tudu, Kisku, Besra, etc. and used "Majhi" as their surnames. They started worshipping Hindu gods and goddesses like, Kali, Lakshmi, Saraswati, etc. in place of their traditional *Marang Buru*. But soon after Independence, the Deswali Majhis were no more treated as Scheduled Tribe like the Santal. In the 1960s they, particularly the younger generations, wanted to re-establish and maintain their separate cultural identity like the Santal in order to avail different facilities and opportunities ensured to the weaker section in the Constitution of India. Since then they have been trying to prove themselves

Table 7.1: Social Interactions between the Santal and the Deswali Majhi

Sl. No.	*Character(s)*	*Santal*	*Deswali Majhi*
1.	Religion	Sari Dharam	Local Hinduism
2	Festivals	Perform their own tribal festivals and worship tribal gods and goddesses.	Perform mostly festivals of the local Hindus
3	Marriage	Within the community. Not with the Deswali Majhis	Within the community. Not with the Santal
4	Preference for neighbour	Own community members. Never treat Deswali Majhis as the members of their community.	Own community members. Treat Santal as their community members.
5	Mother tongue/ Language	Santali (Thar)	Bengali
6	Drinking habit	Habitual drinkers	Ceremonial drinking
7	Social status	Higher than the Deswali Majhis	Higher than the Santal
8	Social visit during ceremonies	Do not invite the members of a Deswali Majhi to their houses during life cycle rituals	Do not invite the members of a Santal community to their houses during life cycle rituals
9	Traditional Panchayat	Own panchayat system. No representation from the Deswali Majhi.	Own panchayat system. No representation from the Santal.
10	Village level co-operation	All are welcome	All are welcome

as a division of the Santal society. The Bihar, Paschim Bangal Deswali Majhi Samaj located at Manbazar, under Purulia district in West Bengal has been fighting for the restoration of their tribal status since 1960s. But they are still treated as a general caste community by the Government of West Bengal.

The Christian Santal: A Case of De-tribalization

The Santal of Bhimpore village in Salboni C.D. Block of Paschim Medinipur district are an example of De-tribalization. Christianity is one of the various factors which have brought tremendous changes among the tribal youths of this region overrunning its virgin territory and eroding its valuable traditions. When the Christian missionaries started their work, all their intentions were evangelical by nature. "They aimed at a final conversion of the people to what they considered to be the only path of salvation" (Troiji, 1978). Christianity gave them an ideology, created a myth and a sense of history sharpened the feeling of separateness and emphasized identity (Singh, 1976). It expanded their horizon of contact not only beyond the village or the tribe even beyond the country. Christianity might have given a new way of life to them, but it could not help in maintaining a separate entity for them. Rather the people feel they have been culturally dispossessed. It is felt that the pragmatic aspect of the tribal culture is still served by the traditional social structure and Christianity could not alter it much. It could only influence the non-pragmatic aspect, particularly those matters of moral value (Das, 1985). It also splits up the tribal community, undermined its solidarity, deepened the gulf and created cleavages between the advanced Christian Santal and the backward non-Christian Santal tribal groups (Jana, 2001).

The Santal: A Case of Contra-acculturation or "Santalization"

The Santal of Bhimpore village in Salboni C.D. Block of Paschim Medinipur district is also an example of Santalization or Contra-acculturation. The main features of Sari dharam are not only propitiation of the traditional gods but also the revival of traditional dance and music; they show their eagerness to bring back their traditional culture and language. A section of the Santal during the 1961 census tried to identify themselves in distinct Sari dharam religious group. This was led by Late Sadhu Ramchand of Silda in Paschim Medinipur district of West Bengal. The younger generations are also now eager to preserve their traditional cultural heritage by observing different tribal rituals and festivals. They are also demanding that the introduction of *Olchiki* in the school curriculum. With their constant efforts, *Santali* language has already

Table 7.2: Social Interactions between the Santal and the Christian Santal

Sl. No.	*Character(s)*	*Santal*	*Deswali Majhi*
1.	Religion	Sari Dharam	Christianity
2	Festivals	Perform own tribal festivals and gods and goddesses.	Perform mostly related to the Jesus Christ
3	Marriage	Within the community. Not with the Christian Santal	Within the community. Not with the Santal
4	Preference for neighbour	Own community members. Never treat Christian Santal as the members of their community	Own community members. Treat Santal as their community members.
5	Mother tongue/ Language	Santali (Thar)	Bengali
6	Drinking habit	Habitual drinkers	Ceremonial drinkers
7	Social status	Feel superior to the Christian Santal	Feel superior to the Santal
8	Social visit during ceremonies	Do not invite the members of a Christian Santal to their houses during any life cycle rituals	Do not invite the members of a Santal community to their houses during any life cycle rituals
9	Traditional Panchayat	Own panchayat system. No representation from the Christian Santal	No panchayat system of their own.
10	Village level co-operation	All are welcome	All are welcome

been included in the VIIIth Schedule of the Constitution of India. The Government of India's decision in the inclusion of the Santali language in the VIIIth Schedule in the year 2004 has given them a moral boost to further revitalize their traditions.

The Jharkhand Movement is also gaining its ground in this area rapidly. The movement demanding that the tribal be allowed to decide their destiny. Sending different memoranda to the Government challenging the erosion of Santal culture are some of the instances of protest and propaganda. Though such protests may be sporadic, they are indicators of reviving traditional identity.

Concluding Remarks

The Santal, Deswali Majhis and the Christian Santal of Bankura and Paschim Medinipur districts of West Bengal have undergone profound changes showing new features of identity.

Prior to conversion, all the members of the tribe were socially equal to one another a larger extent. However, with the process of conversion and sanskritization, the Santal, Deswali Majhi and Santal Converts differentiate themselves from one another. Each of the group, particularly the younger generation within the three segments, tries to establish its superiority over the other and advances several cultural and religious reasons to justify the evaluations. Such attitudes have affected their social relations and created considerably misunderstanding among the three segments.

Caught in between the Church and the Jharkhand movement (demanding that the tribal should be allowed to tribal destiny), the tribal of Paschim Medinipur district are fast loosing their links with the cultural moorings and thereby facing a kind of identity crisis. The "nature worship" cult of the Santal has been replaced by Christianity. The traditional tribal feasts and festivals are no longer observed in the Santal Christian families. Christain songs have replaced the original Santal folk songs. The legends, myths, folklores, and folktales relating to their origins, gods and goddesses are withering away in the fold of Christianity. As more and more Christian Santal children move into the mainstream education, they are slowly forgetting their dialect *Olchiki*. Also prompted by the Church, the Christian Santal deliberately induced mass amnesia in themselves — traditional rites and rituals were all discarded as pagan; the tribal identity were forsaken, the rich cultural heritage was relegated to the background.

REFERENCES

Bailey, F.G. 1960. *Tribe, Caste and Nation — Study of Political Activity and Political Changes in Highland Orissa.* London: Oxford University Press.

Beteille, Andre. 1977. "The Definition of a Tribe," Seminar, (14), October 1968, as reproduced in Thapar, Romesh (Ed.), *Tribe, Caste and Religion in India.* New Delhi: Macmillan India Limited, p. 7.

Bhowmick, P.K. 1980. *Some Aspects of Indian Anthropology.* Calcutta: Subarnarekha, p. 33.

Cohen, Ronald. 1978. "Ethnicity: Problems and Focus in Anthropology," *Annual Review of Anthropology,* 7: 379-403.

Das, R.K. 1985. *Manipur Tribal Scene: Studies in Society and Change.* New Delhi: Inter-India Publications.

David, Kenneth. 1977. *The New Wind: Changing Identities in South Asia.* New York: Mouton Publishers.

Geertz, C. 1963. *Old Societies and New States: The Quest for Modernity in Asia and Africa.* New York: Free Press.

Jana, Shyamal K. 2001. "Christianity and Tribal Identity: A Case Study of the Santal of Bhimpore in the district of Midnapore, West Bengal," *Man and Life,* 7 (3-4): 195-206.

Oraon, M. 1965. *The Santal: A Tribe in Search of Great Tradition.* Detroit: Wayne State University Press.

Singh, K.S. 1976. *Tribal Ethnicity in a Multi-ethnic Society.* Unpublished UNESCO paper.

Troiji, J. 1978. *Tribal Religion.* New Delhi: Manohar Publications.

EIGHT

REJECTING THE SYSTEM AND GETTING REJECTED:

New Generation Juang Adolescents in Search of New Identity

SASWAT PUJARI and JHARANA MISHRA

In any vision of a nation's destiny, the present and future of childhood must be central. The child should be protected and sheltered or should be thrown into the waters of experience to sink or swim. These are questions that we usually ask. Modern work ethic gives much stress to material possessions and material success at the expense of human relations and thc arts. But, growing up in a Juang village one cannot make costly mistakes. The child belongs to the community. The Juang believe the children are inherently imaginative and that they need only be given freedom to evolve rich and charming ways of life for themselves. Most of the things happening in the community are discussed in the *mandaghara.* It is basically experimental learning and not forced learning, the inbuilt cultural mechanism has given the Juang child more freedom in decision-making. The Juang may not be economically sound but they are socially and culturally rich. Every child is gifted, gifted with the inalienable right to explore the world, to seek information, to go beyond what he knows empirically, into the realm of imagination. Foster this with stories and songs, with poems and parables, with love and laughter and in the course of growing up he develops a lively imagination. The various games played by the children of the Juang society cannot be considered as mere play of games; but it is a source of learning apart from being a source of pleasure. All the games have got some social significance. Children become intimately acquainted with their socio-cultural fabric and learn how to play appropriate roles in upholding their age-old traditions. It also helps them in finding their own identity within the ambit of their socio-cultural surroundings

The Scheduled Tribe (ST) population is estimated to have reached 88.8 million in 2001, which is 8.6 per cent of the country's total population. Of this, 1.32 million (1.95%) belong to Primitive Tribal Groups (PTGs) who are more marginalized than other ST population. They have a heterogeneous cultural and economic pattern of life, largely conditioned by the ecological settings and ethnic environment. Inevitably, these leave the effect upon socio-economic development, as well as education. For centuries, the tribal communities lived in isolation from the social mainstream, maintaining the cultural identity and transmitting their skills and knowledge through oral traditions from one generation to the other. However, in India, during the course of the last hundred years or so, the rapid advancement in transport and communications affected these tribes to some extent. It is impossible to isolate these communities from the effect of cultural and technological changes taking place around them. The Juang is one of the primitive tribal groups exclusively found in Orissa. Linguistically they are Munda speaking people (Munda being one of the Austro-Asiatic language families). Each Juang village is an autonomous socio-political unit managed by a set of traditional leaders and a corporate body of village elders called *barabhai*. Their economy centers round shifting cultivation, which is the main source of livelihood. To a large extent this is supplemented by some other economic pursuits such as food gathering, hunting and wage earning. Food crisis is one of their major problems. The Juang family needs the contribution of each and every capable family member in this struggle for their existence and in the struggle the contribution of Juang children cannot be undermined. The Juang are far away from the mainstream. They still stick to their traditional pattern of life style (Rout, 1969-70).

Because children have proved that when they are involved, they can make a difference in the world around them. They have ideas, experience and insights that enrich adult understanding and make a positive contribution to adult actions. When the drive is neither respected nor nurtured, when children are excluded or ignored by adults, their potential to contribute to their communities is compromised. Such children are likely to act as they have been treated, i.e. as social outcastes — with their energies and creativity directed into subcultures and away from creating a cohesive community. It is not if children participate, but how they participate, that is a critical issue now, when so many millions of children are hungry, diseased or exploited. It is quality of their interactions with their social environment that is vital and the paper tries to find out how external forces are influencing the rich Juang tradition; does the changing situation create an identity crisis among the Juang adolescents; are the younger generation in search of new identity; and can a Juang child move into adolescence with confidence and assertiveness. The paper makes a humble attempt in understanding the Juang children, their hopes and aspirations, contribution and participation. The study is part of the ethnographic research conducted by us in a few tribal dominated villages of Banspal block of Keonjhar district of Orissa.

During the fieldwork, we interacted with several children, their parents and the community. We feel too often that research remains silent about the relationships that develop between the researcher and respondents while in the field. It is only through the recognition of the personal and emotional dimensions of fieldwork that we can critically reflect upon the balance of self-analysis and academic discussion in the presentation of data (Coffey, 1998: 140; Lofland & Lofland, 1995). The changing nature of the relationships that develop between researchers and respondents during field work are clearly demonstrated by writings which have pointed out how host population expectations about visiting researchers have shaped the course of various studies, so much so that, the roles visiting researchers have adopted in the field have not necessarily been chosen by themselves (Blackwood, 1995; Caplan, 1993: 21). Immersion in the setting, we found a useful strategy to attempt to view the culture from within. Indeed, living in the village certainly proved illuminating and also paved the way for conducting household survey, interviews and observe the respondents closely.

Nurturing the Natural Way

Close knit communities like the Juang interweave their forms of cultural expressions. Painting, wood carving, songs, festivals, birth, deatn, animals and forests are components of a cycle which metamorphose together to give their philosophy and understanding of the cosmos a holistic dimension.

Ninjiya Gaon (Our Village):

"Uli tulia nal kantua ninjiya san gaon
Ale, alsam, bangru, jambu lagare swad.
Sang jalare man kusire dulite kaleke anje.
Majadang duwar dal adaj kusire ande anje.
Gadag bilte lakuke kiti jati jati pasal"

English

> On the foothills besides the stream lies our small village. Mango, jackfruits, grapes and flowers are so sweet. With a joyous heart I play with my friends. The sound of the *changu* from the *mandaghar* makes me happy, I participate in agricultural activities and reap a rich harvest.

This is how a Juang child describes his social life in the village. The children love their natural surrounding and growing-up in a natural environment makes them capable of playing the future role of an adult. For the Juang, there is an invisible link between the fertility of crops and fertility of their womenfolk. Both are engaged in continuing the creative act that not only brought human life into being, but also made land productive. If a young wife conceives she becomes reciprocally a symbol of blessing to her husbands family land.

The mother has received blessing of her husband's ancestors. The marriage is now secure. She is now pregnant. Her dread of barrenness is removed, for were she barren, after some years the husband would have been within his rights to send her back to her parents and take a second wife. Nevertheless, for nine months (or "ten months") she is creature of two worlds, the bridge between the living and the unborn, who is now known only to the ancestors. Certain safeguards must, therefore, surround her in the form of taboos.

Since food is very limited for most of the year, the Juang women observe very few food taboos during the time of the pregnancy. She may not eat meat from either of the community's source, i.e. from an animal sacrifice or from a kill in hunting. She must also avoid anything that might startle or frighten her, these being "little deaths". She must, in fact, keep away from any reminders of death, for then a pregnancy may lead to a miscarriage, a still-birth or even the death of the mother. These tragedies are believed to be due to the activity of evil spirits. If at any point the pregnant women becomes sick, suffers from debility or has any antenatal problems, the priest or the traditional village medical practitioner may prescribe further taboos and rituals to safeguard her well being. Otherwise she continues her strenuous daily work in the home, the hill fields or gathering wild produce from the forest until the final stages of pregnancy. She also continues sexual relations with her husband until close to her confinement.

The birth of a child is a matter that requires no assistance from outsiders. At the time of childbirth the husband's mother is usually in-charge along with at least one other woman from the village who is call a traditional birth attendant. She does the more minor jobs for the mother and infant, but it is also her privilege to announce the sex of the child to the waiting community and to name it after a deceased member from the paternal grandparents' generation. The paternal grandmother or great-aunt severs the umbilical cord. This is done with a knife. The father buries the placenta behind the house. The birth attendant smears the stump with turmeric paste and ties a protective cord round the infant's neck and another round the mother's neck. These are worn for about two weeks. If the child dies before the umbilical cord has fallen off, it is not cremated but buried without the usual rites because it is not yet fully recognized as a family member. Age-grade plays a vital role in Juang society. The baby is now given a warm bath, and after that is massaged near the fire. The birth attendant receives payment in the form of paddy, a chicken and food. If the child is male the payment is double. This highlights the preference for a male child. In case of a difficult delivery, the patient squats while the attendant messages her abdomen. That failing, the traditional medical practitioner is called in. He offers prayers and tries herbal remedies. If these also fail, it is a sign that an evil or evil spirits are at work. After surmising on what exactly may be the cause — may be an offended ancestor spirit — he takes the necessary steps to remedy the situation. An ancestor is pacified through a chicken sacrifice or offerings of liquor, tobacco and rice; otherwise through reversal procedures directed towards the person believed to be sending out the evil eye.

The birth makes both the parents ritually unclean, so they are not allowed to enter any home, or touch anyone in their homes, or handle things of common use. During and immediately following the birth, the mother must not cook; which is done for the two of them by the husband. Both attend a ritual of purification the next day when they bath and wash their cloths in the stream, and the mother also washes the mat she has been sleeping on. She also throws away her old cooking pots, replacing them with new ones. On return from the stream the father does the Juang' traditional act of self-purification by placing a copper coin in a pot of water. He sprinkles this water around and inside the house and over himself and his wife. Then he offers husked rice and turmeric to the two deities, the Creator (sky) and the Mother (earth). He may also make the sacrifice of a chicken to the ancestors and local deities on behalf of the new born child and his other children if they are already there. Then the parents ceremonially greet the child by dipping their fingers in turmeric powder and very lightly pinching its forehead and chin. The mother duly purified now may resume cooking, but she must observe certain food taboos; she must eat only rice, greens and fried salt, and certainly no meat or fish. She stays in seclusion and is restricted from doing any hard work. She resumes her normal diet and routine work only about four or five months or when the child begins to crawl. These months give her enough leisure to feed and care for the child constantly. The taboos, the baby would suffer from stomach trouble and diarrhea, which are common. These are the most common cause of infant death, because they result in rapid dehydration.

By Juang rule, the child's parents must observe continence until the child begins to stand and tries to walk. Though a name may have been given to the child earlier, a public name giving ceremony marks the end of this probationary period. By staying alive for several months, the infant has proved itself to be no temporary or destructive interloper from the spirit world, but a genuine human birth into the family. Family membership cannot be recognized, however, without a rite of integration for the child and alongside this, the end of the required period of segregation of the mother. Part of the reason for her remaining separate until then is not simply the belief about her earlier physical impurity, but is due to her close tie with the infant during its period of marginality between the two worlds. Difficult labour is ascribed to the evil eye of the enemies or to the ill will of some malevolent spirits dwelling on hills, forests and streams. If displeased the ancestral spirits also create countless troubles in case of childbirth. To counteract the evil eye and to neutralize the effect of sins or ill temper of the ancestors a number of magical rites are performed. The *Raulia* (ghost-finder) is summoned to perform rites to expel the ghosts. He first gives a few medicinal herbs to the expectant mother to help ease delivery. If this fails the *Raulia* gets confirmed that some evil spirits are creating troubles. The *Raulia* measures three reeds to detect the spirit or the person obstructing the delivery. If the evil maker is detected to be a sorcerer the *Raulia* performs magical rites to counteract or to neutralize the evils played by the sorcerer. If the labour pain is believed due to the whim of some displeased ancestor, sacrifice of chicken, tobacco, liquor and cooked rice are made to avert his ill temper. The other spirits causing troubles are also properly propitiated to help easy delivery.

If the baby is male one the *sutrunihari* shouts saying that the child is *sengan* or firewood (meaning male child); and it case of a female child she is referred to as *alak* (leaves). The midwife cuts the naval cord of the newborn, anoints turmeric paste and bathes the baby in tepid water. She cleans the mother and the apartment, and lights a fire to warm the baby and the mother. The mother is advised not to expose herself to rain or cold. The midwife is given remuneration, which consists of five to ten *pai* of paddy; one chicken, and leaf cupful of cooked-rice and curry. In case a son is born she may be given extra amount of one to two rupees and a brass bangle for her services. Though Juang hail the birth of a child as a happy event, there are, however, situations when a birth is not considered desirable, as before a marriage or too soon after a previous birth. But there are also certain elderly women in some villages who supply a root, which can prevent childbirth.

Name Giving Ceremony *(Nimincha)*

A name is given to the newborn after five or six days of its birth, or it may be delayed for three to four months. The ritual called *Nimincha* aims at naming the child and blessing it for a happy future, free of diseases and calamities. The father procures two to three chickens, worships the ancestors and local deities, and offers them dried husked rice, milk, molasses, chicken and liquor. He and his wife smear a little turmeric powder on the chin of the child and kiss it. The father prays:

> *Oh Basumata and Dharam Deveta Boitini Pata, Gramsiri Pitrupitaki.*

English:

> "To day I am performing the *Nimincha* ritual for my child. Let him/her lead a peaceful life free from all calamities."

The priest must be invited to perform certain rituals before this public naming of the child. The names most commonly given in these ceremonies are those of recently dead members of the family who have died at a ripe old age, though this is not obligatory choice. Signs characteristic of that ancestor may have been detected in the child. This is in no way to be confused with the Hindu doctrine of transmigration of souls, for the Juang ancestor so named continues to be regarded as a full member of the ancestors' group. Sometimes a deity's name is also given. In naming the child, the names of the deceased ancestors are always preferred. It is believed that the dead persons take rebirth in the family. The name of the child's father's father (if dead), or father's brother is preferred to in case of a male child. In case of a female child, her father's sister's name is preferred to. At times, the *Raulia* reads omens by measuring three reeds and selects a name for the child from a whole bunch of names. Giving new and fashionable names is more a fancy among the Juang. The children are named after the local trees, flowers, roots and tubers and after certain birds and beasts. Thus we get names like *dunkia* (a kind of cereal), *basandae* (a kind of tuber), *bayam* (a kind of tuber) and so on. Persons named after their physical deformity are not completely unfamiliar. Lame persons are named as *choota* or *chuuti* and blind persons are called *andha*. There are also persons who are named after the name of the day of their birth. Thus, boys born on Monday, Tuesday, Wednesday, Thursday, Friday and Sunday are named as *Sambaria, Mangala, Budhai, Guru, Sukra* and *Rabi* respectively. Likewise the girls are also named as Gurubari, *Sukru* and *Raibari*. After a name is proposed the Raulia measures the reeds and in case the length of the reeds increases the name is considered auspicious and is thereby selected. The day the child is named, the mother cooks rice and the chickens slaughtered in the ritual. Shares of cooked rice and meat curry are distributed among the families of one's own lineage and in case the family can afford to spend more, the same may be distributed among the families of the village. A name once selected is however, not taken as final. It can be changed and a new name be given in case the child with the original name cries insistently and suffers from frequent ailments. Renaming the child does not involve any further ritual, except that the father may offer some liquor in honour of the family ancestors.

Fostering a Child

In order to avoid the premature death of a child whose elder brother and sisters died young the parents may ceremonially hand over the child to the *bara bhaiki* (village elders) and *mabhouniki* (village women). The Juang believe that if the child is ceremonially made over to the care of the villagers it restores health and happiness. On a particular day the father intimates his intention to the villagers, and all the elderly men and women assemble in his house. The *Raulia* reads omens and detects the agency creating troubles to the family members of the affected person. An earthen doll is made representing the evil maker and the *nagam* (priest) makes offerings praying *Basumata* (Earth Goddess). *Dharma Devta* (Sun God), *Gramsiri* (Village Deity) and other deities. He first draws a circle on the floor with turmeric powder. The doll of the troublemaker is placed inside the turmeric circle and the *nagam* offers husked-rice grains, molasses and liquor to him praying for the health of the child. Three pairs of *split sal* twigs, measuring three to four inches in length and about an inch in diameter are kept on the hands of the image and the *nagam* tilts the image to make the split twigs fall down on the floor, while doing this he pours liquor before the image and prays the image to forget anger and take back his curse. All the three pairs of the sal twigs are thrown from the hands of the image pair by pair until all the three pairs fall down in a definite manner that is viewed to be auspicious. Of the two split pieces of the twigs one should fall down with the flat surface down and the other one reversely in order to indicate good luck. After this the women bath the child in turmeric water and make him to sit on the lap of a woman. They contribute one or two beads from their necklace and make a necklace for the child that is tied around his neck. They put turmeric powder on the cheek of the child and bless for his good health. They give a new name to the child and announce him to be their son. The elderly men and women assemble together and perform a liquor ritual. They pour liquor on the ground in the name of the deities and the *pitruki* (ancestors) and sprinkle a little over the head of the child wishing him a smooth life. While performing the liquor ritual they pray:

> "*O Basumata, Dharam Devta, Gramsiri, Pitru Pitaki* (ancestors). From today the child ceases to be the son of his father; he becomes the son of the villagers. From to day we pour all our blessings over him. Let him be free from all diseases and let him lead a happy life, if any body tries to endanger him, let that person be eaten by tiger, let his heart burst, and let his tongue be uprooted."

Though the child is ceremonially handed over to the villagers he still retains all his normal relations with his family members. He continues to remain with his parents, and is fed by them as usual. After he grows up, and before his marriage, his parents present about one or two *khandi* of husked rice, a goat, and liquor worth two to three rupees to the villagers to get back their son ritually. A feast is held and the food is distributed among all the families equally. The community and the family do not duly recognize some of the creative activities of the children. But a person who is good at agricultural operations and household works is always appreciated. *Raulia* is much respected. Gopal Juang, a 17-year-old boy from Gonasika, who is a *Raulia* is in much demand. He cures minor injuries, aliments and snakebites with mantras and traditional medicine.

Solberg (1989) illustrates his argument about the importance of the social construction of time in the analysis of childhood by ethnographic material that focuses on the present, ongoing social lives of children rather than their past or future.

Ethnography has been taken up as a methodology, which has a particular role to play in the development of a new sociology of childhood since it allows children a more direct voice in the production of sociological data than is usually possible through experimental research. Similarly, fieldwork-based research encourages researchers to focus on the ongoing roles that children play and the meanings they themselves attach to their lives. The real aim of the researcher's participation in the lives of subjects during the course of fieldwork is not to yield any research data; it is at best a means to carrying out the proper research activities, which yield such data. Whatever, other research techniques the researcher might imply during fieldwork, the main data yielding procedure is observation. Malinowski (1922) suggested three methods which were the need to achieve the ultimate goal of ethnography, "to grasp the natives point of view, his relation to life, to realize his vision of his world."

Daily Schedule of Activities of Children

Children of age groups 0-6 and 7-12 get up from the bed around 5.00 a.m. but the children in the age group 13-18 (especially girls) usually get up as early as 4.00 a.m. After meeting the calls of nature, the older children (7-12 and 13-18) attend the younger ones (0-6) and girls assists their mother in their household work. After taking their morning meal the older children prepare to leave for work please along with their parents. They do not come back home for the mid-day meal. Small children gather to play around village. After the evening meal the younger ones go to bed but the grown up boys and girls engage themselves in gossiping, joking, dancing and singing.

Buddu Juang, a 13-year-old boy, stated:

> "I don't want to become anything when I grow up. I shall do what I am doing. I don't always enjoy going to the forest along with my father. Especially when I want to do other things".

Laxman Juang, a 15-year-old boy, said:

> "Going to the forest has taught me a lot of things. Things like working in close co-ordination with others and self-reliance. The forest has also given me a lot of beautiful moments. Do you know

there are so many types of animals in the forest? Once I saw a tiger. It was terrifying but exiting. Unfortunately I am not good at sketching so I am not able to get the exact image on paper. Yet, it was quite an experience, one that I enjoyed tremendously."

Work Done by the Children in Different Seasons in a Year

Seasons	*Work Done*	*Age Group*
Sraban to Dasara (July to October)	Watching the crops, weeding fishing in the field, collection of roots, tuber and green kathia and kanou for eating, reaping of *podu,* cultivated paddy, and gulji, maize, suan, harvesting in irrigated lands.	7-12 & 13-18
Ashada to Sraban (June to August)	Collection of mushrooms and green leaf vegetables, mango kernel, jackfruit, watching the crops, sowing *saru* (corn).	7-12 & 13-18
Kartik to Pausa (October to January)	Harvesting, reaping, threshing, winnowing of *rasil, niger* (line seed), tobacco cutting and drying.	7-12 & 13-18
Phalgun, Chaitra Baisakha (February to May)	Harvesting crops like *niger*, mustard, reaping, carring crops from field to house, storing the seeds in straw packs, clearing forest for *podu* cultivation, cutting down trees, clearing shrubs and bushes, firing the cut tree and bushes after drying, spreading the ashes all over the cleared land, *Paridhi* (hunting), ploughing of *billa* (flat land).	13-18

It is found that children are involved in most of the day-to-day activities of the Juang community. The children through informal social group activities are taught their role in their own community. Such activities further help the children to learn the cultural practices of the community. Therefore, it has rightly been said that, a man's culture is what he has, the totality of his life and interests. This is especially true of the Juang people because they are still not much exposed to outside influences. Traditional yet, somewhere open in their attitude, the two mix-ups to give a unique distinction to this tribe. And growing up in a Juang village with its own social system, cultural patterns, customs, religious belief, marriage system all have their own uniqueness.

Juang children's contribution to the family economy often goes unnoticed. The household works are considered to be the domain of the women. The Juang boys are not concerned with this work. The girls from an early age start working at home. They do all the household work such as cleaning the house, washing the cloths, cleaning the utensils, bringing water, etc. Besides they also collect firewood from the forest. But their work goes unnoticed as it is mainly confined to domestic sphere.

The routine work of the Juang children, centre rounds the economic activities. It is very systematic and regular. Work in their society starts before sun rises and continues till late in the evening or early part of the night when they go to bed. In the daily round of labour the Juang extract work from all, young and old, male, female and children by assigning specific works. The women and grown-up children always lend a hand in all food getting activities. There is a division of labour along the sex line. The common practice is that the men attend to more arduous work whereas the women and the children do relatively lighter works. The men do the works requiring strength, whereas women do the works connected with preparation of food. Ploughing, sowing seeds by broadcasting, thatching, tree felling are exclusively the works of men whereas weeding, transplanting, reaping and threshing are done jointly by men and women. Both the sexes including the children and old men and women go to the forest for collection of minor forest produce. During slack season one may see the men spending time leisurely, while the women are always engaged in some work or the other. Grown up boys and girls assist their parents in the field and small boys and girls do lighter work like weeding in the field, looking after infants and collecting fruits. The girls help their mothers in domestic works like cleaning the houses, cooking, grinding, and pounding grains. The Juang support their economy by collecting minor forest produce. Animal rearing, cottage industries and wage earning are their other subsidiary occupations.

Majority of Juang non-school going children are wage labourers. They work in agricultural fields and various construction sites. Some of them also work in hotels of Keonjhar. The school going boys do not work during the school hours and school days but in the long vacations, they earn money by taking up some temporary jobs. Both girls and boys in the age group of 12-18 years go for wage earning. They also help their parents in agricultural field. Children in the age group of 5-11 years mainly collect minor forest produces (MFP). The Juang follow the age and sex-wise distribution of labour. The heavier work such as cutting trees, ploughing, hunting, etc. fall on the shoulder of boys while lighter work such as domestic work, cooking, thrashing are done by the girls. Certain works such as clearing the forest, transplanting, harvesting, and collection of minor forest produces are done by both boys and girls. All these works are seasonal by nature. The construction works are undertaken mainly in summer and winter, but once the agricultural season starts they come back to the field. The pre-agricultural activities start with the selection of hill slopes for cultivation. The children help their parents in their field in felling trees and cleaning bushes, piling of felled trees and firing, ploughing and sowing, transplantation and weeding and finally harvesting. In all these activities children have some contribution to make. Hence, in a Juang family the children start sharing the economic burden of their parents from an early age.

Children, like adults, gain their self-esteem through positive and active engagement with the world. A sense of respect and responsibility for self and others is a value that is lived from the early moments of life and experienced constantly in interaction with the world. Where we see instances of authentic child participation in the family, school, community and society, we hear children and young people tell us that they are more confident in themselves, more aware of the community and its problems, more committed to serving and working with others and more optimistic about the future and their role in it. Here a crucial distinction has to be made between child labour and child work. Child work should be used as the generic term, and should refer to any type of work in any mode of employment relationship. The concept of work, which is description of a physical (or mental) involvement in a job, may be an activity which, rather than being harmful, is beneficial to the child in its formative socialization. The concept of labour, on the other hand, should be restricted to the production and services, which interfere with the normal development of children as defined by the Convention on the Rights of the Child. There is a perception that quite a lot of what has been subsumed under child labour, is actually work performed during a standard process of socialization and not associated with labour exploitation or interfering with the quality of development which the child in the given circumstances could expect.

The School Experience

At school, the experiences of tribal children range from discrimination to a sense of alienation. Students from ST communities encounter a series of problems such as commuting long distance to school in hostile environmental conditions, discrimination by teachers and fellow students from non-tribal backgrounds, difficulty in comprehending the language of instruction. etc.

Children's denominational identities have always affected their school experiences. Ideally, the school teacher must play a vital role in supporting the struggles of first-generation learners. But it is found that although there is formal inclusion in the mainstream education system in the sense that children are officially enrolled, the teachers are often found to question the "educability" of tribal children, revealing that nothing much has changed in the perception held about the "other" by teachers who are generally drawn from mainstream social groups. Our interaction with Tunnu Juang, a student of class V in Gonasika High School was really interesting. When we asked him regarding his birthday he stated:

> "My teacher told me that November 14 is Chacha Nehru's birthday but I don't have any birthday. None of my friends have birthdays. Gopal says only rich people have birthdays."

Research shows that tribal children are often subjected to overt discrimination by non-tribal upper caste school teachers who view them as "slow learners" unable to learn despite several repetitions. Teachers also demean tribal children by calling their parents "drunken", with no interest in schools and education. Untouchability is also found to prevail in schools, where upper caste teachers and students refuse to drink water from the same tap used by the tribal children. Even play activities and school transactions are sometimes segregated on the basis of these identities. The tribal children are repeatedly subjected to verbal abuse at the hands of upper caste teachers and this has a critical impact on the way these first generation students view themselves as learners.

Since the tribal dialects are distinctly different from the medium of instruction in schools (which is Oriya, the State language of Orissa), tribal children often find it extremely difficult to cope with their studies and homework. This lack of language skills acts as a serious impediment when the teacher is a non-tribal and makes no effort to link the two linguistic experiences for the child. Aspirations among the tribal children are also low considering that there are not many formally educated persons in such communities. The inability to secure jobs amongst tribal who have completed formal education has led some to get disillusioned with the education system and question the futility of spending several years struggling to get educated. Some consider them "useless" in their traditional lives. It is important to note here that education among many tribal communities is imparted in a very effective manner through family and traditional organizations. In the absence of any formal educational system, most of the tribes in India have their own traditional institutions for learning, which cater to the needs of their culture. These institutions provide education in the realm of their tradition and culture.

Traditional Youth Organization and its Role in the Learning Process

Youth dormitories are among the oldest of institutions in tribal societies, with great influence on the character formation of their people. This is particularly true of the Hill Juang, whose Community House provides so much more than just convenient sleeping quarters for the boys who are growing up. It is indeed the centre of life for all unmarried males, be they boys of eight or nine (for whom it is taboo to go on sleeping in their parents' homes), marriageable youths, older bachelors, if any, or widowers. Contrary to much outside opinion, there is nothing permissive or promiscuous about the young people's sleeping arrangements. The young boys sleep around the sacred fire, under the presiding eye of their deity, on mats woven for them by young unmarried women. The latter, however, sleep in the homes of the widows, who are also part of the extended dormitory organization.

Throughout life the Juang distinguish between age and sex groups with certain understood privileges and responsibilities attached to each stage. Only small children, before the age of sexual awareness, are undifferentiated. When parents send their eight years old sons to sleep in the Community House, they become formal members of *kangerki;* they nevertheless remain subject to the authority of their own family heads. One of the most important stages comes, at puberty, when they are admitted to full membership of the youth organization. At this point young men must undergo an initiation ceremony in order to belong fully. This is an annual event that follows a celebration known as *Amba Nua Khai* (Eating the First Mango), a ritual in three parts. The first involves the whole village and the ritual elders; the second, the blessing of the drums in the Community House, performed by the ritual elders assisted by the senior young men; and third and final part is also for the same purpose, but involves only the senior young men. The second and the third parts reflect the two uses of the drums, the first by the ritual elders in the celebrations designed for the well-being and productivity of the village the second by the young men, whose inter village drumming visits usher in the period of bride selection. By a much less demanding right of admission the girls become *selanki,* the age set of unmarried young girls. They leave this age set only on marriage.

Interestingly, the boys and unmarried youth have a ritual status similar in many ways to enjoyed by ritual elders. For example, they may eat meat from the heads of sacred animals, something that is taboo for all other males except ritual elders. Also, after a death, an unmarried youth from the deceased person's mother's village performs certain rites in the purificatory ceremony, which is otherwise carried out by the ritual elders. The two groups are treated identically since neither is engaged in the procreation of children, one being too young and the other being too old, whereas all other males in the village are so engaged. Whenever a married man is divorced, the point is again made, for he returns to sleep in the Community House. This means that, from the Juang view point, an inactive sexual life increases one's ritual status whereas an active one increases one's secular status.

Though older bachelors, if any, and widowers are already involved in the system, the *kangerki* chooses one male sponsor to be their particular guardian, supervisor, and moral guide. Based on suggestions made by the council of family heads, the *kangerki* selects him from among the group of married men who have not yet become ritual elders, for; at that point, the sponsor must dissociate himself from the youth organization. His office is recognized by the whole village, and for him, too duties are laid down by traditions, which are responsibilities expected of the organizations

The life of a Juang is based on a nine-fold age-grade classification. According to this the male and female populations are divided into nine classes. The discrepancy between the biological and social age groups is bridged up within the framework of youth organization. The social norms do not favour an ordinary person to joke with anybody who stands in adjacent generation to him or her, but the *kangerki* and *selanki* of own, alternate, and adjacent generations are allowed to joke with each other within their own group. This is because, in a broad sense, all the *kangerki* are considered as brothers and all the *selanki* as sisters to each other.

After marriage, a *kanger* automatically steps into the status of a *kamathara kanger* but he continues to work and co-operate with the *kangerki* till he can afford to get himself detached from the association of the *kangerki* through a special observance. Right after the marriage the groom does not sleep with his wife. A new house is built for him and on the consummation day of the marriage he has to take farewell from the *kangerki* by giving them cakes, tobacco, and a mat.

After this formal observance the boy is permitted to sleep with his wife, but he still continues to be a regular member of the boy's dormitory and fulfils most of the obligations of his association group. When he wants to resign from the group of the *kangerki* he gives some rice and a chicken to the *kangerki* on the *Amba Nua* ritual day. It is after this only that he ceases to be a working member of the youth's group.

Similar is the procedure for a girl to get herself detached from the membership of the youth organization. After her marriage and before she sleeps with her husband, she visits the *kangerki* and *selanki* of her village to take farewell from them and offers them cakes, tobacco and a new mat. Every age group is entrusted with special roles and responsibilities under the purview of the dormitory and youth organization. The boys and girls of the *Majang* choose a sponsor of their own, known as *tandakar* who acts as their guardian and moral adviser. Failing to do the duty, as prescribed by the norms of the society, is considered as a deviation for which the village elders punish the offenders.

The punishments are of the following four kinds:

- Expulsion from the *Majang*.
- Physical punishment like standing on one leg holding the ears, putting the second finger in excreta, etc. in minor offences, and beating in case of adultery and incest.
- Fines of money, liquor, goat and rice.
- Verbal scolding and caution not to repeat the work again.

Both the girls and the boys are punished for failing to discharge their duties properly. The boys are generally punished for not bringing firewood to the *Majang* and for not obeying the village elders similarly the girls are found fault with if they do not plaster the *Majang* and sweep the plaza regularly. If first attracts the attention of the village elders when the boys or girls are found guilty in neglecting their duties, they first accuse the *tandakar* for not supervising the work of the *kangerki* and *selanki*. Sometimes, the *tandakar* is fined one or two rupees for the fault of the boys or the girls after which the blame falls on the actual offenders. One of the main features of the Juang youth organization is collective responsibility of its members. For negligence of one duty or for the failure to carryout any assigned task in case of one member of the dormitory, all the members of the organization are liable to be punished. They are fined, the fine being rice (generally one to two *khandi*), a goat or a pig, and about two to five rupees for liquor for the village elders. They collect these things from their own houses or borrow from some body on an arrangement to pay it off by working on the creditor's field. The fines are used for holding a feast in the village.

Learning through Rhythm and Movement

Children learn in a variety of ways. What is crucial is that the experiences are meaningful to the reality. Children's natural flair for experimenting with body and sound goes beyond the traditional rigor of the classical forms. They incorporate meaningful digressions and suggest "swaying like a tree" or "running like a deer" or "imitating mother when she is angry". Music and dance are effective tools to capture a child's attention. *Changu* drums hold supreme place among the Juang musical instruments due to three factors; the sacred value set upon this type of drum, the importance of rhythm in the Juang music, and the close-knit relationship in the village community calling for the rhythmic drum messages being easily heard and understood by all. The *changu* drums are large, shallow tambourines, two feet or more in diameter, with a single memberance of stretched deer hide, or more often goatskin. The outer hairs are carefully scraped from the hide, which is then stretched over the circular wooden frame and attached all around the sharply pointed hard wood nails. The Juang also use a *kettledrum* and a thin, barrel-shapped double memberance drum, and both of these are of cowhide and resemble those commonly found in Orissa. The *changu*, which is hung from the left shoulder of the drummer and covers the upper half of the body, is beaten with the fingers and palm of the hand. Usually two or three drummers move together, stepping, turning, stooping and straightening in the closest possible harmony. When not in use, the *changu* drums hang from horn or wooden pegs on the walls of the Community House, for they are sacred to the deities residing there and may be played only by the men and the *kangerki*. Their most common uses are two: first is for religious rites and festivals, and second is for the occasion of visits by the young women of *bandhu* village. Always before being played and at intervals throughout a performance, the instruments are warmed at the Community House fire to tighten the skin and so produce the full sound.

Depending upon the tradition surrounding specific occasions, *changu* drums may be played singly or in twos and threes (mostly by youth). They may be played as single instruments, or else accompanied by other percussion or wind instruments. Toy miniatures are made for small boys to beat, both for enjoyment and for naturally talented children to start learning drumming skills. Adult drummers drumming together sometimes display amazing rhythmic complexity. There is always a leader in the team who starts the rhythm, who is followed by one or more secondary drummers who beat a contrasting rhythm. The most commonly used beats are duple (two-time) played by the leader, interchanged with triple (three-time) by the secondary drummers. At specific points, especially during ritual occasions, extremely complicated cross-rhythms and off-beat phrasing are produced to heighten rhythmic tension and to call the attention of all the people and the deities to some particular activity about to take place, e.g. the moment of blood sacrifice. Dances performed by the unmarried young girls are closely connected with their *bandhu* young boy's *changu* drumming. These would never be solo performances, either by a drummer or a dancer; rather they would always be done by small groups, the young girls dancing in a short curved row with their arms closely inter-twined so that they move together as a single body. Their simultaneous foot movements deftly follow the rhythmic patterns of the drums or even produce a stamped cross beat to the pattern. No particular dress is worn, though necklace and other small adornments are donned for visits to other villages, and they always tighten their sarees around the body for neatness of action. Junior girls do not join the older-dancers' row, instead they form their own little age-set, rapidly learning the movements by observation and participation. They do not, of course, go on dance visits to other villages until they become of marriageable age.

The body movements in Juang dances are not limited to linking of arms and deft footwork. The drummers may gradually stoop forward until bent double. The row of girls does not likewise in repeated sequences, bending their knees at the same time though without slow in the pace. Both lines of participants advance and recede or stoop and straighten while still dancing. Although the basic movements are highly repetitive, they are performed with keen concentration and united motivation and always with obvious enjoyment. Similar community involvement, though of a more serious nature, is in evidence when the music forms part of some ritual or ceremonial occasion at a recognized ritual site. On all occasions of drumming, especially when accompanied by dance, the performers display total absorption in their activity, time being of no consequence. The performance may thus go on for several hours without the drummers loosing interest or vitality.

The Juang also possess skills in a variety of arts and crafts, particularly in woodcarving and painted decoration. These are best seen in the elaborately, carved pillars which support the roof on the open front of the Community House. The cross beam of a Community House often shows more varied decoration, with stylized forms of flowers, humans, animals, insects and birds, all of a fairly rudimentary nature. These artistic traditions are not usually found in ordinary houses. The custom of tattooing a traditional pattern on the skin of the forehead, the cheeks and chin by means of countless needle-pricks rubbed with a mixture of soot and castor oil, is becoming rare as the concept of beauty changes. This indeed, can hardly be considered a useful art form, whereas carving skills open the way also to economic improvement.

Some dances are preceded or accompanied by songs in which the young men and the young women may sing the alternate stanzas. In the manner so often found among the hill people of Orissa, the Juang songs usually begin with an introduction sung simply to the words: *Na-ray, na-ray, nar-ray....* In due course this moves into a song, which may be in a story form or may be in the form of a dialogue between the young boys and young girls, or it can be the recounting of some epic. Singing while dancing or drumming appears exhausting, yet they continue for considerable periods before taking a brief break. On the occasions, when sung by the relevant age or sex groups, songs may also accompany agricultural work (usually solo and chorus) or other tasks, and in all the tribal societies there are, of course, traditional lullabies sung by a mother to her child.

Thus the resources which the Juang music provides in terms of expertise, enjoyment and group participation and direct communication of messages are already very great, and their potential for use in community development is immense. It should be remembered, however, that any form of Juang music is related to an activity, which may be of a social, ritual or economic nature and may precede, accompany or follow an activity. In terms of its use the medium should be viewed in the wholeness of context, with social attention paid to the underlying values traditionally derived from its use.

The Changing Scenario and Coping Mechanisms

The anthropological study on education has challenged the traditional ideas regarding education, opened new avenues in the realm of psychological investigation, resulting in the refinement of cross-cultural studies to understand the educational pattern and motivation of any primitive society. Margaret Mead (1928) was the pioneer in this field, whose work attracted a number of psychologists and anthropologists towards the subject. The researcher's emphasis lies on the fact that the child born with a clean state of mind and is molded by its culture to fit into its society. Games played by Juang children has got tremendous educational value, which creates new aptitudes in them and the imitation and pretence practiced by children cultivate power significance and the learning of things they have to do in their practical life (Acharya and Mohanty, 1993). The various games played by the children of the Juang society cannot be considered as mere play of games; but it is a source of learning apart from being a source of pleasure. By playing the games with the playmates they build themselves for their future life. They form some ideas about their social life, such as rituals and the work they have to perform in their matured life. Manipulating, experimenting, trying out, exploring, discovering new things and communicating, the child develops by employing all these strategies. The eagerness to learn is inherent in the child. The Juang believe that providing a suitable environment, assisting, appreciating, supporting and being part of the excitement is what is parenting all about.

In the course of the interaction with the various caste people and their increasing association with the outside world, the Juang have witnessed some changes in their traditional culture. The material aspects of the Juang culture have undergone a great change. The dress and ornaments of the Juang have changed considerably. Bamboo combs which were prized possessions of the Juang girls, and which the unmarried boys made with great care and present those to their sweethearts are fast disappearing and giving away to plastic comb of the market. The traditional ornaments which consisted of a whole bunch of bead necklaces, a number of heavy brass bangles and alloy rings are no more liked by the younger generation. The changes that are taking place among the Juang as a result of acculturation are mostly confined to their material culture. The non-tribal inhabitants living in the Juang villages and the visiting government officials serve as models to the Juang for change in their dresses. According to Nayak *et al.* (1993) the traditional dress of the men and women is slowly being replaced by the dress pattern of the non-tribal. Previously men used to wear loincloths and the women leaf dresses. However, the external forces have least affected the religious life of the Juang. The Juang continue to observe all the rituals and rites in order to avoid the displeasure of the local deities. The varieties of dances as mentioned by Dalton (1972) and Elwin (1948) are no more noticed these days.

The school education is seen as an imposition. The Juang cultural patterns and social values do not have any place in the school education. There is lack of confidence in and mistrust towards the teacher: they are seen as foreigners, intruders, and exploiters like the malaria worker, forest guard, police constable or revenue inspector. There is a growing feeling of insecurity resulting from contradictory values taught in the schools. There is no immediate and concrete benefit from education and the Juang are ignorant about educational opportunities, facilities, or prospects. The school environments are dull, non-stimulating, and boring. Most of the teachers do not know the Juang language and never bother to learn it. They are neither interested nor trained to teach tribal children. Teacher absenteeism is as big a problem as student absenteeism in the schools located in our sample area. In mixed classrooms, the teachers pay greater attention and have greater expectations for non-tribal children. There is insufficient number of teachers in the sample schools. Teachers maintain a very formal and distant relationship with the tribal children. On the whole, the schools and teachers are failing to attract the Juang children to schools and facilitate their educational progress. The present system of primary and secondary education has no relevance to the day-to-day problems experimented by Juang. The Juang dialect is not used at any stage for the education of Juang children. The textbooks do not incorporate the Juang culture, custom and tradition in their content and style. There is no equality of educational opportunity and no accountability. The coordination and supervision of schools of the sample area is far from satisfaction. The socio-cultural, psychological, and educational problems of the tribal children are too many and too serious. Urgent ameliorative measures are necessary to tackle the situation. Our suggestions, however, are based on simpler assumptions, utilization of local resources and talents through the mechanism of available social and cultural norms with the least friction with traditional forces and under the internal rhythm of speed and momentum.

The institutions of society are obliged to defend and support the weak and the vulnerable. Clear expression of the obligation of the state and the responsibility of the society is what has lately come to be called in legal terms the 'rights of the child'. During our fieldwork in the Juang community and interacting with the Juang children, we basically understood it as a moral and practical issue. We could build a legal obligation, but the primary character of the human rights is moral. We would suggest that at the root of the concept of human rights is not so much any political ideology as the primordial sorrow at what man does to man knowingly or unknowingly. And this impulse is a good enough start for respecting, protecting and fulfilling the rights of the child in general and Juang children in particular. Rights are not luxuries. Although rights cannot be realized if needs are not met, simply meeting needs is not enough. The problems faced by vulnerable children might have immediate, underlying and structural causes and common roots. These could be discrimination in various forms, including gender bias, unsafe environments or chronic poverty. The root causes of preventable death and illness, for example, are often a violation of civil and political rights. A poor child dies not simply from a disease but by a poorly functioning health system. A number of underlying reasons, including his or her mother's access to education, health care, credit, jobs, participation in public life and ultimately power over food and other resources are root causes of preventable death. Rights, therefore, cannot be separated from needs. Human rights including child rights are an indivisible cluster. A rights-based approach is therefore an integral human-centered process. There is documented experience to show that this is feasible only in a community context. Children should certainly be allowed to remain children and receive protection necessary to safeguard their health and development. Children should not be forced to take up responsibilities for which they are not ready. But, children's healthy development also depends upon being allowed to engage with making more independent decisions and assuming more responsibility as they become more capable. Where children's views are sensitively solicited and sincerely understood, they often change a great deal. They may reveal things that adults would never have grasped independently. The consultation of every very young child can produce remarkable results.

Growing up in a Juang village is an experience in itself, the children love their natural surrounding and growing up in a natural environment makes them capable of playing the future role of an adult. Traditional yet, somewhere open in their attitude, the two mix-ups to give a unique distinction to this tribe. The children growing up in a Juang village with its own social system, cultural patterns, customs, religious belief, marriage system all have their own uniqueness. Traditional education and youth dormitory in Juang community has a vital role to play in the personality development of a child. Through centuries of wisdom Juang have built up a recognized reward and privileges alongside of obligations and this reward motivate them to perform their duties. Communal and group endeavour is a special feature in the tribal societies and it is in full swing in the dormitory life of the Juang. It is interesting to observe how such group activities are organized and how these are translated into action. Co-operation of the group members and their common interests find full expression in two situations, i.e. dancing visits exchanged between *bandhu* boys and girls, and their common economic pursuits like cultivating common patches of forest land, working as hired labour for wages, collecting oil-seeds from the jungle, etc.

The Juang culture clearly captures their attitude to knowledge and education. Knowledge like the land and the air and water is common property—everyone must share it. The main threat to the Juang culture and religious belief comes from the fact that it does not exclude others. The very nature of the philosophy has left them wide open to exploitation, both material and spiritual. The most difficult threat to deal with however, comes from the onslaught of modern consumerist culture, cinema, popular music, fashion, television, all of which combine to tell the young Juang that in order to be smart and fashionable they should modernize their dress, language, manners and customs. Indeed, this is an onslaught that all of traditional culture is facing. And the change in society is visible. However, romanticizing Juang culture makes little sense, somewhere we need to have a blend. The Juang adolescents are in search of a new identity, they are in a flux, where they are not able to adopt modern culture completely at the same time they are not able to give up some of their own customs and rituals. The first Juang graduate Srikant Juang says, "though I was offered several jobs but I was not interested. Why should I listen to such humiliating statements like 'quota', 'reserved category'? They will not recognize my talent. If I stay back in the village at least I will have my self respect and do something for my community."

Srikant and many such adolescents know it very well that they will get rejected if they reject their system. In spite of their educational status they don't want to loose their identity and become alien in their own setting rather they prefer to participate actively in the affairs of their community.

REFERENCES

Acharya, M. and R. P. Mohanty. 1993. "Games vis-à-vis Socialisation. A Case Study among Kondh Children," *Adibasi*, XXXIII.

Blackwood, E. 1995. "Falling in Love with another Lesbian: Reflections on Identity in Fieldwork," in D. Kulick and M. Willson (eds.), *Taboo: Sex, Identity and Erotic Subjectivity in Anthropological Fieldwork.* London: Routledge.

Caplan, P. 1993. "Introduction to the Volume," in D. Bell, P. Caplan and W.J. Karim (eds.), *Gender Fields: Women, Men and Ethnography.* London: Routledge.

Coffey, A. 1998. *The Ethnographic Self: Fieldwork and the Representation of Identity.* London: Sage.

Dalton, E.B. 1972. *Descriptive Ethnography of Bengal.* Calcutta.

Elwin, Verrier 1948. "An Indian Riddle Book: Orissa, Juang," *Man in India,* XXII (1&2): 64.

Lofland, J. and L.H. Lofland. 1995. *Analyzing Social Settings: A Guide to Qualitative Observation and Analysis.* CA: Wadsworth.

Malinowski, B. 1922. *Aronauts of the Western Pacific.* London: Routledge and Kegan Paul.

Mead, Margaret 1928. *Coming of Age in Samoa.* New York: Blue Ribbon.

Nayak, R., B.M. Boal and N. Soreng. 1993. *The Juang Handbook for Development.* New Delhi: Indian Social Institute.

Rout, S.P. 1969-70. *Handbook on the Juang.* Bhubaneswar: Tribal Research Bureau.

Solberg, A. 1989. "Negotiating Childhood: Changing Constructions of Age for Norwegian Children," (pp.126-144) in Allison James and Alan Prout (eds.), *Constructing and Reconstructing Childhood.* London: Falmer Press.

SECTION II

STATE INRERVENTION

NINE

THE FATE OF THE JARAWA: Some Lessons across Space and Time

SITA VENKATESWAR

Me titiro whakamuri tatou
Kia mohio ai
Me pehea haere ki mua.

We should look backwards
So we can determine
How to go forwards
(Maori adage)

The adage neatly summarizes the process that was underway in India and the events which marked that important year of 2004. It was a period when we proceeded with the hindsight of past errors, not just our own, nor those confined to the boundaries of our nation; but with the clearer vision informed by the histories of tribal peoples across the world, as well as the greater knowledge and resources we had available to us in the 21st century. We were presented with a unique opportunity to undo some of the errors of the past and create a legacy for the future for the Jarawa, setting up a model that we as a nation could feel proud of, and which the rest of the world looked to emulate.

Before I get into the substance of this paper I think it is necessary to situate it, and mark its point of departure from the earlier narrative of my research in the islands, as constituted by my thesis and the numerous papers that have derived from it. At a point in my life when my research in the Andaman Islands was being archived into my past, and my ethnography the closing chapter of it, I was *catapulted* back into active engagement with the Islands and its peoples yet again, as a result of a series of unforeseen events.

But the re-engagement is in a very different mode from my earlier one, which expresses itself in a distinctly different voice, showing no trace of the anguish or the despair that was contained in the earlier rendering of my experiences in the Islands. This one has been written within a far more enabling space that nurtures within it, the seeds of hope as well as a degree of optimism regarding the existing institutions of civil society. Notwithstanding the life changes and the confidence wrought by a decade within academia since I completed my Ph.D fieldwork, the domain of hope is also where I have located my current intellectual undertaking.

The narrative that I present here traces a linear chronology, following the trajectory of an accelerated process unimaginable during my research in the Islands. The tale is a familiar one, following the well-trodden path of disease, dispossession and death common to aboriginal peoples everywhere in the world. But the tale I tell holds the potential for an alternative scenario, creating the possibility of a different ending to this particular story. Therein lies the seeds of hope in this context, in the possibility of envisioning an alternative future for the Jarawa of the Andaman Islands.

In April 1996, I revelled in having successfully defended my Ph.D thesis, and went on to celebrate the continued hostility projected by the *Jarawa*. At that gathering of faculty and students my description of the Jarawa reads as follows and unwittingly presages some of the later developments:

> "What of the fierce Jarawa who eluded the grasp of the British colonialists, keeping them at bay with their bows and arrows? They wield the same weapons still, stronger now, reinforced with iron arrowheads to defend their territorial boundaries as it is continuously remapped by the Indian colonists. And yet, who are lured to remarkably staged encounters by the promise of coconut, bananas, rice, cloth, plastic buckets, beads, pieces of iron. Will the seduction of "goods" finally erode the mystique of the Jarawa, resolutely drawing them into the circuit of commodity fetishism?" (Venkateswar, 2004).

But even as I concluded on that lingering image of the Jarawa, during that same week, a small act of kindness faraway in the forests of the Andaman Islands, was to go on to have profound long-term consequences. In April 1961,[1] an adolescent *Jarawa* boy named En Mei was found immobilized and nursing a fractured leg, along the edges of the forest close to the village of Kadamtala in Middle Andaman. He was taken by the local authorities to the G. B. Pant Hospital, the main hospital at Port Blair and treated there for his injury. The reasons attributed to the cause of his fracture have been varied,[2] from being hit by a truck on the Andaman Trunk Road (Mynott, 2004), or his foot getting caught in an animal trap (Anthropological Survey of India, n.d.), to a fall from a tree (Mukhopadhyay, 2004).

Six months later in October 1996, En Mei was dropped off near the forest where he had been found, laden with gifts and stories of his time spent at Port Blair. Exactly a year after En Mei returned to the forest, an unprecedented event occurred: a group of Jarawa including En Mei in their midst, appeared at a jetty in Middle Andaman during the day, shedding their "hostile" demeanour, and presenting a "friendly" mien instead.

En Mei's injury and the subsequent entry of the Jarawa in the settler villages has become the starting point of a new origin story currently in circulation in the Andaman Islands: the story of the sequence of events that led to the Jarawa's transformation from a "hostile" people existing in a "state of war" with the neighbouring settler population to a "friendly" one, with the Jarawa indicating their willingness to enter into a compact of "peace" with them.

Similar incidents continued to occur in the ensuing months, during which gestures used by the Jarawa, pointing towards their bellies, were understood as expressions of hunger and therefore a request for food. Sekhsaria (2003) reports on the decision to airdrop packets of food into the Jarawa forest. This was in response to the growing belief by the Andaman administration that the emergence of the Jarawa from the forest was a consequence of increasing hunger resulting from food and resource shortages. He goes on to describe an occasion witnessed by him in April 1998 when a large group of Jarawa, including women and children, arrived at the same jetty in Middle Andaman. The inability of the local settler community or the administration to respond with sensitivity to such a situation is noted by Sekhsaria.

The interpretation of food shortages has been countered by anthropologists at ASI who tend to highlight the role played by En Mei in bringing about the transformation of the Jarawa from "hostile" to "friendly." But speculation is rife as to what actually transpired between the Jarawa, or the discussions that may have ensued amongst them during the lapse of a year since En Mei was released into the forest. In a recent discussion, Mukhopadhyay of the Anthropological Survey (2004) is more sceptical. According to him, and purportedly based on conversations that he had with En Mei, the very first instance of the Jarawa emerging from their forest cover during the day came about when En Mei was promised food by some of the settlers if he brought other Jarawa to the jetty in Middle Andaman. En Mei agreed, went on to comply and the rest is history.

Meanwhile, in a bizarre turn of events leading from the perception that the Jarawa were suffering from starvation, a local lawyer in the Islands named Shyamali Ganguli, filed a legal suit against the Andaman administration. She claimed that under the Indian Constitution the Jarawa had the same right to receive and enjoy "the fruits of civilization," as any other "Indian," but instead had been denied the benefits of civilization by the administration in the Islands. She then went on to demand that the Jarawa be immediately provided with all the modern amenities and rehabilitated like the Andamanese and the Onge. As one commentator notes, this was a "classic example of a move undertaken with the right intentions but seeking the wrong solutions".

In response to the writ petition, an awareness and petition campaign coordinated locally by Samir Acharya of the Society for Andaman and Nicobar Ecology, better known as SANE, and internationally by Survival International,[3] resulted in a flood of outraged and condemnatory letters to the administration from noted anthropologists across the world, drawing attention to the dangers of rendering the Jarawa sedentary.

A grimmer and more foreboding set of outcomes were to eventuate from the increased interactions of the Jarawa with the local populations. The warnings that had been issued over the years by the Whitakers' and others, which had been consistently ignored by the Andaman administration finally manifested from July-August of 1999, when a series of illnesses became visible among the Jarawa. The intensified "contact" with the Jarawa, the continuing extension of the Andaman Trunk Road right through the heart of Jarawa territory with its associated clearing of forests, finally took its toll in outbreaks of epidemics of measles and pneumonia, tuberculosis and conjunctivitis among the Jarawa (Ali, 1999; Bedi, 1999; Sekhsaria, 1999). Madhusree Mukerjee (2003) a former journalist with the Scientific American, who had been conducting research in the Islands over the past seven years, notes the bus loads of tourists brought by tour operators up the Andaman Trunk Road to visit the Jarawa. She also reports on the increasing incidence of coughs and colds among the Jarawa prior to the epidemics, noted in passing by anyone who encountered them.

The public outcry that followed threw the spotlight on Indian government policies in the Islands, and spurred the efforts of the medical establishment in the Islands to control the spread of the diseases among Jarawa populations in the forests. The numbers who remained in the forests and succumbed to the epidemics and other related illnesses remain unknown.

Court Cases and Committees

The High Court interim order on the case filed by Shyamali Ganguly, the local lawyer, prohibited all entry into Jarawa areas and further directed that the Jarawa be protected from any encroachments into their reserve, calling for severe penalties to civil servants who failed in their duties. The court directive also required further research to be conducted into why the Jarawa were emerging from their forest areas and to ascertain whether they were subject to food shortages. Expert committees were constituted to provide more information to the courts, the second of which was entrusted with the responsibility to research and formulate a plan of action to deal with the Jarawa. Sekhsaria's (2003) recent book, comprising of a compilation of his observations on the Islands over the years, details the directives of the High Court and the prevailing mood of optimism that ensued among environmental and indigenous rights activists.

It is instructive at this stage to pay closer attention to the process by which the committees who were responsible for providing more information to the Court were constituted, the chronology of events that led to committees being formed and dissolved, and more significantly, the personnel appointed to serve on the committees.

In May 1999, the High Court appointed Special Officers from within the Andaman administration to submit a report on the problems relevant to the Jarawa, and to suggest some means for their welfare cum rehabilitation. In a surprisingly speedy response, given the slow and protracted process of usual governmental functioning within the Islands, the officers submitted a report within a month. The report was deemed unsatisfactory and was unacceptable to the Court. In February 2000, the entire matter was handed over to an Expert Committee, one which was constituted by the Court itself. Moving its range slightly further than it had in the previous instance, the High Court appointed 6 members, all of whom were functionaries of the Government of India, namely the Anthropological Survey of India (ASI) and the Health Services in the Islands, with the Chief Judicial Magistrate of the Session Court of Port Blair to serve as Member Secretary to the committee. On submission of their report six months later, the Court identified a number of key issues that are detailed below:

(a) Whether the Jarawa should be isolated from the rest of humanity and left to themselves to lead their own way of life as they did a few years back, or

(b) Whether the Jarawa should be brought into the mainstream of "civilization," or

(c) Whether to ensure their peaceful co-existence as suggested in the Master Plan[4] for the Welfare of the Primitive Tribes of the A&N Islands prepared by Mr. Awaradi, Director of Tribal Welfare." (Expert Committees Report, Government of India)

These issues were to be settled as a matter of policy by the Government of India after consultation with national and international experts on the subject. In the 60 page judgement that was delivered in April 2001, the Court ordered that the Ministry of Tribal Affairs, Government of India, should constitute [yet another!] Committee of Experts to spell out in clear terms:

(a) Reasons for the sudden change in behaviour of the *Jarawa*, i.e. shedding their hostility, coming out of their forest abode in broad daylight and accepting exogenous items from non-Jarawa, and,

(b) To suggest remedial measures for the welfare of the *Jarawa* (*ibid.*).

Pankaj Sekhsaria (2003) also notes that the report submitted by ASI based on the studies that they had conducted, indicated that there was no shortage of food for the Jarawa in the forests, but highlighted their vulnerability to various infections, and the scale of illegal poaching that occurred within the forest and surrounding coast.

Responding to the Court Order, the Ministry of Home Affairs, Government of India, constituted for the third time a "Committee of Experts." The composition of this particular eight member committee was significant and went on to play a crucial role in the events to come. Yet again, the personnel chosen were various functionaries of the government, some were repeated from the earlier committee, but a few surprises were in store in the final report which was the outcome of their research and deliberations.

While these developments are significant, and are an indication of the efficient functioning of the Indian judiciary, of concern is the terms of reference of the directives. There is no suggestion that the Jarawa are offered any agency in the decisions being made about them, nor is their autonomy ever really under consideration. All of the choices listed in terms of future policy require active intervention on the part of the administration, and welfare measures are always on the cards. They also underscore the contradictions inherent in a process whereby the radical potential of the Indian judiciary is countered by other arms of the government executive, determined to maintain an undisturbed *status quo*. Moreover, the reality on the ground is foreboding and tells a somewhat different story. In an email communication after a visit to the islands in 2002, Mukherjee notes:

> "I learned that a massive team of anthropologists, zoologists, botanists, nutritionists, medical researchers, foresters, social workers and their assorted helpers, a total of sixty to ninety heads, was camped on Jarawa territory. 'Its a picnic,' reported one policemen. Cooks provided meals at three campsites, while other assistants fetched water, washed up and ran errands. (The Jarawa, if no one else were surely learning about social structures). Trash disposal was into the forest or the sea, and although toilet tents had been set up, most of the men preferred the beach, trusting the tide to cleanse it of their droppings."

Mukherjee (2003) goes on to observe, "[t] he judges could scarcely have expected their thoughtful verdict to be put in place on such a thoughtless scale" (pg 212).

At the end of her visit Mukherjee despairingly notes:

> "I was told the Jarawa were getting just about every substance. Some of the women would vanish into the jungle with truckers who stopped on the road, for rewards unknown (and taking a generic route for the spread of AIDS), while young Jarawa men routinely begged for *sukka,* the popular form of chewing tobacco....I heard the aboriginals were getting alcohol and tobacco in exchange for their takings [from the forest], which were discreetly sold back to the public" (pg.218).

In a parallel set of developments, Samir Acharya of SANE together with Kalpavriksh, an environmental action group and the Mumbai-based Bombay Natural History Society (BNHS), had filed another public interest case to stop the illegal harvesting of trees in the Onge reserve areas, documenting the deteriorating state of the environment throughout the entire Islands. The wide-ranging Supreme Court verdict,[5] communicated to me in a celebratory email message from Sophie Grig of Survival International, delivered a blow to commercial forestry business interests in the Andaman Islands, and according to Mukerjee (2002), made Acharya the most hated man in the Islands. Prior to making the ruling, the Supreme Court appointed an environmental expert, Shekhar Singh, "to look into the state of the Islands' forests and other related matters." At the end of the six weeks allotted to him to submit his report, Singh made extensive recommendations, which included many of Survival's key campaign objectives, namely, "removing the settlers from all the tribal reserves and forests, stopping all logging on the islands and the closing of the Andaman Trunk Road which had been built illegally through the Jarawa's reserve" (Grig, 2002).

In an unforeseen move, the Supreme Court endorsed all of Shekhar Singh's recommendations. Sophie Grig conceded that while much had been achieved with the Supreme Court ruling, there were still major obstacles to overcome in terms of the actual implementation of the order, which Survival International would continue to monitor.

On a more sober note are Sekhsaria's (2003) re-considerations in his epilogue, as the time frame given for the implementation of two of the key directives of the Supreme Court of India goes by without any hint of future implementation by the Andaman administration. Appraising the ongoing situation in the islands, Sekhsaria highlights what is at stake for the Jarawa and the future health of the island system in the Andaman administration's non-compliance with the orders. The closure of the Andaman Trunk Road (ATR) in the sections where it transgresses through the Jarawa reserve, the declaration of the Islands as an Inner Line Area with the issue of Islander Identity Cards, are central to protecting the indigenous groups and the fragile island environment, already strained well beyond its capacity.

Of Origins and Genetics

To add to the already complicated state of matters in the Andaman Islands, at the end of 2002 and early in 2003, a number of papers were published almost simultaneously in the journals *Current Biology* and the *American Journal of Human Genetics*. The articles published brought together various lines of evidence suggesting that the Andaman Islanders were the descendants of the earliest populations of modern humans who migrated out of Africa into Asia approximately sixty thousand years ago, remaining genetically isolated for tens of thousands of years through the catacylsms of the Ice Age and its aftermath.

Leaving aside the heated debates that these publications have generated among scholars around the world, we are yet to discern the impact of this information on the existing state of affairs in the Islands and on "the last of the planet's first humans" (Mukherjee, 2003:241). It may provide the final springboard to accelerate the implementation of the Supreme Court order, or in a replay of the scenario described earlier by Mukherjee, bring in its wake scholars of various ilks clamouring for a piece of the action.

Collaborative Anthropology: Policy Initiatives and New Partnerships

I did return to the Andaman Islands in May 2004, a decade after I finished my fieldwork in the Islands.

The narrative of how that came about is located in a different site, in the networks of communication that exist in cyberspace, where scholars, journalists, activists and concerned individuals have shared information and kept abreast of events in the Islands. Initiated and moderated by Pankaj Sekhsaria, this cyber forum was to play a crucial role in shaping events over the course of 2004.

To pick up the threads of the narrative from the preceding section, the Committee of Experts constituted by the Ministry of Home Affairs submitted their report in July 2003. The contents of the report were posted by Sekhsaria in a website[6] that included other reports, along with his own articles on the Islands over the years. This ensured public and widespread access to a document which was deeply provocative in part, and presented a challenge to the Ministry in its efforts to maintain unchanged its administrative operations in the Islands. Sekhsaria's actions countered government efforts to suppress the document, as well as to maintain tight control over and hence, restrict the participants involved in the next stage of the High Court directives, namely a seminar convened to formulate policy on the Jarawa. According to the Court's directives, the seminar(s) were to be convened after widespread public notification and were to include a large cross-section of participants.

In a typical display of bureaucratic bravado, the Ministry dragged its feet about publically announcing the dates for the seminar which was to be convened in the city of Kolkata, cancelling the first proposed dates, and leaving sufficient uncertainty about the next ones in an attempt to stall and discourage potential travellers to the venue.

It is at this point that I was inserted into the narrative by an email from Madhusree Mukherjee, alerting me to the significance of the proposed seminar. As an active participant in Sekhsaria's discussion group, Mukherjee had been following the events in the Islands since she completed her research there, and kept me periodically informed about the most important developments. Initially dismissive of any significant outcomes from such a gathering,[7] I quickly changed my mind as I followed the discussions and comprehended the implications of government efforts to muzzle opposing voices by restricting those invited or permitted to speak at the forum. Exploring the possibility of obtaining funding for the travel from the university where I was located in New Zealand, I finalized my plans to attend the seminar and make myself heard at the proceedings.

A core sub-group developed within Sekhsaria's web-based discussion group, of those who had taken the time to read the expert committee reports and who were determined, at whatever cost, to storm the seminar if necessary, and strategize to ensure that their views would be made known at the proceedings. Coordination with representatives from Survival International meant that they too were apprised of the implications of the forum and could respond accordingly.

It is useful at this stage to pause and examine more closely that part of the report submitted by the Committee of Experts which posed a problem, and the reasons for the consternation it generated within the Ministry and the government bodies whose operations it regulated. The member of the committee who created the stir was Mr. K.D. Saxena, former Secretary in the Ministry of Social Justice and Empowerment. As a retired, but respected civil servant with a reputation for his personal integrity, his inclusion within the 8 member committee did not merit any comment. However, the dissenting note that he submitted revealed the lack of consensus within the committee, and more disturbing, the dynamics of power among its members that impacted on its democratic operation. His note with a separate draft policy attached to it, went on to critique the basis for some of the conclusions arrived at by the Health team and proposed a radical overhauling of the tribal welfare organization (AAJVS). He strongly endorsed the closure of that stretch of the ATR where it traversed directly through the Jarawa reserve, and proposed a constitutional amendment to guarantee for perpetuity the rights of the Jarawa to their forest base. His dissenting stance enabled another member of the committee from ASI to finally put in writing his opposition to the ATR and recommend its closure too.

Far-reaching in its sweep and intent, Saxena's note provided the peg to rally together all the opposing voices and give them a blueprint for an alternate and humane policy. The fact that such a policy had emerged from within a committee constituted by the Ministry, posed a problem of sufficient magnitude for the government to attempt to suppress the document and limit its dissemination.

The sub-group of 5 that emerged from Sekhsaria's discussion group of whom I was one, consisted of an interesting mix of academics, activists, journalists and NGO's, located in India and overseas. Brought together by our research and writing about the Islands and its peoples, we were energized by our awareness that here was an opportunity to finally make a difference to the lives of the islanders, one in particular, the Jarawa.

Our presence at the Kolkata seminar, despite attempts to block our entry, completely changed the tenor of the proceedings. We were the only ones present who had actually read the report or were familiar with its contents, and as a coordinated pressure group raised questions and insisted that we be permitted a space to speak to the proceedings. Hence, the challenge provided by Saxena's report could not be hidden from public view. At a gathering that received coverage by the national media, our presence changed the agenda of the conference and ensured that the forum had to take note of the dissenting reports and the alternate policy framework proposed therein. Furthermore, the press conference that we organized for the following day meant that the issues we raised continued to be covered by the media in the ensuing weeks, and reminded the government that we were serious about making ourselves heard.

The conclusions from the Kolkata seminar were well short of the recommendations contained in Saxena's draft policy, or those pressed for in Survival International's campaign. Some significant gains had been achieved but it was clear that the government reserved for itself the right to intervene in the lives of the Jarawa, and would not condone the closure of the ATR. While grudgingly admitting the need for more accountability within all the administrative bodies pertaining to tribal welfare, the framework of welfare itself remained unaltered. Hence, there was much more work yet to be done, and it would have to be accomplished before the next proposed seminar where the final policy recommendations were to be hammered out.

Return to Port Blair

The next seminar was to be convened 6 weeks later in Port Blair. And that is how I returned to Port Blair just as the monsoon arrived in the Andaman Islands late in May 2004. But this time with a formal invitation from the Ministry of Tribal Affairs and as a guest of the Andaman administration, along with the others who had stormed the first seminar in a bid to present a united but opposing front there. It meant making a second trip from New Zealand, a point that generated a degree of amazement from the authorities, who also noted the determination to ensure that our views and recommendations be documented and heard.

Still enthused by the awareness that the situation presented an important opportunity that should not be lost, the group that crystallized prior to the first seminar continued to work together and in tandem with each other. Madhusree Mukherjee, on consultation with Saxena, drafted an alternate policy framework for the Jarawa and the other islanders, which was to be submitted jointly at the Port Blair gathering. The rest prepared individual submissions that built on the points contained in the alternate framework, and continued to strategize on how best to insert them into the proceedings if we were not allotted individual slots as speakers within the forum.

As the flight skidded to a halt on the runaway at Port Blair, I noted the first point of difference, the runaway had been extended: the hill that had stood at the end of the earlier much shorter one had disappeared. There was no further need to sit nervously at the edge of one's seat wondering whether the brakes would apply in time before the face of the hill loomed before the nose of the aeroplane. I scanned the streets and buildings trying to reconcile my mental map with the current configuration of the town. Port Blair has been enormously built up over the decade since my departure from its shores, it was virtually unrecognizable. I had 4 days in Port Blair, two of which would be spent at the seminar, and the other two planning strategy with the others of the group, to once again ensure that we presented a coordinated and coherent set of interventions into the seminar.

On the first day of the seminar, in a shrewd move calculated as a pre-emptive strike, the organizers had filled the entire morning's agenda with speakers and elected representatives from the settler communities in the Islands, everyone of them arguing, vehemently and loudly against the closure of the ATR. If the extent of resistance to that recommendation was to be demonstrated by the volume of sound generated, and the numbers stacked against it, the administration had succeeded very well.

In another surprising move over the course of the rest of the proceedings, the Ministry accepted in entirety the Alternate Policy Framework drafted by Mukherjee and submitted jointly by us, as well as the draft policy recommendations drawn up earlier by Saxena in his dissenting note. The 3 key concepts of sensitivity, minimality and accountability which had informed the joint submission, and around which the policy recommendations had been constructed, became the administration's new catch phrases for referring to their future plans for the Jarawa. Perhaps that should have warned us, but the bubble of euphoria that buoyed us along as we savoured our success at the seminar was to evaporate slowly only later, as reality crept in with the other developments in the months to come.

The Battle Ahead

Sekhsaria's cyber forum remains active, keeping abreast of the developments in the Islands. Its membership has swelled to number about 400, many actively involved in debating and articulating their views. And there is much to debate in the subsequent months, with the government announcing its plans for tourism developments in the Islands, followed by a proposal to embark on oil exploration. "It's an all-out assault," despaired Mukherjee in a recent email. The Ministry's strategy of coopting and silencing the opposition was demonstrated in its announcement of the new board for the tribal welfare agency, which entailed a mere expansion of the existing board with a chosen few who could be relied on to speak the administration piece and not cause too many ripples. The new structure for the overhauled organization proposed in the joint submission and in Saxena's recommendation, which would ensure that it remained accountable and efficient is never mentioned and has disappeared altogether from the administrations plans. Saxena, who remains grimly watchful of these developments, cautions that the only recourse is to go back to court. Samir Acharya, too, is waiting and biding his time, wary of the shape of things to come.

And what of the Jarawa who remain invisible and distant from the scene of these strategies and maneuvers that will impact on their lives and determine their futures? While unwilling to tolerate the closure of the ATR, the administration has increased the area allocated to the Jarawa by including a section to the right of the ATR, in another typical gesture that looks good on paper but resolves nothing.[8] But what of their day-to-day lives and their futures? Or the Sentinelese, how safe are they in their remote island fastness? My brief visit to Port Blair allowed me access to some recent and revealing footage that underscored the continuing vulnerability of both the Jarawa and the Sentinelese, despite any decisions that are taken in the political centre-stage. One showed the ongoing clearing of a section of the denotified forest[9] within the Jarawa reserve by a forest officer who, when queried about his actions, responded that he was only following orders from higher authorities within the administration. The other footage, equally gut-wrenching in what it presages, was taken when the former Chief Secretary to the Islands commissioned a trip for his visiting family and friends to North Sentinel islands, the sound track recording his voice urging the boatman to go closer ashore where the Sentinelese were lined up, while observing that there was nothing to fear from them any longer, the fierce Sentinelese were harmless.

As matters stand, the Andaman Islanders, and in particular the Jarawa, are poised on the threshold of a precarious future that could utterly destroy them. But, if the coalitions that have been forged over the past months can withstand the several battles that lie ahead, the Jarawa may yet have another lease of life, perhaps finally on their own terms, as they venture into the new millennium.

Finally, I want to move on to a wide-ranging discussion with Sydney Possuelo, head of the Brazilian government's Department for Uncontacted Tribes or FUNAI. Possuelo was responsible for a major change in the approach towards the Amazon tribes. In a wide-ranging interview, he discusses his experiences working with the uncontacted tribes, the political problems that he confronted, as well as the other vested interests with a stake in the Amazon forests much like in the Andaman Islands. Possuelo's success was in his ability to create an empowered and accountable structure responsible for enforcing the protection and defence of the various Amazon groups and their territories, both by land and water. The interview from which I am quoting below will appear in a book that is to be published soon. In response to a question regarding the future of such people.

Sydney Says

> "What happens to them depends on who we are tomorrow. What's important is time...I am talking about gaining time for white society, so that we can rethink the dramatic conditions which historically we have imposed on these peoples. We need time to rethink the whole process of colonization, the rights of these people to land, health, peace, life, in short, happiness. All this is smashed with the arrival of the whiteman. So, now, the stronger society, the more intelligent society, the society which can make aeroplanes and rockets-must think of an approach which is more intelligent and which respects these peoples. Across the last 500 years we were not wise enough for that. But every year our values move. Our society is constantly transforming itself. Ten years can mean a revolution in the way our society thinks. So all the time we can gain now is important to create spaces in our society for these peoples. Will we permit this last handful to be happy? Can we avoid aggression on their environment? Can we prevent our enormous paraphernalia

of technology, tractors, communication, transport-from changing their whole environment? When there's a contact in the future, will we be more brotherly, more human, less violent?" (Ross, 2004)

I want to end this account with a proverb that garners the wisdom from another indigenous people, the Maori, whose own ongoing battles provide an example of what can be achieved:

Hutia te rito o te harakeke
Kei hea te komako e ko
Ki mai ki ahau
He aha te mea nui o tenei ao
Maku e ki atu
He tangata, he tangata, he tangata

The proverb translates as: if you pull out the central stalk of the flax plant, (so that it dies),[10] where will the bell bird sing?[11] If you were to ask me, what is the most important thing in this world, I will say to you, it is the people, it is the people, it is the people.

NOTES

1. In the same week that I revelled in successfully defending my Ph.D thesis, which is narrated in the preceding pages, and went on to celebrate the continued hostility projected by the Jarawa, a small act of kindness faraway in the forests of the Andaman Islands, was to go on to have profound long-term consequences.
2. Thus pointing to the continuing lack of clarity in communication with any of the indigenous groups in the islands, despite claims to the contrary.
3. An organization based in London that advocates for the rights of indigenous peoples.
4. Mr. Awaradi's Master Plan had been gathering dust within the tribal welfare agency over the past 2 decades. It is interesting that it should be referred to at this time by the High Court as a basis for future policy. It also makes one wonder about the directives emerging from the courts, simultaneously progressive but also limited in its terms of reference where policy pertaining to the Jarawa is concerned.
5. See Sekhsaria (2002) for a more detailed discussion of the various cases brought to court pertaining to forestry in the Andaman Islands, and the court rulings on the matter.
6. The informative website is an excellent public source of the reports from the various committees.

7. I reminded her of the junket I had participated in during my research and the futility of taking such events seriously. "This one is different," she insisted, there will be people listening and taking note of what is said.
8. As noted by Sekhsaria recently in an email communication, the change merely reinstated the area previously demarcated as Jarawa reserve forests.
9. Sekhsaria's presentation at the Port Blair seminar using satellite imagery, was a stark illustration of the extent to which the only original and intact forest cover left in the Islands was the area demarcated as the Jarawa reserve. Hence, as he demonstrated in his compelling argument, the twin needs of environmental protection and the protection of the Jarawa life-world neatly coincided.
10. The flax is a very important plant for the Maori, it has sacred, medicinal and very practical uses, and many protocols for how the plant is harvested. The leaves that are used are always taken from the sides of the plant, never from the centre, because that is the heart of the plant.
11. The song of the bell bird is one of the most beautiful and haunting sounds of the NZ native bush and forest.

REFERENCES

Ali, F.I. 1999. "Official Kiss of Death for Ancient Andaman Tribe," *The New Indian Express,* Sunday, October 17.

Anthropological Survey of India. n.d. Jarawa Tribes - Confluence of the Present with the Past. Electronic Document, http://www.angelfire.com/az/ausaf/jarawa.html

Bedi, R. 1999. "Modern World may be Death of Tribe." *Dominion,* October 11

Grig, S. 2002. Personal communication by email.

Mukherjee, M. 2002. Personal communication by email.

____. 2003. *The Land of the Naked People: Encounters with Stone Age Islanders.* Boston, New York: Houghton Mifflin Company.

____. 2004. Personal communication by email

Mukhopadhyay, K. 2004. Personal communication.

Mynott, Adam. 2004. Unique Tribe on Edge of Extinction. Electronic document, http://news.bbc.co.uk/2/hi/programmes/from_our_own_correspondant/3593989.stm

Ross, M. 2004. Personal communication by email.

Sekhsaria, P. 1999. "Embracing Disease," *Down to Earth,* October 31: 16.

____. 2002. *Troubled Islands. Writings on the Indigenous Peoples and Environment of the Andaman and Nicobar Islands.* India: Kalpavriksh and Lead India.

Venkateswar, S. 2004. *Development and Ethnocide: Colonial Practices in the Andaman Islands.* Copenhagen: International Work Group for Indigenous Affairs.

TEN

FORGOTTEN COMMUNITY AND INDIFFERENT STATE: The Case of Santal in Bangladesh

MANZURUL MANNAN

Introduction

Bangladesh, along with all the states of the South Asia, is the creation of the British colonial authority. A linear nationalist sentiment and idea construes the notion of post-colonial state, which aims at assimilating, homogenization and conformity with a fairly narrow ethnic and political range for creation of the illusion of a single nation-state (Nagengast, 1994: 109). The nation-state has both a narrow and expanded sense. In the narrow sense, the state is equated with government, functions by command and coercion. In the expanded sense the state is equated with political and civil society wherein the state exercises hegemony protected by the armour of coercion (Gramsci, 1971: 263). The coercive power of the state promotes class hegemony of the ruling elite from the dominant ethnic group. The ruling elite from both political and civil society of the dominant ethnic group not only establish hegemony over the poorer sections, it also shows indifference to the minority ethnic groups. The domination of a single class from a major ethnic group also constructs the identity of the state, which is continuously shaped by the image of poverty and opposition of ethnic groups to the state (Ali, 1993: 162-203).

In Bangladesh, Bengalis represent 98 per cent of the population and the different ethnic communities account for the rest. This constructs a skewed relationship between domineering majority Bengali and dominated minority ethnic groups. The formation of Bangladesh state has implication on the different ethnic groups. Until recently, states were indifferent to the interest of different ethnic and tribal groups which not only resulted in the marginalization of ethnic communities, but also alienated them fro the state.

The relationship of indifferent state to various ethnic and tribal groups in many ways is dysfunctional. More particularly, the state is unable to articulate and deal with the ethnic situations. The explanation for the inability of the state to create space to accommodate the interest of ethnic groups in its state and development policies lies in the several factors. First, the root problem lies in the processes of state formations by curving ethnic territories in order to create territorial boundaries of Bangladesh (erstwhile East Pakistan), Bhutan, India, Myanmar, Nepal, and Pakistan by the British authority in 1947. This territoriality represents political project rather than mere empirical fact (Ludden, 2003: 2). The territorial map is shaped by the contention of religious nationalisms—Muslim versus Hindu—to the direct detriment of population belong to different religions and ethnic entities. The territorial maps have also split the different ethnic and tribal groups only to distribute them into the political boundaries of different post-colonial states. Many of these groups have accepted the territorial maps imposed on them, but others have reservation on such distribution which often leads to the aspiration for struggle to form independent nations by themselves. In case of Bangladesh, Bengali Muslims form a home with fairly homogeneous ethno-linguistic population, but it has also incorporated ethnic groups whose ethnic trees are spread over to the political maps of India and Myanmar. There are also notable exceptions whereby a few ethnic groups live inside the plain land of Bangladesh.

Secondly, the makers and enforcers of territorial boundaries use maps to construct a political reality based on the nationalist sentiment of dominant Bengali ethnic group. This sentiment to make the political reality generates tension between the "totalizing dimension" of state formation and the "individualizing dimension" of state formation.[1] The totalizing dimension emphasizes plurality by creating space wherein all ethnic groups will equally flourish. The best example of totalizing effort of the Bangladesh state is cited in its recognition to the non-Bengali ethnic groups of Chittagong Hill Tract. Under the peace agreement of 1996, Bangladesh government allowed the ethnic population to form their own autonomous administration within the framework of the Constitution and no Benglai will be allowed to be elected as political representative from the three political districts of Chittagong Hill Tracts (Ramkanta, 2003: 233). As an outcome, the state gives more access to patronage to the ethnic groups of the Hill, who were once termed as insurgents and rebellious groups. Such recognition came as a result of prolonged resistance movement which made the state to recognize the legitimate identities of ethnic groups at the Chittagong Hill Tracts.

On the contrary, the individualizing dimension squeezes space for non-Bengali ethnic groups by emphasising Bengali class, ethnicity and locality. The space for non-Bengali ethnic groups further narrowed down with the development of state sponsored capitalism and liberalisation of market forces (Mannan, 2005, 1990). For example, the ethnic groups in the plain, particular in the northern and central Bangladesh, are virtually non-existent as they are unable to voice their opposition or place demands on the state for their well-being. These ethnic groups become a forgotten or marginalized community. Now they are fast disintegrating. For example, the Santal in the plain is unable to oppose the state; they are virtually non-existent in the paradigm of the state.

Overall, Bangladesh state remains historically indifferent to indigenous, but non-Bengali ethnic and tribal community. Because of the indifference of state, even after the 34 years of independence, one gets the following three images on the question of locating non-Bengali ethnic groups.

- The ethnic groups are termed with various appellations like *adivashi* (primitive inhabitants), *upa-jati* (sub-nation), *khudro jati sattha* (small nation), *pahari* (hill people), etc.
- They belong to isolated and stagnant societies, hidden in the jungles, averse to change, hardly with contacts with the outside world (Mey, 1984: 325)
- Bangladesh is unsure about the number of ethnic groups in its territory. It varies from 45 to 57 groups (Ramkanta, 2001: 40).

The indifferent state becomes aware of the existence of ethnic groups only when natural resources are discovered in the territory historically inhabited by one or other non-Bengali ethnic groups. The predominant approach of the ruling elite is to use regulative and coercive power of the state to exploit these resources without considering the interest of the ethnic groups. On the contrary, the ethnic groups expect both accesses to and protection from the state. This paper explains the location of Santal in the state; how state-sponsored economic development marginalizes the Santal and how Christianity erodes the community spirit of animist Santal. It also seeks an explanation why the state is indifferent towards Santal and why they fail to emerge as a strong community despite their rich cultural heritage (Mannan, 2004).

State and Santal

Historical indifference marks the relationship between the Bangladesh state and the Santal community.[2] The indifference attitude of the state toward the Santal lies in the attributes partly to the nature of state formation and partly to the territoriality. There are few Santal in Bangladesh, but more Santal resides in India. The territoriality which became the geographic expression of power of the state, as a common strategy for exercising political control fails to represent the interest of Santal or any other weak minority groups within the power structure of the state. As a result, every thing in the world has acquired a single national identity within the territoriality of Bangladesh. The Bangladesh state is a product of nationalist movement. However, the national identity of Bangladesh is shaped by the contested between the idea of Bengali nationalism and Bangladeshi nationalism. The evolution of nationalism in Bangladesh has gone through two distinct phases. First, present Bangladesh was known as East Pakistan, which emerges in 1947 as a constituent part of Pakistan. Religious nationalism played a catalyst role in dividing Pakistan and India. As soon as Muslim Bengalis became the member of Pakistan, a new phenomenon of language based Bengali nationalism surfaced, which eventually led to dismembering of Pakistan to create a new state of Bangladesh in 1971.

The religious nationalism of 1947 which created the East Pakistan was transformed into linguistic Bengali nationalism of 1971 to create Bangladesh. The evolution in the politics of nationalism also in hindsight created a problem for Bengali nationalism which is unable to take into cognizance the existence of various non-Bengali ethnic groups. As an outcome, the post colonial state in 1972 that framed the constitution of Bangladesh defined nationalism as:

> The unity and solidarity of the Bengali nation, which, deriving its identity from its language and culture, attained sovereign and independent Bangladesh through a united and determined struggle in the war of independence, shall be the basis of Bengali nationalism (Article 9, CPRB, 1972: 5).

Further, the Article 6 (Part 1) of the Constitution declares the citizens of Bangladesh are to be known as Bengalis. The imposition of these clauses upon entire population turned the non-Bengali population of the state into ethnic minority (Mohsin, 2004:10). Article 3 adopted Bengali as a state language. The ethnic groups have repulsed imposition of Bengali nationalism only to see the rise of ethnic rebellion in the Chittagong Hill Tracts.

However, the post-1975 government to correct the problem ensued from the Bengali nationalism has adopted "Bangladeshi" nationalism as a state policy. Bangladeshi nationalism incorporates the elements of race, the war of independence, the Bengali language, culture, religion (Islam), land (geographical area) and economy. However, Bangladeshi nationalism paradoxically produced double meanings. In the first place, Bangladeshi nationalism sought to build rapport with the alienated non-Bengali ethnic groups. In the second place, the Bangladeshi nationalism is also interpreted as a beginning of Islamisation of the Constitution. The proclamation of Order No.1 of 1977 inserted, "Bismillah-ar-Rahman-ar-Rahim" (In the name of Allah, the Beneficent, the Merciful), in the preamble Constitution. The same proclamation replaced the Article 8 as the principle of secularism with the principle of absolute trust and faith in the Almighty Allah. Further, the Eight Amendment to the Constitution on 7 June 1988, Islam was declared as the state religion of Bangladesh (Article 2 Clause A).

In a short, the shift from Bengali nationalism to Bangladeshi nationalism has deep rooted implications on the ethnic population. It further alienated and marginalized ethnic communities on the following two grounds.

- Bengali nationalism turns non-Bengali ethnic population into "ethnic minority," but recognizes the religious freedom of ethnic groups.
- Bangladeshi nationalism turns non-Bengali ethnic population into "religious minority," but recognizes the legitimate and cultural rights of the ethnic entity.

Moreover, the problem is that Bangladesh state has developed a democratic model for political governance that is based on the rule of majority, and not on the principle of plurality. This model created spaces for the representation of ethnic population of the Chittagong Hill Tracts, but is unable to provide space to ethnic population like Santal who live in the plain land of Bangladesh. As a result Santal, Munda, Mahili, etc, are missing in their representation in the parliament and their interests are never voiced at state level. Until recently, Government formed Adivashi institutions to project and protects the indigenous culture, but these institutions have yet to go far.

State, Economic Development and Marginalisation of Santal

Bangladesh state is indifferent to the question of promoting and protecting tribal community. This indifference has two implications. First, the development plan that state takes without comprehending the tribal social, political and economic structure bound to have negative consequences on the ethnic polity and society. Secondly, state is not a sole agency in the development. State allows market forces to promote the economic activities of the country (Mannan, 1990). The growth of liberal market and capitalism that link Bangladesh to the global economy has dire consequences on the Santal as the latter is unable to cope up with market economy resulting in the becoming of the labour forces and wage earner in the market. To capture the impact of state and market on Santal, it is important to categorically discuss the implication of local government on the historically evolved traditional Santal administrative system; development activities on the traditional economy of Santal.

Local Government and Santal Traditional Panchayet

Santal has historically developed a religio-historical administrative system that governs their daily discourse of life. The village is evidently the key political unit, but the largest formally organized territorial unit is the *Pargana,* a loose confederation of approximately a dozen villages bound together to settle certain judicial issues. The historically evolved traditional religio-judicial system glues the organization of clan and sub-clans. The judicial system brings cohesion to the Santal social and moral orders. The traditional judicial system is constituted by four layers of organizations.

1. *Gram Panchayet: Gram Panchayet* is the first layer of the judiciary system, which is comprised of five members. These members are *Manjheram*[3], *JogManjhe*[4], *Jogparanic*[5], *Godeth*[6] *and Naikeye*[7].
2. *Porgona Panchayet:* The second layer *Porgona Panchayet* is formed by recruiting the village heads of a few villages as well as *Manjhe Harams* of those villages. The head of *Porgona Panchayet* is known as *Porgona. Porgona Panchayet* may have five or six members, but there may be exceptions.
3. *Desh Manjhe Panchayet:* Santal usually term a particular territory as *desh* and each *desh* has its own head. This head is known as *Desh Prodhan*. He might control five or six, may be more, *Porgona* and *Manjherams*.
4. *Lo bir or higher court.* The fourth layer is the Lo bir, which sits once a year. Usually, all the complicated matters of Santal community are solved here. At present Lobby has become dysfunctional.

The *Porgona Panchayet, Desh Prodhan* and *Panchayet Lobby* became dysfunctional in the light of emergence of *Adibashi* Association and the increased influence of Union Parishad Chairmen. In the study area, the last *Porgona Panchayet* took place in 1980 which mitigated conflict resulted from an event whereby a Santali girl fall in love with a Bengali lad. The problem started when a Santali man teased the said Santali girl over the love affair. However, Santali girl was fined Taka 1,200 as she violated the Santali norms and tradition.

In recent years, the state has expanded its administrative reach to Santal areas aiming, among other things, to develop grassroots democracy and promote the representative character of local political organs. A proper electoral representative body is seen as necessary to administer state-sponsored development activities. The local political organ is known as Union Parashads (UPs) and covers an average population of 25,000. A position in UPs provides access and linkages to the local government bureaucracy. UPs oversee both political functions and development activities. The political function of the UP chairperson and members is of strategic importance in the formation of rural power structure. The chairperson and members are elected by direct voting which gives them legitimacy to govern local political institutions. Given the importance of UPs, the subsequent political government tried to reform UPs to suit their interests. Two important policy changes in the 1990s have put further spotlight on this organ. First, the government streamlined the representational base of the UPs by demarcating a Union into nine wards instead of the previous three, with each ward having its electoral representatives. The new system broadens the base of political representation, as members are elected from constituent villages within the boundary of respective wards. Second, the government has made the representation of women mandatory in the UPs, each UP having to reserve three seats for women (Rahman, 2001: 2). However, female participation has brought critical changes in local electoral politics along gender lines.

While this allow Bengali political elites to widen their power-base from micro-village to meso-village higher forums, the Santal are unable to take the advantage from such political system. The expansion of the local government administrative reach has deep implication on the traditional Santal religio-judicial administrative system. The consequence is the disintegration of Santal traditional system. UPs do not recognize the role and position of *Manjheram*, *JogManjhe*, *Jogparanic*, *Godeth* and *Naikeye*; rather it recognizes the representatives of Santal as Chairmen and members. On the question of representation in UP, Santal may have representational problem in the decision-making process on the following grounds? Except for one or two UPs, Santal do not have major representation in different UPs. As result they might be elected as "members" from different wards. Importantly, when Santal elect members and Chairmen, they no longer become interested in strengthening their traditional *Panchayet*. This has corresponding affect on the traditional function of *pargana* and *lo-bir*.

Economic Activities and Development

From days immemorial, the economy and livelihood of Santal have evolved within the broader organization of clan. Because of clan culture, Santal harnessed a collective sense of going together and reciprocity (Mannan, 2004). Prior to the nineteenth century, the basic Santal subsistence pattern was hunting. The present settlement area of Santal was largely covered with forests, *bushes* and *jungles*. These forests, *bushes* and *jungles* were the niche to the Santal. Santal depended on these bushes and jungles for their livelihood. They hunted extensively wild animals and birds which met their protein requirements. Birds (*céré*) were found in abundance. Among these birds are *garur, kurit, pajhar, gidi, tetengoe, kikir, sarali, bata, pankauri, kokor, dundu. Meru, caicir, gundri, jhik, bardhurue, cutia, bardhurue,* etc. Their main weapons to kill animals and birds were the bows and arrows. They used two types of arrows, namely, the arrow pointer is made of flat-head wood and of sharp metal spear. The flat-head pointer arrow was used to kill birds. The reason of using the flat-head arrows is that it would not let the blood out of birds' bodies, and thus, preserve the blood of the birds. It also means birds will die less painfully. Santal also used dogs extensively to identify and chase animals. Dogs played important roles in bringing wild animal in some selected and convenient hunting spot from where hunters could kill the animal easily.

Jungles also supplied wild fruits and foods. Forests are vital source of food and vegetation. The following wild plants were available: *ulè alañ, catom, dhurup, gadle arak, poraine, garudi.* They relied on wild potatoes, which were extinct, for supply of energy. They also rely upon wild indigenous variety of rice and cultivated rice on a limited scale. Santal as a community participated in all hunting, gathering foods and cultivation. At present, hunting is of little economic importance, but it becomes an important element of the cultural heritage of Santal. Every year on December 28, that is, in the winter months of *Agrahyan* and *Paush,* they commemorate annual hunting festival locally known as *Sendara*. The Santali male goes to distance place of Dinajpur district where some jungles and forests are still left.

It seems that the Santal spirit of collectivism has suffered erosion with the introduction of the Permanent Settlement in 1793. The Permanent Settlement introduced private and individual ownership of land to the direct detriment of collective ownership of land by clan. The British also consider the settlement of Santal as schedule areas. Such policy had dual purposes. First, it would protect the Santal community from outside intrusion. Secondly, it also enabled the colonial rulers to extract revenue from the Santal. However, the Santal have since turned to agriculturalists with ever-increasing population, the transformation of jungles into arable lands, and the rapidly decreasing supply of forest animals and foods. As the Santal gradually became agriculturalists, they also made effort to domesticate wild animals. Today, pigs, sheep, goats, oxen, buffaloes, cows, etc. are raised to some extent. These animals are used as supplementary sources of protein in the diet, as well as for other purposes (e.g. rodent control).

Currently, most of the Santal are agriculturalists and agriculture is the main source of their livelihood. The income of Santal is tagged to crop production cycle. *Zaminders* (Feudal Landlord) brought Santal into Dinajpur and North Bengal to clear and transformation of jungles and bushes into arable lands. Santal cleared the jungles against a very low rent. However, as soon as jungles are converted into arable land, *Zaminders* increased the rent. This made most of the Santal as the rent paying peasants or *Pattoni Proja* (Rahman, 2002: 25). Lately, the British government allocated these lands, through *Zaminders,* to the Santal by the decree of Permanent Settlement. As a result, a lot of Santal became the landowner. Many Santal still nurture from their social memory that their ancestors held lands up to 700 acre lands, but in course of time they lost their ancestral lands and properties.

There are many reasons why class of labourer has emerged among the Santal, some of which is related to the process of inheritance. With the increase of population, lands are distributed in equal portions among the heirs. The successive inheritance over a few generation lead to the fragmentation and division of large lands into smaller one. Inheritance follows the following formula: The basic family unit is the extended patrilocal family. This means that inheritance play an import role in fixing the nature of family. Inheritance follows along male line, and women do not inherit any parental property as they, upon marriage, become the member of husband's lineage. In most cases, inheritance takes place, among the male heirs of the family, posthumously, i.e. after the death of parents. The devolution of property in Santal society follows male bias custom. Sons inherit in equal shares and daughters do not inherit parental property. If a person does not have sons, then his brothers get property. If there is no brother, then his male agnates inherit. If there are no agnates, the daughter inherits with succession to her children. If man dies leaving young sons, his widow manages the property till all the sons are old enough to divide and start separate households. She then moves into her youngest son's household. If the widow moves outside the family, the male agnates take the property in trust till the sons become matured and she gets nothing. One cannot give property to his son-in-laws (Risley, 1998).

Apart from the inheritance, many Santal fall into trap of land transfer by the local touts. Santal are in general simple people and illiterate. Many Bengali touts deceived them and forged their documents in order to takeaway their lands. Importantly, after the abolition of *Zamindary* system in 1950, many of the Santal were driven off from their land by the land grabbers and village touts (Rahman, 2002: 25). The settler Muslim migrated from neighbouring district like Rajshahi, Noaga and they made aggressive ploy to grab lands by all deceitful means.[8] The land grabbing was a historical problem for which the British government even enacted law to protect Santal land. The chief protection of Santal land is provided by the "Chota Nagpur Tenancy Act of 1908", which prohibits the transfer of lands to non-tribal without the permission of District Commissioner. Bangladesh government recognizes special tenure status, but there are many loopholes through which land could be transferred. For example, a dominant practice among Santal is to give land as mortgage in exchange of money. Lands remain in the passion of money lender until the borrowed money is returned. In most cases, they are unable to pay back the borrowed money resulting in the possession of land permanently in the hand of money-lenders. A few wage labourer Santal reported that they have 40-50 *bigha* of lands which are mortgaged, but they are unable to raise the required money to release the lands. The rate of land mortgage varies depending on the negotiation among the parties. At present, the rate varies from Taka 1,000 to Taka 5,000 for mortgaging one *bigha* (33 decimal) of land.

Many Santal even did not bother to own lands. They thought it was a cumbersome job to deal with *Zaminders* and pay rent and taxes to the *Zaminders.* Instead they prefer to remain as *Adiaer* and were happy to share the crops with landowners. The landowners are known as *Malik* and the sharecroppers are known as *Adiaer*. Two types of *Adiaer* are seen. First, landowner who, have sufficient lands, cannot cultivate lands by their own labour. They rent out land to *Adiaer* for cultivation. Secondly, many who have some lands and use their own labours for tilling, they prefer to take *Adiaer* from others who have lands. The normal negotiation and agreement between *Malik* and *Adiaer* is that the *Malik* will give the land and *Adiaer* will give his labour. *Adiaer* must supply cow or ox, plough, and other agricultural tools required for tilling lands. On top of it, both *Malik* and *Adiaer* will share equally the cost of production like the prices of seeds, fertilisers, pesticides and water for irrigation. The harvest will be shared into 50:50 ratio between the *Malik* and *Adiaer*. Apart from *Adiaer* sharing contract, there also exist crop-sharing agreement. In this system, *Malik* and *Adiaer* enter into verbal agreement and *Malik* gives lands to the *Adiaer*. *Malik* do not provide any agricultural input for production, which remains the responsibility of the *Adiaer*. In exchange of land, *Malik* receives annually 10-13 maund rice. After the harvest, they have to enter into new agreement for the next agricultural season and in this case, *Malik* is not obligated to give land to the same *Adiaer*.

The majority of Santal are agricultural labours. The rate of agricultural wages varies from season to season. Currently, daily wage is Taka 50 with food during the pick agricultural season, but it goes down to as low as Taka 20 during the off seasons. It seems that most of the Santal become, eventually, the labourer class and wage earners as they lost their lands over the period of time. Table 10.1 reflects the present wealth ranking and economic stratification in one village.

It is clear that although historically Bengalis considered land as not only a critical source of subsistence, but was also considered to be a symbol of wealth and prestige (Mannan, 2001:82). But to Santal land was never appeared as either critical source of subsistence or a matter of prestige. However, this centrality of land in current context of market development is disappearing as it is neither a basis of status, nor does it represent a single livelihood source for the rural population. In a recent estimate, household income from agriculture had dropped to under 50 per cent (Rahman, 2001: 10). This decline of household income from land is compensated with multiple livelihood systems and opportunities for the rural poor both in the agricultural and non-agricultural sectors, resulting in the circulation of money in poor households.

The second factor is the gradual importance of the mechanized tiller over the traditional plough; use of both deep and shallow tube wells that rely a great deal on seasonal rain fall; use of fertilizer and pesticides instead of traditional cow manure; and replacement of traditional with a high-yielding variety of seeds. All these shifts, induced by the introduction of new technology, have brought fundamental changes to the social organization of the Santal peasantry. The technological extension initiated by public agencies (which are

Table 10.1: Wealth Ranking

Category	*Number*	*Land size (bigha=33 decimal)*	*Household (HH) Resources*			*Professional*
			Livestock	*Natural resource*	*Others*	
Rich	09	50-60	Cow, Hens Buffalos, Pigs, Dogs	Trees, Bamboo bush, Palm tree garden	Tin and mud house, power tiller, Motor cycles, shallow Shallow machines Cycles	Jobs at Government & Mission office
Middle	08	10-15	Cow, Goat Hens, Ducks	Trees, Bamboo bushes around HH	Tin and mud house Shallow machines Cycles	Petty jobs, Sharecro-ppers
Poor	13	2	Few goats, cows	A few trees	Cycles in fes HH	Agricultural labours
Ultra Poor	60	Only homestead lands	Hens, Ducks	—	HH made of grass straws	Men and women sell labours van & rickshaw pullers

now in the process of privatization) has gone hand in hand with the establishment of many peasant co-operatives dominated by Bengalis that have encroached upon the scope and work of Santal community. This new technology has created additional arenas of contention among the peasantry, since it has become a lucrative business to gain control over mechanized tube wells and the increased quantum of water. New ties are established between people from different villages and social groups—for example, the people who have operational plots within the command area of the same tube well. At times, heterogeneous groups are required to work out a system of joint management to reconcile various competing as well as conflicting interests.

The marginalization of Santal has also influence by the role of the Department of Forestry which pursue a policy that brings destruction to traditional forests, but recreate one with exotic species. The activities of the ministry have negative consequences on the Santal primarily because of the fact that these ministries largely fail to understand the importance of forest based economy of Santal. The traditional knowledge of Santal helped them in preserving common property resources like forest. They knew how to manage the resources without destroying the forest. This knowledge of forest conservation has been in decline due to the intervention of forest department as they also involved in illegal logging. The Santal are dispossessed from their lands through a policy of non-recognition of their customary rights over land and forest (Mohsin, 2004: 14). Government policy of reservation of forest technically uproots the indigenous community from using the forest resources. Government has three categories of forests such as Reserve Forests (RF), Protected Forest (PF) and Unclassified State Forests (USF). In the early 1980s, the Forest Department gets hold of 1,500 acres of land belonging to Santal in Dinajpur. Santal are the owner of 90 per cent of this land. The forests, which are a niche to Santal, are being systematically destroyed by the Department of Forestry (DoF). The DoF has recreated forest with trees of exotic varieties. As a result, hardly any birds and animals are seen on the trees, nor any bushes or shrubs in and around the forest. Because of the exotic plant species, the forest becomes unfriendly to environment. It appears to us that this forest is without spirit. DoF destroys the traditional forests full of animals and birds and recreated a forest with foreign exotic spices of trees devoid of birds and animals.

Christianization and Erosion Animist of Santal Spirit

The state, despite the adoption of Islamic principle in the Constitution, always remains unconcerned about religion. This could be the reflection of broader sentiment of Bengali Muslims who are secular and non-communal in character (Huq, 1975; Roy, 1983). As an outcome, the state ignores the activities of other religions, which proselytes tribal and ethnic groups into a particular religion. The State policy of indifference is advantageously utilized by a particular monotheistic religion sponsored by Europeans and North Americans churches. This religion, although is very successful to proselyte large members of the ethnic community, also causes erosion in the community spirit built upon an animistic religion.

Santal believe that their ancestors had come from a far-off place somewhere from the East — the land of Sun-rise. Thus, the sun becomes on of the main deity of the Santal. Traditionally, Santal religion is characterized by a belief in a pantheon of supernatural beings represented by the supreme god *Thakur (Chando, Chando Bonga, Sing Bongo,* or *Kando).* There are also six other major gods, a host of nature and ancestral spirits. Although the Santal have no idols or temples, the sacred groves or springs represent to them the place of residence of the supernatural powers. It is in these sacred groves or springs prayers and sacrifices are made, usually by a priest, to avert the ill will of the gods and to bring upon themselves, their crops, and their animals the blessings of the supernatural spirit. In addition, each family has two gods of its own, the *Arakbonga* (household god) and the *Abgebonga* (secret god), whose names are never divulged to anyone except the eldest son in the family. Generally the *bongas* or spirits were friendly toward man, but at times could inflict misery and trouble.

Magic and witchcraft have figured prominently in Santal religious practices. Santal strongly believe in the existence of witches in the society. Witch is motivated by envy and operating through the medium of the "evil eye" or other magical practices, cast sickness, death, and other calamities upon members of the village community. By means of divinatory practices exercised through the offices of the witch-finder and the *Ojha* (exorcist), the causative agents of the disease are determined and ritually removed, and the identity of the witch revealed. Often invisible witch mediates through individual. There is elaborate ritual to identify the name of witch. Once the name of the witch is known, that person is often beaten, fined, driven out from the community, and not infrequently killed. Witches in Santal society are inevitably *female,* while the *Ojha* and the witch-finders are male.

The non-Christian Santal, like the Hindus, observe 13 *Pujas* (worships) in twelve months. In the month of *Baishakh* (15 April- 15 May), Santal observe the ritual called *Holi*. On that day, people sprinkle coloured water through a bamboo made large syringes on their family members, friends and neighbours. The members of the Santal community sing and dance on that day. In the month of *Jaistha* (15 May- 15 June) the Santal observe the *Jaistha Puja* (need to get more information). In the Bengali month of *Ashar* (15 June - 15 July) the Santal observe *Amad*. This ritual is related to mango and jack fruits as the members of the community receive these food in large amount on that particular day. The family members receive the food and they also send these fruits to their neighbour's houses. In the month of *Sraban* (15 July- 15 August), the Santal have no particular rituals, but they observe *Dala Puja* in the month of *Bhadro* (15 August-15 September). They gather some vegetables and worship those during this *Puja* period. The Bengali month of *Ashin* (15 September-15 October) is famous for *Durga Puja*. Sometimes it is observed in the month of *Kartic* (15 October-15 November). *Durga Puja* is thought to be a pan-Bengal phenomenon. It is not observe in other part of South Asia. According to Hindu text Durga is the wife of Shiva. The Santal people say they just dance and enjoy the day of this particular *Puja*. In the same month *Lakhi Puja* is also celebrated by the community. They often observe *Kali Puja* during the new moon night. Kali is one of the appearances of Durga. She has nine appearances. Santal identifies only one of her appearances. They also observe *Kali Puja* in the month of *Agrahayan* (15 November-15 December). It depends on the availability of resources. In the month of *Poush* (15 December-15 January) they observe the *Poushna Puja.* This is relating to the paddy harvesting period. In the month of *Falgun* (15 February-15 March) *Holi Puja* is observed again.

The main differences in the ritual procedure between Hindus and Santal are that the Hindus require statues (*Murti*) for their gods and goddesses, but the Santal have no use of the statue. Some members of the Santal community who obtained formal education think they are sort of animist by born. They used to worship sun, water sources and different parts of the nature. Later this was misinterpreted by a few Hindus as they consider this act as influences of Hinduism on the Santal. This notion has been strongly opposed by Santal and they think their heritage of religion is much older than Hindus. However, the *Manjheram* also plays the role of the ritual leader. Some *Naikeye* follows him during the ritual period. There is a small platform made of mud in each *Manjheram's* house. The platform is called *Manjhethan. Manjhethan* — place of *Manjheram* — is thought to be a sacred place for all.*Manjheram* performs all rituals as he sits in front of the *Manjhethan*. During each of the *Puja* he needs some flowers, offerings and leaves of the wood apple tree, paddy and grass to perform the main rituals. Different flowers are used in different rituals and the number of wood apple's tree leaves varies *Puja* to *Puja*. In some *Puja* a pair of flowers used by *Manjheram* whereas single flower used in other *Puja* rituals. For example, a lotus is required to perform the *Kalipuja*. The *Manjheram* utter the *Montro* (spell) during the *Puja* as he leant the whole procedure from his father. He has learnt everything verbally as there is no written text available. During most of the rituals common people dances and drink rice wine (*Chuani*).

We paid visit to the house of two *Manjheram* at *Amtala* in the village of Basidebpur. There was a stake of the stems at the homestead which had been separated from the harvested paddy very recently. The house of the *Manjheram* has been constructed with mud. The house has a few rooms including a kitchen. It seems very clean and the mud walls of the house are very good-looking. Each of the walls is decorated with some art designs and the art is done with a lot of care. This reveals the creativity and aesthetic sense of the Santal, particularly of women. During a discussion with the mother of the *Manjheram* and other fellow members (in absence of her sons) we have been informed that banana and vermilion also have a significant use in *Puja*. The mother of *Manjheram* is called *Panu Besra*. She has two sons and both of them got the power of *Manjheram* as her husband had played the same role. It is significant that *Manjheram* inherits their power hereditarily. Now-a-days this has become less strict. Some one else instead of the sons of *Manjheram* can also hold the similar power. However, there are two *Manjhethan* founded by two brothers at the same homestead. Both of the *Manjhethan* had some vermilions on them at that time. It reveals that a short while ago they had observed the *Akhipuja* on the *Manjhethan*. The mother of *Manjheram* reported that they had observed the ritual on that morning. *Manjheram* took his bath a bit earlier and got prepared to lead the rituals. Volume of rituals observances was pretty high during the British period. This tradition has declined as there is a lack in food security. They also blame the decline in agriculture for this deterioration. During different rituals the villagers gathers at the house of the *Manjheram*. In most of the cases they cook rice pudding and *khichury*. All members of the community contribute for this according to their ability.

Christianity and Santal Animistic Religion

Hinduism[9] has had only nominal influence on Santal religious practices as has Christianity. Currently, Santal are going through the process of Christianization. Despite the fact that Christian missionary have been functioning among the Santal since 1862, until 1947 only 52 Santal became Christians (Ali, 2002). The process of Christianization has to be viewed from the background of the policy of Christian missionaries who in 1974 took decision to proselyte all the aboriginals and indigenous population from their animistic beliefs into Christian faith (McNee, 1976). This policy has deep rooted implication on the Santal community. The conversion of Christianity does not mean that Christianity has modified their traditional culture. Christianity primarily confined to the religious order, and within the framework of Christianity, they are reproducing their cultural practices. However, as majority Santal embrace Christian faith, primarily to escape their ever increasing poverty, it creates pressure on those Santal who have yet not accepted Christianity. For example, the non-Christian Santal find it difficult to marry-out their daughters to the grooms belonging to the non-Christian clans where they have shortage of grooms. However, grooms are available from Christians Santal, but the latter put conditions that they cannot marry from non-Christian Santal. Thereby, a social pressure is going on the animistic Santal to accept Christianity and many, indeed, submit to such pressure only to become Christians.

Although many Santal have accepted Christianity, they have not abandoned their traditional animistic religion. Rather they have developed a syncretistic tradition between Christianity and animistic religions. For example, in many Christian Santal village, we discover that a pig's jaw is place on the branch of a jackfruit tree. It is believed that if pig's jaw or skull is placed on the top of the tree with proper rituals, it would protect the community and households from the demonic affect of *Sukri-datha* (evil eye). Many Santal frequently swing their religious faiths between Christianity and traditional animistic religions.

There exists a lot of antagonism against Christian Church. An informant opined,

> "Missionaries are interested in making Santal Christians. They are working in our areas over 100 years. During these times they have only opened primary schools, and are not interested to see educated Santal. On the contrary, they have opened high schools, colleges, etc. for the Bengali Christians."
>
> "Churches are a main source of confusion. There exists contest among Churches to establish their supremacy. They discourage Church members not to visit members to different church. There are Catholic, Protestant, Nazarene, etc. American Churches are better than the European Churches."

Christianisation is causing erosion in the community spirit to fight back which make them more marginalized and alienate from the state.

Concluding Thought

During the British rule, that is, before 1947, the natural habitat of Santal and other ethnic groups was given the status of a scheduled area so that they could preserve their separate identities without being assimilated into the other community. During the last three decades, the former policy of segregation has been replaced. Ownership of land has been introduced in these areas resulting in the transfer of tribal and ethnic lands to non-tribal population. This land transfer has increased sufferings among the minority ethnic community. In recent years, the ecological degradation has caused further sufferings to the people of this area. Once, Santal used the rivers and *beels* (depressed lands) as a main source of fishing. The fishing is now seriously threatened due to lack of water in the rivers. Most of the Santal have become wage labourers and share croppers. Most of them support their livelihoods from agriculture. The problem with agriculture is that agriculture sector as a whole is becoming non-viable. The agriculture is not giving them sufficient income to support their families. This means that Santal as agriculturalists are also sufferings and becoming more marginalised community.

Santal is a cause for concern for two reasons. First, the numbers of affected persons are very high; secondly, the chain of exploitation is impeding the social and economic development of the Santal. They are subjected to the discrimination in the labour market. It has been observed that discrimination in the labour market is prevalent. Bengali labourers have a fixed time to work whereas Santal labourer works 2-4 hours more than the Bengalis. Although the type and the load of the work is same between Bengali and Santali labour, the latter is paid fewer wages for their labour. The daily wage of Santal labour during the off season goes down to Taka 20 per day, but increases up to Taka 50 per day during the seasons. However, Santal find it difficult to believe that their cause of marginalization is not due to market exploitation, but due to their fate. Santal are subjected of exploitation by the broader Bengali population which gradually is making them pauper and marginal landless. The exploitation is forcing them to migrate elsewhere in search of livelihood.

Santal now have a very low community spirit which is also a main reason why they are failing to protect their rights and identity. The reasons for low community spirit are related to at least two dynamics. First, forests are vital element to the sustenance of the clan structure. They hunt together; they share the prey together; and they maintain ecological balance of the forest. As the forests are depleting and recreating with foreign exotic species, it affects the whole clan structure. Inheritance, further, brings disintegration to the Santal community. Since parents' properties are distributed among the descending generation, it results in the rise of individual families and clan structures are unable to glue these families. Secondly, the Christianization has also contributed to the loosening of the community strength. There are several Christian churches which compete with each other for Santal members to be kept under their control. A way to keep under church's control is to encourage Santal to forget and abandon their own Santali language, but to adopt the Bengali language. Many people have followed the church's prescription. As a result, many Santal did not have access to their linguistic and ritual based animistic religion, but to follow the rule and rituals of Christianity. Churches introduce primary education (five year education) and almost all Santal children attend the primary schools. Here students are taught Bengali and learn Christianity. However, when the Santali children complete primary education, they do not receive further higher education. Higher education means these children will go beyond the control of churches. In the last instance, Santal community is fast disintegrating because of the indifference of the state which hardly aware of the plight of Santal, who are again subjected to the exploitation of market controlled by Bengalis and religious aggression of Christianity.

NOTES

1. The idea of "totalizing dimension" and "individualizing dimension" of state formation is borrowed from Joseph and Nugent (1994: 20).
2. Santal came to picture as coal mine project is positively thinking on how to rehabilitate the dislocated Santal.
3. *Manjheram* is the head of *Gram Panchayet*. He adjudicates all the legal matters and enforces traditional rights in the community. Besides these specific functions, he also oversees all social functions, marriage, death rituals, etc. in the community. *Manjheram* is a central to all activities and all actives revolve around him. No functions are complete without the presence of *Manjheram*. However, it is impossible for one person to look after and response all the events of village, *Manjheram* usually delegates his authority to four other key actors, namely, *JogManjhe*, *Jogparanic*, *Godeth* and *Naikeye*. These actors support the Manjheram to execute his responsibility. Traditionally *Manjheram* is a hereditary position. Usually, eldest son become the *Manjheram*, but in many situation, others sons could also become *Manjheram*. The hereditary position of *Manjheram* is being challenge by the disgruntled community members and since 1970 they have adopted a practice through which a non-hereditary *Manjheram* could be selected by the consensus of the community.
4. *JogManjhe* especially looks after all the village festivals and it is his responsibility of organize cultural events of the community. If any unpleasant incident takes place during the festivals, *JogManjhe* takes active role in mitigating the problems. Beside this, *JogManjhe* also keep watchful eyes on the behaviour of the young men and women. He gives warning to any young persons, if he finds that they deviate from the cultural rule of the community. These roles of *JogManjhe* create space for young men and women to let know the *JogManjhe* about their problems. Often, *JogManjhe* also seeks advice from the young persons. In other word, he is the representatives of youths of community.
5. *Jogparanic* mainly extends support to *Manjheram* in all activities. He plays the role of *Manjheram* when the later is absent, due to illness or for any other reasons, from any functions and events.
6. *Godeth* is like a guard of the community. Upon receiving instruction from, *Godeth* takes the responsibility to initiate and organize the social festivals and traditional judiciary for conflict resolution.

7. *Naikeye* is a religious priest or *guru* of the community and his main role to perform religious rituals and sacrifice animals and birds on religious events.
8. Santal and original Muslim population of Dinajpur maintain very cordial relations.
9. In primary schools, Santal children are bound to take lesson on Hinduism, since no book is available on Santal religion.

REFERENCES

Ali, Mehrub. 2002. *Dinapurer Adibashi* (Original Inhabitants of Dinajpur) (2nd Edition) Dinajpur: Sun Computer and Printers

Ali, S.M. 1993. *The Fearful State: People, Power and Internal War in South Asia.* London & New Jersey: Zed Books

CPRB. 1972. *The Constitution of the Peoples Republic of Bangladesh,* Dacca, Government of Bangladesh.

Gramsci, A. 1971. *Selections from the Prisons Notebooks.* New York: International

Haq, M. Enamul. 1975. *A History of Sufism in Bengal.* Dhaka: Asiatic Society of Bangladesh.

Joseph, G and D. Nugent. (eds.). 1994. *Everyday Forms of State Formation: Revolution and Negotiation of Rule in Modern Mexico.* Durham, NC: Duke University Press. pp.3-23.

Ludden, David. 2003. *Where is Assam? Using Geographical History of Local Current Realities.* Ceniseas Paper 1. Sanjib Baruah. Series Editor, Guwahati: Center for Northeast India, South and Southeast Asia Studeis.

McNee, Peter. 1976. *Crucial Issues in Bangladesh. Making Missions More Effective in the Mosaic of Peoples.* California: William Carey Library

Mannan, Manzurul. 1990. "The State and the Formation of a Dependent Bourgeoisie in Bangladesh," *South Asia Journal,* 3 (4): 389-410

____. 2001. "South Asia's Experience in Land Reform: NGOs, State and Donors," (pp.81-102) in K.B. Ghimire (ed.), *Whose Land? Civil Society Perspectives on Land Reform and Rural Poverty Reduction.* Rome: IFAD/PC/UNRISD,

____. 2004. Santal: An Anthropological Profile of Indigenous Community. Report submitted to SMEC International Ptv. Ltd. 2004, Dhaka.

____. 2005. "Rural Power Structures and Evolving Market Forces in Bangladesh," (pp. 271-298) in K.B. Ghimire (ed.), *Civil Society and the Market Question.* London: Palgrave Macmillan.

Mey, Wolgang. 1984. "Implications on National Development Planning for Tribal Concepts of Economy and Politics: A Contribution to a Critique of Concepts of Development," (pp.325-337) in M S Qureshi (ed.), *Tribal Cultures in Bangladesh.* Institute of Bangladesh Studies, Rajshai: Rajshai University.

Mohsin, Amena. 2004. "State of Indigenous Community in Bangladesh: An Overview," paper present at a seminar "Indigenous People of Bangladesh" organized by the Independent University of Bangladesh at IDB Bhavan, November 25, 2004.

Nagengast, Carole. 1994. "Violence, Terror, and The Crisis of the State," *Annual Review of Anthropology,* 23: 109-136

Rahman, Hossain Zillur. 2001. "Re-Thinking Local Governance towards a Livelihoods Focus," PPRC Policy Papers, Power and Participation Research Centre, Dhaka.

Rahman, Mizanur (ed). 2002. *In Search of a Withering Community: The Santal of Bangladesh.* Dhaka: ELCOP

Ramkanta, Singha 2001. *Bangladesher Nritattic Jonogusthi (Ethnic Peoples of Bangladesh)* Dhaka: A.H. Publishing House

____. 2003. *Tribal Law of Bangladesh.* Dhaka: A.H. Development Publishing House.

Risley, H.H. 1998 [1891]. *The Tribes and Castes of Bengal.* Vol.II. Calcutta: P. Mukherjee

Roy, Asim. 1983. *The Islamic Syncretistic Tradition in Bengal.* Prinston: Princeton University Press.

ELEVEN

SELF-RELIANCE TO ENDANGERED COMMUNITIES:
Consequences of Interventions in the Life of Foraging Tribes of Andaman & Nicobar Islands

JAYANTA SARKAR

Sudden interaction of two or more societies, having widely varied technological base and different mindsets, generates uneven reaction among them. Mindset of the people who survive in almost complete isolation pursuing age-old foraging activities, based on simple technology, often gets severe unbearable cultural shock. In the urge to survive, some of such societies may opt to maintain a symbiotic relation or withdraw from their adverse surroundings as has happened in the case of the Birhors (Adhikary, 1984) or the Cholanaickan (Bhanu, 1989) of the main land India. Where scope of adjustment does not exist, the ill-fated communities virtually collapse.

The present paper seeks to unfold destine of the endangered small tribes of Andaman and Nicobar Islands, namely the Great Andamanese, the Onges, the Jarawas (Ang), the Sentinelese and the Shompens, as has taken shape due to the interventions of the State.

Intervention during Colonial Period

The Great Andamanese Situation

Though for many centuries the Malayas of the peninsula have used these islands for their piratical practices and the Chinese and the Japanese knew about thc islands, it was the British who in the year 1789 first intervened in the way of living of the foraging tribes of the South Andaman. Convicts were brought to these islands from the main land India to establish a Penal settlement near present Port Blair, which was then known as Port Cornwallis. The settlement, however, was abandoned in 1794, as the climate did not suit the people brought from the main land.

After this the British rulers again intervened in the life of the tribes of the islands in 1858. They had brought convicts and other people from the main land and established the Second Penal settlement. The development of infrastructure facilities resulted into mass scale deforestation reducing the resource areas of the tribes.

At the beginning of the Second Penal settlement the Great Andamanese, who originally had ten territorial groups, tried to protect their resource areas through several attacks on the settlers with the help of their bows and arrows but could not continue their uneven fight for a long time. The Colonial rulers intervened in the normal living of the tribes by arranging several punitive expeditions into their habitats. This approach was discarded subsequently and a policy of reconciliation was adopted. "Andaman Home" was established at the Ross Island in 1863 with the objective to bring the Andamanese in the Home and treat them as guests, offer them many gifts and allow them to return to their habitats whenever they so desired. The Colonial rulers could bring a few willing persons of this tribe at the Home. But the consequences proved to be fatal for the tribes. Through this contact they had acquired several dreaded venereal and other diseases from the outsiders. The Colonial Administration could not save them from the fatal diseases (Sarkar, 1990). As a result there was alarming decline in the population of this tribe and by 1901 they were reduced to 625 from a population of about 3500 in the year 1858. This resulted into extinction of many of their territorial groups. In spite of such depopulation they could not come together to live in a place. It seems they were not prepared to give up their age-old strong feeling of territorial separateness even at the cost of biological extinction.

The Onge Situation

Like the Great Andamanese, the Onges of Little Andaman tried to defend their resource areas initially from the Malayan pirates or the Chinese or Burmese traders. The British rulers did not allow them to live in their own way, though this 731sq. km Island is situated at a distance of 122 km south of Port Blair. In order to bring the Onges within the fold of Colonial rules punitive expeditions used to be sent. Several original inhabitants of this island perished in encounters. The policy of befriending this tribe, like the Great

Andamanese also continued. It was Portman, an administrator of Andaman succeeded in establishing friendly contact with the Onges in 1886. His method was to bring the captured Onges at Port Blair and treat them very nicely keeping at his residence and then whenever they wanted to go back they were taken to their island after entertaining with a large number of gifts. The British administrators kept visiting the Little Andaman in order to maintain friendly contact with the Onges. This tribe was fortunate to some extent as the Colonial rulers spared their territory from the policy of colonization. Even then they could not escape the consequences of their contact with the outsiders, their population declined from an estimated number of 572 in 1901 to only 250 in 1931(Census of India 1931).

The Jarawa Situation

Prior to establishing friendly relation with the hapless Great Andamanese the British Administration probably had no clear knowledge about the existence of a separate tribe like the *Jarawas* (we now know that they identify themselves as the Ang) and could not think to take care of the *Jarawas* separately. Once Colonial rulers completed counseling the Great Andamanese, perhaps they came to know about the existence of the Jarawas in the deep forest as a separate tribe. The intervention of the British administrators in the Jarawa territory began with the help of their new friend the Great Andamanese. Several punitive expeditions were arranged in order to suppress their unfriendly activities and to expand the habitation area around the Penal settlement. The Jarawas did not surrender instead they retaliated against the members of the expeditions causing several casualties of both sides. By the time the British administrators changed their policy from punitive measures to friendly contacts with the Jarawas a lot of encroachment and deforestation had taken place in their neighbouring resource areas of the Great Andamanese. The *Jarawas* must have watched such activities with great fear and suspicion. The Colonial rulers adopted the policy of capturing a few Jarawas and treat them with friendly gesture as they successfully did in case of the Onges. However, this method did not work with the Jarawas. Therefore, the encounter with the Jarawas continued.

The Sentinelese Situation

The Sentinelese, whose number has been estimated about 100 persons only, is perhaps the most isolated tribe in India. The 47 sq.km North Sentinel Island is situated at a distance of 64 km southwest of Port Blair. The British administrator Homfray was first to make an attempt to enter in the North Sentinel Island unsuccessfully in the year 1867. Police and a small group of Andamanese escorted him. The Island was left undisturbed for nearly 13 years. Later Portman, accompanied by Andamanese paid several visits to this Island during 1883 to 1887 with the hope to establish friendly contact. He, however, was greeted every time with the arrows of the Sentinelese. Such attempts were abandoned in course of time (Sarkar, 1993).

The Shompen Situation

The Shompens of Great Nicobar, a 1045 sq km island and located at a distance of 544 km from Port Blair, did not experience any intervention of worth mention from the Colonial rulers, though they were not unfriendly to the visitors in their island. It is reported that like the Onges, the Shompens also had to face the atrocities of the pirates from the neighbouring countries. In fact they could retain their isolation in the almost inaccessible terrain where they live (Awaradi, 1990).

Intervention after the Independence of India

The most significant change in the nature of intervention was from the punitive expeditions of the Colonial rulers to the welfare of the friendly tribes and befriending the unfriendly populations. The first reported intervention after the independence was an attempt by the Forest Department of Andaman in the 1949 to initiate general welfare of the Great Andamanese. Initially to put them as buffer against the Jarawas and then to protect them from the exploitation and to improve upon their condition of living the Forest Department brought the few dispersed Andamanese from various islands and put them in the Bluff Island. However, as the surviving individuals of this tribe could not find any viable resources to exploit for their survival or the initiator of the scheme could not provide them adequate infrastructure facilities ensuring availability of foods and other requirements to live on, the attempt did not succeed (Census of India, 1951).

In order to protect the tribes of the islands, the State introduced the Andaman and Nicobar Islands (Protection of Aboriginal Tribes) Regulations 1956 and the district administrators were vested with the responsibilities of both protection and welfare of the tribes of the islands. After 1950 various government and non-government agencies initiated welfare activities for the benefit of the Onges.

In accordance with the Act of 1956, the habited areas of the tribes had been declared as "Primitive Tribal Reserve Areas". However, there was no welfare programme for the tribes of the islands in the First Five Year Plan. During the Second Five Year Plan a fair weather dispensary was set up at the Little Andaman for providing medical aids to the Onges under the sector "Welfare of the Backward Classes". Besides the following activities were included during this Plan period (Sarkar, 1993).

- Dropping of food gifts in the areas inhabited by the Jarawas and the Sentinelese with a view to establishing friendly contacts with these tribes.
- Establishing contacts with the Shompens of Great Nicobar.

There were no dearth of policies of the State towards welfare and development of the endangered tribes of the Union Territory. When the Census of India enumerated the Andamanese population to be only 19 individuals in 1961, the State once again intervened. In order to prevent the tribe from physical extinction, on the advice of the experts, a scheme to bring the disintegrated and dispersed 19 individuals at one place was included in the Fourth Five Year Plan. The primary objectives were to encourage these individuals of different territorial and dialect groups to live at one place and interact with each other so that they may get a scope not only to create a sense of oneness but at the same time can establish marriage among themselves keeping aside their age-old territorial bondage and *beyera* (community hut) affiliation, under a compulsive situation. This time provision for all facilities like residential huts, supply of free ration and clothes, creation of coconut plantation and orchards as viable alternate economy; adequate medical care, formal education for the children had been included in the programme. The 19 individuals who had been eking out their existence either working as labour or as servants in some Burmese families, ultimately were rehabilitate at the Strait Island in 1970. The small 5 sq. miles island located at a distance of about 60 km from Port Blair has finally become their homeland, who were the proud and vibrant inhabitants of the whole of South and North Andaman Islands prior to 1858 (Sarkar, 1993).

This intervention of the State has two sides. The first and foremost being arrest of alarming decline in the population, preventing extinction of the Great Andamanese. The significant achievement of such intervention helped this people to grow their population from 19 to 43 in 2003, overcoming their social and demographic constraints, through marriages within themselves and even establishing marriages with non-Great Andamanese. This should be considered as an encouraging positive intervention on the part of the State.

However, the other side of the intervention cannot be accepted to be very encouraging. Easy availability of almost all the provisions required for day-to-day living, including foods and clothes at their doorsteps in the island itself, has made them completely dependent on the State. As a result they have lost their desire to exploit the surrounding marine and forest resources for survival. Regular contacts with the non-Great Andamanese at their island and also in other places caused emergence of an inferiority complex among the members of this tribe whose forefathers once mastered the Great Andaman Islands.

The larger society could not accept them within their fold. On the contrary they consciously maintain a distance with this population. The basic objective of the State to bring this endangered community nearer to the so-called main stream remains unfulfilled. This kind of failure, however, is not unexpected. In fact when the State had intervened in the life of the Great Andamanese her prime objective was to save the hapless population from being extinct, which could be achieved with satisfaction. Under the critical demographic situation this tribe lost the very urge to survive. Therefore, the State immediately extended all kinds of doles in order to undo the adverse effects of the erroneous policy of the Colonial rulers.

The steps taken by the State in case of the Great Andamanese seems to be justified in a critical situation, though it had many shortcomings. But it is very much difficult to understand why the State had facilitated creating a situation, which caused severe disturbances in the life of the Onges of Little Andaman and also of the Jarawas of South Andaman.

When the policy of populating these islands was accepted by the State, the members of the larger society knew the consequences of introduction of such schemes. The eye-opening example of the ill-fated Great Andamanese was before them. Even then, refugees from erstwhile East Pakistan (now Bangladesh), Tamil repatriates from Sri Lanka and Myanmar had been brought to these islands and rehabilitate in the vicinity of the Jarawa and the Onge territories. Intention was welfare of the displaced persons of the larger society. The lesson learnt from the sad episode of the Great Andamanese could not resist the State in taking such decision. For the sake of argument one may points out that such a policy was adopted on the basis of recommendations of some high-level expert committees. However, if one looks at the recommendations carefully, one may find that creation and maintenance of buffer zones between the tribes and the new settlers was the most important precondition towards implementation of the rehabilitation programme (Sinha, 1952). This, however, remained unattended. The people of the larger society, on the other hand, constantly make efforts to encroach upon the resource areas, both marine and forest, of these tribes in order to raise their own standard of living.

In the Little Andaman Island rehabilitation of the Bengali refugees started in 1969, which continued till 1979. Intermittently a few Nicobarese of the Car Nicobar Island came to settle here (1973), the Tamils from Sri Lanka and Myanmar were rehabilitate in 1977, where as the Moplahs were brought to settle in this island in 1979 (Danda, 1987).

The entire programme necessitated induction of several State machineries and manpower, which caused influx of population and disturbed the ecological balance. Prior to 1967 the Onges were the sole inhabitants of the 731sq km island and were distributed at three broad areas spread over the island. The programme of rehabilitation caused large-scale deforestation. Till March 1987 an area of 1117.64 hector was reclaimed through deforestation of which 816.00 hector was allotted for settlement of 398 families (Sarkar, 1993). Population of the island was 7,214, the Onges being 100 only. Considering the intensity of influx of population it may be assumed that the population might have reached around 15,000 by 2001 and thus overwhelmed the already endangered tribe of the island.

In order to protect the Onges from the adverse effects of such influx the State again intervened. The tribe was provided with settlements at Dugong Creek and South Bay. Though the intention of the State was to provide benefit of welfare measures, it cannot also be denied that the resettling of the Onges at two places, facilitated reclaim of forest for rehabilitation of the outside population.

In other word, the larger society's interest became more prominent at the cost of the existence of an ancient population. No one can deny that a number of welfare measures have been implemented for the betterment and development of the Onges. But the only positive result was the arrest in the rate of their population decline. Like the Great Andamanese they have also become totally dependent on the State for their livelihood and have been giving up the foraging activities in the context of interference of the people of neighbouring larger societies.

Had there been no intervention, barring the measured medical aids, the Onges could have survived with self-respect and honour like the Sentinelese. But the larger societies thought other wise. They always claim that interactions with them have protected this tribe from physical extinction, without accepting the hard reality that such interactions have been pushing the tribe towards extinction. The sea depth difference in the mindsets of this ancient tribe and their neighbouring larger societies would never be on same wavelength. Thus, becoming the dependants, the Onges would rapidly loose their confidence and vigor, essential to survive with honour as component of India's composite culture.

With the same intention to populate the islands, refugees from the then East Pakistan (now Bangladesh) were first brought to rehabilitate in the South and North Andaman Islands. Immigrant populations increased at Mayabander, Rangat, Port Blair and Ferrargunj, the adjacent tahasils of the Jarawa territory from 83,998 in 1971 to 2,17,719 in 1991. Population in the Andaman District became 3,14,239 in 2000 (Directorate of Economic and Statistics 2000 & 2001). This once again resulted into large-scale deforestation. Forest measuring 828.28 ha and 202.00 ha was cleared in the South and Middle Andaman respectively (Andaman & Nicobar Basic Statistics, 1987). Earlier 2,49,30 ha of forest had already been cleared during the Penal settlement (Bonington, 1908). Reduction in the resource areas pushed the Jarawas further inside the forest. The marine vessels also disturbed the aquatic resources of the tribe.

Even after observing all the ill effects on the Great Andamanese the democratic State decided to rehabilitate thousands of people near the habitat areas of the endangered tribes ignoring the probable fatal consequences on the life of this small population, nurturing ancient culture through ages.

The Jarawas did not accept the interference of the people of the larger societies and therefore retaliated with their bows and arrows in their own ways. The conflict intensified with the calculated encroachment into their forest resources by the neighbouring settlers. The process of resettlement had to face many problems for such frequent encounters with the Jarawas.

In order to overcome such situation of conflict, the old method of conciliation and befriending was adopted by the Administration. Though, in administrative parlance such programme was adopted to bring this foraging community in to the fold of larger societies so that they may also get the benefits of welfare measures, the ultimate objective was to pacify the unfriendly Jarawas, so that the interest of the larger societies to live undisturbed, is not jeopardized. With this mission Contact Party used to visit the Jarawa areas in the west coast to establish friendly relation with them. Such acts were expected to ease out the conflicts between the tribe and their neighbouring non-tribes (Sarkar, 1987).

The conflict reached at its peak when the State took a decision to connect the islands of the South Andaman with those of North Andaman by constructing Andaman Trunk Road (ATR) that passes through the Jarawas' resource areas. No one can claim that this ATR was constructed for the benefit of the Jarawas. It is the interest of the immigrant people of the larger societies, which received attention of the State since demand of the majority needs to be honoured in a democratic country no matter whatever consequences the small already endangered population had to face. The unexpressed underlined simple logic was perhaps that "for a handful of about 260 odd Jarawas the development process in the infrastructure and thereby in the life of about more than one lakh people cannot suffer".

Introduction of the ATR through the Jarawa territory virtually shattered the way of life of the tribe. They had to ultimately give up their unfriendly behaviour with the intruder to their areas, which shielded them so far from being victim of the sudden exposures to several unknown alien vices. The consequences of showing friendly gesture were almost similar to that of the Great Andamanese and the Onges. Diseases spread alarmingly, though that times the alert State machineries could prevent the small population from any serious casualty. But the several other activities like plying of vehicular traffic, frequent visit of outsiders including tourists, poaching and supply of alien food items have been in operation in the area. These would likely to push the Jarawas to a stage of total dependency on the larger societies like the Great Andamanese or the Onges.

After initiating measures those have tremendous adverse impact on the life and culture of the Jarawas, the State has once again shown concern about the survival of this endangered population. In fact the Administration has to initiate actions again in the interest of the larger societies.

Barring a few, almost the entire population, whether living in the vicinity of the Jarawa territory or elsewhere, demanded immediate steps by the Administration to prevent the Jarawas from coming out of their forest and entering in the villages or squatting on the ATR.

The Bench of Kolkata High Court intervened on the basis of Public Interest Litigation. The Government of India had to intervene by one more Expert Committee (Sarkar, 2003). It is apprehended that whatever may be the recommendations of the Expert Committee, the final implementation would have the same fate as had happened in case of earlier recommendations. The interest of the larger societies would receive the prime attention, as these endangered tribes are not in a position to voice their grievances before the authorities of the larger societies, who matters.

The story of the Shompens is no different. The Great Nicobar Island with an area of 1045 sq.kms, has been experiencing influx of outsiders since 1969 when 303 families of the Ex-Servicemen from mainland India had been resettled in this home land of the Shompens (Sarkar, 1993). This was followed by continuous increase in infrastructure development and in-migration of people. An area of 1499.66 ha of land was reclaimed through deforestation (Andaman & Nicobar Basic Statistics, 1987). Unlike the negrito tribes of the Andaman Islands the Shompens had never been unfriendly to the outsiders. In order to avoid the emerging situation they have been withdrawing themselves in the deep forest. However, it seems a matter of time when this self-reliance small tribe would also follow the foot steps of the other present day endangered tribes of the Andaman and Nicobar Islands.

Summary

In sum, the small tribes of Andaman and Nicobar Islands, when put into multiple external pressures by the influx of immigrant diverse populations from different parts of India, initially reacted in two different ways. The negrito tribes at the first instance retaliated to protect their resource areas and their societies as well. On the other hand the Shompens started withdrawing themselves from the contacts of the alien populations. However, except the Sentinelese, the other three negrito tribes could not succeed to resist tremendous continuous pressure of the alien people, equipped with advanced technological knowledge and ultimately succumbed to the latter's desire.

The legacy of befriending the unfriendly independent tribes by the Colonial rulers for successful colonization continued, though in different form. The apparent intention of present authorities is welfare of the tribes. However, this has other side too.

This process helped in pacifying the self-reliance tribes to a considerable extent, which ultimately facilitates smooth encroachment in to the resource areas of the tribes. The immigrant people through their several acts, consciously or unconsciously, intend to subjugate these once most active groups and transform them to fully dependant communities so that the larger society's life may prosper with out any hindrance from the earliest inhabitants of these islands.

Interventions at such stage by a welfare State like India, with a view to safeguarding the interest of small communities, in all respect, unfortunately often do not give the desired result for many reasons. Being a democratic country, the Nation aims at bringing all her citizen, irrespective of their levels of living, within the fold of, what in the State parlance, is known as "main stream" and providing them the benefits of welfare measures initiated by the State. In such endeavour, the Nation has to take due cognizance of both the recipient and the dominant populations as deemed fit for a democratic State. However, where the societies at the receiving end are not in a position to express their will and sentiment to the people of a completely different mindset, the latter decide the fate of the former without jeopardizing self interest. The present grave situation, in which these endangered tribes have been struggling from being extinct, is not their creation. The onus lies on several acts of both the Colonial rulers and the people of contemporary larger societies.

The lesson learnt from the past experiences could not change the mindset of the larger society. As a result, these small early inhabitants of the islands are destined to struggle for their biological survival. They are hardly accepted within the fold of the neighbouring larger dominant societies and are placed even beyond the periphery of the so-called "main stream" where they rapidly loose their ancient cultural heritage.

The other cultures, with relatively complex technological know-how and mindsets, get pleasure in demonstrating their dominance, no matter if such acts push the societies at the receiving end towards verge of extinction.

REFERENCES

Adhikari, Ahsim Kumar. 1984. "Hunter and Gatherers in India: A Preliminary Appraisal of their Structure and Transformation," *Journal of the Indian Anthropological Society,* 19 (1): 8-16.

Andaman and Nicobar Administration. 1987. *Andaman and Nicobar Islands. Basic Statistics.* Statistical Bureau, Port Blair: Andaman and Nicobar Administration Publication

____. 2000 & 2001. *Andaman and Nicobar Islands: At a Glance.* Directorate of Economics and Statistics, Port Blair: Andaman and Nicobar Administration Publication.

Awaradi, S.A. 1990. *Master Plan* (1991-2021), Port Blair: Andaman and Nicobar Administration.

Bhanu Ananda. 1989. *The Cholanaickan of Kerala. Calcutta*: Anthropological Survey of India.

Bonington, M.C.C. 1908. *Gazetteers of Andaman & Nicobar Islands.* Calcutta: Government Printing.

Census of India. 1931. *The Andaman and Nicobar Islands.* Vol.II, Part-I & II, Calcutta: Central Publication.

____. 1951 [1955]. *The Andaman and Nicobar Islands*. Vol. XVII, Part I & II, Delhi.

Danda, G. Dipali. 1987. "Little Andaman and the Onge," *Human Science*, 36: 66-91.

Sarkar, Jayanta. 1987. "Befriending the Jarawa: A Challenging Task," *Human Science*, 36: 1-12.

____. 1990. *The Jarawa*. Calcutta: Seagull Books on behalf of the Anthropological Survey of India.

____. 1993. "Endangered Tribes and their Development in Andaman and Nicobar Islands," (pp.1-45) in Arabinda Basu *et al.* (eds.), *Andaman and Nicobar Islanders: Studies on Small Populations*. Calcutta: Indian Anthropological Society.

____. 2003. "The Jarawa Destine: A Critical Appraisal of Some Recommendations," *Journal of the Indian Anthropological Society,* 38 (2&3): 167-172.

Sinha, Surajit Chandra. 1952. *Resettlement of East Pakistan Refugees in Andaman Islands: Report on Survey of Further Possibilities of Resettlement:* January-March 1952. Calcutta: Government of West Bengal.

TWELVE

LAND RELATIONS IN TRIBAL AREAS IN ORISSA: A Critical Assessment of State Interventions

PRASANA KUMAR TRIPATHY and NIBEDITA NATH

I

The land relations in tribal areas centered round rights over resources, land and forests. Land is the most important source of livelihood of the tribal people……Their economy being multiple loci, revolves round cultivation in donger and plain land, wage earning as agricultural labourer, collection of forest produces, hunting wild games, etc. in the forest land (Behera and Nath, 2004: 6). Forest is a resource to these people not merely in terms of fulfilment of basic needs and drives but also in regard to livelihood. Traditionally around 80 per cent of their food came from these sources and from shifting cultivation on forest land (Fernandes, 1997: 82). The forest is not only a source of food and medicine for the indigenous people and their domesticated animals but also it provides them with raw materials required for the construction of their houses. In their forest-based economy, activities like cultivation in the hill slopes, collection from the adjoining forest and hunting and trapping are interwoven (Behera and Nath, forthcoming).

The "plains" in tribal areas witnessed emergence of various land revenue systems in a similar pattern as evolved in case of other settled agricultural systems in plains. The "forests" in tribal areas also witnessed changing system of management with gradual, continuous and increasing control of the state. Both these processes affected the lives of people inhabiting in these areas particularly those who were culturally dependent on the latter and were losers being marginalized in the processes under the former. While the process of survey and settlement during the colonial period (Rao, 1990) and the land laws formulated during the post-independence period truncating the notion of "land to the tiller" (Tripathy, 2003) contributed towards process of marginalization of people who cleared the forests and established settled agricultural systems over generations. The tribal areas ever since early 19th century thus were subjected to British colonialism and through it to internal colonialism resulting in transfer of resources from the natives to the immigrants from the plains. The natives were gradually converted into resource less position ready to provide labour to the newly established owners. Similarly the changing rights over resources in tribal areas has been summarized by Sharma (1990) in the foreword of the Report of the Commissioner on Schedule Caste and Schedule Tribe,

> "The primary resources other than agriculture in the traditional economy are forests, *pastures* (wasteland and water) on which the ordinary people depend for their living. The wrong entitlement over resources of all descriptions started getting established during the British period. It was in that period that the intimate relationship between the resources and the local community, which was like that between a mother and the child, was ended and the State acquired monopoly rights there on. This colonial process of centralization has unfortunately got further reinforced under the tutelage of the new paradigm of development, which has been adopted in our country after independence. The full implications of this colonial developmental process are becoming clearer only now. Everywhere the lives support system of the local community and the common man at the moment is being snatched away by the abstruse state institutions and big people without any qualms of conscience. In this situation the people are engaged in a fierce struggle of their right to life. But the system is branding their current use of those resources as illegal and is driving them away taking undue advantage of its authority."

The role of State in the evolution of the modern sector has been significant in different parts of the globe. However, the process of evolution of modernity and modern sector has not been uniform. Capitalist state in general performed a progressive role in the transformation of traditional economy. Indian state like in many of the ex-colonial countries however lacked the progressivity in transforming the traditional economy. While the origin of modernity in the Indian context may be attributed unequivocally to the Indian State during the colonial period, it was through a process of co-integration of the traditional sector. Even freedom from colonialism did not qualitatively result in the change in the character and role of the state. The state historically performed a singular role in protecting the interests of the ruling sections and stabilizing their cultural (socio-economic-political) dominance. The state in performing the stabilizing role protected the valuation systems whose basis centred round the solitary factor "scarcity" of factors of production. In such a framework, primitive society can be characterized through tribal communities that existed in nature-abundant regions. The salient features of such societies can be characterized through similar activities by families of the community. Here acquisition of knowledge is based on perceptive sense experiences and the knowledge transmission, though acquired individually, is free without any costs. Low level of technology, high dependence on forests, shifting cultivation, minimum integration with rest of the economy, consumption based production, low accumulation, low division of labour with the exception of natural division of labour associated with low specialization, women occupying the center of economy, exchanges with other families through labour are some of the characteristics" (Bharathi, 2002).

In such a society the interaction of men with nature was in the most natural form and the level of forces of production was at the lowest level. Thus perceived scarcity if at all in such a society was in the sphere of knowledge of nature. The state was either non-existent or non-functional. The second stage may be perceived through the evolution of settled agricultural system and hence the emergence of "land scarce system". With the evolution of family, private property and state, the context of "scarcity" got introduced and people with lack of possession of any factor of production perceived scarcity of that factor. Thus, with the growth of settled agricultural systems, the perceived scarcity was in terms of land, which became fixed and limited. However, the perceived scarcity of a slave or a landless producer was dominantly land, while perceived scarcity of proprietors still continued to be knowledge of nature. However to the extent the proprietors' acquired control over resources through institutions of state and ideology, the dominant ideology centered round a system of land-based valuation, providing authority to owners of land. The process of acquisition of knowledge was private and the level of knowledge was also low. The other characterizations are "Land accumulation, bondedness, existence of agricultural labour in excess, share cropping, male superiority, non-separated households with interlinked consumption and production decisions, in active markets for resources of production are some of the characteristics of a land scarce system" (*ibid.*). The state under such a scenario represented the interests of owners of land (the scarce factor). In contrast the capitalist state evolving through a process of dissolution of the traditional state projected capital as a scarce factor and maintained a valuation in favour of capital. Such a society evolved through a long process of evolution of guilds, industries and markets based on socialization and division of labour. This resulted in the growth of productive power of labour. There was separation of labour from the means of production. Labour became free in a double sense, one from the means of production and the other from all factors contributing to their getting tied to the owner and/or means of production. This apparent freedom of labour was in fact a freedom for capital with the decline in the control of feudal owners over the material resources and organization of production. The socialization of labour and production resulted in enormous growth of knowledge, which became the property of owners of capital given the basis of private property and private appropriation of surplus and the perceived scarcity of knowledge of nature vanished. This empowered capital and the owners propagated capital scarcity as the dominant scarcity in society.

Given such a framework of analysis, one can perceive the changing role of state and the transitional problems can be visualized to be minimum when nature of transition is through a movement from one type of scarcity to the other, specifically from "land scarce system" to "capital scarce system". Problems of transition became enormous for societies where both the valuation systems co-existed along with communities least integrated to both the systems and the State turned out to be a dualist state protecting the interest of both owners of land and the owners of capital.

II

The role of State institutions in the transformation of the tribal societies thus relates to how much they have been integrated into the "land scarce systems" and "capital scarce systems" and in what status. In this chapter, an attempt has been made to examine the nature of integration of tribal communities in three districts of Orissa, which were historically part of three different geographical and administrative divisions under British administration. The district of Koraput with Jeypore *Jamindari* was under Madras Presidency, the district of Kalahandi with Feudatory state and *Jamindaries* was under Central Provinces and the district of Mayurbhanj was purely a Feudatory state. These three districts together contribute a share of 53.28 per cent of the tribal population of the state as per 1981 census. The major tribes inhabiting in the district of Mayurbhanj are Bathudi, Bhuiyan, Bhumij, Gond, Ho, Kolha, Munda and Santal. These tribes together constituted 91.83 per cent of the total tribal population in the district. The tribal population is about 56.67 per cent of the total population of the district. The dominant tribes of Kalahandi district are Gond, Kandha and Shabar/*Lodha*. Together they constitute 77.99 per cent of the tribal population of the district. The tribal population has a share of 30.95 per cent in the total population of the district. Similarly, the important tribes of Koraput are Bhottada, Gadaba, Gond, Kandha, Koya, Paroja, Saora and Shabar/*Lodha*, who constitute about 84.24 per cent of the tribal population in the district. The tribal constitute 54.31 per cent of the total population in the district (Census, 1981).

The level of development of the three districts and the land distribution can be examined from the Table 12.1. It is interesting to note that there is expansion of gross cropped area in the districts over time and the higher rate of expansion compared to the State average is noticed in the district of Koraput. There is expansion in the irrigated area in all the three districts, though relatively higher growth of irrigated area is noticed in the district of Koraput and least expansion is noticed in Kalahandi district. The irrigation level however remains much lower compared to the State average. In terms of production of food grains one observes relatively higher growth in Koraput district and lowest in case of Kalahandi district. Similar pattern is also observed in case of non-food crops production.

Table 12.1: Level of Development of Tribal Districts of Orissa.

Index	*Kalahandi*			*Koraput*			*Mayurbhanj*			*State*		
	59-60	93-94	% Increase	59-60	93-94	% Increase	59-60	93-94	% Increase	59-60	93-94	% Increase
GCA 000 hect	369	555	50.41	556	827	48.74	751	1188	58.19	6379	9747	52.79
Production Food crops 000MT	298	482	61.96	344	437	26.95	272	569	108.86	4137	8307	100.78
Non-food Crops	9	24	172.54	7	16	136.18	10	84	783.13	101	335	229.22
Per cent Irrigated Area	9.62	19.64		9.32	11.73		4.23	16.92		14.87	25.0	

There is a tendency of increasing proportion of Marginal Farmers (MF) in the State during 1970-71 to 1995-96. Though Mayurbhanj registered higher proportion of MF in total cultivating households compared to the state in 1995-96, the proportion is much less for the districts of Kalahandi and Koraput. However, one finds higher growth in proportion of MF overtime in the districts of Kalahandi and Mayurbhanj. One also observes decline in the proportion of Small Farmers (SF) over time at the state level as well in the three tribal districts. Together MF and SF constitute 80 per cent of the cultivating households having 45 per cent of total operated area. Only the district of Mayurbhanj registered higher proportion of MF and SF with 84 per cent households having 56 per cent of the operated area in the district. The lowest proportion is observed in the district of Kalahandi. (Agricultural Census, 1970-71 & 1995-96).

Apart from the MF and SF who possess limited access to land resources, the category of households who have fallen in the world is agricultural labour. Their numbers have increased significantly over time. They constituted 27.76 per cent of total main workers in 1981 at the state level. All the tribal districts registered higher proportion of agricultural labour with 33.60 per cent, 35.59 per cent and 28.47 per cent respectively for the district of Mayurbhanj, Kalahandi and Koraput. One also finds higher proportion of agricultural labour population among the main workers of tribal population with 39.46 per cent, 38.66 and 31.09 per cent respectively for the three districts (Census, 1981).

In the context of predominance of agricultural labour persons and growing number of marginal farmers in these districts, it will be of interest to analyse the educational status of tribal population. It is noticed that in 1981, while for the state the rate of literacy was 34.23 per cent, it was found to be 19.42, 16.10 and 25.66 per cent for the distrcts of Kalahandi, Koraput and Mayurbhanj respectively. The access to education is found to be significantly low for the tribes as indicated by the rates of 11.54, 6.31 and 14.50 per cent for the three districts respectively (Census, 1981). (Table 12.2).

The context for the landless and the marginal farmers to fall back on dependence on forest resources is found gradually reduced over time. As on 2002 out of the total forest area of 58135.47 sq. km 45.32 per cent are under Forest Department bulk of which (99%) as Reserve forest and the rest under Revenue department (48.84% of which are Protected Forests). The Reserved Forests and Protected Forests constituted 71.99 per cent of the total forest area in the State, while it is found to be 81.40, 85.59 and

Table 12.2: Land Distribution in Tribal Districts of Orissa

Land Size	*Kalahandi*				*Koraput*				*Mayurbhanj*				*State*			
	1970-71		*1995-96*		*1970-71*		*1995-96*		*1970-71*		*1995-96*		*1970-71*		*1995-96*	
	% No	% area	% No	% area	% No	% area	% No	% area	% No	% area	% No	% area	% No	% area	% No	% area
Marginal	17.58	2.8	39.60	12.01	32.67	9.33	41.45	14.11	44.17	14.41	56.91	23.88	43.3	11.95	53.66	19.73
Small	28.64	11.82	22.99	20.35	32.84	21.70	29.01	23.73	31.77	27.82	27.95	32.75	32.89	26.41	26.22	26.93
All	100.0	100.0	100.0	100.0	100.0	100.0	100.0	100.0	100.0	100.0	100.0	100.0	100.0	100.0	100.0	100.0

62.39 per cent for the three districts respectively. While in the tribal areas the access to forestland and resources is gradually denied, the diversion to non-forest use in the interest of the plains people is also evident. During 1982-2002 as per Economic Survey there has been officially approved transfer under 252 projects involving an area of 27563.18 hectares forestland for non-forest use (Economic Survey of Orissa, 2003-04). This is not the case in the State of Orissa only. The total forestland in the Indian nation is also reducing in an alarming rate. India has a total geographical area of 328.8 million hectares, out of which 74.78 million hectares, i.e. about 22.7 per cent

Table 12.3: Tribe-wise Proportion of Agricultural Labour in Main Workers in Tribal Districts of Orissa, 1981 Census

Tribe	*Population*	*% Agril. Labour in Main Workers*
Kalahandi		
Gond	233916	27.60
Gadaba	56413	28.38
Gond	88579	.4178
Shabar/Lodha	49900	45.15
Total	326594 (77.97)	
Mayurbhanj		
Bathoda	82478	40.97
Bhuiyan	41580	47.76
Bhumij	94214	53.95
Gond	21757	26.92
Ho	24967	32.55
Kolha	143724	37.14
Munda	25645	35.88
Santhal	403423	34.96
Total	837788 (91.83)	
Koraput		
Bhottada	233916	27.60
Gadaba	56413	28.38
Gond	88579	20.98
Kandha	366231	33.76
Koya	87052	7.34
Paroja	247304	35.13
Saora	45940	48.71
Shabar/Lodha	29970	50.81
Total	1155405 (84.24)	

were occupied by the forests at the time of Independence. They represented 2.2 per cent of the world's land area. The National Remote Sensing Agency (NRSA) reported 14.1 per cent of the total land area in India as forests while other studies indicate a still lower value of 10 per cent in 1990. Thus India is losing forests rapidly at the rate of 0.5 per cent per year. India's forests have been shrinking by 1.5 million hectares per year (Dash and Mishra, 2001: 19). (Table 12.3).

III

The plains in the tribal areas with settled agricultural systems were subjected to survey and settlement during the British period and created the basis for the growth of private property and growing importance of non-tribal in the region. The various land tenures existing in the feudatory States subsequently constituting these three districts was guided by British settlements.

The Feudatory state of Mayurbhanj witnessed the existence of tenure of village headmen as *Padhan* and above him *Sabarkar*. Together they were responsible for collection of rent, and to remit to the King after deducting a share of the collection. They enjoyed *Jagir* lands, which were settled against them on produce rent later on after conversion of *Sabarkar* into *Sardars*. The *Jagir* grants were also given for religious, social and service purposes (Religious—*Barheri Jagir, Bhaka Jagir*, *Raiguru Jagir*, *Social—Babuan Jagir* to Kshatriya, *Mahal Jagirs* to collecting agents in *Debottar Mahal, Dalai Jagir, Dakua Jagir*). Apart from these *Jagirs* there existed *Lakhiraj* tenures and service tenures granted for religious and social purpose. The religious grants were *Debottar, Brahmottar*, grant for social purposes were *Datta-Mahatram* and for service purposes such as *Datta-panpika*. The tenants were guided by Mayurbhanj Tenancy regulation of 1909 regarding occupancy status with continuous possession for 12 years. But this regulation did not apply to lands held in lieu of wages or to the *Nijote* (self-cultivated) land of a *Lakhirajdar* or any other landholder.

The present district of Kalahandi comprises the ex-feudatory state of Kalahandi and Khariar Zamindari. In the ex-state of Kalahandi the various tenures were *Zamindars* (proprietors of the estates) but under the control of the King, Gaontia, village headmen, enjoying *Bhogra* land (equivalent to 20 to 25 per cent of the total rental of the village). The *Gaontia* had power to evict a tenant for non-payment and the reclaimed land from waste or ejectment constituted *Khudkast* land. Apart from *Gaontia* tenure there was *Sikimi Gaontia, Jagir* holders for services to the community (washerman, barber, blacksmith etc.). *Nalia Jagirs* for national militia and later on engaged as dak carriers or attending to officers. In the ex-state some *Gaontias* were also collecting revenues from persons resorting to shifting-cultivation particularly in the Khalsa area. In the ex-*Zamindari* of Khariar there existed Maufi tenures (*Maufi Khariati* and *Maufi Khidmati,* for personal services to *Zamindar*). *Thekadars* were the village head to collect rents from tenants for the *Zamindar*. They were granted Sir lands.

The present district of Koraput comprises of Jaipur ex-estate and other semi-independent *Zamindaries* such as Pachpenta and Bissamcuttack. Some parts like Kodpat Pargana and Salami Mutta were under Bastar. These areas were known as agency areas as they were put under the special control of the Collector or agent to the Government. The estates were administered partly on *Royatwari* system and partly on village rent system known as *Mustajari*. In the *Royatwari* the tenant paid systems rents to officials of the King directly, while the *Mustajari* system was similar to *Gaontia* system of Central provinces enjoying rent-free land known as *Hetha bhumi* or a percentage of the collection. There were other tenures like *Inam* lands are gift to Brahmins, mokhasadars to relatives of King and service grants for service extended to the King. These regions were governed by the Madras Estates Land Act, 1906. In the *Mustajari* system the tenants were completely at the mercy of the Mustajars.

Prevalence of various forms of intermediaries enjoying authority during the British period on the one hand served the colonial interest of revenue expansion and on the other growth of non-tribal interests in the regions. The state interventions in providing occupancy rights to tenants and abolition of intermediaries during the post-independent period emerged not as a measure of structural change but only restructuring of the erstwhile established owners of land solitarily due to adoption of definition of "to cultivate" which meant "to till" or husband the land for purpose of raising or improving agricultural produce, whether by manual labour or use of cattle or machinery or to carry on agricultural operation thereon, as a result of which "to cultivate personally" meant to cultivate on one's own account:

(i) by one's own labour
(ii) by labour of any member of one's family or
(iii) under personal supervision of one-self or any member of one's family by hired labour or by servants on wages payable in cash or kind but not in crops share (Report of the Land Reforms Committee Orissa, 1958: 14).

While such a definition provided the context for continuance of the traditional non-peasant owners in the new disposition, it completely negated the norm of 'land to the tiller' and resulted in the stabilization of the marginalization process initiated earlier "The survey and settlement operations identified different categories of land, determined tribal rights on land, fixed rent and thus grafted concept of private property in land into the tribal system. Settlement operations turned land into a saleable commodity. Tribal lost its non-negotiable character and could easily pass from tribal to non-tribal under certain circumstances" (Tripathy, 2003: 84).

The forest laws were no exception. As observed earlier:

> "The forest laws at first regulated and later denied tribal rights on the forest and the produce of forest. *Shifting* cultivation was adversely affected and the forest products no longer belonged to the tribal but were appropriated by the state for the use of the class it represented. The tribal were alienated from the forests, which had provided over ages, fodder, fuel, building materials, agricultural implements, medicines and even the most important requirement of existence-food to them. A section of tribal who earlier depended on forest became marginalized and joined the ranks of unemployed, casual labour in search of wage employment. This ensured a cheap and elastic supply of labour to industries and mines and at the same time turned the 'natural' tribal into a 'factor' for sale in the market" (*ibid*).

The various Forest Acts used by British India were Forest Act, 1865 followed by Forest Act, 1878 and the First Forest Policy Resolution promulgated in 1894 and the subsequent Forest Act of 1927. The objectives of various Acts passed by the British authority may be summed as (1) establishment of monopoly power over forests (2) exploitation of the forest for commercialization (3) curtailment of the rights of local people to use the forests and its products. The post-independent State Forest Act, 1972 and subsequently Government of India Forest Act of 1980 amended in 1988 continued the legacy in a more systematic manner resulting in the present status of tribal as "intruders into forests". As forests have always been an intrinsic part of the economy of the indigenous people, their reservation by the state has reduced the self-provisioning ability of local peasants (Baviskar, 1995).

The other important state intervention in the region is opening of railways and roadways resulting in the migration of peasants and traders from crowded plain areas who settled permanently in tribal areas and also the emigration of cheap labour.

> "The introduction of communication network also generated demand for forest products. The opening process also resulted in the growth of mining and industry, which resulted in large-scale dispossession of tribal lands and forests. The important consequences of opening up of tribal economy was that the hitherto closed tribal economy was infected by the culture of market economy whose rules of game were in contradiction to internal dilactics of the tribal economy - the tribal mode of production was swallowed by the superior mode of production of the non-tribal, which provided a very marginal place for the tribal" (Tripathy, 2003: 84).

The other instrument for acquisition of land by the State was the Land Acquisition Act of 1894 and subsequently amended in 1984, which enabled the State not only to acquire land in the name of "public purpose" but also for companies. So far as Public purpose is concerned "it is not necessary that land when taken should be made available to the public at large, but it is enough if it is in the general interest of community as opposed to individual interest" (Land Acquisition Act, 1995). This perspective resulted in the displacement of large number of persons in the tribal districts through projects which adversely affected the landless agricultural labour households and persons dependent on forestland and forests for which they possessed no record of rights.

Most of the mega dams, mines, wild life sanctuaries and heavy industries were set up in the remote areas, which displaced the tribal people on a massive scale (Fernandes, 1991; Mohapatra, 1990; Mishra, 1996). The big dams submerge vast land and displace thousands of people from their original habitations in the name of "national development," without considering the views of the Project Affected Populations (Mohan, 2002: 2). Most of the development projects in Orissa are invariably located in inland hilly terrain, basically inhabited by ethnic communities belonging to STs, SCs and OBCs (Swain and Panigrahi, 1999: 164-165). It is needless to say that big dams and irrigation projects are the largest source of displacement of the people from homelands in Orissa. It has been calculated that during the last forty years about 56,377 families comprising roughly 2.7 lakhs people have been displaced due to construction of dam/irrigation projects in Orissa. In other words, on an average 5,000 persons have been displaced in a year (Dalue, 1993: 25). Tribal people cultivate on hill slopes and government lands. They have only customary rights and no legal rights over those lands. The tribal people own very little landed property according to the modern legal norms or rules of the Land Acquisition Act 1984 (Nath and Behera, 2005). But only cultivation on lands does not make them eligible for any compensation package under Land Acquisition Act that recognizes only such persons who possess legal rights on land (ORG, 1998). Significantly, the Land Acquisition Act 1984 only recognizes individual and not collective or community rights. The indigenous people have only customary rights over land and no legal rights. For the purpose of payment of compensation the customary rights are not recognized under the Land Acquisition Acts (Swain and Panigrahi, 1999: 170). A total area of 3,943,53 acres of forestland was submerged in the three districts, viz. Koraput, Kalahandi and Nawarangpur due to the construction of the dam on the river Indravati (Behera, 2003: 24).

IV

The village level data on land particulars obtained from three unirrigated villages of Mayurbhanj, Kalahandi and Koraput are analyzed in the Table 12.4. While the sample village of Kalahandi has tribal population and people belonging to SC and OBC categories, the sample villages of Mayurbhanj and Kalahandi have only ST and OBC groups. As per Census data, 1981, the sex ratio is found to be highest for sample village of Mayurbhanj followed by Kalahandi and Koraput. High sex ratio in these villages indicates importance of women among people and may also be due to aspects of male emigration from the village. The Kalahandi village has high agricultural labour population followed by Mayurbhanj and the least in Koraput village.

Table 12.4: Forest land Distribution in Tribal Districts as on 2002 (sq. km)

District	*Forest Land under Forest Department*		*Forest Land under Revenue Department*			*Total*
	RF	URF	DPF	UDPF	Other forests	
Kalahandi	1449.03	0.98	1992.51	313.37	631.81	4387.70
Koraput	2138.26	2.01	3758.15	661.92	3950.13	10510.47
Mayurbhanj	3330.14	2.20	245.06	—	814.73	4392.13
State	26329.12	20.55	11685.68	3838.78	16261.34	58135.47

The land utilization pattern in the villages indicates relatively higher importance of reserved land and cultivable waste in the sample village of Koraput followed by Mayurbhanj. (Table 12.5). Among the households high proportion belonged to agricultural labour in the sample village of Mayurbhanj and high marginal farmers category in the sample villages of Kalahandi and Koraput. The inequality of land distribution is found very high for Kalahandi followed by Koraput. Regarding dependence of villagers on forests and availability of state sponsored programmes it is observed that relatively higher allotment of ceiling land is found in the Koraput village and lowest in the Mayurbhanj village. The relatively lower level if agricultural labour households in Koraput and Kalahandi may be due to allotment of ceiling land converting them into marginal farmers. The degree of encroachment of land by the various households is found very high in the Koraput village and Kalahandi village and least in Mayurbhanj village. None of the households in all the three villages reported that they enjoyed freedom to fell trees. Relatively higher proportion of households reported freedom to collect forest products in Mayurbhanj village followed by Koraput village, though such freedom to collect from outside the village is found low in all the three villages. The payment of penalty for collection of forest produce to the forest officials is found highest in Kalahandi village followed by Koraput village. A sizeable proportion of households (about 70%) indicated unpleasant relationship with forest officials and the highest being in the Kalahandi village. Relatively higher allotment of State sponsored programmes is noticed in Kalahandi and Mayurbhanj villages.

Table 12.5: Profile of Study Villages

<table>
<tr><th>Sl. No.</th><th colspan="2">Particulars</th><th>Kalahandi</th><th>Koraput</th><th>Mayurbhanj</th></tr>
<tr><td>1</td><td colspan="2">No. of Households</td><td>67</td><td>115</td><td>51</td></tr>
<tr><td rowspan="3">2</td><td rowspan="3">Caste</td><td>SC</td><td>14</td><td>—</td><td>—</td></tr>
<tr><td>ST</td><td>45</td><td>86</td><td>44</td></tr>
<tr><td>OBC</td><td>8</td><td>29</td><td>7</td></tr>
<tr><td>3</td><td colspan="2">Population</td><td>309</td><td>616</td><td>163</td></tr>
<tr><td>4</td><td colspan="2">Sex ratio</td><td>1116</td><td>1033</td><td>1203</td></tr>
<tr><td>5</td><td colspan="2">Proportion of Agril. Lab in Main workers</td><td>45.28</td><td>1.33</td><td>32.83</td></tr>
</table>

V

The profile of the un-irrigated villages of the three districts testifies that the agricultural labour households and marginal farmers in one monsoon determined agriculture find themselves unemployed or underemployed in major part of the year. (Table 12.5) The continuing dependence on forest and forest land without consent of the state and payment of penalty has implications in terms of inadequacy of resources, which can ensure a decent living with basic amenities of life as enjoyed by people in the plains. The state interventions in the shape of anti-poverty measures are inadequate and often misplaced as they fail to increase the resource base of the beneficiaries, though they serve the market interest through increasing demand for consumer goods. The interventions of the state, which acted inimical to the interests of the marginalized sections in tribal areas are the land laws based on a definition of 'personal cultivation'. Sharma (1990) in the Report of the Commissioner for Scheduled Castes and Scheduled Tribes noted,

Table 12.6: Land Utilization Pattern in the Village

Sl. No.	*Particulars*	*Kalahandi*	*Koraput*	*Mayurbhanj*
1	Ryoti land	331.86	400.81	105.93
2	Rserved land (*Rakshit*)	63.32	443.77	58.82
3	Public land (*sarba sadharana*)	8.22	16.87	4.28
4	Cultivable waste(*Abad jogya*)	0.48	73.80	15.41
5	*Abad ajogya*	6.40	44.25	3.98
	Total	410.28	979.50	188.42

> "The first step for protecting the right to life related to land will have to be to ensure that, whatever may be the law, or even if the law is silent on this issue, the person who is cultivating a piece of land continues to be in possession of that land. This principle should be openly promulgated and the fact of possession through cultivation should be entered in government records".

Next in order are the various forest laws, which systematically denied access of tribal and other marginalized sections into forest and forestlands. The Report (1990) also noted,

> "In the new frame, the symbiotic relationship between the forests and forest dwellers was not recognized and the forests became the property of the state. After the state acquired monopoly rights over the forests, a formal system was established for their management which gradually became comprehensive and also strong. The biggest irony of this change was that the forest dweller who has a life long relationship with the forests- which are their very homes, their religion, their culture and their everything was conspicuous by its absence in that frame. In this formal structure, which recognizes only administrative and market relations, an all-out effort has been made to see that these live-long mother-child relationships are transformed into market relationships.....It is on account of this basic lack of understanding, that there is a state of confrontation and regime of destruction in almost all the tribal areas which in final analysis means great injustice to the tribal people".

The forests, the mainstay of tribal economy, were reserved in the interest of the nation and the indigenous people remained in the mercy of the officials from the plain land. The forest resources were taken away from the remote areas for the development of the people of more advanced communities (Vyasulu, 1985; Mohanty, 1997). The instrument through which state acquired any land in any area, particularly in tribal areas was the provisions under Land Acquisition Act of 1984, which very often ignored the claims of toiling people, producers who either had no resource or no record of possession of resources, on which they were dependent. This is largely due to the inability of the forest dwellers and people's groups to reach the court and set a new legal discourse on natural resources and traditional rights (Pathak, 1994). Sharma (1990) in the above-mentioned Report nōted.

> "The biggest irony is that a 19th century colonial law like the Land Acquisition Act is being used indiscriminately in the great voyage of development. This law does not admit the concept of right to life and the will of the Raj has been accorded the hoary status of 'public purpose'. He further noted "Acquisition of land becomes a certainty, once a decision is taken about establishment of a project. Invitation of objections in accordance with the law thereafter is a mockery of the whole system. Thus, even though the letter of law may be followed but its intention is not being honoured".

State interventions in the context of a dualistic valuation system, in which the interests of traditional owners of land and new owners of capital are protected, become devoid of the finer human sensibilities to protect the interests of the weakest sections of the society. Indigenous people, or people with characteristics similar to that of indigenous people, are in many places regarded as somewhat backward, and are thought to "not know what is best for them". Phrases like this are used by government/state to defend encroachments on indigenous people's rights, by saying that the intention is to "develop" these people (Behera, 2003: 6). The dominant classes are able to articulate their demands whereas the indigenous people being poor and unorganized lose much than the dominant vocal section of the society (*ibid*). It will be pertinent to highlight the observations made by Sharma (1990) in his report which states:

Table 12.7: Land Ownership in Villages

Sl. No.	*Particulars*	*Kalahandi*		*Koraput*		*Mayurbhanj*	
		% hhs	*% area*	*% hhs*	*% area*	*% hhs*	*per cent area*
1	Landless	20.89	—	7.83	—	31.37	—
2	Marginal Farmers	52.23	15.73	41.74	24.34	21.57	12.18
3	Small Farmers	11.9	7.45	35.65	42.21	43.13	70.94
4	Medium & Big	14.93	76.81	14.78	33.45	3.92	16.86
	All	100	100	100	100	100	100

> "The state can broadly be said to have three primary responsibilities viz., law and order, protection and development. In the anxiety to maintain order and in the hurry for development as also in the dazzle of its glitter, the dark lanes of the state's responsibility for protection of the poor, particularly the SCs and STs, have been forgotten. Moreover, there is no hesitation in supporting the vested interests entrenched in the old as well as new structures under the cover of policies, principles and laws and even in striking against those whom the state is expected to protect'.

The overriding power of the "eminent domain" of the state is clearly reflected in the whole process of displacement and rehabilitation of the indigenous people of the UIHEP ((Behera, 2003: 34). In case of UIHEP private lands (both *patta* and *non-patta*) were forcefully acquired under the Land Acquisition Act, 1894 for the mega dam. But this forced eviction violated the basic right as enshrined in Indian Constitution. Article 21 of the constitution guarantees the right to livelihood apart from meaning the right to live with dignity (Behera and Nath, 2004: 6). It is a pity they the State imposed many policies in the area without consulting the people. People were forced to accept some decisions, which were detrimental to their life and livelihood.

Thus, looking from the perspective the marginalized sections, the appropriate state interventions would be to consider the stark reality of communal basis of tribal life and reorganize their production systems on collective framework rather than individual framework. Extension of the same principle to plains can also generate the basis for reorganization based on norms of 'land to the tiller' and generation of productive power through collective action. With such an understanding, the state can reorient the development paradigm with inclusion of interests of local people part of 'public purpose' in any development project.

Table 12.8: Dependence on Forests and State sponsored programmes

Type		*Kalahandi*		*Koraput*		*Mayubhanj*	
		No.	*Area*	*No.*	*Area*	*No.*	*Area*
No. of landless		14		9		15	
No. of hhs receiving ceiling land		15	25.76	31	53.0	8	11.10
No. of house-holds encroaching land		19	28.9	51	83.2	3.	5.5
No. of hhs reporting that they are free to fell trees		—		—		—	
No. of hhs reporting that they are free to collect forest product (per cent)	Inside	61.19		69.56		78.43	
	Outside	11.94		12.17		17.64	
No. of hhs reportedly paid penalty (per cent)	Inside	19.40		3.47		—	
	Outside	16.41		22.61		17.64	
No. of hhs reporting relationship with forest officials	Unpleasant	83.58		63.47		66.66	
No. of hhs received IRDP assistance (per cent)		41.79		26.08		35.29	

REFERENCES

Agricultural Census. 1970-71 and 1995-96

Behera, D.K. 2003. *Impact of Upper Indravati Hydroelectric Project on the Indigenous People.* Report submitted to Winrock International India, New Delhi.

Behera, D.K. and Nibedita Nath. 2004. "Impact of a Mega Dam Project on the Land Sources of the Project Affected Indigenous People of Kalahandi District, Orissa," *Man and Life,* 30 (1&2): 1-18.

Behera, D.K. and Nibedita Nath. 2004. "Resource Conservation and Utilization through Indigenous Knowledge in a Tribal Community of Orissa, India," paper presented in the international conference "Orality, Literacy and Cultural Diversity" held at University of Jululand, South Africa

Bharathi, M. 2002. *Philosophical Essay on Crisis and Development in Marxian Framework.* Thesis submitted for De Lit Degree to Ambedkar Open University, Hyderabad.

Census of India, 1981.

Dash, M.C. and P.C. Mishra. 2001. *Man and Environment.* Kolkata: Macmillan India Limited.

Daula, A. K. 1993. *Environmental Impact of Large Reservoir Projects on Human Settlement.* New Delhi: Ashish Publications.

Fernandes, Walter. 1991. "Power and Powerlessness: Development Projects and Displacement of Tribal," *Social Action,* 41 (3): 243-270.

____. 1997. "Displacement of Tribal: Struggles and Implications for Resettlement," in George Pfeffer and D.K. Behera (eds.), *Contemporary Society: Tribal Studies.* Vol. 2. New Delhi: Concept Publishing Company.

Mishra, Nita. 1996. "Tribal Resistance in the Chhechhari Valley: A Report," *Economic and Political Weekly,* 31 (24): 1539-40.

Mohan. M. 2002. *Development, Displacement and Rehabilitation: A Study on Project Affected Populations of Somasila Irrigation Project.* Unpublished Ph.D. Dissertation, Department of Anthropology, S. V. University, Tirupati.

Mohanty, B.B. 1997. "State and Tribal Relationship in Orissa," *Indian Anthropologist,* 27 (1): 1-17.

Mohapatra, L.K. 1990. "Rehabilitation of Tribals Affected by Major Dams and Other Projects in Orissa," in A.P. Fernandes (ed.), *A Report on the Workshop on Rehabilitation of Persons Displaced by Development Projects.* Myrada (Bangalore): Institute for Social and Economic Change.

Nath, Nibedita and D.K. Behera. (forthcoming). "The So-called Development, Displacement, Dispossession: An Analysis of the Forest and Land Rights of the Project Affected Tribal People," in R. M. Sarkar (ed.), *Land and Forest Rights of Tribal.* New Delhi: Serials Publications.

Operations Research Group (ORG). 1998. Socio-Economic Survey of DPs of Upper Indravati Project. Report submitted by ORG to UIHEP, Orissa Hydro Power.

Orissa District Gazetteers (Kalahandi. 1980. Gazetteers Unit. Department of Revenue, Cuttack: Orissa Government Press.

Orissa District Gazetteers (Koraput) 1966. Gazetteers Unit. Departmentof Revenue, Cuttack: Orissa Government Press.

Orissa District Gazetteers (Mayurbhanj). 1967. Gazetteers Unit. Department of Revenue, Cuttack: Orissa Government Press.

Pathak, Akhileswar. 1994. *Contested Domains*. New Delhi: Sage Publications.

Rao, R.S., 1990. *History of an Ahistorical People in Peoples History,* a Booklet published by ISSC, Jyoti-Vihar, Burla.

Report on Operational Holdings in Orissa, 1995-96, Agricultural Census Commissioner, Board of Revenue, Govt. of Orissa.

Report of the Land Reforms Committee Orissa. 1958. Revenue Department. Government of Orissa.

Sharma, B.D. 1990. Report of the Commissioner for Scheduled Castes and Scheduled Tribes, Twenty-ninth Report, 1987-89. Faridabad: Government of India Press.

Swain, M. and N. Panigrahi. 1999. "Development, Displacement and Rehabilitation in Orissa," *Man and Life,* 25 (3&4): 163-175.

The Economic Surveys of Orissa. 2002. Directorate of Economics and Statistics, Government of Orissa.

The Economic Surveys of Orissa. 2003-2004. Directorate of Economics and Statistics, Government of Orissa.

The Land Acquisition Act. 1995. Allahabad: Central Law Agency.

Tripathy, P. K. 2003. "Political Economy of Tribal Systems," *Journal of Humanities and Social Sciences,* 2 ( ): 82-89.

Vyasulu, V. 1985. "Under Developing Koraput," *South Asian Anthropologist,* 6 (1): 63-71.

THIRTEEN

EMPOWERING THE TRIBAL BARGADARS*: A Case Study from Malda District in West Bengal

MD. BASAR ALI

Background

This paper is mainly based on the case studies of the tribal people of Malda District in West Bengal, belonging to a specific socio-economic category. This socio-economic category is termed as "sharecropper" or "*Bargadar*" in West Bengal. A bargadar is a person in the land tenure system in West Bengal. *Bargadars* are also known as *Bhag-chasis,* who is not the owner of the land but cultivates the land and gets a portion of the crop after the harvest. Traditionally they are tied to the landowner's family and in many cases to the absentee landlord. But before the introduction of 'Bargadar act', the bargadars did not enjoy any record of right in the land, which they cultivated. Bargadars are the actual cultivators of the land without having any ownership right. In rural West Bengal bargadars constitute a substantial portion of the peasantry.

Before the introduction of West-Bengal Land Reform Act there was no legal protection of the bargadars from being evicted by the landowners. Even after the promulgation of the Land Reforms Act in 1955, the landowners continued to exploit the bargadars in various ways by using their superior

* This paper is an outcome of a research project entitled "Rural Poverty, the Developmental State and Spaces of Empowerment in Bihar and West Bengal, Eastern India" which was funded by Economic Research Council, U.K. and was conducted by the University of Cambridge and University of Keele, U.K The fieldwork was conducted during October 1998 and continued up to December 1999.

position in the existing socio-political system. The left parties took a major role in West Bengal in upholding the interest of the bargadars by organizing peasant movements and through the implementation of the legislation under a specific governmental programme named "Operation Barga" taken up after the Left Front government came to power in 1977. The Left Front Government gave serious attention to the problem of safeguarding the interest of the weaker share croppers in the West Bengal. The cause of the sharecroppers was taken up in right earnest. According to Bhaumic (1993), tenancy reforms under Left Front rule actually take the shape of an organized struggle of the share tenants. The programme Operation Barga was launched for the quick recording of the names of bargadars in order to secure their legal rights against rent-enhancement and eviction by the landowners and which also enabled the sharecroppers to claim a share of the crop. The crop sharing according to law can be of two types, which are: (i) when the bargadar gives the agricultural inputs like plough, manure, seed etc. then he gets 75 per cent of the crop, and (ii) when the landowner supplies the agricultural inputs then the bargadar gets 50 per cent of the crop. This was also accompanied by several other measures such as providing the bargadars the facility of institutional finance (Pramanic 2004). The whole idea was to alter the existing power structure in the countryside through an organized movement of the bargadars in order to free them from the grip of the exploiter-landlords and village moneylenders.

In the initial years this programme recorded spectacular success in terms of the number of registered bargadars. The recently published West Bengal Human Development Report (May 2004) by the Development and Planning Department of the Government of West Bengal reported that the total number of recorded Bargadars in the state in 2000 was 1.68 million, which accounted for 20.2 per cent of the agricultural households. The report further stated that the land covered under the cultivation of registered bargadars is 8.2 per cent of the arable land in the state. But the same report as well as an earlier one observed that the initial political activism regarding the recording of the bargadars declined over the years and as a result, the pace of the Operation Barga programme "tapered off in the mid-1980s and since then the rate of additional registration has been negligible" (WBHDR, 2004: 30-32; Mukharji & Bandopadhyay, 1993: 41). An interesting projection was presented in the Mukharji and Bandopadhyay report which calculated the rate of recording of the bargadars during December 1981 to September 1992 and projected the rate to see how much time would it take to bring the then remaining 5 lakh odd Bargadars under registration. They found that it would take more than 15 years to record those bargadars. The authors of the report observed: "…. the unfinished task is still considerable….The rate needs to be accelerated".

Under this background, we would now bring in the issue of the exploitation and eviction of bargadars in terms of deprivation from the agricultural land in which they have been enjoying traditional and recorded rights. It should be mentioned in this context that the eviction of bargadars have been taking place either through the maneuverings of the local elites or by the State itself as the state has failed to provide the existing legal safeguard. In this study we would deal with the case of bargadars who belongs to schedule tribe population of West Bengal. But before going into the details let us again look into the pages of the West Bengal Human Development Report. In pages 39-42, under the second chapter of the Report entitled "Land Reforms" a "disturbing feature" is noted. The disturbing feature refers to the rapid increase in landlessness among the rural households in West Bengal despite land distribution and registration of bargadars. To quote from the report: "There have been recent reports of increasing land alienation by *Pattadars*, and of eviction of bargadars, thus suggesting that the benefit of the land reform have been relatively short-lived at least for some rural household" (WBHDR, 2004: 40). Interestingly, the WBHDR did not make any attempt to classify, let alone analyze the cases of the eviction of bargadars on the basis of the types of sources that caused such impoverishments to this important category of reform benefited peasantry (Guha, 2004). The report however, quoted some statistics from another study sponsored by the State Institute of Panchayats and Rural Development, which found that as a whole 14.13 per cent of the recorded bargadars have been evicted since land reform began in West Bengal. The district-wise figures of bargadar eviction have also been quoted from the same study, which show that percentages vary between 31.6 in Jalpaiguri to 5.66 in Malda (Chakrabarty *et al.*, 2003). We should note that all these eviction figures refer to recorded bargadars. No mention or hint is given about the eviction of unrecorded bargadars who are one of the most vulnerable groups among the peasantry in rural West Bengal.

Study Area

Our study area consists of three villages, namely, Kantabari, Narioli and Jhajra, which belongs to Mangal Bari II Gram Panchayat under Old Malda block of Malda district. The village Kanta Bari consists of 93 households, which contains mixed ethnic population. There are 19 households in Narioli, all of which belong to the Santal Community and Jhajra consists of 132 households, which is a multiethnic village.

Objectives of the Study

This study has the following objectives:

- To make an exploration into the pattern of occupational changes of the tribal populations from cultivation to other occupations from the past to present generations.
- To present a few case studies of the tribal bargadars regarding the problems of their empowerment in the field of agriculture at Old Malda block of Malda district.
- To formulate some suggestions so that the bargadars could be empowered under the changing socioeconomic and political conditions.

Methods and Materials

For this study genealogical data have been collected from 1 86 households of Santal and Malpaharia community of Kantabri, Jhagra and Narioli villages of Old Malda block of Malda district of West Bengal. This exploratory research is mainly based on some case studies and field observations.

Table 13.1: Age Group Distribution of Occupation of Living and Dead Persons of Tribal (Santal and Malpahari) Families of the Village Kantabari, Jhagra and Narioli

Age group	*Agricultural labour*	*Owner cultivator*	*Share-cropper*	*Cultivator on contract*		*Non-Agricultural labour*	*Skilled Technical worker*	*Total*
				share cropper's land	*Owner cultivator's land*			
16 -20	47(2.06)	16(0.70)	27(1.18)	9(0.93)	10(0.43)	82(3.60)	21(0.92)	212
21 -25	44(1.93)	14(0.61)	33(1.44)	15(0.65)	11(0.48)	98(4.30)	28(1.22)	243
26 -30	48(2.10)	17(0.74)	29(1.27)	15(0.65)	18(0.79)	84(3.68)	12(0.52)	223
31 -35	56(2.45)	14(0.61)	31(1.36)	10(0.43)	25(1.09)	68(2.98)	15(0.65)	229
36 -40	59(2.59)	17(0.74)	41(1.80)	28(1.22)	22(0.96)	52(2.28)	7(0.30)	226
41 -45	64(2.81)	34(1.49)	44(1.93)	31(1.36)	28(1.22)	38(1.66)	7(0.30)	247
46 -50	57(2.50)	38(1.66)	46(2.02)	37(1.62)	22(0.96)	34(1049)	4(0.17)	228
51 -55	59(2.50)	36(1.58)	29(1.27)	10(0.43)	40(1.75)	54(2.37)	2(0.08)	230
56 -60	57(2.50)	27(1.18)	22(0.96)	11(0.48)	42(1.84)	48(2.10)	2(0.08)	216
60 +	69(3.30)	29(1.27)	13(0.57)	15(0.65)	44(1.93)	50(2.19)	3(0.13)	223
Grand Total	560 (24.59)	242 (10.62)	315 (13.83)	181 (7.94)	262 (11.50)	608 (26.70)	1012 (4.43)	277

Note : Figures in parentheses represent percentages.

Findings of the Study

Table 13.1 has been compiled from the genealogies of the Santal and the Malpaharia individuals of the study area. So, there are both living and dead persons (male and female) within the total population. The data show that in the earlier period most of them were cultivators, and non-agricultural labourers were fewer in number. Over time, the number of owner cultivators has declined with an almost simultaneous increase in the number of day labourers. The first three columns of Table 13.1 show an interesting trend. If we observe the age group-wise distribution of the number of agricultural labourers, then we find that in the earlier period there were more agricultural labourers but the number of owner cultivators increased from 60+ to 41-45, then declined among the tribal of the study area. In case of bargadars the number shows almost a jump from 60+ upto the age group 36-40 and after that the number suddenly drops at the age group 31-35. The rise in the numbers of non-agricultural labourers as well as skilled technical workers from the earlier to the recent period can be called spectacular which reveals displacement of the tribal from their own land as well as sharecropping rights. The increase in the number of technical workers shows that the younger generation is also gradually trying to acquire modern skills outside the orbit of agriculture to earn their livelihood.

This Table 13.2 has also been compiled from the genealogies of the Santal and the Malpaharia individuals of the study area. The data for the table reflected the chronology of available occupational statuses of living and non-living individuals of the said tribes in four different phases with specific intervals in years since 1972 to 1999. The Table 13.2 shows that over time, the number of owner cultivators have declined with an almost simultaneous increase in the number of day labourers. It also reveals that during 1972 to

Table 13.2: Changing Pattern of Occupation among the Tribal of Old Malda Block

Interval in Years	*Owner Cultivator*	*Recorded Share Cropper*	*Unrecorded Share Cropper*	*Cultivator on Contract*	*Day/Wage Labour*
1972 - 1978	159 (26.81)	00	126 (42)	12 (26.45)	157 (24.19)
1979 - 1985	151 (25.46)	58 (25.32)	83 (27.66)	05 (11.11)	142 (21.87)
1986 - 1992	144 (24.28)	89 (38.86)	62 (20.66)	09 (20)	153 (23.57)
1993 - 1999	139 (23.44)	82 (35.80)	29 (9.66)	19 (42.22)	197 (30.35)
TOTAL	593	229	300	45	649

Note : Figures in parentheses represent percentages.

1978 there was no registered sharecropper though there was huge numbers of unrecorded sharecroppers and a few contractual sharecroppers. During 1979 to 1992 numbers of recoded sharecroppers have increased, whereas numbers of unrecorded and contractual sharecroppers have decreased in comparison to the earlier phase. During 1993 to 1999 the number of both registered and unrecorded sharecroppers has decreased, though the number of contractual sharecroppers have increased in comparison with the last two phases (1975 to 1984). It has also been observed that the number of day labourers had also increased during 1986 to 1999.

The genealogies of the Santal and the Malpaharia families tell us a story of displacement of these tribal from the occupation of cultivation in their own land on the plains of North Bengal, which had downgraded their conditions of livelihood over time. This displacement is not caused by any natural disaster but has a history of exploitation of tribal sharecroppers traditionally attached to the farmland of landowning non-tribal families. Through some case studies and field observations our findings revealed that landowners in this area are depriving the recorded bargadars and their legal heirs in various ways, which is severely affecting the livelihood of this poor and underprivileged section of the rural society. We would now narrate the cases of two Santal families and one Malpaharia family, who after being empowered as registered bargadars had been transformed into wage labourers over the generations.

Case-I

This is the case of a Santal family. About ten years ago Munshi Hembram and his elder son Surai Hembram had been cultivating their land as recorded sharecropper. Munshi had two sons, Surai and Dulu. At that time Dulu was a minor, so Munshi could not register his name officially as a bargadar. The owner of this agricultural land (a non-tribal named Dinesh) lived at Rathbari, Malda town. When Munshi and Surai were alive and cultivated the land, the landowner used to come frequently at Munshi's residence to collect the crop and also for other agriculture related purposes. According to Dipa Kisku (Wife of late Dulu Hembram), she herself, Rabi Hembram (son of Late Surai Hembram) and other family member are very much familiar with landowner.

After the death of Munshi and Dulu the right of registration according to barga inheritance rule did not transfer to Dipa and Rabi due to their lack of initiative. But then Dipa and Rabi had cultivated mustard (an oil seed) in the land by employing wage labour. At the time of harvesting, the landowner visited surprisingly with some labour and took away the entire mustard crop with him. Dulu, Rabi and some villagers tried to stop the owner and his team but they failed. After this incident, Dipa and Rabi did not seek the help of any political since they had no faith on any party. They went to the local police station but the police did not take any complaint against the landowner. Ironically, after the collection of crop the landowner filed a case against Sinul who worked as a wage labour of Dipa and Rabi for performing illegal cultivation on the land of the former. Sinul then came to Dipa and requested to visit Dinesh and to ask him to withdraw the case. Dipa along with Rabi and Sinul went to the residence of Dinesh and requested the latter to recognize them as the legal heir of the sharecropper of the land. But the landowner refused to comply and ordered them to leave his house. The landowner also threatened them not to come to his residence in future. He even said that if they come further with this demand then he would inform the police. Poor Dipa was very much scared and left the house of the landowner.

After these incidents, Dinesh made an attempt to sell the land to a company Messrs. Mahindra Pvt. Ltd by paying advance money. The company then constructed few pillars on the land and then put a signboard. But then some Malpahari villagers of Kantabari village, who had a good relation with Dipa and her family members, forced the company to vacate the land and demolished the pillars and the signboard. During this time the villagers and some local political leaders requested Dinesh and other adjoining landowners to donate some portion of their land for the connection of the Kantabari *Kaccha* (unmetalled) road with NH-34. But Dinesh denied the proposal and that led to a conflict and finally the concerned owner filed a case in the court. Then some political leaders went to Dipa and Rabi and told them that they will help them to get back the land in exchange of some money and some land for the development of the village road. According to Dipa any political party or leader would never try to help anyone without own or the interest of the party. Dipa also told that she does not belong to any political group, and she has no contact with any political person and she added that she hated political personalities. Meanwhile, Dipa lost the official documents relating to the barga record of her husband. They however applied for a duplicate copy through a lawyer but did not yet received it at the time of our fieldwork. When we enquired about the case of this tribal woman bargadar at the Block Land and Land Reforms office the concerned officials stated that they were not aware about problems of Dipa Kisku and her family. Then we requested the officials to show the govt. records of the concerned land. But to our utter surprise we found that the particular page, which contained Dipa's records, was missing from the register. At present Dipa and her family members are engaged as day labourers for earning their livelihood.

Case-II

Sukul Soren was a Santal bargadar of Narioli village who had been cultivating three and half bighas of land as a registered bargadar of two owners, Adhir Karmakar and Sanjay Karmakar. Adhir is the elder brother of Sanjay. Adhir and Sanjay each had 1 bigha and 15 khata of agricultural land. Sukul had no problem with Sanjay. But during our fieldwork we came to know that for the last 5 years Sukul was facing problems with the other owner, Adhir, regarding the distribution of crop. Sukul alleged that Adhir was not following the terms and conditions of the Bargadar Act of the Government of West Bengal. Sukul told us that since Adhir did not supply the inputs for agriculture to him, he as sharecropper should get 75 per cent of the crop but at the time of sharing. Sukul alleged that one day, Adhir took away the major portion of the crop, which was nearly 75 per cent of the total produce. Sukul demanded that the crop sharing should be in accordance to the law. Then Adhir told him that he could forcefully evict Sukul from his right since he had money and power. With this threat of Adhir, Sukul became very much scared and he had stopped to protest and agreed with landowner that the crop sharing would be on a 50:50 basis.

Then Sukul went local members of the major political parties, the CPI (M) and Congress, to get some assistance and suggestion towards the legal safeguard as registered bargadar but both party's members ignored him. Sukul told that he had no faith on political party and on concerned authority (BLLRO office and police station). Sukul also told that he does not belong to any political party and that is why no political party leaders helped him to get back the land, which he cultivated as a legal sharecropper. Sukul told that he never lodged a complaint against his landowner as he thought that the concerned authority would not take any action as the owner could stop the authority by paying some bribe. Sukul was also scared, if his landowner had come to know that he was going to complain, and then the owner, Mr. Adhir could forcefully evict him, as Adhir was a rich person and had a good relation with government officials and local political leaders. Finally he didn't complain in the BLLRO office about the problem. Following this, Sukul gradually became less interested in cultivation as a sharecropper and stopped cultivation and finally became an agricultural labourer.

Case-III

This is a case of a Malpaharia family. During the year 1979, father of late Deben Mal, called Late Lohina Mal, used to cultivate 12 bigha and 15 katha land of Mr. Biseswar Kundu, at Jhagra as a sharecropper. In the year 1980 Deben's father, Late Lohina Mal with the help of C.P.I. (M) had succeeded to become registered bargadar. After two years of barga recording, Mr. Lohina Mal died. Late Lohina Mal left his three sons, Deben Mal, Chetan Mal and Panchu Mal. In the year 1983 on the merit of Barga record inheritance rule, his sons became the legal registered sharecroppers. The land (12.5 khata) was divided into three equal measurements among them in the capacity of sharecropper. During the study, only Chetan Mal was alive. Name of the wife of Late Deben Mal was Sankari Mal. Sankari Mal and his family were active grass root level C.P.I. (M) party workers and they had good relation with local C.P.I. (M) party leader. Sankari had three sons and two daughters. During the fieldwork Sankari's two sons had been working in the shop a local wholesale cement dealer as a labour. Late Panchu Mal had left only one son, Sagar Mal. Few years back of our fieldwork period, Sagar lost mental balance. After long treatment, he had recovered his normal mental position in the end of the year 1998.

Approximately in the year 1990 or 1989, late Panchu Mal had handed over unofficially the sharecropper right of 2.5 bigha from his total 4.5 bigha recorded barga land to his elder brother's wife's name, Sankari Mal on a plain paper in exchange of two thousand rupees. After getting the share right, Shankari had then a total of seven bigha land for cultivation.

Seven or eight years back Sankari Mal was seriously ill and she had no money to run her family and for her treatment. Under this situation she had mortgaged her land to Ananda Ghosh of Naldubi village in exchange of seven thousand rupees. They had a written negotiation that when Sankari will return the money with interest to Ananda Ghosh then the latter would return the land. Chetan Mal also had handed over the share right in the same way to Ananda Mal in exchange of five thousand rupees. And by taking the advantage of Sagar Mal's (son of Late Panchu Mal) mental disability, Ananda Ghosh succeeded to motivate Sagar Mal to hand over his barga right in writing to Ananda's name without any money. Then Ananda had been cultivating the total land in the capacity of sub- sharecropper (Bandhaki chas in local parlance), which has no legal recognition.

When the landowner, Biswanath Kundu came to know about the land problem and failed to evict the illegal sub-sharecropper then he had sold out the land to three different persons. These three new joint owners were actually business partners of "land purchase and sell business". The main objective of these three owners was to buy registered barga land and to make the land free from bargadar in various illegal ways. Now when the new owners visited the land they found that the land had been handed over to sub-sharecropper in mortgage. After listening the whole disputed matter, new landowners suggested to the sharecroppers to pay back the money to sub sharecropper to free the land from sub-sharecropper. Then the sub-sharecropper tried to become an original recorded sharecropper, through the help of some political leaders. But the local political leader refused him as he had a good relation with Sankari Mal. Then the local CPI (M) leader arranged the money and went to Ananda Ghosh to pay the same for the barga land. But Ananda Ghosh refused to take the money back. Next day Sankari forcefully paid the money and had taken the possession with the help of local CPI (M) party leaders. But during the capture of the barga land, a violent conflict took place, which was initiated by Ananda Ghosh.Then police and local leaders came over there and decided that the original sharecropper would take the possession of the land. But Ananda Ghosh applied to BLLRO office to allow him as registered Bargadar. After three years, the BLLRO office decided that the Anada Ghosh had no right over the land as a bargadar. Sankari told that if they did not have political connection then they would not get back the sharecropper rights.

Concluding Remarks

This brief exploration revealed the ground realities of the empowerment of sharecroppers in West Bengal under a pro-peasant government. The empirical data and the case studies show that the enactment of a pro-bargadar legislation may not be a sufficient condition for the empowerment of this category of peasants who became vulnerable to the exploitative manipulations of the rural elites. It was found that the most crucial aspect of the empowerment of the bargadars hinges on the proactive role of the government administration as well as the left political parties. The three case studies narrated above are not exceptions rather they represent the general pattern of all the cases, which we have collected from the field. In fact, during the early years of the Left Front Government, the positive role of the left political parties as well as the government administration created a congenial milieu wherein the empowerment of the bargadars took place. The policy makers of West Bengal should immediately review the situation not only in terms of the number of registered bargadars over the years but also the micro-level qualitative changes that have been taking place in the relationship between the bargadar and the landowner in the different regions of the state.

Acknowledgements

I am greatly indebted to the Economic Social Research Council (ESRC), University of Cambridge, University of Keele of United Kingdom and the EASRC project "Rural Poverty, the Developmental State and Spaces of Empowerment in Bihar and West Bengal, Eastern India" for providing me the chance to work in the project and for their helpful cooperation, without which I would not have been able to prepare this paper. I would also like to thank Dr. Glyn William, Department of Geography, University of Keele University and Prof. Stuart Corbridge Sussex College. I would also like to thank Rene Veron, London School of Economics and Sri Manoj Srivastab, Senior I.A.S. and visiting fellow of University of Cambridge. I would also like to thanks to other colleagues of the project.

I am also indebted to Dr. Abhijit Guha, Department of Anthropology, Vidyasagar University, who always inspired me to write down the paper. I am also grateful to the organizers of the International Conference on 'Tribal Society in India and Beyond', held during 17-19 December 2004 at Sambalpur University, Sambalpur, Orissa for giving me the chance to present this paper. Last but not the least I would like to express my sincerest thanks to Dr. Jayanta Sarkar for giving me useful suggestions for the improvements on the paper.

REFERENCES

Bhaumik, S.K. 1993. *Tenancy Relation and Agrarian Development: A Study of West Bengal.* New Delhi: Sage Publication India Pvt. Ltd.

Chakrobarty, A.K. *et al.* 2003. *Beneficiaries of Land: The West Bengal Scenario.* Kolkata: State Institute of Panchayat and rural development, Kalyani, Nadia, West Bengal, and Spandan Kolkata.

Guha, A. 2005. "Eviction of Bargadars Under State Patronage in Leftist West Bengal: A Policy Perspective", in R.K.Das, A. Basu and A. Guha (eds.), *Perspective in Rural Development Problems and Prospects.* Kolkata: Indian Anthropological Society and Paschim Medinipur: Department of Anthropology, Vidyasagar University.

Pramanick, A.K. 2004. *The West Bengal Land Reforms Act,* 1955. Kolkata: Tax N Law Publication.

Mukarji, N. and D. Bandopadhyay. 1993. *New Horizons for West Bengal's Panchayats.* Kolkata: Department of Panchayats, Government of West Bengal.

West Bengal Human Development Report. 2004. Kolkata: Development and Planning Department. Government of West Bengal.

FORUTEEN

BEHIND BOW AND ARROW: A Look into the Tribal Unrest on Forest Movement of East and West Singhbhum, Jharkhand

ASHIS KUMAR DAS

India is a large country. Approximately 8.3 per cent of the total population of our country belongs to the scheduled tribes. As per 1981 census, Bihar is the third biggest state in India so far as the density of the population of scheduled tribes is concerned, and the population of scheduled tribes in Bihar itself is 58,10,867. The population of scheduled tribes out of the total in the districts of Ranchi, Singhbhum) and Santal Parganas are 54.4 per cent, 44.1 per cent and 38.3 per cent respectively (Hopkins, 1981). The plateau region of Bihar, which is the main habitation of these Kolarian and other tribes, is connected with the tribal populated parts of Madhya Pradesh, Orissa, and West Bengal. The total area becomes a place wherein we find a high concentration of these tribal. Now a separate Jharkhand State has been formed where most of the tribal population is concentrated.

Historical Background

Throughout the colonial ascendancy, the tribal of Jharkhand had rebelled time and again in their traditional ways against the socio-economic injustices meted out to them by the outsiders whom the *adivasis* called *diku*. Periodical tribal uprising against the *dikus* throughout the nineteenth century were brutally crushed by the colonial rulers. During 1798-99 the Bhumijs of Manbhum and the other tribal communities of Jharkhand rose against the oppression by the *dikus*, which include British colonialists. The effort was described as antisocial and anti *status quo* and to discredit the uprising the colonial rulers described it as "Chuar Rebellion". The word *chuar* has originated from *Chor-Chuhar* meaning thieves and nasty people. In 1800 Cheros and Khewars of Palamau revolted against the British. Again 5000 Mundas of Tamar revolted under the leadership of Dukhan Manki in 1807. Rahe, another leader, followed the same path in 1812. During 1819-20 a massive movement took place under the leadership of Rudu and Konta Munda. During "Kol" Rebellion of 1831-32 led by Singhray and Bindray against the Thikadars the British defended the oppressive Thikadars with troops under the East India Company. Similarly, the "Santal Hul" led by Shido and Khanhu in 1855-56 against the non-tribal moneylenders, big landlords, and British merchants was crushed by troops of the British government. The prolonged "Sardari Larai" or "Mulki Larai" of the last quarter of the nineteenth century and Birsha Munda movement were the two other remarkable uprisings of the tribal of Eastern India.

Social Movement and Political Movement

The essential characteristic of social movement is that they are oriented to a certain definite goal or objective. A social movement is essentially a phenomenon of mass mobilization on specific issues or problems concerning social life. Moreover, social movements must develop sooner or later a comprehensive ideology and theory, which should be convincing to the participants of the movements. This usually involves the following (Paul, 1989):

- The goals or ends of the movements.
- The ways and means by which the goal has to be attained.
- The rationale for the participants for joining the movements.

We find that the tribal reacted fiercely when their economic interest got affected, religious beliefs scoffed at and their freedom attacked. They got infuriated when their traditional customs and manners, civic rights were curtailed and their judicial system and tribal codes were ignored. During the independence movements tribal did participate with other non-tribal in their common goal of driving out the colonial government from India.

The tribal do display a distinct cultural and demographic position in Indian society even when they are comparatively insulated; they are maintaining a unique place in the history and civilization in India. They are ecologically more or less isolated and demographically concentrated in certain contiguous geographical regions. Economically, their life is wedded to land and forest. Culturally too, they enjoy a distinct style of life, distinct language and cultural heritage; forms of religion, love for freedom and respect for self-identity.

The self-awareness might be of limited range and depth but there are numerous instances of their participation in the socio-cultural life of the country as a whole. For more than last two centuries, the tribal have been undergoing diverse socio-economic changes and much of these were initiated by the penetration of British colonialism. The British introduced a new economic system gradually in consonance with their own economic system. It was characterized by commercialization of land and state ownership of forest, well-defined property rights, occupation structure and marketing of agricultural surplus. These in turn produced unprecedented contradictions in the tribal society, which was earlier based on economic relations and collective mode of productions and consumption. The colonial penetration had diverse purpose and motives to exploit the socio-economic resources of the native economy and this introduced new social tensions and conflicts in the society. In other words, the colonial intervention resulted in the gradual encroachment upon their entire communal way of living.

On numerous occasions there were riots, revolts and uprisings, against colonial rule and its exploitive socio-economic network. In almost all pockets of India, tribal were surging resistance of this sort against deprivation of their traditional rights over land and forest. Surface observation of this phenomena may lead us to categorize them as scattered "events or episodes" and not as "movements". But these events of resistance by the tribal people were centered on the issue affecting their existence itself. Resistance, as we know "is a characteristic of a social movement" (Singh, 1978).

Viewed from a particular period of time and space it may not look like a "movement" in the proper sense of the term but these "events" were surely indicators of a "movement" where persons in hundreds and thousands rose against the high handed exploitative forces. Over a period of time, during the colonial rule, such movements in tribal society might have taken different nature, forms, dimensions and magnitudes. But these were surely sustaining attempts on their part to oppose the exploitative system, which affect their existence in one way or the other.

Forest Movement in Singhbhum: The Theme

In the year 1978 the Sadar subdivision of Singhbhum district witnessed the outbreak of a well-organized *andolan* known as 'Tree War' or forest *andolan* started by the tribal of these areas. The *andolan* took the form of felling of tree in these forests by the *adivasis* or tribal as a symbolic protest against the threat to their livelihood and identify. It spread like wildfire in the whole sub-division and vast areas of forests were cut down by the *adivasis*. Their argument was that these lands once belonged to them and were illegally taken away by the Forest Department.

Causes of Forest *andolan* in Singhbhum

In order to understand the present forest *andolan* we have to go into the root causes of tribal unrest in the forest areas of Singhbhum. Areeparampil has described some of the basic reasons for this movement, which are described below (Narayan, 1992).

Encroachment by the Forest Department on Adivasi villages and their Customary Rights on Forest

The Ho and Munda tribes of Singhbhum lived in present day Ranchi district. Gradually the Hos, who preferred to remain independent, left Ranchi and migrated to the southeast. They started settling in the ghat areas of Bandgaon block of Singhbhum district. From there they slowly migrated in to the Singhbhum plains. That the Hos once settled in these ghat areas is evident from the numerous villages, which exist in these areas whose names correspond to the name of Ho *kilis* or *gotras*. When the British declared this area to be a reserved forest many of the *Khuntkatti* villages were uprooted and included in the reserves without considering the legitimate rights of the *adivasis* who resided there. As a result, many of the Hos left their original villages and moved to south Singhbhum. When the *adivasis* were forced out their *Khuntkatti* villages they left behind them the burial places (*sasans*) of their ancestors with huge stones placed on the graves, their worship places (*desaulis and sarnas*), the paddy fields which they had made and tamarind and mango trees which they had planted as signs that once they lived there. Actually the adivasis are closely united not only with the living members of the tribe but also with their dead ancestors. When their villages were uprooted and their *sasans* included the reserved forests, it adversely affected their clan unity and created a traumatic situation in their mental world and culture.

Exploitation and Harassment of Tribal by Forest Officials

From the time of reservation of forests the *adivasis* have been constantly harassed and exploited by the officials of the forest department, especially by the lower level officials. However, not all the villages were removed from the reserves. Some of them were taken over from the Civil department and the residents of these villages were kept as bonded labourers by the Forest Department. These are the so-called forest villages of which the sole malik or owner is the Forest Department. At many places the adivasis were allowed to settle down and cultivate land within the forest demarcated areas and in lieu of it they supply everything right from milk to rice to the forest officials. Further, they are forced to work for the department during the forest cutting season. The adivasis who live in this forest villages as bonded labourers to the forest department live under constant threat of attracting the fancies of the forest officials. Sometimes, their beautiful womenfolk become prey to the lustful forest officials. The condition of these adivasis is miserable. They have no basic amenities like schools, dispensaries, drinking water facilities, etc.

It is astonishing that even after the enactment of the Abolition of Bonded Labour Act in the year 1976 many forest villagers are still kept as bonded labourers by the forest department in forest areas of Bihar.

Commercialization of Forests and the Resultant Pauperization of Tribal

The life of the Hos and other tribal is centered on the forests in which they live. There is a symbolic relationship between the culture and life of the *adivasis* of the forests (Verma, 1995). Besides their need of parts of certain trees for traditional religious rites, the tribal villagers, especially the poorer marginal farmer, depends on the wealth of the forest for his livelihood. He makes his own house, getting the wood from jungle; he makes his own ploughs (except the ploughshare which he gets from the village Lohar); he makes the yokes, which he needs as well as the wooden part of other agricultural utensils, *pickaxes, kudalis,* etc. In most houses they keep a couple of cots by procuring the wood and the rope from the jungles. Their womenfolk make mats from trees of the jungles. During the lean part of the year, when the main crops are not growing, cattle are let free in most villages. These means that those who have vegetable gardens must fence from off. The frameworks used to support vegetables, which grow on vines, come from the jungle. Many cultivate lac on certain trees of the jungle, and even more cultivate silk worms. This gives an important supplementary income to many poor families. They get their oil from trees of the jungle. Many get an important supplementary diet from various parts (fruits, leaves, flowers) of trees from the jungle. Also some collect and exchange such items for rice or cash. The leaves of certain trees of the jungle are used not only for religious rites but also serve as plates for serving meals or cups for serving rice beer. Different types of herbs, roots, tubers, which are helpful as medicine to the poor patients, are collected from the forest.

Therefore, the village tribal who are poor and who live near the jungle satisfy practically all the basic needs from the jungle. About the only essential item, which he has to buy, is salt. His life is poor and hard, but he has independence and dignity. He prides himself that he is a landowner, however small his holding may be. Obviously such a person feels threatened when he finds that parts of the jungle are being transformed in a way, which will deprive him of what he needs to subsist as a village landowner.

In absolute disregard for the very survival needs of the *adivasis* a massive programme was started in the year 1975 to replace the existing forest with fast growing industrially useful trees like teak. In that year the Bihar State Forest Development Corporation Limited was set up for the purpose of commercial exploitation of forest. It was decided that the "future production programme should concentrate on clear-felling of valuable mixed forest, mixed quality forest and inaccessible hard wood forest and planting these area with suitable fast growing species yielding higher return per unit area". An area of 39,968 hectares of Porahat forest division was leased out to the FDC for this type of development. The Corporation began to replace Sal, Mahua, Kusum and other useful and fruit bearing indigenous trees by teak in the traditional mixed forest, which included *Khuntkatti* forests, in which adivasis enjoyed traditional communal rights. Thus vast areas of natural mixed forest on which the tribal communities depended for their survival were clear-felled and replaced by monocultures of commercially useful species such as teak. The felling of teak trees during the *andolan* by the *adivasis* was, therefore, a protest against this anti-adivasi programme of the forest development corporation.

Looting and Destruction of Forests by Contractors in Collusion with Forest Officials

Another reason for the unrest in the forest areas is the large-scale loot of the forest by contractors, timber merchants and other vested interests in collusion with the police and the forest officials. The guardians of the forest became the main culprits for its destruction in the eyes of the Forest Department. The tribal resented the wanton destruction and loot of their life support system by these vested interest groups. For a long time even now the Bihar Government has been spreading the story that the tribal are destroying the forests on a large scale.

Some Other Causes for the Tribal Unrest in the Forest Areas of Singhbhum

Besides the factors mentioned which are directly connected with the forest some other factors have also contributed considerably for the sudden outbreak of turmoil in the forest areas of Singhbhum. These are:

- Large-scale legal and illegal alienation of tribal land.
- Displacement of tribal due to various development projects without proper rehabilitation and adequate compensation.
- Increasing unemployment in the area due to closure of mines and the frequent drought conditions existing in the area.
- Thousands of *adivasis* got unemployed due to the closure of Chiriburu quartzite mines, asbestos mines at Roro and at other places.

The increasing pauperization of the *adivasis* forced them to search for alternate means for survival. Some of them migrated to the brick-kilns in search of jobs. Others took recourse to illegal felling of forests for the purpose of cultivation or for the selling of firewood or timber. The real reason behind the illegal felling of trees is extreme poverty and hunger of the tribal people who live in and around the forest areas.

Different Phases of Forest *Andolan*

We have described the basic causes behind the beginning of a militant phase of the Jharkhand Movement, which took the form of a *jungle katai andolan* in Singhbhum. This *andolan* broke out suddenly from the second half of the year 1978. The immediate cause for the sudden outburst was certain actions of the government, which the tribal felt were detrimental to their interest. In the year 1973, the government nationalized the Kendu leaves trade; in 1976 it took over the *Sal* seed trade and in 1978 trade in all the Minor Forest Produce (MFP) was taken over by the government. In 1975 the Forest Development Corporation was formed and a total area of 1.92 lakh hectares was leased out to the Corporation for the purpose of clear felling and planting these areas with fast growing and high yielding varieties like teak. Soon after these actions by the government the entire Chotanagpur plateau was rocked by violent tribal uprisings demanding the denationalization of MFP and the closure of the work of FDC. The first major incident of this uprising took place at Simdega on 4th August 1978, when police fired at a non-violent crowd of *adivasis* killing one person. They were protesting against the State take-over of MFP trade.

In the context of these developments, let us now examine the various phases of the *andolan* in Singhbhum where the forest question became the most important issue of the *andolan*. For this study, we shall consider the years between 1977 and 1987.

Period of the Samyukta Mancha: (October 1977-November 1979)

The intensification of *alag pranth andolan*, which started in October 1977, had its impact in Singhbhum too. More than 11 incidents in connection with the *andolan* were reported from different parts Singhbhum during the period October 1977 to June 1978. Large public meetings, big processions, seminars of youth and students, formation of different parties, and student organizations have been reported in the name of Jharkhand movement. As the *andolan* progressed the forest question gained greater importance. The forest *andolan* in Shinghbhum had its origins first in the Porahat area. The tribal of Porahat region were very much agitated by the operations of the Forest Development Corporation. On 17th June 1978, a group of about sixty *adivasis* led by Mora Munda of Darong village hijacked a jeep carrying some forest officials and kept them in confinement for several hours at a village. The agitators demanded that the officials should give them in writing that the work of the Corporation would be stopped.

On 28th August a crowd about 5,000 *adivasis* gheraoed the SDO office at Chaibasa. They came from the forest areas of Sonua, Goilkera, Bandgaon, Chakradharpur, etc.

As this was going on a group of *adivasis* started a movement of felling trees in the forest areas for the purpose of preparing arable lands on the ground since they believed that they enjoyed the traditional right to reclaim forestland for cultivation. The *jungle katai andolan* for reclaiming land for cultivation was first started by Machua Gangarai in the Karaikela area. He had organized about 67 villages for this movement.

During the *forest andolan,* the *adivasis,* therefore, tried to reclaim their ancestral lands taken over by Forest Department. This movement spread further under the leadership of Magi Dorai and Jogo Munda in the Serengda area.

The *Sanguan Katai Andolan* spread like wildfire in the forest areas of Sonua, Goilkera, Monoharpur, Chakradharpur Police Stations. Teak plants were uprooted, huts in the nurseries were razed to the ground and costly pump sets belonging to FDC were destroyed. After destroying the teak plants, the *adivasis* started ploughing the area for cultivation. The entire roads in the forest areas were closed down and operations of FDC came to standstill. On 9th October 1978, a public meeting of *Jharkhand Alag Rajya Samyukta Morcha,* Porhat Unit was held at Goilkera market. About 7,000 villagers from nearby villages with their traditional weapons like bow and arrow took part in this meeting.

Looking at the agitation as a law and order problem the administration reacted strongly by deploying forces in the forest areas. Many leaders were arrested. The *adivasis* were refused to pay Masul or toll in the market, as they complained that no facilities like drinking water, urinals, etc. were provided in the market place. Fifteen adivasis were arrested on that day. On 6th November 1978, the police indiscriminately fired at a crowd of *adivasis* at Ichahatu village in Goilkera block. Again on 25th November 1978, the police fired 12 rounds at a crowd of *adivasis* who had gathered for the weekly market at Serengda. The Samyukta Morcha organized a big public meeting at Jamshedpur on 21st January 1979 in support of their demand for a separate Jharkhand State. On 14th July the adivasis from Jonko village in Bandgaon burned down the forest bungalow in relation to the arrest and firing at an adivasi who had taken some wood from the forest for making a plough.

After the announcement of election to the Parliament a meeting of the Samyukta was held on 10th October 1979 at the house of N.E.Horo, the president of the Morcha. In this meeting leaders from four parties were present. Mr. Guria from Birsa Seva Dal proposed that they should fight this election under one flag and symbol and have a common manifesto to which Mr. Horo did not agree. As a result Samyukta Morcha broke up and Horo slowly alienated from the *andolan* scene in Singhbhum.

Period of Election Politics (November 1979—September 1980)

After the break up of the Samyukta Morcha the leadership of the *andolan* in Shinghbhum was taken over by Jharkhand Mukti Morcha. The party selected Devendra Majhi, the leader of the *forest andolan,* as its candidate for the mid-term parliamentary election from Shinghbhum. Devendra began his election campaign on 29th November 1970 with a big public meeting at Chaibasa, where more than 10,000 *adivasis* with their traditional weapons attended. They submitted a memorandum to the D.C. (Deputy Commissioner) demanding the immediate starting of relief work for the drought-affected people, the changing of forest policy for the benefit of the forest dwellers and the separation of Jharkhand from Bihar. In the assembly elections the JMM had an agreement with the Congress (I) at the state level.

During this period Singhbhum faced one of the worst famines in its history. There was widespread corruption in the food for work and other relief programmes. Black marketing and profiteering thrived and there was food shortage and increase in the prices of essential commodities. Robbery and other crimes increased.

During this period the *jungle katai movement* gathered momentum and started spreading to other areas under the leadership of JMM.

Gua Firing and After (8th September 1980—January 1981)

As the *jungle katai movement* gathered momentum the repression by the State also increased and became brutal. A strong contingent of BMP (Bihar Military Police) was deployed throughout the forest areas. BMP jawans harassed the *adivasis* by breaking into their homes lifting chickens and vegetables without payment, indiscriminately arresting people from public places like hats and even misbehaving with *adivasi* women.

Against such oppressive actions of the BMP and the police the adivasis decided to mobilize public opinion. On 8th September 1980, under the aegis of JMM they called a public meeting at Gua aerodrome to prepare a memorandum to be handed to the local authorities.

After a short meeting at the market the *adivasis* started dispersing. But suddenly without any provocation BMP accompanying the *adivasis* surged forward, arrested their leaders and dragged them out from the gathering, which led to a clash. On this spot 59 rounds were fired and the place is so congested that it is unbelievable that only three *adivasis* would be killed on the spot.

But what is most dastardly happened afterwards. In the IISCO hospital half a km. away some of the injured policemen were brought for treatment and shortly after some injured *adivasis.* But as soon as the first batch of 9 *adivasis* were brought into the hospital they were surrounded within the hospital, assaulted and then shot dead. As per official version 9 rounds were shot killing 9 *adivasis* within the hospital.

Immediately after Gua firing a reign of terror was let loose by the police and the administration especially in areas where the tribal were better organized like Chakradharpur, Goilkera, Sonua, Monoharpur and Noamundi Blocks.

Thousands of innocent adivasis were dragged out of trains, buses, etc. or picked up from weekly hats, courts or from their places of work and put in prison. Villages were raided and women raped and beaten up. On the night of 19th September Mora Munda and Machua Gagarai, two leaders of the JMM were beaten almost to the point of death in Chakradharpur police station.

In spite of the furore these firings created in the State Assembly and the Parliament no judicial enquires were made and no action taken against the guilty officials. The massacre at Gua stands apart from other such tragedies because of the ruthlessness and the reign of terror that followed the actual firing.

Emergence of Kolhan Raksha Sangh (January 1981—September 1983)

Kolhan Raksha Sangh (KRS) founded on November 1, 1977 (Das, 116: 1992). As the *jungle katai* and *alag pranth andolan* spearheaded by the Jharkhand Mukti Morcha was spreading throughout Singhbhum, another movement for an autonomous Kolhan nation by an organization known as Kolhan Raksha Sangh (KRS) was gradually emerging in the Kolhan area of Singhbhum.

Their activities are confined mainly to the Saranda area where they are involved also in the *jungle katai* movement. The police raided many villages in these areas to arrest the leaders. During these raids houses of several innocent *adivasis* were destroyed. On 25th April 1981 the police fired at a crowd of *adivasis* at Tonto. The next day 59 men were arrested from the villages around there. On 18th May an armed police party went to Tansera village and destroyed the house of K.C. Hembram and took away his belongings. On the way back the police beat up an *adivasi* woman named Lembo Kui. Another *adivasi*, Pai Hembram, was arrested by the police and taken to Chaibasa where he died in police custody. On 22nd May 1982 the police force went to Bandabera village and looted and fired at the villagers.

In March 1983 the KRS sent an appeal to the President against the increasing repression in Singhbhum. A case was also filed in the Supreme Court by KRS against the repression. On 9th February 1983 KRS made a demand for Kolhan Regional Parisad. Gradually they have changed their demand for a separate nation into one separate identity within the Indian constitution.

The economic situation of Shinghbhum during this period was miserable. There was near famine situation all over Shinghbhum. During this period the *jungle katai* movement began to spread more and more to Saranda areas. The fellings were mostly done by the followers of KRS.

The Tribal Welfare Commissioner, Ranchi made an inquiry of this incident and sent a confidential report to the government asking for CBI inquiry. But nothing has been done to punish the guilty officials.

Emergence of Gram Raksha Dal (September 1983—September 1985)

From September 1983 onwards a strange and frightening phenomenon began to appear on the socio-political scene of the village areas of Shinghbhum, especially of the Kolhan — Porahat region. It is the phenomenon of self-annihilation by the exploited and was started by a new organization called the Gram Raksha Dal in the name of getting rid of dacoits, witches and other anti-socials. The administration did practically nothing to stop these crimes; in some cases it colluded with the criminals. As a result the villagers began to take the law into their own hands and the Gram Raksha Dal was formed in every affected village, to get rid of the criminals and anti-socials.

Soon killings in the name of *chor kato dain maro* (i.e. kill thieves and witches) began to spread through out Kolhan Porahat areas. In this way hundreds of innocent people including women and children were killed.

Writ Petition against Human Rights Violation in Singhbhum

On 7th April 1983, Director, Tribal Research and Training Center, Chaibasa and four *adivasis* of Lonjo village in Shingbhum District filed a Writ Petition in the Supreme Court of India. In their petition the petitioners had pointed out the gross violations of the fundamental rights of the adivasis of Shinghbhum by the police, the administrations, the forest officials, mines owners and other vested interest groups.

After hearing the Writ Petition the Honourable Court took the following actions:

- Stayed the two cases against the petitioners.
- The court also stayed all the forest cases (1,623 cases) filed against the adivasis in Singhbhum during the period 1978-83.
- The court asked the Deputy Commissioner, Shinghbhum to submit a report regarding the killing of Bidar Nag at Gua on 1st June 1983.
- The court ordered their respondents to produce the confidential report of the Tribal Welfare Commissioner, Ranchi, asking for CBI inquiry regarding the murder of Gangaram.

- Further, the Court asked for a report of all the cases against the adivasis pending in the various courts in Shinghbhum District.

Demand to Declare Chotandgpur and Santal Parganas a Centrally Administrated Territory (September 1985-1987)

This period is characterized by the movement to make Chotanagpur and Santal Parganas a centrally administrated territory. As regards the forest *andolan* two important events have taken place during this period. One is the entry of Jharkhand Kranti Dal (JKD) in this sphere. They have started a movement against eucalyptus plantation in Dhalbhumgarh subdivision of Shinghbhum. Thousands of JKD volunteers uprooted eucalyptus trees and planted mahua, sal, and other fruit bearing indigenous trees in all over seventy villages in Chakulia and Baharagora from the 1st to 15th August 1986.

The other event is an order passed by the Ranchi Bench of Patna High Court in connection with a Writ Petition filed by Mora Munda and others regarding the adivasi lands illegally taken away by the Forest Department. In this case, the Honorable Court directed the Deputy Commissioner, Shinghbhum to either hold an inquiry by himself or get the inquiry done by any competent officer appointed by him in this behalf about the rights of the petitioner and the residents of villages.

Strong Points of the Andolan

- The *forest andolan* in Shinghbhum is a struggle of the *adivasis,* who have been oppressed for hundreds of years, for their self-identity and self-determination.
- This is people's movement. We see the emergence of people's power in this *andolan.* It is not a movement of the leaders only. The emergence of people's power resulted in the rejection of traditional political parties. They have become irrelevant.
- It is a struggle guided by socialistic ideals.
- A major strong point of this andolan is the participation of women on a large scale. The students were also involved very much in the beginning.
- It received the active support of human rights organizations such as Shinghbhum Ekta and other action groups.
- The movement also received the strong support of leftist forces.

- There was wide publicity through media, inquiries, reports, etc. and the fortnightly Shinghbhum Ekta played an important role in this movement.

Weak Points of the *Andolan*

- No cohesive unity in the movement could be observed. Mushrooming of too many organizations for the same cause. Everyone wanted to get on to the bandwagon; no one wanted to be left out.
- The traditional political leaders and parties took an ambiguous stand towards the *andolan*.
- Except in the beginning the support of the student community did not remain also strong.
- The movement remained confined mainly to the forest areas. There was little support from the plains living tribal and non-tribal.
- Another weakness of the movement was there was no proper alignment with national movements. Devendra got isolated and confined himself to small areas.
- Involvement in election politics led to the downfall of the movement. Elections brought out the real colour of the leaders. Leaders became separated from the masses and became busy in election politics at Delhi and Patna. They became opportunists and selfish. Fight for chair and position became their main concern. Groupism became strong; there were as many groups as there were leaders.
- In the run for elections leaders became involved in agreements and adjustment with large national parties like Congress I sacrificing their own regional interests.
- The leaders moved away from the struggle and became reformists.
- The movement lost its leftist character, which gave birth to it.
- As a result of all these the movement became weak and took a reactionary form.
- Later on the movement was confined only to meetings, processions, demonstrations, memoranda, petition, etc.
- Forcible collection of Chanda and its misuse by leaders led to the loss of faith of the people in the movement. Those who tried to oppose were gotten rid of.
- People were cheated by the leaders saying that cases are filed in the court; orders have been received, etc. when in fact nothing of the sort happened.

- Another major weakness of the andolan was that the leaders did not care about the victims of repression, about those killed or wounded or about those who were embroiled in many cases.
- Land hunger of the *adivasis* became the main motive force. Other aspects of the movement weakened, e.g. the demand for alag pranth.

REFERENCES

Das Victor, 1992. *Jharkhand Castle over the Graves.* Delhi: Inter-India Publication

Hopkins, Edward W.1981. *Census of India* 1981. Government of India, Manager of Publication

Narayan. S. 1992(Ed.): *Jharkhand Movement and Evaluation.* Delhi: Inter-India Publication

Paul, Madan. C. 1989. *Dimension of Tribal Movement in India: A Study of Udayachal in Assam Valley.* Delhi: Inter-India Publication.

Singh, K.S. 1978: "Colonial Transformation of Tribal Society in Middle India," *Economic and Political Weekly,* July 29. pp.12-29

Verma, R.C. 1995. *Indian Tribes Throughout the Age.* Publication Division, Ministry of Information and Broadcasting. Government of India.

FIFTEEN

OF A UNIVERSITY, A TRIBAL VILLAGE AND POLICY-MAKING: (De)construction of a Development Dialogue

ABHIJIT GUHA

Establishment of a University or How the Myth was Constructed: The Jural Level

Universities have become inseparable from the socio-political reality of a nation-state. They bring in varieties of socio-economic groups within the campus cutting across region, class, caste, religion and gender but at the same time universities also marginalize some people particularly the underprivileged by a kind of elitism, which is built into the structure of the university. Ironically enough, these centres of highest learning also champion high ideals regarding the elimination of poverty, illiteracy and various forms of social inequality. The university campus is one of the physical symbols of the elitism of a university. The campus is an enclosed space often encircled by boundary walls, which separates the university from its surroundings. The university administration makes sincere efforts to protect their campus with high walls and security forces but not through participatory management by involving the local inhabitants. Under this background, let describe the case of the establishment of Vidyasagar University in the erstwhile Medinipur district of West Bengal.

Vidyasagar University was established by an Act passed in the West Bengal State Legislative Assembly in the year 1981. The University Grants Commission (UGC) recognized this University on condition that it should develop in a non-traditional line incorporating subjects, which would have rural development oriented bias. Accordingly, departments like Economics with rural development, Political Science with rural administration, Anthropology with tribal culture, Commerce with farm management, Applied mathematics with oceanology and Library and information science were introduced in 1985-86 academic session. The Vidyasagar University Act, 1981 in its section entitled "The University and its officers" mentioned in its clause 4 (2) that the institution shall have the power to "to organize specialized diploma, degree or post-graduate courses... in such subjects as tribal languages, habitats and customs, rural administration forestry... regional resources planning, ecology and environmental studies" (The Vidyasagar University Act, 1985). The clause 4(5) in the Act is more remarkable which emphatically stated that the University shall have the "power to make such academic studies as may contribute to the improvement of economic conditions and welfare of the people in general and the tribal people in particular" (*ibid.*). With this pro-poor and pro-tribal legislation passed in the state assembly of the Left Front Government (LFG) of West Bengal and taking its name after the famous nineteenth century social reformer Pandit Iswar Chandra Vidyasagar, the non-traditional University started its journey by affiliating 30 undergraduate colleges from Calcutta University within the administrative jurisdiction of the erstwhile Medinipur district. This was a sufficient load on this new University in terms of routine works related to examination and others to detract it from the stated objectives enshrined in its Act. This also reveals the populist policy decision of the LFG, which passed a progressive Act in the state assembly without giving any serious thought towards its implementation.

The Construction of the Myth: The Physical Level

The location of the Vidyasagar University campus was also selected on a non-conventional site at a distance of about 3 kilometers from the Medinipur railway station (about 34 metres above the Mean Sea Level) on the Western side of the Medinipur town under the municipal ward 21. This ward and its adjoining one, ward 20, represent the recent municipal extensions of the town into the into the rural areas characterised by vast open land, agricultural fields, woodland and lesser number of administrative offices, residential houses as well as trade and commercial activities. The National Atlas and Thematic Mapping Organisation (NATMO) calculated the densities of population in wards 20 and 21 as 12.84 and 23.65 persons per hectare respectively in 1981, while the town's average population density was 47.50 persons per hectare (NATMO, 1992).

The administrative, academic and residential buildings of the University are built on the vast open 150 acres of uncultivated lateritic upland (*tanr land* in local parlance) donated by the state government. Formerly, this land, which was probably regarded as "non-agricultural waste" by the colonial administration was owned by one revenue paying *zamindar* belonging to the illustrious "Khan" family of Narajole of Paschim Medinipur district. The big palace of the Khan family and its adjoining garden lie on the south west side of the Vidyasagar University campus and the palace has become the Raja Narendra Lal Khan Women's College which is affiliated to Vidyasagar University. The campus of the N.L. Khan College provides a marked contrast in terms of the vegetative cover on this lateritic and undulating landscape. The campus of the College harbours a wide variety of old indigenous fruit bearing and other kinds of big trees like mango, jackfruit, arjun, neem, wood-apple, kul, guava, lemon etc. The Vidyasagar University campus on the other hand, still looks like a forest department office with *krishnachura, sirish* and debdaru trees and patches of eucalyptus and *akashmoni* plantations. There is also an area measuring a few acres, which contain some cashew trees. Recently, some well-protected gardens containing mahogany, sal and segun have been developed within the campus. And that is all. No systematic attempt has yet been made by the University authority to plant and protect a good number of local varieties of fruit and other kinds of trees on this vast open land since its inception. Till today only some ritualistic gestures have been made by the University authority (sometimes by the units of the National Service Scheme) to plant some indigenous trees during the onset of the monsoon. But a large number of such trees are eaten up by the grazing cattle of the surrounding settlements which include the tribal village named Muradanga. Even some eucalyptus and *akashmoni* trees which the grazing animals do not eat have been felled by the local villagers who used them as fuelwood. But despite all these kinds of uncomfortable interactions of Vidyasagar University with its neighbours, the myth of the non-traditional and rural University catering to the needs of the local people survived at least in the initial stage. The myth however began to pass through a process of deconstruction over the years. The published statements of the Vice-Chancellors of Vidyasagar University revealed that the University is gradually deviating from its mandate. Let us examine the narratives in some detail.

Deconstruction of the Myth

Voices from "Us"

The idea of developing a non-traditional University in a rural milieu having a substantial number of tribal communities was placed before the policy-makers not by the anthropologists but by Dr. Anil Kumar Gayen, a Professor of Mathematics and Statistics of the Indian Institute of Technology at Kharagpur. The University Grants Commission approved the idea of Dr. Gayen but unfortunately the chief planner of Vidyasagar University passed away before the establishment of the University in 1985. After the establishment of the University, Prof. Bhupesh Chandra Mukherjee, a former history teacher in Presidency College and an administrator in the state education department was appointed as the first Vice-Chancellor of this non-traditional University in West Bengal. Professor B.C. Mukherjee published a communication in the UGC' *Journal of Higher Education* in 1987-88 entitled "Vidyasagar University: Its Objectives and Character" (Mukherjee, 1987-88). Let us look at what he wanted to communicate about the aims and objectives of this University. In his communication, apart from reiterating the VU Act regarding the upliftment of the "backward areas and removal of regional imbalance" and the rationale behind the establishment of the University, Prof. Mukherjee stated: "The overall emphasis of the university is not to perpetuate the traditional nature of other universities but to emerge as a distinctive entity with a special nature of its own having an orientation towards non-traditional and specialized teaching and research" (ibid.).

Interestingly, just after seven years of difficult run owing to fund shortage and non-availability of capital grants from the UGC, another vice-chancellor, Dr. Satyanarayan Ghosh, in the First Convocation Address delivered on 9 January 1995, frankly admitted: "The university started with the objective of teaching and developing non-conventional subjects, but had later to stray a little away from this original idea in the case of some subjects which did not find ready employment. A brief but disenchanting experience more or less forced some of the departments to revert to teaching what is called traditional or conventional subjects" (Ghosh, 1995). It appeared from the statement of Dr. Ghosh that the university has already made enough innovative experiments in developing along non-traditional lines and its students have been refused jobs and/or fellowships for pursuing the original objectives of the institution. Suffice it to say that nothing could be far from the truth about the pursuance of the ideals and the real spirit of the University as depicted in Dr. S.N. Ghosh's narrative quoted above. The next vice-chancellor of the University,

Professor Amiya Kumar Deb in his Second Convocation Address on 4 April 1997 did not mention the words "non-conventional" or "non-traditional" like his predecessors. Professor Deb had a different kind of answer to the problem. Throughout his speech, he went on narrating the tale of opening new undergraduate and postgraduate courses by the University which have both application and job for the students. In his own words: "Our interest in vocationalisation and application orientedness of education has also led us to giving affiliation to a course in Master of Social Work...." In another place of his Convocation Address Professor Deb elaborated his arguments in the following manner:

> "In pursuit of the third dimension of university education, we have set up an extension centre in which self-financing certificate and diploma courses are going to be given from the coming academic session in such fields as Computer Application, Laboratory Technology and Seed Technology to begin with. The courses are being designed in such a way as to impart full application oriented training to those who offer them in search of a career or for the sake of career improvement. This is only the initiation. We plan to fare further, in answer to the developmental and career needs of the region" (Deb, 1997).

The narratives produced by these three vice-chancellors of Vidyasagar University over a period of twelve years show the evolution of the deconstruction of the myth of a non-traditional University constructed by the Leftist Government, which found its expression in the Vidyasagar University Act of 1981. At Vidyasagar University, non-conventional now means opening of self-financed and distance education courses by which the University can generate its own funds and resources. The trend was set during the tenure of Professor Amiya Kumar Deb. Not a single experiment was conducted by the University to directly involve its faculties and students towards the upliftment of the weaker sections of the region, some of whom live right under the nose of the University community and regularly visit the campus in search of fuel and fodder.

University Campus for "Us", Common Pool Resource for "Them" and How the Gap Really Widens

The 150 acres of non-agricultural land on which the Vidyasagar University campus was constructed is still being perceived by the inhabitants of the neighbouring villages as a reservoir of common pool resource on which they have been enjoying customary usufructory rights for several generations. The adjoining villages named Muradanga, Tantigeria and Phulpahari are inhabited by poverty stricken Munda, Oraon and other Scheduled Caste people. On the northeastern side of the campus there is a small settlement of after cure leprosy patients belonging to Scheduled Tribes and Castes who live a highly marginalized existence in the town and represent one of the weakest sections of the locality. Closer observation reveals that the people around the campus of Vidyasagar University do not present a homogeneous entity in terms of economic and socio-cultural features but they share at least three interesting characteristics, which are important for the present discourse. These characteristics are enumerated below:

- All these groups of people used to enjoy usufructory rights of grazing, firewood and other non-timber forest product collection and rights of passage through this land without getting any resistance from any quarter before the establishment of Vidyasagar University. The present campus land was a kind of open access resource and/or common pool resource to these groups of people.
- Since the establishment of the University all these groups of people are experiencing resistance from the University although the responses towards this resistance are not similar for all the groups.
- All these groups of people distinguish themselves from the University community, although no specific term has been found to emerge yet in the vocabulary of these people to designate the paired opposition: "University Community" vis-à-vis the "Local Community". The Levi-Straussian binary opposite does not seem to be very much helpful in this context. (Guha, 2001).

Voices from "Them"

Under this broad background let me present my own interactions with some of the tribal villagers of the locality for whom our campus is their commons. Let me begin with an old Munda villager of Muradanga. His name was Raghunath Singh. He was about sixty years old when I first met him in the year 1987. He was a dark skinned lean man who was strong enough to pedal a three-wheeled cycle rickshaw with passengers in its seat in Medinipur town. It was his occupation since he could not engage himself in cultivation. Raghunath was a man of wit and humour. He used to tell stories of the past.

He narrated his childhood when this Gopgarh area was covered with big sal and other trees and people from the Medinipur town did not dare to come to this place even during the daylight hours. This was a heaven for the large snakes, wolves and jackals and occasionally also used to roam in this area. "The land of your university was never used for cultivation". Raghunath went on saying "It is the grazing field of our cattle, our women collect fuel from your ground and our children play here. The Rajas of Gop gave this land to us. We defended our village from the attacks of the robbers with our bow and arrow and village unity". "But" Raghunath used to continue "now your guards are creating problems for us". He frequently lamented over the rapid weakening of the collective strength of the inhabitants of his village. I later learnt that Raghunath's sons did not look after him properly. After four or five years, he suddenly became much older and could not pedal the rickshaw anymore. Raghunath started to beg on the streets of Medinipur. Every Sunday morning he reached our campus limping with the help of a stick and collected some coins from the residents of the University quarters and then used to go to the town. After not seeing him for some weeks, I enquired with a young man of Muradanga and came to know that Raghunath had died a few days ago. In 1997, few years after the death of Raghunath, the university authority employed a Calcutta based private security agency to protect and guard the campus from the "encroachers". The university authority had also started a plantation of *akashmoni*, eucalyptus, *sirish* and some fruit trees on the western residential side of the campus. The cost of employing of employing the security agency was Rs.4,80,000 not a negligible amount for the University. The main task of the security guards was to drive away the grazing animals of Muradanga and Saltola. The people of the neighbouring villages adopted interesting strategies to continue the grazing of their animal on this traditional common pool resource base. One strategy was to play a hide and seek game with the security guards and the other was to send the grazing animals in night to the campus land when it was very difficult for the security men to locate the animals. The proposed plantation of the University, however did not materialize due to various reasons. For example, the grazing animals ate up many saplings; some were also taken away by the villagers any some died for the lack of proper care and protection. There was no attempt on the part of the University to involve the tribal villagers in the protection of the plantation of the University although a specific proposal was submitted by the Anthropology department of the University in this regard.

I would now narrate the anecdote of "Saltola", which is the name of the settlement of leprosy-affected patients who have been living by the side of the boundary wall of the University on the east. If one comes through the metal road of Tantigeria to reach Vidyasagar University in the night one may not even know the existence of this group of people who have planted a good number of indigenous varieties of trees. They do not have electricity, latrines and supply of safe drinking water from the municipality. They are of course voters and their settlement is known to the general public and the district administration as a settlement of lepers or *kusthapally*. They also graze their cattle and collect the fuel from the University campus. In course of my anthropological encounters, I came to know about the indigenous name of this settlement. The inhabitants of this place call their settlement by two interesting appellations, one is *thutapara* which means "a hamlet of physically handicapped people" since "thuta" in spoken Bengali means a person whose limbs, particularly the hands have become non-functional. *Thuta* symbolizes a person affected by leprosy. This has a derogatory connotation and many people of the town designate this colony by this term and the inhabitants also use it in their daily conversation although they would not usually mention this name of their settlement to a newcomer. The other name by which the inhabitants refer to their settlement is "Saltola". Saltola means "a hamlet where on can find sal trees" (*shorea robusta*). And here comes the anecdote. In one evening, while I was discussing the problems of getting *patta* (a deed of right over land awarded by the state government to landless and poor families) for the families of this settlement with its inhabitants, a very energetic cultivator, Nagen Ari who belonged to the Sabar tribe narrated an incident. Let me translate Nagen's narrative in verbatim: "When I came from Gokulpur to this area there was a very big *sal* tree at this place. We used to enjoy its cool shadow and our children played beneath its huge canopy. It was about twenty years ago. But one day few men from the Tantigeria panchayat office came to this place and told that they would hack down the tree for using its wood to make the furniture of their office. We objected by saying that you won't get much wood from this tree because it has already been bored by the termites." Nagen continued, "The panchayat men didn't care since they were unable to understand this from outside. They brought their men and felled the tree but not much wood was obtained. Our prediction was correct." Then Nagen said with an emphatic smile, "you see, although the tree has gone but we call this place 'Saltola', which means that this was the abode of the huge *Sal*." Three years ago, the district administration made a move to rehabilitate the inhabitants of Saltola in another place in Tantigeria, which is about 1 kilometer from Saltola. The district administration seemed to be more interested to shift these families from near the University campus than giving them pattas on this land and the general attitude of the University community was not also favourable to these after cure leprosy patients although, we have not found any individual in Saltola currently affected by the disease. We carried out a socio-demographic survey at Saltola and another adjoining colony in 1995 among the 74 households in collaboration of an NGO who runs a hospital for the leprosy patients. We have found that there were 100 deformed persons (47 males and 53 females) who were once affected by the disease and no individual below twenty years of age was neither found to be deformed nor affected by leprosy (Bhuniya, Guha and Das, 1996). With the effort of the district administration 12 families from Saltola were shifted in a resettlement colony and all these families now lament for leaving Saltola since in the resettlement colony they could not continue the village life of Saltola. Moreover, very recently in 2004, the district administration has given land *patta* to the families whom they could not resettle. Here we may recall one interesting incident regarding the attitude of the University community towards the marginalized families of Saltola. In the year 1997, the members of the University community decided to organize a procession on the occasion of the celebration of the 50th year of country's Independence and they had also resolved to distribute some fruits and sweets to the poor people of the locality. Interestingly, neither Muradanga nor Saltola was selected for this purpose. Someone suggested the name of Saltola but it was rejected on the ground that many members of the University community might not like to visit a "leper colony" on such an occasion. On 15th August 1997, the procession, under the leadership of the then vice-chancellor Professor Amiya Kumar Deb passed by the side of Saltola (I also participated in it) and traveled some important parts of the Medinipur town and finally donated the fruits and sweets to the authority of the district hospital for its distribution to the patients.

This in brief constitute the deconstruction of the myth of the non-traditional University at Medinipur in West Bengal. The narratives of Muradanga and Saltola signify how the process of disempowerment and marginalization of the rural tribal and the poor families have been taking place in and around Vidyasagar University which was established to contribute to the improvement of the socio-economic conditions of the rural poor and particularly the tribals of the region.

From Policing to Participation: A Prelude to Campus Anthropology

During 1995-96, Vidyasagar University got about 40 acres of land from the District Land and Land Reforms Department on the Western side of the residential campus right within Raghunath's village Muradanga. The University executive council decided to utilise the plot (this land has been designated by the University authority as the "third plot") through the extension of some of its academic departments and accordingly suggestions were invited from those departments. The Department of Anthropology submitted a proposal to involve the tribal people of this village for this purpose (Department of Anthropology, 1997). We reproduce here a summarized version of the said proposal.

Anthropological enquiries revealed that the tribals of Muradanga still perceive the plot given to the University as their common pool resource. The tribals of this village are basically agriculturists who depend upon monocrop rain fed cultivation, collection of non-timber forest produce and daily wage labour in the neighbouring township. The basic needs of the people of Muradanga revolve around supply of water for irrigation and pasture for their cattle. A canal dug by the state irrigation department runs through their village, but it remains dry throughout the year. It has been found through interviews of some villagers and field observations that the "third plot" is also being used by the people of Muradanga as grazing field as well as for the collection of minor forest produce. It was reported that some families of the village also occasionally cultivate paddy on this plot. On a more intimate level, the villagers have expressed their grudge towards the irrigation department for not being able to supply water for cultivation of their subsistence crop. They were not also found to be happy with the District Land and Land Reforms Department for not distributing patta lands to the families of the village who really need it. This is the wider context under which the huge plot of common land (which is legally placed within the domain of State property) was given to Vidyasagar University.

Under this background, the Department of Anthropology strongly felt that it would be more economical as well as in tune with the needs and age-old customary rights of the people of Muradanga, if the academic departments of the University could involve the villagers in the protection as well as sustainable development of the third plot. This could be done by extending the twin principles of (i) benefit sharing and (ii) social fencing as enunciated in the 1985 National Forest Policy of The Government of India. This will be also in line with the objectives of Vidyasagar University.

A derailed plan for the parcicipatory management of the third plot was also worked out in the proposal that ran as follows:

Benefit sharing and social fencing could be done through a step-by-step gradual process. In the first step, an area of grazing field may be enclosed within the third plot where the villagers would graze their cattle and attention should be given to grow sufficient fodder on this area. In lieu of this gesture the villagers may be motivated to take part in developing a garden for the University outside the enclosed area based on the principles of joint forest management since this is a well-known phenomenon for the villagers. In the next stage, the University may involve the villagers to harvest rainwater in ponds and start pisciculture and the latter could also use the water in irrigating vegetable gardens. In order to do this kind of participatory management of the "third plot" the various departments of the University may conduct empirical studies on the different dimensions of the socio-economic life of Muradanga and its surroundings. These empirical surveys would require good rapport and interaction between the University community and the villagers and would also help in gaining the confidence of the people who have been marginalized by the establishment of the University.

The proposal of the Department of Anthropology was submitted to the University authority in July 1997 and the authorities admired the proposal and shelved it in the proverbial red file and the villagers are using the "third plot" as a common land till today (Guha, 2004).

Postscript

In this connection, it may be relevant to mention the case of Manomanium Sundaharnar University in the Tirunelveli district of Tamil Nadu. According to a report published in a national daily, this small and young University has set an example in conducting action oriented research projects by involving the local people in many rural development schemes which include organic farming, wasteland development and acquaculture. Dr. N. Sukumaran, Head of the Centre for Environmental Sciences of this University said in a training-cum-seminar programme in the Agricultural Science Centre at Kapgari in West Medinipur: "The key to our success lies in the fact that the faculties and the students of the centre regularly meet the locals to understand their problems and solve them" (*The Statesman*, 1998). Interestingly, two faculties of Vidyasagar University from its Botany and Zoology Departments were sent to M.S. University to get an exposure on organic farming through vermiculture in collaboration with the Centre for Women's Development Studies, New Delhi. Ironically, neither the tribal women of Muradanga nor the women of Saltola were involved in developing vermicompost by the Botany and the Zoology Departments of Vidyasagar University.

Acknowledgements

I would not have been able to write this paper without the help of the villagers of Muradanga and Saltola who provided me with much valuable information about our University campus and its surroundings. I remain greatly indebted to them. I am also thankful to my colleagues, particularly, Gopal, Falguni, Rajatda, Ambarish, of the University who gave me many useful information and made critical comments on the earlier drafts of the paper. I owe a lot to my wife Priti and my sons Roni and Ruru who always take part in the discussions on our campus, which have become our family affair! My colleagues and the members of my family are not of course responsible for the shortcomings of the paper. Finally, I would like to express my sincerest thanks to Deepak Kumar Behera and Georg Pfeffer for inviting me to present the paper at the International Conference on Tribal Society in India and Beyond held during 17-19 December 2004 at Sambalpur University, Orissa.

REFERENCES

Bhuniya, S., A. Guha and R.K. Das. 1996. "Beggars May Have Choice: A Socio-demographic Study of the Lepers in Medinipur Town, West Bengal," *Journal of Indian Anthropological Society,* 31: 273-278.

Deb, A.K. 1997. "Convocation Address of the Vice-Chancellor," (delivered on 4 April 1997), Vidyasagar University, Midnapore.

Department of Anthropology. 1997. "Proposal" (Submitted to the Registrar, Vidyasagar University dated 10.07.97) [unpublished] Midnapore.

Ghosh, S.N. 1995. "Convocation Address of the Vice-Chancellor," (lecture delivered on 9th January 1995 at Vidyasagar University, Midnapore.

Guha, A. 2001. "An Anthropological Enquiry of Vidyasagar University Campus: Myth and Reality." *Journal of Indian Anthropological Society,* 36: 251-255.

____. 2004. "Wither Civil Society?" *Down To Earth,* 13 (12), November 15, 2004.

Mukherjee, B.C. 1987-88. "Vidyasagar University: Its Objectives and Character," *Journal of Higher Education,* 13 (1-3): 125-126.

National Atlas and Thematic Mapping Organization. 1992. "Medinipur" (Urban Studies Series) New Delhi.

The Statesman. 1998. "A Tale of Two Universities: Hundreds of Miles Apart": 9 July 1998 (p.3), Calcutta.

The Vidyasagar University Act, 1981. Section entitled "The University and its Officers" Vidyasagar University, Midnapore.

SIXTEEN

INTERVENTION AND POLITICAL CULTURE: A Case Study of the Kanwar Tribe of Chhattisgarh

A.K. SINHA and B.G. BANERJEE

In the profession of anthropology, the concept of interventionism is not something new. Lisa R. Peattie (1968) in her article, "Interventionism and Applied Science in Anthropology," had pointed out a typical anthropological approach towards interventionism. She has referred to an article way back in 1882 mentioning about the first French anthropological society to be active in this direction. Later anthropological societies of London and Paris took interest in this topic *vis-à-vis* applied anthropology. She has dealt in detail the topic of interventionism and the role of applied anthropologist world over. She raised certain viable questions. To what extent is it proper for present generations to undergo discomfort in the interest of the (presumed) advantage of future generations? To what extent has one man or group of men a right to exert power over others, even in their own interest? To what extent may men ever be said to have free choice, and in what circumstances?

The intervention philosophy, an ideal justification for outsiders guide native people in specific directions, seems to be the guiding force for economic development. Bodley (1988) argues that the basic belief behind interventions—whether by colonialists, missionaries, governments, or development planners—has been the same for more than 100 years. This belief is that industrialization, modernization, westernization, and individualism are desirable evolutionary advances and that development schemes that promote them will bring long-term benefits to natives. In a more extreme form, intervention philosophy may pit the assumed wisdom of enlightened colonial or other First World planners against the purported conservatism, ignorance, or "obsolescence" of "inferior" natives.

Anthropologists dispute such views. We know that for thousands of years bands and tribes have done "a reasonable job of taking care of themselves" (Bodley, 1988: 93). Indeed, because of their low energy needs, they have managed their resources better than we manage our own. Many problems that people face today are due to their position within nation-states and their increasing dependence on the world cash economy.

Sometimes when natives are reluctant to change, it is not because they have unduly conservative attitudes but because powerful interest groups oppose reform. Many Third World governments are reluctant to tamper with existing socio-economic conditions in their countries (Manners, 1973 cf. Kottak, 1997: 426).

Conflicts between governments (colonial or post-colonial) and natives often arise when outside interests exploit resources on tribal lands. Driven by deficits and debts, governments seek to wrest as much wealth as possible from the territory they administer. This goal helps explain the worldwide intrusion on indigenous peoples and their local ecosystems by highway construction, mining, hydroelectric projects, ranching, lumbering, agribusiness, and planned colonization (Bodley, 1988).

Studying people at the local level, ethnographers have a unique view of the impact of national and international planning on intended "beneficiaries". Local-level research often reveals inadequacies in the measures that economists use to assess development and a nation's economic health.

Today, many government agencies, international groups, and private foundations encourage attention to local-level social factors and the cultural dimension of development. Anthropological expertise is important because social problems can doom the projects to failure. A study of fifty development projects (Lance and McKenna, 1975) judged only twenty-one to be successes. Social and cultural incompatibilities had doomed most of the failed projects (Kottak, 1997: 426).

However, ethical dilemmas often confront applied anthropologists (Escobgar, 1991, 1995). Our respect for cultural diversity is often offended because efforts to extend industry and technology may entail profound cultural changes. Foreign aid does not usually go where need and suffering are greatest. It is spent on political, economic, and strategic priorities as national leaders and powerful interest groups perceive them. Planners' interests do not always coincide with the best interests of the local people. Although the aim of most development projects is to enhance the quality of life, living standards often decline in the target area (Bodley, 1988).

In the backdrop of the discussion the authors have endeavoured to explore the extent of benefits of governmental intervention that a small tribal group, called the Kanwar, of Chhattisgarh State, through the concept of political culture. It is imperative that one must delineate the threads that weave the concept of political culture. Hence discussion on the conceptual orientations towards political culture has been contained in the subsequent discussion.

The study of the concept of political culture constitutes an examination of the anthropological aspect of the subject of political development. At the broadest level political culture refers to the meanings attributed to politics (Aronoff, 2001). Even since this term was popularized by some leading writers like Beer and Ulam (1962) and Almond and Verba (1963), it has come to stand as a very important touchstone for a morphological study of the political system. It had influenced the system-theorists to assert that one political system is distinguished from another not only in terms of its structure but also in respect of the political culture in which it lays embedded.

Although the term "political culture" is used primarily by political scientists and historians (Gendzel, 1997), interest in the relationship between politics and culture — including the investigation of the extent to which each constitutes an autonomous realm — is of interest in fields in which the practitioners use the term less frequently; for example, anthropology, sociology (Swidler, 1984) and cultural studies.

The two major approaches to political culture are semiotic (via anthropology) and cognitive (via social psychology). Wilson (2000) subdivides them into five approaches. Hermeneutics, influenced by the work of Clifford Geertz, is an important bridge between traditional and postmodern approaches. The interpretative semiotic approached has been very influential in the social science and humanities—the boundary between these two having become increasingly blurred in recent decades.

Scott (1990) utilizes this approach to investigate the boundaries of the political. The culture theory approach builds upon the work of Mary Douglas. Developed by Thompson, Ellis, and Wildavsky (1990), it postulates a universal division of polities into four ideal-type subcultures based on two criteria. Analysis focuses on the contestation within polities between competing subcultures, and explains change in terms of their different competencies and biases.

Social character is the third approach influenced by anthropology, but it also draws heavily from social psychology. It emerged from studies of culture and personality, and national character. Personality variables are analyzed in terms of types of significant value orientations, including attitudes towards and dependence upon authority, fear of disorder, and various religious and ideological positions. These studies generally are based on the analysis of the relationship between norms and behaviour in specific cultural contexts. The social learning approach, based more directly on psychological theories, utilizes social surveys to analyze values and beliefs to explain the role of socialization in determining values and behaviour. Inglehart's (1997) work on the relationship between generational change and post-materialist values illustrates this approach well, following the tradition of the Civic Culture. Other cognitive approaches incorporate Piaget's theories and conceptualize value orientations very differently from social character studies. Analysis focuses on the reciprocal relationship between individual development and social life. In some of this work moral reasoning and development is at the centre of analysis.

Political cultures are dynamic because they are embedded in changing historical, social, economic, cultural and political environments that shape them, and which are in turn shaped by them. The relationship between these variables is dialectical.

The behaviour of political systems, and of the people within them, is a function of ideas about politics. People have pictures in their heads about what constitutes appropriate political behaviour, and will evaluate the performance of their governments accordingly.

A political culture "is composed of the attitudes, beliefs, emotions and values of society that relates to the political system and to political values" (Ball, 1971: 56). It is also defined as "the pattern of individual attitudes and orientations towards politics among the members of a political system" (Almond and Powell, 1966: 50). The people of a given society share a common human nature like emotional drives, intellectual capacities and moral perspectives. This common human nature expresses itself in the form of certain values, beliefs and emotional attitudes which are transmitted from one generation to another, though with greater or lesser modifications, and thus constitute the general culture of that society. "Certain aspects of the general culture of that society are especially concerned with how government ought to be conducted and what it shall try to do. This sector of culture we call political culture (Beer and Ulam, 1962: 32 cf. Johari, 1976: 155). It "is that set of attitudes, beliefs and sentiments that give order and meaning to a political process and that provides the underlying assumptions and rules that govern behaviour in the political system" (Pye, 1966: 104).

From the above, one may discern the point that the political culture has certain components having their place in the world of anthropology. They are: values, beliefs and emotional attitudes of the people towards their political system. We may observe that the people have, in general, certain political values as elections should be held periodically and also in a free and fair manner, that the ministers should resign if they forfeit the confidence of the people or their chosen deputies, that no person should be made to suffer in body or in goods unless a verdict is given by a competent court of law following a procedure established by the organic law of the country etc. Closely linked with political values is the component of political beliefs about the actual behaviour of men. It includes certain norms such as that adult population of a country has the right to take part in the political discussions. The significant cause of the beliefs should also be traced in this fact that ideas that "do not appear at first glance to have relevance to politics may be intimately connected with it through the belief system of the political culture" (Beer and Ulam, 1962: 32 cf. Johari, 1976: 155).

A political culture hinging on the fact of people's attitudes and beliefs towards the political system, whether homogenous or heterogenous, is a product of several inter-related factors — historical, geographical and socio-economic. Moreover, it is not static; it is dynamic and thus responds to the needs generated from within political system or imparted or imposed from outside.

Political culture can be classified according to whether the members of a society take an active or a passive part in the political process. That is, whether they play a part with an ardent expectation of tangible benefits from the governmental activity, or whether they have very little, or almost no knowledge of the decision-making process and thus have no hopes for a share in the power. Almond begins with this assumption that political culture and political structure are intricately interrelated as one is affected by the other and the operation of one is conditioned by another. In order to elucidate the relationship between the two, he introduces the concepts of roles and orientations to political action. He looks at the political system as a set of interactive roles, or a structure of roles in which each individual or group is taken as a political actor. The second assumption of Almond is that a political system operates within a framework of set of meanings — attitudes of the people towards political activity. Thus, there appears a thing like the pattern of orientations to political action that may be described as another name for political culture.

Almond presents a classification of political cultures on subjects-participants basis and his classification of the political systems on the basis of different political cultures. In the classification of political cultures the basic touchstone is his emphasis on the roles of the subjects and the participants. Persons aware of the political system may be either subjects (those individuals who are oriented to the political system and the impact which its outputs, such as welfare benefits, laws, etc. may have upon their lives, but who are not oriented to participation in the input structures) and participants (those individuals who are oriented to the input structures and processes, and engaged in or view themselves as potentially engaging in the articulation of demands and the making of decisions). Almond further states that orientations to politics include the notions of the individual about himself as a political actor (Almond and Powell, 1966: 53-54).

Yet Rosenbaum (1975) feels that "the concept of political culture offers a potentially powerful, and almost always useful, approach to daily political events by identifying the underlying psychological forces that shape much of civic life".

"Political culture can be defined in two ways, depending upon the level at which we want to study political life. If we concentrate on the individual, political culture has a basically psychological focus. It entails all the important ways in which a person is subjectively oriented towards the essential elements in his political system. We want to know what he feels and thinks about the symbols, institutions, and rules that constitute the fundamental political order of his society and how he responds to them. In effect, we are probing the psychological dimension of a person's civic life; we ask what bonds exist between him and the essentials of his political system and how these bonds affect his behaviour".

"The second definition of political culture refers to the collective orientation of people towards the basic elements in their political system. This is a "system level" approach. We are interested in how large masses of citizens evaluate their political institutions and officials. To say, for example, "that a nation's political culture is largely 'integrated' means that most people within the system have similar, or compatible, political culture orientation, which are congenial to the political institution within which they live. When political culture is discussed, it usually refers to these mass political orientations across the whole political system" (Rosenbaum, 1975: 3-4). Some operational definitions of political culture orientations, put forth by Rosenbaum (1975) is given in Appendix-I.

Chhattisgarh and the Kanwar

Chhattisgarh, carved out of India's largest state of Madhya Pradesh came into being on 1 November 2000 as the 26th state of the Union, consisting of 16 districts, namely Bastar, Bilaspur, Champa, Dantewara, Dhamtari, Durg, Jashpur, Kanker, Korba, Koriya, Kwardha, Mahasamund, Raigarh and Raipur. This new state lies between latitudes 17°85'N-24°10'N and longitudes 80°20'E-84°25'E and has an area of approximately 1,35,194 sq. km. It is elongated from north to south with an extension of about 400 km. and widens upto a distance of about 385 km. from east to west. It is bound by southern Jharkhand and Orissa in the east, Madhya Pradesh and Maharashtra in the west, Uttar Pradesh and Western Jharkhand in the north and Andhra Pradesh in the south. Area-wise Chhattisgarh is the ninth largest state and population-wise it is seventeenth state of the nation.

The total tribal population of Chhattisgarh state is 46,41,104 which constitutes 33.13 per cent of the total population of the Nation (Census of India 2001). It is noticed that the tribal communities have sizeable population almost in all the districts of the state except Raipur. As a result these districts are notified as tribal districts of the state. There are 43 tribal communities concentrated in the districts of Bastar, Bilaspur and Surguja.

The Kanwar are the inhabitants of the districts of Raigarh and Raipur of Chhattisgarh. "In Bilaspur the name is always pronounced with a nasal tone Kanwar" (Russell and Hira Lal, 1975: 389). They believe that the term Kanwar has been derived from Kaurav, the ruling clan of the *Mahabharata*, and state that they are the descendants of one of the Kauravas. Trivedi (1971) reports that the term Kanwar appears to be a corruption of the word Kauravas, who were trusted soldiers of the Haihaibansi chiefs of Ratanpur. There are about twelve endogamous divisions among them, a few of which are Rathia Kawar, Paikara Kawar, Dudh Kanwar, Tanwar Kanwar, Cherwa Kawar and Kamal Vansi Kanwar. They are notified as a scheduled tribe in Chhattisgarh along with a few groups such as the Kanwar, Kaur, Cherwa, Rathia, etc. They are predominantly a rural-based community (98.54%).

Singh observes: "The Kanwar, in general, are of below medium stature, and show a long and narrow head shape with long face and broad nose (Ahmad, 1963). Their skin colour is light brown to dark brown and they have scanty hair on the body and face. According to Negi (1953), they show a relatively higher incidence of gene B (34%) than gene A (21%). Thus, on the whole, they maintain a distinct biological identity from the numerically dominant central Indian tribal group of Gondid strains.

"The Kanwar are divided into a number of exogamous clans (*gotiar*) like Tilasi, Darpan, Bama, Sandhur, Sagar and Sonvani. These people are generally monogamous.

"The Kanwar are landowning cultivators. As a subsidiary occupation, they work as labourers. According to the 1981 census, 44.85 per cent of them have returned as workers (68.80% males and 29.11% females). Of them, 77.41 per cent were cultivators and 18.18 per cent were agricultural labourers. The remaining 4.41 per cent were engaged in other services. The Kanwar selects a person to head the community council for several villages. He is assisted by elderly members of the community. The council looks after the social order within the community. They worship their principal deity, Dulhadeo, village deities like Mahamai, Thakurdeo, Gaongosai, etc. their clan gods and other Hindu gods. In the 1981 census 99.91 per cent of the Kanwar returned as followers of Hinduism, 0.06 per cent as Christians and 0.01 per cent as Sikhs.

"The Kanwar employ agricultural servants from their neighbouring communities. They accept cooked food from the Gond, Rout and Bhaina communities but not from any other community. Some members of the community have taken up salaried jobs in organized sectors and a few have become traders. They favour education for their children, especially for the boys. The girls usually discontinue their education to get married. According to the 1981 census, 19.03 per cent of them were returned literate. While the male literacy rate was 32.36 per cent, the female literacy rate was 5.86 per cent. Politically the community has come into prominence and few of them are members of the Legislative Assembly of the state. They avail the modern medical facilities, but also have faith in traditional methods of cure. Their attitude towards the family planning programme is positive" (Singh, 2001: 484-486).

The Rationale

The total population of the Kanwar tribe in Chhattisgarh is 6,47,659 (1991 Census), out of which 1,65,862 lived in Bilaspur district (Bhatt, 2003). Bilaspur district was selected as the regional locale for the present study. Out of the 15 Tehsils of Bilaspur district (undivided Madhya Pradesh then), two Tehsils—Katghora and Korba—have 80 per cent of the Kanwar population and, therefore, these two Tehsils have been chosen for the study. Two villages out of each block of these two Tehsils were selected and from each of the villages (listed in Chart-1), twenty informants were selected following random sampling technique. Thus, the entire study is based on interviews of 200 people, including educated and uneducated men and women, some of them associated with politics. In order to add to the value of the survey, people were also interviewed in groups.

Chart 16.1: Villages selected for fieldwork

Sl. No.	*Tehsil*	*Block*	*Name of the Selected Villages*
1.	Katghora	Katghora, Pori, Uprora Pali	Malgaon, Marvadodha Tanakhar, Tuman, Amgaon, Hardi Bazar
2.	Korba	Korba Kartala	Bhaisma, Chitapali, Beharchuan, Barpali

The authors are aware of the difficulty of applying the concept of political culture in any analytical study. The difficulty from an analytic point of view is that identifying exactly how political culture exerts its influence in political life is difficult. Too often the cultural elements of politics become a residual explanation—when more objectively demonstrable variables are unsuccessful in explanation then the outcomes must be the consequences of political culture. Several of the approaches to political culture do provide some objective measures of culture, but even with those it is difficult to establish a clear link between the indicators of individual political values and the behaviour of whole political systems. Making this linkage remains one of the major challenges for the advocates of political culture (Ball and Peters, 2000: 89).

In the field of political anthropology the concepts of politics as well as culture are significant. The discipline of political science has a significant theoretical as well as conceptual contribution to make in the dynamics of present politics. In an era of interdisciplinary approach the authors contemplated to fruitfully utilize the concept of political culture as enunciated by Rosenbaum. The framework and the schedule seemed appropriate to analyze the political culture of a tribal group — the Kanwar of Chhattisgarh. Also it is of much consideration that the people under study had many of their tribal political leaders permanently residing within the same habitat. It was also to test whether their presence made any positive influence on their political culture. After a perusal of existing literature relating to the analysis of political culture and various conceptual framework we turn to the work of Rosenbaum and the theoretical model postulated by him. This model is being tested in this article for the Kanwar, presently settled in Chhattisgarh.

Kanwars and Political Culture: The Past

The characteristics contained in the concept of political culture, as per Rosenbaum, are "political identification", "political trust", "regime orientation", "rules of the game", "political efficacy", "political competence", and "input-output orientation".

Political Identification

This attribute relates to notion of citizenship; political units and groups towards which one feels positively or negatively; and political units and groups with which one is most often involved. In other words it relates to an individual's political affiliation which may be at the national, regional and local levels.

The investigation reveals that the Kanwar had little or no political awareness. Whatever, little political awareness existed, it was at the local level and never at the national level. They respected their own customary law and no one dared to disrespect them.

Political Trust

This concept relates to different arrangements/structure of political system and their faith/beliefs and participation in it. According to operational definition it is willingness to collaborate with various groups in different types of social action; group memberships; and rating of groups in terms of trustworthiness, political motives, type of membership, etc.

The study reveals that the Kanwar were totally committed to their traditional gram panchayat and customary law. The settlement of disputes and related problems were resolved in their own community and would hardly look forward elsewhere for their resolutions. They did not care for governmental judicial system.

Regime Orientations

It is belief in the legitimacy of the regime; feelings towards, and evaluations of, major political offices and regime symbols; and involvement in political activity supporting to opposing the regime.

Their worldview regarding national political system was far from the existing reality. There was total apathy towards it. This could be because of their lack of knowledge regarding political administration. No governmental institution like a police station or a bank was there in their rural setting.

Rules of the Game

It covers how one feels political opinions should be expressed; concepts of political obligations for oneself and others; concepts of how political decisions should be made by government; and attitudes toward political deviation and dissent.

The Kanwar had full faith in a person of their community. The election of a headman (*Mukhiya*) was made through consensus. The elected person would thus enjoy the confidence of his fellowmen. The rites and rituals like marriage, etc. were performed as per their traditional and contemporary norms. Home-made remedies dominated in case of a person falling sick.

Political Efficacy

It is believed that government is responsive to one's opinions; belief in importance of civic activism and participation; and belief in possibilities of political change.

Political efficacy means awareness and activity of the government towards local people. Lack of education was the prime reason for their ignorance towards political system and its attributes. Hence the question of political stand or influence did not arise.

Political Competence

It includes frequency of voting and other types of political activity; knowledge of political events and their influence on oneself; and interest in political affairs. Lack of communication and mass media, and formal education could be attributed to be detrimental for such a situation.

Input-Output Orientation

It relates to satisfaction with governmental policy; knowledge of how political demands are made on government; and belief in effectiveness of policy inputs and outputs. There was an utter dissatisfaction with the governmental policy. Also the knowledge of how political demands were made on the government was totally missing.

To conclude, in the past there was a total ignorance of the Kanwar towards political trust, political efficacy and political awareness. Lack of education, mass media and a firm conviction and commitment towards their own community were the major determinants for them to refrain from becoming a part in the mainstream of Indian way of living at the time of Independence. There is yet another reason for this state of affair — isolation from other communities. The villages used to be totally void of outsiders and outside influences. There was hardly any communication between the community and the outside world. Those who were considered elite among the community because of their better economic and educational attainment also toed in line with the sentiments of their villagers.

Kanwars and Political Culture: The Contemporary Scenario

Assuming Rosenbaum's working definition as our base we endeavour to assess and understand the extent and magnitude of political culture of the Kanwar. According to Rosenbaum (1975: 6) what the core elements appears to share is of fundamental importance in shaping a nation's political order. Wherever analysts offer such a list they are, in effect, using a rule of thumb: those dimensions of an individual's thoughts, feeling, or behaviour that are linked to the creation and maintenance of a society's fundamental political order, belong to the label "political culture". Thus, insists one observer, political culture must be limited to the "attitudes, beliefs and sentiments that give order and meaning to the political process and provide the underlying assumptions and rules that govern behaviour" (Pye, 1966: 104-5).

It is helpful to think of these core components as orientations towards different elements in the political order. Such a list commonly includes the following particulars:

Orientations towards Governmental Structures

Regime Orientation

How an individual evaluates and responds to the basic government institution of his society, its symbols, officials, and norms (collectively, the "regime"); this may include a more detailed investigation of orientations towards specific institutions and offices or an investigation of preferences for alternative governmental structures.

What type of orientation do the Kanwar have towards specific political institution and offices like corporations, administrations, courts and those who work for administrations, the way they work, their individual capacity and effectiveness are worth probing. People were asked whether they liked traditional system of customary law or constitutional law. According to the assessment it was found that 76 per cent was in favour of traditional system; 17 per cent preferred the constitutional law; 4.50 per cent were with both the systems and 2.50 per cent did not answer.

Orientations towards Governmental Inputs and Outputs

How individuals feel and respond towards various demands for public policy ("inputs") and policy decisions made by government ("outputs") are major concern towards political orientation; this may include an inventory of a person's knowledge concerning how these processes operate, what demands he may make upon government, and how effective he believes governmental policy to be.

People were asked whether the government had made any special policy/policies for their education or not. 80 per cent had knowledge about this; 11.50 per cent had no knowledge; and 8.50 per cent did not answer. Thus, it is evident that a majority of people had knowledge of the governmental policies, showing a definite rise in interest of people towards various policies and programmes run by the government.

Orientations towards Others in the Political System

Political Identifications

The political units (nation, state, town, region), geographic area, and groups to which one feels he belongs, that are in some significant subjective sense a part of his own social identity; in particular, these include those units and groups to which he feels a strong loyalty, obligation, or duty.

Some respondents were asked whether they are citizens of India or Chhattisgarh. The responses showed that 70.50 per cent were correct while 14.50 per cent were wrong. 7 per cent said that they belonged to both and 8 per cent did not respond.

Political Trust

The extent to which one feels an open, cooperative, or tolerant attitude in working with other in civic life; essentially, political trust expresses the intensity of a person's conviction that other individuals or groups mean him well (or ill) in political life.

To study people's participation and trust in various aspects of political system like law and order, people were asked whether they liked laws governed by their own community or by the state/nation. The results showed that 60.50 per cent were in favour of laws governed by their own community. Only 13.50 per cent showed faith in government while 10.50 per cent agreed on both, 15.50 per cent were not very clear in their mind.

The response pattern clearly indicates that the Kanwar have more faith in their own community's rules and regulations rather than Indian constitutional law. Their political identification is strongly in favour of their own community norms.

Rules of the Game

An individual's conception of what rules should be followed in civic life; these subjective preferences may or may not be consistent with prevailing law and other norms supposed to govern civic conduct.

In light of the above statements it was asked whether they felt that education is necessary for both girls and boys or not. 73.50 per cent responses were for both girls and boys; 18 per cent for boys only, 8.50 per cent did not answer. It also confirms their faith with the prevailing law and other norms of the community.

Orientations towards One's Own Political Activity

Political Competence

How often, and in what manner, a person participates in civic life, the frequency with which he uses the political resources available to him in civic affairs is the domain of political competence; this may include some evaluation of his knowledge of his political resources.

To measure political competence a question was asked from them to name the ruling political party in the country. 54.5 per cent replied correctly; 11.5 per cent incorrectly and 34 per cent did not respond.

Hence, it is clear that amongst Kanwar tribe only 54.5 per cent people have information regarding national political system. While the rest have no knowledge of this. The situation is indicative of a transition through which the Kanwars are slowly getting themselves acquainted with various national political activities and happenings.

Political Efficacy

"The feeling that individual political action does have, or can have, an impact on the political process" this includes a belief that political change is possible and that one can accomplish change through civic action — individuals are customarily ranked on a scale according to whether their "sense of political efficacy" is "high" or "low".

To measure political efficacy people were asked whether they were satisfied with the special safeguards made for them in the constitution or not. It was found that 45 per cent of them were satisfied; 33.5 per cent less satisfied; and 21.5 per cent did not respond.

From this it is clear that a high percentage of people had no knowledge of the constitutional safeguards made for them. Hence a low sense of political efficacy.

State Intervention and People's Response

Apart from the analysis, based on Rosenbaum's model of the political culture that exists in the Kanwar, it is worthwhile to observe if the Kanwar have directly or indirectly have been politically alive to the governmental intervention and the infrastructure there in. In the subsequent discussion this has been highlighted.

Governmental Welfare Scheme

It was found out that more than 80 per cent of the respondents had never heard of any welfare scheme being run by the government. According to them, "we do not know anything about the governmental schemes, but yes what we can recall is that at the time of the last election the politicians were discussing about these schemes." Only 20 per cent people, who were literates and whose financial condition was stable, were found to be aware of these schemes. They had knowledge about the various schemes run by the government.

Beneficiaries of various Schemes

It was realized that the various schemes prepared by the government for the scheduled tribes and their benefits were found unsatisfactory by these people. 60 per cent of the respondents admitted that, "the schemes have benefited them but due to a lot of problems cropping up while getting the benefits, the schemes have not been able to deliver as much as desired." As far as the questions of others are concerned they have fully benefited from the schemes. But it is important to mention here that these people are a part of the upper strata of that area and are the elites. Due to this a commoner living in these areas has formed an opinion that the benefits of these schemes go only to those people who are already self-sufficient.

The Status of Present Education System

The level of education has progressed to a certain predicated limit due to the schemes, but they are dissatisfied with the present education system. The senior citizens of the village believe that the future of the children is at stake. It has been found through the literates that mostly people are not aware of the facilities which are being available for education. The aged and the elderly believe that they are better off being less educated as compared to the present literate youth. According to Shri Ganesh Ram Kanwar (male/60) who is one of the most respected persons of their society narrated, "I have attained education only up to class four. We (I) have all those qualities which are missing in students who have passed present day matric or M.A". There are four alphabets in class four, which are explained by him in the following way:

Ka, Kha, Ga, Gha

Ka: *se karma karo* (always do your work).
Kha: *se khali mat raho* (Do not sit idle).
Ga: *se Govind ka nam lo* (Always remember God).
Gha: *se Ghari ke samaya anusar kam karo* (Always be punctual).

Thus, we see that they are not satisfied with the new education system. Traditional agriculture is facing an adverse effect due to the out-migration of the young members of the families. The number of agricultural labourers is decreasing day by day. In this type of society where most of the people depend upon agriculture for a living, their kind of view is seen appropriate.

Education versus Employment

It has been revealed that the people of Kanwar tribe are presently aware of the significance of getting educated. Yet after being educated, they are still unemployed. On asking Shri Ganesh Ram Kanwar, whether education has led to some change in their society, he replied:

"Matric wala meta gaya
B.A. wala baya gaya
M.A. karne per na eme ke na ome ke"

To further explain this, he added that it takes a person around 15 to 16 years to complete matric. In present times they do not get any job even after completing their matric. Instead, had he spent this much time to practice their traditional work or agriculture he would have learnt something to earn his livelihood. Unfortunately he is nowhere now. Likewise those who have done their B.A. have high hopes, neither are they capable to do agriculture nor are they successful in getting good jobs. This makes them insane. Those who have passed their M.A. get jobs in the cities which are far away from their village. They do not want to come back to the village and are not even satisfied with the amount of money they earn or get. Thus, they are "neither here nor there".

Reactions to Education System

Although the elderly and aged people of the village are dissatisfied with the new education system, yet on conducting a survey amongst them, it is realized that some elements of change has come in their thinking process. Lately, every village has a primary school and they send their children to these schools to get education. Also, people were mostly aware of the facilities extended by the government for education. In this way, it can be said that even if they are not completely satisfied with the existing education system and are not being able to benefit from it completely, still there is an iota of awareness about education in them and their interest towards it has increased.

Financial Schemes and their Implementation

Although the governmental interventions through various policies are aimed at upliftment of the tribal people, there are certain shortcomings which are revealed at the implementation level. Consequently, the tribal are not able to get the full benefit of the various schemes meant for them because of the apathy of the government officials.

When we look at the problems faced by these people while trying to reap the benefits from the schemes it is evident that half of the amount that is sanctioned and granted to them goes to the mediators or the influential local people. Many tribal are frustrated so much so that they back out in the middle of the process of envisaged financial gains and leave the idea of continuing with the beneficiary governmental welfare programmes.

It is relevant to cite a glaring example here. Shri Prem Singh Kanwar (Male/55) narrates the story thus. A pair of bulls was given under the cooperative village welfare schemes. Soon he realized that they were not as valuable as they were projected to be at the time issuing the loan. Under the said scheme, 50 per cent of the amount is given by the government in the form of a donation and the rest has to be taken from the trustees. According to his narration, it is impossible that hard earned Rs.5000 which was paid by him could match for the pair of bulls he received. In the open market the pair of bulls could have cost much less.

The bank sanctions loans for buying bulls, etc. the tribal were not aware of the scheme under which the loan was sanctioned. In order to get a loan sanctioned they have to be in regular touch with the bank and the competent and sincere bank officials. However, these tribal find the bank officials totally indifferent which disappoint the tribal. Under such a state of affairs the people do not think in terms of what and where did they go wrong, but project their utter disappointment and dissatisfaction towards the schemes and their implementation.

The Problem of Rehabilitation

Many schemes are being established in the name of industrial progresses which, in effect, prove to be dysfunctional to the tribal. A citizen of the country cannot be justifiably be deprived of his sole source of livelihood in the name of development and progress. There are provisions for compensation in matters relating to land-acquisition but the provision is silent on their rehabilitation, particularly in the sphere of livelihood and a steady source of livelihood for the tribal. Definitely, it goes against the fundamental rights enshrined in the Constitution.

The various other schemes which are being established for the progress of tribal have not been able to attract them. The main reason behind this is the issue of suitable rehabilitation. The villages under Katghora tehsil, namely, Malgaon, Jhingatpur, Ratiya, Bailtikri, and Aamgaon village of Pali tahsil were to be taken under the Gewra project in near future. The residents of Amagaon which also include the Kanwar tribal have been given money in the form of cash, some have also been provided with land in Nehru Nagar for the purpose of rehabilitation which is not liked by them. They feel that money would shortly get exhausted. But their land had been a steady source of livelihood for them for generations. The tribal are utterly disappointed and unhappy about the felling of trees and cutting of forests and their rehabilitation elsewhere.

They do not want to part with their land, a symbol of attachment that they have with their ancestors, and place. Any extent of money cannot compensate for the bondage and the emotional sentiment that the tribal have for their ancestral land and forest. The intended industrial development and their consequent benefits to the tribal is a matter of prolonged discussion. What is paramount presently is a suitable rehabilitation programme acceptable to the displaced tribal of the area.

Owing to a gap between the existing system and the implementation policy, the tribal face problems. Sequel to this state of affair the faith and conviction against the governmental administration is deteriorating. This statement is proved through the underline instances.

The minimum wage that has been fixed up by the government is contested by the people. They cite an example that in a government organization the officers get a salary much above the other subordinate staff. But this yardstick is not followed in case of wages to the workers. The agricultural labourer, the carpenter, the artisan etc. all are made to have equal wages. Their resentment is further extended. Shri Ganesh Ram Kanwar states that "we grow the commodities yet levy on them is fixed by the government. This is an act of injustice. The difficulty and hardship that we confront during the agriculture operations should put us to decide what is good for us." He also cites an instance when late Rajiv Gandhi, the then Prime Minister of India, visited Anjani village where he himself stated that out of a development grant of Rs.100, in effect only Rs. 5 reaches the people for whom the development is meant. He stresses this point vehemently to state the gravity of the wrong-doings and corruptions that are existing in our system. While commenting on the efforts of Adim Jati Kalyan Vibhag it was pointed out that the grants are received in the names of villages and their development but actually it is the concerned department which benefits the most.

The Summing Up

It is heartening to note that the administration through its various infrastructures have not been able to win the confidence of the people. Thus it is evident that developmental programmes aimed at tribal welfare and upliftment are not sufficient enough unless they are supported and backed by the tribal's commitment and faith for whom the development is meant for. It is imperative that one must evolve strategy of people's participation in every welfare project. This can be achieved only when the implementers and the receiver has a good extent of understanding and confidence.

Nevertheless it cannot be doubted that because of the governmental policies that socio-cultural changes have been brought about in these people. General awareness prevails amongst them on account of these changes. Today they are in a position to put across their needs and demands to the competent authorities. Illiteracy, as we know, is the root cause of many maladies that exist in this society. With the improvement in literacy, the community is making steady overall progress. Shri Shiv Kumar Kanwar (professionally a curer) admitted that the educated need not necessarily benefited in governmental jobs on the lines of reservation all the times, yet this has widened the worldview of the Kanwars. Even the tribal now are themselves aware of the changing circumstances and scenario. This has motivated them to accept newer innovations and new developmental programmes which in a long run going to benefit them the most. They have now come out of their laziness and lethargy to become a part of Indian mainstream.

It can be safely stated that though the tribal in question have not been able to reap the maximum harvest through the various development programmes, yet it is a truism that the quality of life and living has tremendously changed over these years to their benefit. Now, they are in the path of an overall development of their people and surroundings.

To sum up, it can be stated that the Kanwar because of their relative geographical isolation and strong adherence to the norms and values including their customary law were politically docile and the political governance started and ended with their traditionally elected leaders and the elites of their community. But since Independence the scenario is changing, though at a slow speed. Opening of the frontiers to the outside world and agents and agencies of political socialization, directly or indirectly, started impinging upon their ways of living. Education, mass media, interactions with other tribal and non-tribal in the surrounding areas have marked influence on them. While the elderly generation tends to cling on to their age-old tradition, norms and values, the younger generation moves on with their open mind. Education is a prized possession of an individual, they assert. Unfortunately, education and the various governmental interventions through various welfare schemes have not been able to out rightly win the hearts of the people.

REFERENCES

Ahmad, S.H. 1973. "Anthropometry of the Kawars of Surguja District," *Man in India*, 53 (2): 170-175.

Almond, G.A., and G. Bingham Powell. 1966. *Comparative Politics: A Developmental Approach*. Boston: Little Brown.

Almond, G.A. and Sidney Verba. 1963. *The Civic Culture*. Princeton: Princeton University Press.

Aronoff, M.J. 2001. "Political Culture," (pp.11640-11644) in Neil J. Smelser and Paul B. Baltes (eds.), *International Encyclopaedia of Social and Behavioural Sciences.* Vol. 17. Oxford: Elsevier.

Ball, A.R. 1971. *Modern Politics and Government.* London: Macmillan.

Ball, Alan R. and B. Guy Peters. 2000 [1971]. *Modern Politics and Government.* London: Macmillan Press Ltd.

Beer and Ulam.1962. *Patterns of Government.* New York: Random House.

Bhatt, S.C. 2003. *The District Gazetteer of Chhattisgarh.* New Delhi: Gyan Publishing House.

Bodley, J.H. 1988. *Tribal People and Development Issues: A Global Overviews.* Mountain view, CA: Mayfield.

Campbell, Angus, Gerald Gurin, and Warren E. Miller.1954. *The Voter Decides.* Evanston III: Row Peterson.

Census of India. 2001.Chhattisgarh Series-23, Provisional Population Totals, Paper-1 of 2001. Chattisgarh: Director of Census Operations.

Escobar, A. 1991. "Anthropology and the Development Encounter: The Making and Marketing of Development Anthropology," *American Ethnologist,* 18: 658-682.

____. 1995. *Encountering Development: The Making and Unmaking of the Third World.* Princeton, NJ: Princeton University Press.

Gendzel, G. 1977. "Political Culture: Genealogy of a Concept," *Journal of Interdisciplinary History,* 27: 225-50.

Inglehart, R. 1997. *Modernization and Postmodernization: Cultural, Economic and Political Change in Forty-three Societies.* Princeton NJ: Princeton University Press.

Johari, J.C. 1976. *Comparative Politics.* Delhi: Sterling Publishers Pvt. Ltd.

Kottak, C.P. 1997. *Anthropology: The Exploration of Human Diversity.* New York: The McGraw-Hill Companies, Inc.

Lance, L.M., and E.E. McKenna. 1975. "Analysis of Cases Pertaining to the Impact of Western Technology on the Non-western World," *Human Organization,* 34: 87-94.

Manners, R. 1973 [1956]. "Functionalism, Realpolitik and Anthropology in Underdeveloped Areas," *America Indigena,* 16 .

Negi, R.S. 1963. "ABO Blood Groups, Sickle Cell Triat and Colour Blindness in the Mana of Bastar, Gond and Kawar of Bilaspur," *Bulletin of the Anthropological Survey of India* 13: 149-53.

Peattie, Lisa R. 1968. "Interventionism and Applied Science in Anthropology," (pp.1-10) in L.P.Vidyarthi (ed.) *Applied Anthropology in India.* Allahabad: Kitab Mahal.

Pye, Lucian W. 1965. "Introduction: Political Culture and Political Development," (pp.7-14) in Lucian W. Pye and Sydney Verba (eds.), *Political Culture and Political Development.* Princeton: Princeton University Press.

____. 1966. *Aspects of Political Development.* Boston: Little Brown.

Rosenbaum, Walter A.1975. *Political Culture.* Great Britain:Thomas Nelson and Sons Ltd.

Russell, R.V. and R.B. Hiralal. 1975. *The Tribes and Castes of the Central Provinces of India.* Vol. III. Delhi: Cosmo Publications.

Scott, J.C. 1990. *Domination and the Arts of Resistance: Hidden Transcripts*. New Haven, CT: Yale University Press.

Singh, K.S. 2001. *People of India. National Series Volume-III*. The Scheduled Tribes. New Delhi: Oxford University Press.

Swidler, A. 1984. "Culture in Action: Symbols and Strategies". *American Sociological Review,* 51: 273-86.

Thompson, M., R. Ells and A. Wildavsky. 1990. *Culture Theory*. Westview: Boulder, Co.

Trivedi, Uma Kant. 1971. *Ethnographic Note: Kawar, Census of India,* 1961, MP, Vol. VIII, Part V-B. Delhi: Manager of Publications.

Wilson, R.W. 2000. "The Many Voices of Political Culture: Assessing Different Approaches." *World Politics,* 52: 246-73.

APPENDIX-I

Some Operational Definitions of Political Culture Orientations

Orientation	*Operational Definition*
Political Identification	Notion of citizenship. Political units and groups towards which one feels positively or negatively Political units and groups with which one is most often involved.
Political Trust	Willingness to collaborate with various groups in different types of social action Group memberships Rating of groups in terms of trust worthiness, political motives, type of memberships, etc.
Regime Orientations	Belief in the legitimacy of the regime. Feelings toward, and evaluation of, major political offices and regime symbolsInvolvement in political activity supporting or opposing the regime.
Rules of the Game	How one feels political opinions should be expressed. Concepts of political obligations for oneself and others. Concepts of how political decisions should be made by government. Attitudes towards political deviation and dissent.
Political Efficacy	Belief that government is responsive to one's opinions. Belief in importance of civic activism and participation. Belief in possibilities of political change.
Political Competence	Frequency of voting and other types of political activity. Knowledge of political events and their influence on oneselfInterest in political affairs.
Input-Output Orientation	Satisfaction with governmental policy. Knowledge of how political demands are made on government. Belief in effectiveness of policy inputs and outputs.

Source: Rosenbaum, 1975: 9.

SECTION III

DISPLACEMENT AND REHABILITATION

SEVENTEEN

REMOVAL OF A BLACK SPOT ON A WHITE SHEET: Impact of Forced Removal on Social Structures at Riemvasmaak

P.A. ERASMUS and M.J. SEREKOANE

Introduction

The sustained policy of demolishing homes and forcibly moving people from the land on which they had been living was for a long time one of the most reviled practices of the South African state (Desmond, 1986; Du Toit, 1982; Harris, 1970; O'Regan, 1989; Tatz, 1962). Well known examples that can be mentioned in this regard are district six, Skipskop and Sophiatown. Contrary to this, Riemvasmaak, although one of the earliest forced removals in the Northern Cape, has never been thoroughly researched. It was/is an isolated community in the harsh environment of the Northern Cape, near the Namibian border. Riemvasmaak may be described as a very arid region: the average annual rainfall is about 211mm with a peak rainfall season during December-April. The highest temperatures are recorded during December-February. The daily maximum mean temperature exceeds 32°C along the Orange River, while extreme temperatures well in excess of 40°C occur (Van der Walt, 2000: 2).

Land is (and always has been) of particular significance to humankind. Without it people would not have homes, building materials, grazing areas, places to cultivate crops, etc. The economic value of land is accordingly viewed as its "real" value; it represents a sense of security and is a key asset in its own right. However, the point regarding the meaning of land for the Riemvasmaak people is that besides the economic aspect, a series of values (cultural, social, political and aesthetic), histories, identities and symbolic meanings are found in and on land, or are attached to it (cf. Hydén, 1999: 152; James, 2001: 1; Schneider, 1981: 33, 111 & 165; Svedin, 1999: 164). Put differently, the consequences of the Diaspora of the Riemvasmaak people cannot be evaluated in terms of financial losses only.

Conceptually it is not possible to separate culture and the environment. On the one hand, culture provides a grid for understanding nature, including concepts, normative rules (as well as the institutions encompassing and codifying such rules), practices (e.g. lifestyles and the tools developed for these purposes) and knowledge systems. On the other hand, the converse is also true. De Beer (1997: 233 & 1999: 21-22), for example, points out that land not only provides human beings with access to resources, but also creates the frame of reference which people employ to evaluate, categorise and assign meaning to other people, things, events and even natural phenomena such as mountains, rivers, trees, and soil.

A central expression of cultural values, norms and meanings is found in people's world-views (Erasmus, 2000; Forde, 1976). World-views are implicit in maps of the world (*mappa mundae*), among other things. The process of creating a *mappa mundi* includes specific choices and certain aspects. Choices relate to components to be included and excluded (and why such selections are made), as well as to scale, opinions on philosophical ideas of time, relevant knowledge and *foci* of interest. Aspects include ways of modelling contemporary geographical understanding, the interplay between craftsmanship and theoretical knowledge, personal narratives, available technology, and the prevailing religious and political situations. When considering the values appropriate to developing a *mappa mundi*, it must be realised that values (although highly subjective) provide a frame of reference and are often made visible by means of the choice of boundary conditions (Svedin, 1999: 167-169; De Beer, 1997: 233-234).

As the South African *mappa mundi* was created largely in terms of discriminatory institutional allocation and administration of land within an overall state of repression, the present process of land reform, restitution and redistribution represents attempts to reverse these inequities and, in doing so, to reconstruct the South African *mappa mundi*. James (2001:15) distinguished two different governmental approaches in this regard: the first favoured the restitution and redistribution of land to those removed from it or denied access to it. This approach enjoyed a brief period of influence under the previous

Land Affairs Minister, Derek Hanekom, who established a legal framework to facilitate the reclaiming of land by those unfairly deprived of or evicted from it. The second approach (under Minister Thoko Didiza) has a more developmentalist focus: it recognises the primacy of the market, and favours the development of small through medium to large-scale agriculture. Despite the differences between these two approaches regarding policy frameworks and outcomes, they largely correspond in so far as they acknowledge the interrelation between economic process, political system and political action.

The Sol Plaatje Education Trust (Kimberley) requested the Department of Anthropology, University of the Free State, to conduct research on how the Riemvasmaak people have experienced their forced removal. The presentation of the data on the removal, the subsequent land claim, and eventually the return of the community focuses, to a lesser extent, on the components of the process (political economy as well as legal and racial aspects), while the experiences of the people who were involved, are the main focus point. Focusing on individual experiences (life histories) is, according to Babbie & Mouton (2001: 501-502), Coetzee & Wood (1997: 2), Mair (1984: 121) and Segar (1989: 1), of increasing relevance in our present-day situation, which is not only characterised by the implications of globalisation, but also by the rise of particularism and by renewed emphasis on the individual.

Fieldwork commenced on 26 May 2003 when the first research visit of two weeks was paid to the Riemvasmaak mission station and its inhabitants. The second visit (which took place from 22 September—2 October 2003) was to the predominately Xhosa community of Vredesvallei. Qualitative data was collected by means of recorded interviews with 58 individuals (27 from Riemvasmaak (mission station) and 31 from Vredesvallei). In order to ensure that the collected data represents the views of all different sections of the community, open, unstructured, in-depth interviews were conducted with the following categories of people:

- Those people who left Riemvasmaak as adults (today they are the elderly and the majority of interviews were conducted with them);
- Those people who left Riemvasmaak with their parents as youngsters (in other words the next generation) and who have only vague memories of Riemvasmaak;
- Those people who were born in Namibia or the Ciskei and who came to Riemvasmaak for the first time during 1994 (or thereafter) and have no direct memories of their forefathers' homes (in other words

the third generation);

- Elected leaders, either trustees of the Riemvasmaak Community Development Trust, or traditional leaders [*goas* (chief) Sarie Dawids and members of her council]; and
- Men as well as women who were selected from the above-mentioned categories.

Various research projects, voluminous in terms of collected information and primarily with a developmental focus, have already been conducted in Riemvasmaak. This kind of research has always created certain expectations and valuable as it may be, it often seems to the people involved that nothing is happening on the ground. The "continuous" presence of researchers who interfere with their daily lives could easily have resulted in resistance. However, with regard to the present research project the researchers (who became involved as empathic "insiders") experienced only goodwill and co-operation. The detailed in-depth discussions of the trauma which the people experienced when they were forcibly removed from their land, gave them for the first time a vehicle to speak out freely about an incident which dramatically influenced the rest of their lives, and of which the consequences are still very much with them.

Origin and Early History

Oral history suggests that people of Khoekhoen (Khoi) and San origin lived a hunter-gatherer existence in the vicinity of the southern part of the Molopo River (later known as Riemvasmaak) since time immemorial. Around 1870 Riemvasmaak[1] was surveyed and proclaimed as crown land and grazing rights were leased to any interested white party (Surplus People Project (SPP) sa: 4; Van der Walt, 2000: 32). When British Bechuanaland Colony was declared British Territory in 1885, Riemvasmaak lay within its boundaries. It was annexed to the Cape Colony in 1895 (*Annexation Act*, 1896, Nr. 41 of 1895) (Smith & Bozalek, 1993: 4).

No one quite agrees on how Riemvasmaak got its name (Du Pokoy, 1995: 65; *Mail & Guardian,* 2000-04-07; Van der Walt, 2000: 32; Winberg, 1995: 28-29 and 8 SA Infanteriebataljon, 1994). Oral history, however, suggests that for different reasons either a person (stranger/traitor/criminal) or an animal (probably a goat) was tied up with a leather thong.

Available evidence suggests that during the wars between Jonker Afrikaner and the Herero (1860-1892) in the former German South West Africa (now known as Namibia), as well as during the Herero and Nama rebellions of 1904-1906[2] a number of families of Nama, Damara and Herero origin who were subjugated by the Nama fled their masters and moved south of the Orange River (Marais, 1957: 99; Smith & Bozalek, 1993: 3; *Volksblad*, 1995-01-05). One of the groups involved was that of "Koning" Dawid. It is believed that he must have been the younger brother of Hosea Kutako,[3] an Omuherero who was suppressed by the Nama[4]. "Koning" Dawid led his people and a group of Nama speaking Ovaherero[5] (*Herero Oorlam*) through southern Namibia to the region of Augrabies in the Northern Cape. On 15 May 1912 "Koning" Dawid succeeded in renting a piece of land for 5 years from a white leaseholder, Lenhoff, at Riemvasmaak (Smith & Bozalek, 1993: 6; SPP, sa: 5). While at Riemvasmaak, other families joined "Koning" Dawid. The Damara family was, according to tradition, the first family to join "Koning" Dawid. Frederik Damara, the head of the family, was of Herero origin and his surname was originally Sererob[6]. The Basson family, who had changed their surname from Afrikaner to Basson, and Jacob Loeriesfontein, originally Tjongombe, fled together over the border to South Africa during First World War. After the war they received permission from "Koning" Dawid to settle at Riemvasmaak. Adam Adams and his family, who had fled Namibia during the Bondelswarts war (1894-1895), also settled at Riemvasmaak (SPP sa: 4-5). Together with "Koning" Dawid, the families Damara, Basson, Loeriesfontein and Adams are thus regarded as the founders of Riemvasmaak.

It appears that "Koning" Dawid left Riemvasmaak during First World War (probably for security reasons because they were too close to the Namibian border) and moved with his homeless people up and down the southern side of the Orange River. Here, in 1923, Father O. Fages of the Roman Catholic Church (he was from the mission station at Keimoes) found them at Warmsand (cf. Burger, 2002-03-05; Du Pokoy, 1995: 69-70; *Windhoek Advertiser*, 1984-11-05). He informed the magistrate at Upington about their poor living conditions and requested permission for them to settle at Riemvasmaak. Permission was granted, they resettled at Riemvasmaak (Du Pokoy, 1995: 1) and "Koning" Dawid invited the Roman Catholic Church to establish a mission station at Riemvasmaak. It became a thriving Roman Catholic mission[7] community. Since a high priority was placed on education, the Church applied in 1929 for permission to establish a school for Coloured[8] children at Riemvasmaak (Smith & Bozalek, 1993: 7).

"Koning" Dawid (and later his successors) ruled as chief and was assisted by a chief's council (representing the inhabitants of Deksel, Melkbosrand, Bok se puts, Blok 2 (currently known as *Vredesvallei*),

Wabrand and Xhubuxap) acting in an advisory capacity. The magistrate from Kakamas paid regular visits to Riemvasmaak to hold meetings with the inhabitants. The council had the authority to give permission to outsiders to settle at Riemvasmaak ("sitplek gee"), but nevertheless also needed the approval of the magistrate. The community had to pay poll-tax ("*kopbelasting*") and grazing licences. In the absence of any permanent white officials the chief and his council were responsible for law and order in the area.

Jakob Booysen was another leader who fled from Namibia during the Herero and Nama rebellions. It is believed that he was originally Hampera from Okahandja, and that he changed his name when he tried to get work at the copper mines in Okiep, South Africa. Oral history has it that he later trekked to the vicinity of Kuruman, where he got permission from "Koning" Dawid during the early 1930s to settle at Riemvasmaak. A very good relationship developed between "Koning" Dawid and Jakob Booysen and before "Koning" Dawid died in 1940 at the aged of 103 years (he was born in 1837) he decided to hand the "throne" to Jakob Booysen and not to one of his sons. Jakob Booysen died during 1972 (1890-1972) and had no children of his own. Jakob Basson (a sister's child of Jakob Booysen) then became headman. According to several informants, Jakob Basson was appointed by the community during a meeting attended by the magistrate of Kakamas, GJJ Jordaan (Hattingh *et al.*, 2000: 2).

Although it was nothing like a homeland Riemvasmaak was proclaimed during 1936 as a Native Reserve in terms of the *Development Trust Land Act,* 1936 (No. 18 of 1936) (Smith & Bozalek, 1993: 17). The first Xhosa speaking people shortly thereafter, in 1939, (SPP sa: 6) received temporary permission from "Koning" Dawid to work at the tungsten and beryl mines at Koolmanskop. When the mines closed down in the 1950s, permission was given to those who requested it to settle permanently at Xhubuxap.

In order to understand the origin of the above-mentioned Xhosa speaking people, it is necessary to go back to the year 1839 when the government of the Cape Colony, according to Marais (1957: 85), resettled about 500 Xhosa at Pramberg (Bushmanland, near the current Williston). In order to prevent robber Bushmen from entering the Colony, about 350 Xhosa were resettled further north at Schietfontein (later Carnarvon). In 1855 the government removed the Pramberg Xhosa to Schietfontein in order to avoid unpleasantness with the neighbouring white farmers. Here the Xhosa settlers gradually became landless. They owed considerable sums to European creditors who simply took over their land. The Xhosa had no other option but to go off towards the north and settle near Prieska (Marais, 1957: 88). However, by 1866 white Boers and "Basters" had begun to encroach seriously on the grazing lands of the Xhosa and once again they were forced to move. This time they settled at a place called *De Tuin* (south of Kakamas). The government started to lease crown lands to Europeans without, apparently, enquiring whether they were being used by the indigenous people or not (Marais, 1957: 93). The Xhosa people were forced to cross the Orange River, and under the leadership of one Donker Malgas, they threw in their lot with the Korana and fought on their side in the second Korana War, 1879.[9] After the war Koranaland became known as the Gordonia Settlement and only "Basters", because they had fought against the Korana and had been Promised Land, received land in the new settlement. The Xhosa who had supported the Korana, were excluded.

As a result of the oral histories, a clear picture can be drawn of the general way of life at Riemvasmaak between the years 1930 and 1970. Four villages existed, Riemvasmaak (mission station), Deksel, Melkbosrand and Xhubuxap, together with a number of cattle posts. Families usually stayed in the villages, where they could attend church services and schools, while men and the elder boys looked after the livestock at the cattle posts (SPP sa: 7).

Large flocks of sheep, goats and cattle formed the basis of the economy. Apart from providing for their own consumption, livestock was sold to people in surrounding areas such as Kakamas and Marchand. Vegetables gardens and cultivated fields were found beside the Orange River and men did seasonal farm work or worked on nearby mines. The Riemvasmaak people proudly claimed that they had tamed "this piece of land".

The schools at Riemvasmaak (mission station), Deksel and Melkbosrand were Roman Catholic, while the one at Xhubuxap was under the administration of the African Methodist Episcopal Church. These schools were recognised and funded by the former Department of Coloured Affairs.

It may be concluded that although Riemvasmaak has been a gathering place for many cultures over the centuries, it became an integrated community which could not easily be categorised racially or ethnically (*Eastern Province Herald*, 1984-11-10 and Hattingh *et al.*, 2000: 2). Most of the people spoke Afrikaans, were devoutly Christian, placed a high priority on education, and were pastoralists with sheep and goats or worked as migrant labourers. Despite the harsh conditions, the Riemvasmaak people succeeded over the years in securing and sustaining their livelihoods.

Forced from Riemvasmaak

The Riemvasmaak people lived for more than thirty years under the proverbial Damocles' sword of relocation. According to Du Pokoy (1995: 98) 1941 marks the first attempt to remove them, when a piece of land near Kuruman was offered to Jakob Booysen in exchange for Riemvasmaak. After he refused it, another piece of land, this time in the Kalahari, was offered, which he also turned down. The next move came in 1957 when the Riemvasmaak people were told to take out Bantu passbooks. If they refused, they would be fined R25 and would have to leave anyway. In 1966, this time from the Department of Coloured Affairs, they were again informed that they were to move and that the schools would be closed down. The reason provided by the Department was that the majority of the children were not Coloureds[10] (*The Cape Times*, 1984-11-15). Legal loopholes, however, prevent the Department from carrying out this threat, but five years later once the legal loopholes had been closed the magistrate from Kakamas (Jordaan) and the Chief Native Commissioner, Mr Archie, informed the people on 7 December 1971 that they had to leave and should start selling their livestock. The same day Father W. Simon (from the mission station at Riemvasmaak) wrote to Mr S. Cloete, Executive Management, Representative Coloured Council, expressing his dissatisfaction about the classification of Riemvasmaak as a Bantu Reserve, as well as about the intended removal. He also emphasised that the Riemvasmaak people did not want to move.

The protests of the Riemvasmaak people were in vain, however, and July 1973 was set as the date for the people of Xhubuxap to be moved, with January 1974 set for the people from the mission station (Southern Cross, 1973-10-14). Before that could happen, government had to classify the Riemvasmaak people racially and ethnically and the help of government ethnologists was called in. Although, as mentioned, inter-married and settled in Riemvasmaak for more than 100 years, the Riemvasmaak people were classified either as so-called Nama-Damara, Xhosa or Coloured (*Eastern Province Herald*, 1984-11-10, Southern Cross, 1973-10-14 and *The Cape Times*, 1993-08-24)[11]. Those people who were classified as Nama-Damara were to be sent to Khorixas, 1 300 km away in Damaraland, Namibia - in other words across international borders. The Xhosa, although some could not speak the language, were to be moved 900 km to Welcomewood, a barren part of the former Ciskei.[12] Those people regarded as Coloured were to be scattered in surrounding townships like Marchand, Augrabies and Keimoes.

Government officials claimed that the Riemvasmaak people were happy to be moved and that no pressure had been used to persuade them (Smith & Bozalek, 1993: 12; *Southern Cross,* 1973-10-14 and *The Cape Times*, 1984-11-15). Oral testimonies of the Riemvasmaak people, however, confirm that they were under extreme stress during this period[13] and that they had never been consulted about the removal in the first place. They did not know why they had to move — they were just informed that they were a black spot on a white sheet. The objectives of the relocation were formulated and the process conducted by, for the respondents, faceless white officials whose cultural frame of reference with regard to the importance and meaning of land, kinship, the extended family, peer-group membership, neighbourhood ties, etc. differed from these of the Riemvasmaak people. Secondly, the people were dissatisfied at having to leave familiar surroundings where they had lived in close proximity to each other, had enjoyed a collective community life, and where crime had been virtually non-existent. Despite promises made by government to persuade the inhabitants to move[14], they certainly did not want move[15]. The relevant point here is that the resettlement took place during the apartheid era, when restrictions were increasingly imposed and enforced on powerless, vulnerable people. The Riemvasmaak people only reluctantly moved because they were not politically empowered and were not allowed to organise themselves. Petrus Loeriesfontein says he was "bloed bedonnerd" (furiously angry) about the removal, but fear and enforced submissiveness by the white government at the end of the day explains the lack of any organised resistance.

According to Du Pokoy (1995: 98-101) the Riemvasmaak people had one request: they want to see the places where they would have to go for themselves and requested permission to undertake reconnaissance trips. The Xhosa Johannes Phillips, Tom Vass, William Andrieas, Jack Swelindawo, Steve Vas and Frederik Bosman went to the Ciskei, while Jakob Basson, Gawie Adams, Jan Roman, Koos Steenkamp and Booi Magani undertook the journey to Namibia. After the delegates returned from Namibia, Jakob Basson, without the support of the rest of the group, agreed to move. When asked why, he allegedly said: "Because the white man wants us to trek". Du Pokoy (1995: 100) accused Jakob Basson of betrayal, while some of the respondents that were interviewed claimed that he was bribed to do it.[16]

As the departure date drew nearer, more and more prayer and churc h services were conducted during which the people prayed for the decision to be changed. The fears of the Riemvasmaak people drew them even closer to their religion and the removal became a matter of the greatest concern between them and God. People still recall the uncertainties of those days and more or less everybody in the community tells of what Jordaan (the magistrate) is alleged to have contemptuously said: "Even if the Lord comes down from that mountain, you shall move!"

The first group to leave Riemvasmaak were the forty-five families who were declared Xhosa. They were removed to the Ciskei and were mainly from Xhubuxap. They left on 24 July 1973 (SPP sa: 12). GG (Government Garage) trucks moved in and people, their possessions and livestock were loaded up. They watched as their houses were torn down and burnt. Maria Vas says: "My Here! Ek hoor nog vandag hoe skrou die kat in die brandende huis" (My God! I still can hear the cat screaming in the burning house). Anamarie Mango was a little girl at the time of the removal. She can remember how they cried when their doll's house was set on fire because, as the white official said: "We cannot load this lot of rubbish".

When they arrived at Kakamas the train was already waiting for them. The name of the train was written in big letters: "Hambakhaya" (go home). Magistrate Jordaan came to greet them. Many people were crying, but some of the younger men shouted to him: "Jou sleg Boer wat soek jy hier" (you bad boer, what are you doing here).

Magrieta Bosman (a Coloured woman) was sick in the hospital at Kakamas. Her parents advised her not to move and asked her to divorce her husband. She loved him and would not divorce him, and was taken from hospital to the train. The journey was a nightmare and she was taken back to hospital at Mount Coke. Martha Bosman (another Coloured woman) who was married to Dick Bosman (a Xhosa) tells a similar story. She had to undertake the journey with a seriously sick child of three months who was, at the time of the removal, in the hospital at Kakamas.

During January 1974 the second group of people, those designated to go to Namibia, were removed. The air was filled with cries and chorals, and as the first lorry passed the big camelthorn tree at the mission station it started to rain. It was an unusually rainy year and it rained for three weeks. The loaded trucks could not leave for Kakamas, and the trek was delayed. "It was the tears of the angels," said Maria Silwer, "who were crying about all the injustice." Niklaas Adams, an elderly male respondent, replied by saying that the Lord looked down and answered Jordaan: "No, they will not move today."

The Riemvasmaak people were forcibly removed in terms of the Black Spot clearance programme under (section 5 (1) (b) of the *Blacks Administration Act*, 1927 (No. 38 of 1927) (Smith & Bozalek, 1993: 16;

SPP sa: 12-13). Before the removal an official spokesperson for the Department of Bantu Administration and Development promised that compensation would be paid for any buildings which the people left behind (*Southern Cross,* 1973-10-14). According *The Cape Times* (1984-11-15) compensation was paid by the State. Du Pokoy (1995: 101) considered the R5.00 per household not adequate, while Smith & Bozalek (1993: 13) maintain that interdepartmental compensation to the amount of R68655.90 was paid by the Department of Public Works to the Department of Development Aid. The Roman Catholic Mission Church received R60000.00 in compensation for its improvements to the land, leaving only R8655.90 to the victims of the removal. The overwhelming majority of respondents, however, insisted that they never received compensation of any nature and that they sustained damages during their removal. This included the breaking of crockery, damage to furniture and the loss of livestock. Respondents maintained that their livestock had to be sold to white cattle-dealers for prices far below market value (cf. also SPP sa: 14).

After the removals had taken place, Riemvasmaak reverted to the Department of Public Works, which held the land for the benefit of the South African Defence Force (SADF) who used it for military training purposes. An agreement was entered into between the SADF and the National Parks Board. The agreement provided for the declaration of the land as a contractual National Park in terms of Section 2B (1) (a) of the *National Parks Act*, 1976 (No. 57 of 1976), and the joint environmental management thereof, specifically the conservation of the Namibian Black Rhino. In terms of Proclamation 44 of 1982 and under section 2 (2) (b) of the *National Parks* Act, 1976 (No. 57 of 1976), a small subdivided portion of Riemvasmaak land (in extent 4 270 hectares and known as Melkbosrand) was declared as part of the Augrabies Falls National Park[17] (Smith & Bozalek, 1993: 14).

Strangers in a Place Called "Home"

For the children, who could not understand why their parents were unhappy, the journey by train was immensely adventurous, while each day's rations, consisting of brown bread, jam and bully beef were a feast. Adults, however, tell a different story. There are the following "stories".

Firstly, there were the Xhosa people who arrived on 26 July 1973 by train in King William's Town. Rain was pouring down and it was a miserable day for the people from the dry and hot Riemvasmaak. Buses transported them to their new destination. It was a long journey and each time they passed a township, they anxiously wondered whether this was their new home. The longer the duration of the journey the quieter they became, women started to cry, while others prayed for consolation. It felt like an eternity, and the road was zigzagging deeper and deeper into the bushes. Maria Vas could see how the first vehicle disappeared time and again over the next hill. Eventually they stopped at a miserable resettlement camp called Welcomewood, near Mount Coke, in the King William's Town district (*Eastern Province Herald,* 1984-11-10).

A white official gave each household head a key; each one then had to go and find the door of the wooden hut into which the key fitted. The huts were without flooring and inside them, weeds were growing to window level. Their possessions were unloaded in different bundles and they had to walk from bundle to bundle to search for their property. Some local residents came and introduced themselves and the women warned the newcomers against snakes with stings on their tails. The first night they pushed their beds together and lay the children in the centre in order to protect them from the snakes.

The Riemvasmaak people were never accepted by the local Ciskeian people because they are Afrikaans speaking and were unfamiliar with the customs and beliefs of the locals (*Mail & Guardian,* 2003-08-12). Magrieta Bosman and Sofi Voko (Coloured women who married Xhosa men) were sworn at and called Boesmans and were not allowed to take the bus to town. One night, Magrieta told, her husband asked her to bake brown bread in future instead of white bread. When she asked why, because she had been baking white bread for many years, he told her that the men at his workplace taunted him, saying that his sandwiches looked like his wife. According to Daniel Vas the local children always ran away from them. They couldn't understand why and one day decided to chase them and to catch one. To their great surprise they were told by the local children that they were afraid because their parents had warned them that the Riemvasmaak people were cannibals.

The Riemvasmaak people had many difficulties surviving in the Ciskei. Local diseases destroyed most of their stock and their grazing land was taken away when the government subdivided it so that other locals could use it. (*Mail & Guardian,* 2003-08-12). They couldn't make a living from farming and decided to take the matter up with the magistrate at Bisho, where they were told that they were welcome to leave if they were not happy. Four out of every ten household heads were unemployed and many men were forced to look for work elsewhere (SPP sa: 17). Freddie Bosman was one of them. He worked for Cosatu in Cape Town.

Secondly, the Damara people from the mission station arrived at Otjiwarongo after a three-day journey by train. However, nobody seemed to know what to do with the new incomers (*Burger*, 2002-03-05). The people themselves, as one respondent put it, acted like cats in a strange house—they wanted to jump, but didn't know which way. Eventually government trucks took them to Khorixas where they were initially housed in tents.

When the first Riemvasmaak people arrived in Khorixas there was a storm of protest from the local Damara people. The local community argued that the arrival of the Riemvasmaak people would exacerbate conditions of overcrowding in the area (*The Cape Times,* 1984-11-15). Because they did not speak the local dialect they were not easily accepted (*Mail & Guardian*, 2003-08-14), and they were called all kinds of names such as "egoist", while the free accommodation and services provided by the Khorixas municipality also became a bone of contention (*Business Day,* 1995-01-19).

In 1978 the Riemvasmaak United Party[18] (in alliance with the Namibia People's Liberation Front and the Federal Convention of Namibia), was founded with the purpose of lobbying for the restoration of Riemvasmaak, the improvement of the lot and rights of the Riemvasmaak people, to promote their separate identity, and to demand that they be treated on a par with other groups in Namibia (*Weekly Mail & Guardian*, 1994-03-30). The differences between the Damara and the Riemvasmaak people were also accentuated during the political run-up to the elections for the independence of Namibia. The United Democratic Front (UDF) of the local supreme chief Justus Garoep enjoyed the general support of the local Damara, while the Riemvasmaak people under Jiems Basson mainly supported the Democratic Turnhalle Alliance.

Families with livestock were moved from Khorixas to the farms Otjihavera, De Riet, Bergsig and Middelpos (*Volksblad*, 1995-01-05). Conditions on these farms were, to say the least, not very "user friendly". They were isolated, the infrastructure was poor, and virtually no communication with the rest of Damaraland existed. There were also the lions and elephants. Sarie Dawids says she thought they were dropped in the middle of a game park because where they had come from there were only jackals. Remuitius Adams and his young friends saw a lioness and her cubs in the veld and, believing that it was a dog with her puppies, tried to catch them. Lions killed hundreds of livestock, while elephants destroyed gardens, fences, boreholes and windmills. The situation continued deteriorating and in 1984 the Riemvasmaak people sent a petition to the Administrator General of SWA/

Namibia asking to be resettled either in the Bondelswarts area in the southern part of the country or the Augegas area near Windhoek. The petition stated that their livestock had been killed by droughts and wild animals and that it was difficult to find any jobs (*The Cape Times*, 1984-11-15 and *Windhoek Advertiser,* 1984-11-05).

Over the course of time young people met new friends at school, relationships developed between neighbours, intermarriages took place, differences started to vanish, jobs became more available and in the early 1990s the government of Namibia offered citizenship to all Riemvasmaak people (*Die Republikein*, 1991-06-04). Many Riemvasmaak people made use of the opportunity, while others like Anamarie Roman's father, refused to take it up, because he was afraid to lose his South African citizenship. Officially, Namibia was their new fatherland. Late one evening Jan Adams was listening to the radio. He was at his cattle-post at Bersig when he heard for the first time the news that there was a possibility of going back to Riemvasmaak. His son worked at Rössing and when he came to visit his parents for the weekend the family discussed the issue and decided that they wanted to go back to Riemvasmaak. However, a lot of water has to pass under the bridge before this could happen.

Thirdly, those Riemvasmakers who had been classified as Coloureds were moved to places like Kakamas, Marchand, Keimoes, Upington and Augrabies. Because they could stay in an environment where the culture was well known and where they could speak Afrikaans, they probably suffered the least of all Riemvasmaak people. However, they lost their houses, livelihoods, families and friends and had to try and make a living in an area with an already high unemployment rate (SPP sa: 17).

There was a fourth group of Riemvasmaak people, although a small one, who should also be mentioned, namely those people who could not see their way clear to going to Namibia or the Ciskei and who decided that if they could not stay in Riemvasmaak, they would rather move at their own expense to places of their own choice. Moffie Hendriks, for example, took his 360 goats, 2 cattle, 4 mules and 10 donkeys and found work at one of the surrounding "white" farms. Daniel Vas told Jordaan that he would not trek and was informed: "Hel toe of Port Nolloth toe, maar jy sal trek" (to Hell or to Port Nolloth, you shall move). Daniel didn't fancy either of the two places and decided to go to Springbok where he found work at the mines.

Back to Where We Belong

In the light of the political transformation in South Africa during the early 1990s and the subsequent struggles of many communities to reclaim their land, Freddie Bosman and a small group of fellow Riemvasmaak people approached a lawyer from the Legal Resources Centre in Cape Town to find out what chance they had of reclaiming Riemvasmaak. They were part of the group of Riemvasmaak people who were classified Xhosa and sent to the Ciskei. On 28 August 1992 their lawyer advised the Secretariat of the government's Advisory Commission on Land Allocation (ACLA) that the Riemvasmaak people intended to apply for the return of their land in terms of the *Abolition of Racially Based Land Measures Act,* 1991 (No. 108 of 1991).

A workshop under the guidance of the Surplus People's Project was held on 7-9 May 1993 at Upington. The purpose of the workshop was to discuss strategies on how to assert their claim for restitution of land and payment of compensation for losses and deprivation. Forty-seven delegates attended the workshop and the Riemvasmaak Co-ordinating Committee was established to promote and co-ordinate their collective interests and shared objectives. Freddie Bosman was elected chairperson, Lawrence Bosman the vice-chairperson and Daniël Vaas secretary. To inform the people about their strategies and to draw support sub-committees were also established for Marchand and Welcomewood (SPP sa: 1-2).

During this time members of the Riemvasmaak Co-ordinating Committee travelled to the Eastern Cape, Namibia and the Northern Cape and spoke to former residents of Riemvasmaak about restoration. In the beginning there was all kind of obstacles. In the Ciskeian case Maria Vas and members of her committee could not find any documentary proof of their removal at the magistrate's office at Bisho. Only after a second visit to the magistrate at King William's Town was it possible to obtain the necessarily documents. Their headman and former Riemvasmaker, Aaron Malgas, opposed repatriation because, to his mind, job prospects at Riemvasmaak were too bleak (*The Citizen*, 1995-01-12).

The Namibian situation proved to be even more complicated. According to Monica Adams "propaganda spread by those opposed to the whole repatriation question" delayed the process (*New Era*, 1994-09-21). The viewpoint of headman Jacob Basson, who had in the meantime been appointed headman in the Damara Council for ward 11, was that no one had approached him about the matter. "I am here to stay in Namibia" he said. "Those who wish to return to South Africa can do so provided they follow the right procedures" (*New Era*, 1994-09-21). Mike Booysen, later to become the chairperson of the Riemvasmaak Community Development Trust, was wary and said that there were "many unanswered questions and a growing suspicion as to whether there [was] no hidden agenda" (*New Era*, 1994-09-21). At this rather late stage, the Namibian Ministries of Foreign Affairs, Home Affairs and Lands, Resettlement and Rehabilitation all denied knowledge of the planned repatriation, while a spokesperson for the South African Ministry of Land Affairs said that there had been no official contact with the Namibian government over the matter (*New Era*, 1994-09-21). Meanwhile, unpaid bills for accommodation and services delivered by the Khorixas municipality also nearly derailed the process. The Namibian Regional and Local Housing Ministry refused to write off the money or to let the people repay the money after their settlement (*Business Day*, 1995-01-19).

After various meetings and discussions (cf. Du Pokoy, 1995: 119-121) it became clear that many of the Riemvasmaak people in the Ciskei and Namibia wanted their land back and wanted to move back as soon as possible. This time the people were well informed and they took a voluntarily decision.

The ACLA turned down the first application of the Riemvasmaak people. This prompted the people to write to the state president, to organise the largest (and perhaps the first and only) protest march in the history of the small, conservative Kakamas[19], to join a demonstration at the World Trade Centre on 23 August 1993[20], to submit a memorandum to the SADF demanding the return of their ancestral land, and to hold explanatory talks with the Parks Board (*Weekly Mail & Guardian*, 1994-03-30). The then Minister of Land Affairs requested the Commission on Land Allocation to reconsider the Riemvasmaak issue. The Commission sat to hear evidence in Upington on 1 December 1993. The Riemvasmaak Co-ordinating Committee submitted evidence based on archival research, showing that their forebears had lived on the land since pre-colonial times. Reports by the Legal Resources Centre, the Surplus People Project and the Land Development Unit of the University of the Western Cape were also submitted in support of their claims.

The SADF opposed the claim, saying the land was required for military purposes. Local farmers (Knydas Farmers' Association and Blouputs Farmers' Association) and the Department of Agriculture said they feared the land would be mismanaged. The Parks Board, however, supported the claim and said that they would stay on the land only if the people invited them to do so (Du Pokoy, 1995: 128). On 11 February 1994 the Department of Land Affairs announced that, on the recommendation of the Commission, the land rights of Riemvasmakers would be restored and that they could return to most of the lands: 50 000 of the original 74 000 hectares (cf. Du Pokoy, 1995: 132; Hattingh *et al.*, 2000: 6; Van der Walt, 2000: 33). The Commission recommended the restoration to the community of land in State ownership on the basis that a trust should be established to hold and administer such land on behalf of the members of the community. The Riemvasmaak Community Development Trust was established during April 1995[21] (when it was registered) and the Riemvasmaak Co-ordinating Committee was dissolved.

The Riemvasmaak people vowed to challenge the SADF for the remaining 20000 hectares. However, after the 1994 elections the SADF decided to return the 20000 hectares to the Riemvasmaak community (*Die Gemsbok*, 1994-07-01; *Volksblad*, 1994-11-17; Du Pokoy, 1995: 137).

On 11 January 1995 the first 17 families returned to Riemvasmaak. They were from Welcomewood. The first group of Riemvasmaak people from Namibia returned on 6 March 1995 (Rapport, 1995-02-19). The transport costs for the South African government for the Damaraland people were R1,5 million (*Business Day*, 1995-01-19).

Current Situation

The Riemvasmaak people were the beneficiaries of the new South African government's first resettlement project (*Mail & Guardian*, 2003-08-14). Media reports sketch different and sometimes confusing images about the land restoration and development process at Riemvasmaak. *The Sunday Independent* (1995-10-22), for example, reports that while the people were delighted to be back on their land, a growing sense of frustration and anger emerged over the lack of development. "Community representatives claim the lack of progress is the result of unwillingness by government agencies to accept responsibility or to take decisions. A Central Government official, however, claimed the community was not playing its part in the development process, that divisions were emerging between the Namibian and Eastern Cape parts of the community and that certain leaders were misusing their positions." *Beeld* (2002-03-02), *Burger* (1997-12-02) and *Die Patriot* (1999-04-16) refer to the sufferings of the people, the urgent need for help, the real danger that the resettlement project may collapse, and that there are many lessons still to be learnt. *Volksblad* (1997-12-22) and *Mail & Guardian* (2003-08-14), on the other hand, say that people are participating in development projects, that they are satisfied with government's involvement and role, that money from overseas is becoming available[22], and that new houses and other infrastructure have been built for them in a new, formally planned township[23].

In a report on the macro development of Riemvasmaak, Hattingh *et al.* (2000: 8) emphasises that differences of opinion existed among the inhabitants and identified the following contributing factors: land usage, utilisation of resources, and the role, functions and decision-making powers of those trustees who are not living in Riemvasmaak.

The origin of the ethnic tension between the Xhosa people and the rest of the community is not clear, but it is surely of great relevance. It is reported by the *Thina Committee* 1996 (paragraph 5 (1)) that Freddie Bosman, at that time the chairperson of the Trust, accused the Namibian Riemvasmakers of not being part of the "struggle" and that apartheid favoured them. They also, according to Hattingh et al. (2000: 49), viewed themselves as different and objected strongly to the Roman Catholic nature of the school at Riemvasmaak[24]. The Namibian Riemvasmakers retaliated, accusing the Xhosa of discrimination, racial insults and that they had never wanted to be part of the community (*Rapport*, 1997-11-16). It was said by respondents that the Xhosa believed because Mandela is a Xhosa they have the right to rule over everybody. For them, "Koning" Dawid established Riemvasmaak, he was the true and first leader and ruled from the beginning over the Xhosa. "So waar kom hulle nou vandaan". (So, where do they think they came from). Tensions were running high, protest marches were organised and political leaders at provincial level worked hard to try to solve the problems. Eventually the Xhosa decided to take their children out of the school and to move 17 km away to the mouth of the Molopo River where they lay out a new settlement, called *Vredesvallei*. Although numbers could scarcely justify it[25], a new school was erected. After twenty years of separation the once harmonious community was divided, there was a lack of cohesion and solidarity, and no longer a collective vision, decision-making and leadership. Interviews confirmed that community members experience the ethnic division as a burning and real issue. According to respondents the last election of trustees, for example, represented ethnic support.

The issue of leadership and local politics is a strong dividing factor and can be seen as one of the major reasons for economic stagnation. Not everyone trusts the trustees of the Riemvasmaak Community Development Trust. Numerous accusations were made spontaneously in almost every interview: nepotism (bursaries are only awarded to the children of trustees);

money is not being spent properly and in accordance with the specifications of the donors (e.g. sport facilities are not being built and vehicles are misused); there is too much talking and no delivering; and that the trustees are autocratic and self-enriching. One of the things that was pointed out in the interviews is that some of the trustees (this applies to previous trustees as well) stay outside Riemvasmaak and it is believed that they are not well-informed about local issues. Some of them have received RDP houses, which are either empty for most of the year (they are used for holidays only) or rented out to people like teachers who stay elsewhere and work temporarily in Riemvasmaak. What makes community members unhappy is the fact that there are many of them who are living in corrugated iron or reed shanties.

During 1996 the Premier of the Northern Cape appointed the Komitee van *Ondersoek na die aantuigings aangaande die Riemvasmaak Gemeenskapstrust* (Committee of Investigation on the allegations regarding the Riemvasmaak Community Trust) (under the chairmanship of G. Thina). A great number of allegations were investigated. The Committee concluded, inter alia, that regulations regarding the allocation of mineral rights were not followed, that funds were not used appropriately, that funds could not be accounted for and that financial irregularities had occurred. They questioned the administrative abilities of the trustees. It is not clear what happened to the recommendations of the Thina Committee. Daniel Vas believed together with other community members: "Die Thina Komitee het bevind dat almal het gesteel, maar niemand is skuldig nie" (The Thina Committee found that everybody has stolen, but nobody is guilty).

Trustees were asked about the above-mentioned accusations and the fairly general perceptions amongst the community members. Apart from assigning the blame elsewhere, the Trust claimed success for projects such as electricity, water and roads, and the establishment of the vineyard of 10 hectares at Vredesvallei, which the District Municipality Siyanda, at Upington, actually provided (cf. *Siyanda District Municipality Newsletter*, September 2003, Volume 5). As proof of their competency trustees responded by referring to their successful tourist project[26] and claimed that the majority of the Riemvasmaak people had rejected the inauguration of the so-called traditional leadership.

Leadership is a sensitive issue in the community. Apart from the cloud surrounding the Trust, it is said by respondents that the traditional leaders were more in contact and in touch with the needs of the people. Goas (chief) Sarie Dawids (claimed to be a great, great-grandchild of "Koning" Dawid 1)[27] assumed office in 1998 when the community took a decision to re-instate their indigenous leadership. Her inauguration as member of the Khoi Tribal House took place on 11 Augustus 2001 and the following council members were elected to assist her: Gys Simon, James Basson, Lucas Basson, Petrus Isaacs, Pieter Malgas, Benedict Dawids and Maria Awaras. As wards and portfolios are not yet allocated (June 2003), it is questionable whether the traditional council is presently involved in any major activities.

The traditional leadership visualises, as does the Riemvasmaak Community Development Trust, development as their major objective, and apart from that, the conservation of the traditional Khoekhoen culture. Overlapping with regard to development objectives, strategies and competing for the same funds will obviously create conflict and tension between the two mentioned institutions-after all each of them has to justify their existence. Conservation of the traditional culture is something that needs attention and could provide the *raison d'etre* for the existence of traditional leadership. After twenty years in foreign parts, Riemvasmaak people have to rediscover their own identity. "We thought that with our land we would able to heal the culture that is the soul of our people. But we find instead that our language is dying. At least while we were in exile we were able to read and speak our language (Nama is recognised in Namibia). We now realise that, in the act of regaining our land, we may have destroyed our culture" (*Mail & Guardian*, 1997-09-12).

Other distinctive characteristics to be mentioned about the present situation in Riemvasmaak, is the importance of the extended family which functions as a household. Unemployment forced especially men and younger people to work outside Riemvasmaak.[28] This explains why nuclear families largely do not (cannot) exist, why grandchildren are often left in the care of their grandparents, why women are the head of many households and why they are playing such an important role in community life. According to Hattingh *et al*. (2000: 37) pensions (mostly welfare and old age) are the sole income of 53 per cent of the households.

The Roman Catholic Mission station is the central point of community life and social, educational and religious activities take place there. Sport and recreational facilities are non-existent, while the abuse of alcohol and drugs, as well as crime and teenage pregnancies are increasing (Hattingh *et al*., 2000: 31; *Mail & Guardian*, 2000-01-02).

Respondents generally feel positive, and sometimes nostalgic, about the "good old days". Dreams confront reality as people struggle anew to come to grips with their land. They believe life was better then, that they are worse off now and that they will never recover economically. People are frustrated and disenchanted because-they believe—the Trust is not doing "enough", unemployment is high and Riemvasmaak is deteriorating. However, in answer to the question: "Looking back and having the same choice again, what would you do?" the overwhelming majority of respondents replied by saying that they would certainly make the same decision. "Riemvasmaak is our place, here we feel at home. I not only married a man from Riemvasmaak, I am also married to Riemvasmaak", says Maria Koppers.

Conclusion

The removal of the Riemvasmaak people was particularly dramatic in terms of symbolic meaning and distance. It took place during the apartheid era, when restrictions were increasingly imposed on blacks by the authorities. As is often the case with forced removals (Du Toit, 1982; Fernandes, 1997; Gans, 1991), the decision to move was not taken voluntarily, but was forced upon them. Irrespective of the supposed rationale, the displacement of the inhabitants of Riemvasmaak was a major violation of their human rights.[29] Government was responsible for a protracted, inhuman uprooting period, which actually started with the first rumours of resettlement. It conducted no preliminary investigations, nor was there any support during either the transition period or the rerouting period. For the people of Riemvasmaak, "benefits" from the resettlement were limited (serious economic disruption was the order of the day, while no compensation was paid) and they experienced their removal negatively.

To lose one's home is a deeply disturbing experience. The apartheid government demolished a community; it was bereft of its identity and character. Before the removal it was a well-functioning and sustainable socio-cultural unit. People cared for each other and supported one another. These structures did not automatically revive after the restoration. Riemvasmaak people became strangers to each other and it was not possible for the old subsistence economy, based on close proximity, to provide security of livelihoods as it had in the past.

Not everybody returned to Riemvasmaak (*Mail & Guardian,* 2000-01-02), which means that families were ripped apart for the second time. Each time they think about or talk to relatives who stayed behind, the Riemvasmaak people go through the trauma of their removal once more. The experiences of the past sedimented themselves as a very prevalent memory that directs their daily lives. Through their oral histories they carry with them the memories of the trauma of their removal right up to today.

It may well be asked whether the anthropological recording of people's experiences contributes to the knowledge and understanding of removals and resettlements in particular or of socio-cultural realities in general. Individuals are attached to social and cultural values and experience forms part of the individual's "experiential inside of reality". According to Barth (1994: 5), any existential human problem "will have found diverse solutions, which must be worth knowing about, thinking about and comparing". Therefore, when, with due allowance for the context, the analytical outsider makes generalisations and turns experience into expression, it becomes part of ethnography. In this regard Hastrup & Hervik (1994: 10) maintain that "(w)hile the scope of anthropology lies beyond the retelling of local stories, these and their experiential grounding remain the foundation of anthropological knowledge".

Many of the hardships and problems described by the people of Riemvasmaak were features of everyday life in South Africa (Desmond, 1986; Erasmus, 1998; Segar, 1989). It was the fate of millions of black people to be obliged to live in foreign areas. However, as the experiences of the Riemvasmaak people have never been thoroughly researched, they are relatively unknown and may soon have been forgotten. Forced removals are traumatic, undignified experiences which occupy people's minds. To give the Riemvasmaak people the opportunity to talk about (and thus become reconciled to) their past and to have their experiences heard will help to restore their dignity, because it validates the fact that their life histories are worth telling and worth knowing.

NOTES

1. Also known as Bokvasmaak Native Reserve 498-Smith & Bozalek (1993: 3) and Van der Walt (2000: 32).
2. The great uprising of the Herero broke out on 12 January 1904 under the leadership of Supreme chief Samual Maherero (Malan, 1995: 68-71). The systematic expropriation of the Herero by German imperialism is indicated by Drechsler (1980: 132) as the main reason behind the insurrection (cf. Drechsler, 1980: 176-181; Malan, 1995: 70 for the reasons for the Nama uprising under Herdrik Witbooi).
3. Petrus Hosea Kutako was of a noble Herero family. After the German army slaughtered ± 80 000 Herero between 1904 and 1907 he gathered together the remaining ±13 000 and was installed as chief in 1917. He became Paramount chief (Okahandja Herero) on 1 June 1925 and hold the position till his dead on 18 July 1970 (when he died at the age of ± 100 years).
4. Du Pokoy initially stated that he was a Nama-dama (1995: 1), but later (1995: 68) confirmed that Dawid was the brother of Hosea.

5. They were in conflict with local Nama communities who were in alliance with Jonker Afrikaner and it is possible that these Ovaherero could be direct descendents of prisoners of war of the Nama.
6. It was a common phenomenon amongst refugees to change their surnames in order to avoid the German police who were on the lookout for "war criminals" (cf. Drechsler, 1980: 201), or to try to find work. The general expression of the Riemvasmaak people in this regard is that they: "het hier kom broodvanne neem".
7. According to Du Pokoy (1995: 144) 97 per cent of the people are Roman Catholic. The majority of people in Vredesvallei, on the other hand, belong to the African Methodist Episcopal Church (AME).
8. Concepts like "Coloured", "Bantu", "Baster", etc are used in their historical and political contexts.
9. Towards the end of the war J.H. Scott, the Special Magistrate, wrote as follows: "There are a good many natives scattered about the country who must live somewhere, and I am quite sure that the way in which they have been driven about, first from Carnarvon, then from Prieska, and so on, has had a great deal to do with this war" (Marais, 1957: 94).
10. Although Riemvasmaak was officially declared a Bantu Reserve, government was not sure of the identity of the people; administratively Riemvasmaak was run by the Department of Bantu Administration and Development; but the schools were administered by the Department of Coloured Affairs.
11. Racial classification of people in terms of physical characteristics is generally viewed as scientificly inappropriate (Haviland, 2000: 348-349; Kottak, 2000: 136; *et seqq* and Turnbaugh, Jurmain, Kilgore & Nelson, 2002: 23 *et seqq*). The classification of the Riemvasmaak people, therefore, can be regarded as not scientific and insignificant. Members of the same family, for example, were differently classified (SPP sa: 14). Mr Dawid Dawids was classified as a Coloured, while his brother and a sister were classified Bantu. In the case of Christene Jantjies the police wanted to arrest her father (who was a Xhosa) under the *Immorality Act*, 1957 (No. 23 of 1957) because they thought he was married to a white lady.
12. According to the *Eastern Province Herald* (1984-11-10) 920 people were resettled in Damaraland and 45 families in Welcomewood.
13. During an interview with Cornelius Adams (2003-09-26) he became emotionally so upset about the injustice and humiliation that he had suffered during the removal that he burst into tears and the interview was stopped temporarily.
14. Mr. Jannie de Wet, the then Commissioner-General for the Indigenous Peoples of South West Africa, for example, promised primary and higher schools for the Riemvasmaak people, the building of a Catholic church, and he said that the proposed area of settlement was good stock farming country and that there would be work for the men in the nearby Uis tin mine (*Southern Cross*, 1973-10-14).
15. This view is supported by the newspapers Burger (2002-03-05), *Mail & Guardian* (2000-01-02), Hattingh *et al.* (2000: 6) and SPP (sa: 11).
16. These allegations were discussed with Rita Maasdorp, a daughter of Jakob Basson who still stays in Namibia. She lives at Riemvasmaak, is in regular

contact with her father, and is aware of the allegations which she has discussed with him. To the best of her knowledge he only received R400 compensation for his brick house. She insisted that her father acted the way he did because "the white man instructed him accordingly".

17. Melkbosrand has become a focus of unsolved conflicts. The various stakeholders differ on how the land should be developed and used, and the community itself is divided on the issue. Technically, the title deed of Melkbosrand is in the name of the Riemvasmaak Community Development Trust, while the National Parks Board is responsible for its management as a conservation area.

18. Dawid Dawids was the president and Petrus Loeriesfontein (today living at Riemvasmaak) the vice-president.

19. Respondents who participated in the march remembered very well the tension of the day. Security police took position on the roofs of nearby buildings, while white residents followed the events from behind half-closed curtains.

20. Freddy Du Pokoy enjoyed telling how he was leading the march with his saxophone when a police officer put the barrel of an R4rifle to his stomach and said: "Hotnot, vandag skiet ek jou vrek" (Hotnot, today I'll shoot you dead).

21. Mike Booysen was chairperson until June 2003. Trustees are elected every two years. On 27 June 2003 the following trustees were elected: John Simon (chairperson), Richard Roman (vice chairperson), Daniel Vass, Sarah Dawids, Jiems Basson (who is also a traditional headman), Romeo Adams, Thomas Steenkamp, Thandiwe Voko and Magrieta Isaks.

22. Food and Agriculture Research Management Africa (Farm Africa) from Britain donated R6 million and the Irish government R1.260 million. The money was used, inter alia, to start a quarter of a hectare of vineyard, to buy two tractors with implements, two vehicles, an irrigation pump, a TV, video and a musical keyboard for the local school, as well as equipment for the manufacturing of cement bricks. B. Scott was the project manager. There were accusations of mismanagement against Scott and his redeployment was requested. The Irish government, however, threatened to withdraw their donations if this happened.

23. Subsequently, the fact that the Riemvasmaak Community Development Trust opted for the establishing of a formally planned town was pointed out by respondents as unacceptable and they indicated their unhappiness about it. It prevented them from returning to their original homesteads where their ash-heaps and cattle-kraals were. They feel that although it is their land (they received their title deeds during 2002), they have no say about it. Traditionally the Khoekhoen buried the umbilical cord of a new-born baby in the ash-heap of the house where he/she was born, which symbolised his/her birthright to be at his/her birthplace. For security reasons and for the sake of convenience the cattle-kraal was always built as near the homestead as possible.

24. As was mentioned earlier (section 3) the Roman Catholic Church received R60 000 for their buildings, including the school, when the people were removed. As part of the restoration ruling, the land as well as the buildings was transferred to the Riemvasmaak Community Development Trust. However, the Riemvasmakers (excluding the Xhosa) viewed the situation differently. For

them, it was their original property and therefore the Trust should have no jurisdiction over it.

25. More or less 59.4 per cent of the total population is staying at Riemvasmaak (mission station), 21.7 per cent stay at Vredesvallei and 18.9 per cent somewhere else at Riemvasmaak (Hattingh *et al.*, 2000: 19). Currently (October 2003) the number of school children are: Riemvasmaak (mission station): 118 with 6 teachers; and Vredesvallei: 70 with 3 teachers.
26. The income from tourism has increased from R40000,00 in 1997 to a peak of R92000,00 in 1999. During 2002 1 660 tourists overnighted in the chalets built with donor funds near the hot springs (*Mail & Guardian*, 2003-08-14). The Siyanda District Municipality and the Riemvasmaak Community Development Trust have entered into an agreement where the Siyanda District Municipality provided assistance to the Trust in developing and upgrading of the tourist infrastructure (*Siyanda District Municipality Newsletter*, September 2003, Volume 5).
27. In a letter to the newspaper *Rapport* (8 April 2001) F. Du Pokoy said that there is difference of opinion in the community about Sarie's election as *goas,* that the Dawids family had not elected her, that her election was without the knowledge of the Riemvasmaak people, and that the majority of the Riemvasmaak people rejected her as leader. However, research confirmed that members of the Dawids family actually went around establishing the most senior family member and thus the most possible successor. It also seems that the greatest resistance comes from the Xhosa section of the population.
28. Men represent 45 per cent of the population and women 55 per cent (Hattingh *et al.*, 2000: 19).
29. During recent years human rights and environmental organisations have come to consider displacement a major violation of the right to life, particularly of the poor.

REFERENCES

Babbie, E. & J. Mouton. 2001. *The Practice of Social Research.* Oxford: Oxford University Press.

Barth, F. 1994. *Balinese Worlds.* Chicago: University of Chicago Press.

Coetzee, J.K. & G.T. Wood. 1997. "Life History Research: A Fragmentary Method," *Acta Academica,* 29 (3): 1-13.

De Beer, F.C. 1997. "Values, Resources and Development: A Perspective from the Northern Province of South Africa," *Journal of Social Sciences,* 1 (3): 229-238.

_____. 1999. "Mountains as Cultural Resources: Values and Management Issues," *South African Journal of Ethnology,* 22 (1): 20-25.

Desmond, C. 1986. *The Discarded People.* Braamfontein: The Christian Institute of South Africa.

Drechsler, H. 1980. *'Let Us Die Fighting': The Struggle of the Herero and Nama against German Imperialism* (1884-1915). London: Zed Press.

Du Pokoy, F. 1995. *Riemvasmaak*. Pretoria: Benedic Boeke.

Du Toit, B.M. 1982. "Involuntary Migration and Government Policy: Population Displacement in South Africa," (pp.139-158) in A. Hansen & A. Oliver-Smith (eds.), *Involuntary Migration and Resettlement: The Problems and Responses of Dislocated People*. Boulder: Westview Press.

Erasmus, P.A. 1998. "Waaihoek: Resettlement without Light," *South African Journal of Ethnology*, 21 (3): 135-139.

____. 2000. "Wêreldbeskouing: betekenis en kruis-kulturele vergelykbaarheid," *South African Journal of Ethnology*, 23 (1): 14-20.

Fernandes, W. 1997. "Displacement of Tribals: Struggles and Implications for Resettlement," (pp.78-91) in G. Pfeffer & D.K. Behera (eds.), *Contemporary Society: Tribal Studies*. New Delhi: Concept Publishing Company.

Forde, D. 1976. *African Worlds: Studies in the Cosmological Ideas and Social Values of African Peoples*. 5London: Oxford University Press.

Gans, H.J. 1991. *People, Plans, and Policies: Essays on Poverty, Racism, and Other National Urban Problems*. New York: Columbia University Press.

Harris, P.B. 1970. *Studies in African Politics*. London: Hutchinson University Library.

Hastrup, K. & P. Hervik. 1994. *Social Experience and Anthropological Knowledge*. London: Routledge.

Hattingh, W.J., A. Senekal, N. Nel & R. Hattingh. 2000. *Riemvasmaak: Makro-ontwikkelingsplan*. Aucklandpark: AGS Teologiese Kollege in ooreenstemming met Randse Afrikaanse Universiteit.

Hydén, G. 1999. "Environmental Awareness, Conflict Genesis and Governance," (pp.150-163) in T. Granfelt (ed.), *Managing the Globalized Environment. Local Strategies to Secure Livelihoods*. London: I.T. Publications

James, D. 2001. "Land for the Landless: Conflicting Images of Rural and Urban in South Africa's Land Reform Programme," Unpublished paper read at joint conference of AASA and SASCA. Pretoria: University of South Africa, 9-11 April, 2001.

Kottak, C.P. 2000. *Anthropology: The Exploration of Human Diversity*. Boston: McGraw Hill.

Mair, L. 1984. *Anthropology and Development*. London: Macmillan Press.

Malan, J.S. 1995. *Peoples of SWA/Namibia*. Pretoria: HAUM

Marais, J.S. 1957. *The Cape Coloured People 1652-1937*. Johannesburg: Witwatersrand University Press.

O'Regan, C. 1989. "No More Forced Removals? An Historical Analysis of the Prevention of Illegal Squatting Act," *South African Journal on Human Rights*, 5 (3): 361-394.

Schneider, K.H. 1981. *The Africans. An Ethnological Account*. Englewood Cliffs: Prentice-Hall.

Segar, J. 1989. *Fruits of Apartheid: Experiencing 'Independence' in a Transkeian Village*. Bellville: Anthropos Publishers.

Smith, H. & L. Bozalek 1993. Riemvasmaak: Application to the Commission on Land Allocation. By Riemvasmaak community. Legal Aspects and Status of Riemvasmaak Land. Prepared by the Legal Resources Centre, Cape Town.

Surplus People Project. sa. 'n Aanspraak op Riemvasmaak. 'n Voorlegging aan die Komissie vir Grond Toekenning namens die gemeenskap van Riemvasmaak.

Voorberei vir die Riemvasmaak Koordineringskomitee deur die Surplus People Project, Athlone.

Svedin, U. 1999. "Culture, Cultural Value, Norms and Meanings-A Framework for Environmental Understanding," (pp.164-172) in T. Granfelt (ed.), *Managing the Globalized Environment: Local Strategies to Secure Livelihoods*. London: IT Publications.

Tatz, C.M. 1962. *Shadow and Substance in South Africa*. Pietermaritzburg: University of Natal Press.

Turnbaugh, W.A., R. Jurmain, L. Kilgore & H. Nelson. 2002. *Understanding Physical Anthropology and Archaeology*. Belmont: Thomson Learning.

Van der Walt, P. 2000. *Augrabies Splendour. A Guide to the Natural History of the Augrabies Falls National Park and the Riemvasmaak Wildlife Area*. Pretoria: Info Naturae.

Winberg, M. 1995. *Back to the Land*. Johannesburg: The Porcupine Press.

SA Defense Force.1994. "8 SA Infanteriebataljon. 21-19773-1994 Riemvasmaak Opleidingsterrein en Ooreenkoms Nasionale Park," unpublished brochure of the SADF

Newspapers

Beeld, 2002-03-02. Gaan die bruilofsbok weer flou gedans word?

Burger, 1997-12-02. Mense vol vertroue terug in "harde wêreld".

____. 2002-03-05. Riemvasmaak se mense kry steeds swaar.

Business Day, 1995-01-19. Unpaid Bill Keeps Land Out of Reach.

Die Gemsbok, 1994-07-01. Weermag onttrek - los alles.

Die Patriot, 1999-04-16. Riemvasmaak se rieme kom los.

Die Republikein, 1991-06-04. Riemvasmaak Burgers.

Eastern Province Herald, 1984-11-10. Resettlement Tragedy.

Mail & Guardian, 1997-09-12. Words that Click and Rustle Softly like the Wild.

____. 2000-04-07. Tightening the Noose in Riemvasmaak.

____. 2000-06-02. Finding Prosperity in the Desert.

____. 2003-08-14. First Resettled Rising Slowly from the Dust.

New Era, 1994-09-21. Riemvasmakers' Departure Derails.

Rapport, 1995-02-19. Riemvasmakers terug na SA.

____. 1997-11-16. Woonbuurte uitgelê, kuddes kom aan - maar dit lol tussen Xhosas, Namas. Steeds 'n "rasse-ding" op Riemvasmaak.

Southern Cross, 1973-10-14. January Date for Community Move?

The Cape Times, 1984-11-15. Riemvasmakers Ask AG to Let Them Move.

____. 1993-08-24. Victims of Forced Removal Speak Out.

The Citizen, 1995-01-12. Uprooted Folk Quit Ciskei.

The Sunday Independent, 1995-10-22. Flagship Land Restitution Project Runs Around on Squabbles and Confusion.

Volksblad, 1994-11-17. SA, Namibië praat oor Riemvasmakers.

____. 1995-01-05. Eerste groep binnekort terug na Riemvasmaak.

____. 1997-12-22. Riemvasmakers vol geloof terug op grond.

Weekly Mail & Guardian, 1994-03-30. A Black Spot Turns into a Green Spot.

Windhoek Advertiser, 1984-11-05. Riemvasmakers Want to Move.

EIGHTEEN

THE TRIBAL WOMEN IN A CHANGING ECONOMIC FRONTIER: A Case Study of Lower Suktel Irrigation Project of Balangir District, Orissa

REETUPARNA DAS and DEEPAK KUMAR BEHERA

Introduction

River valley projects for irrigation and other purposes have been a characteristic feature of India's development stand since independence. These projects have induced, and are still inducing a massive amount of human displacement with huge materialistic and non-materialistic losses in the lives of the affected people. This fact has been hardly properly considered by the government concerned (Mohapatra, 1998) with due sensitivity. Despite this, to agree with Arundhati Roy (a Booker Prize winner and also an activist for human rights), whether we love the dam or hate it, it has become the symbol of national progress (Roy, 1999).

The State of Orissa has already experienced a number of dam projects, either completed or ongoing, and subsequent displacement of huge number of people triggered off by these. Till date, there are about seventy odd major and medium dam projects in this State. Some of these major projects are: Machhkund Dam Project, Upper Kolab Dam Project, Rengali Multipurpose Dam Project and Upper Indravati Hydro Electric Project (Barik, 1997; Behera and Patel, 1997). Out of the total number of displacement caused by all the dam projects in Orissa, the tribal population alone constitutes about 35 per cent (Ota, 1998). It is noteworthy here that till 1973 in Orissa, there was no provision of any rehabilitation assistance for the affected people.

The Lower Suktel Major Irrigation Project is finally going to take its shape in the coming years, in Balangir, a predominantly drought affected district in the western part of this State. This has simultaneously pushed a large number of families towards those unavoidable uncertainties as a result of prospective dislocation. As per the current Status Report of the study project, there would be 1222 displaced ST families, which is more than 29 per cent of the total displaced families. This percentage has every possibility to rise after total completion of the survey.

"Continuity in terms of social life depends on structural continuity, that is, some sort of continuity in arrangements of persons in relation to one another" (Radcliffe-Brown, 1971:10) — this basic truth, responsible for the existence or non-existence and strength or weakness of the structure of a society, has been studied since long by the pioneer anthropologists. Today's anthropologists and sociologists have been studying the social and economic benefit as well as the loss caused by these so-called development projects, through detailed ethnographic research over few decades. This has been, however, diverted into more focused and diagnostic research by the current scholars in this field of study.

Amongst the stakeholders those who get most affected by these projects, are the tribal people. So, they have been focused by several activities and environmentalists as they get differently affected unlike their non-tribal counterparts, due to their distinct socio-cultural and economic entities (Fernandes, 1997; Baboo, 1997). The specific reason is again that the livelihoods of the tribes are very much associated with nature, even amidst the process of deforestation. Apart from the males their womenfolk also play a major role in making the natural resources productive and usable in manifold ways (Indira and Shanthi, 1997). Such contributions of these women not only act as complementary to that of their male counterparts, but also often prove to be more productive. But the women of these communities do not receive much separate attention in this respect. Especially, their economic status and role within their own set-up and the effects of changes in the same under displacement, have unfortunately escaped serious scholarly concern. Hence, incorporation of gender dimension becomes an indispensable part of the analysis of the possible outcome of such projects from economic point of view; and is especially relevant when viewed from the point of tribal existence (Fernandes, 2005). This is because of the fact that, economy is one of the major aspects in their lives that is most likely to get a severe blow from the issue of displacement.

Objective, Universe and Methodology

The womenfolk of the tribes in the study area — mainly Gond, Saora and few Kondh, Binjhal and Luhra-have been studied from an angle of double-folded marginalization. That is, on one hand, they are the indigenous disadvantaged people whose livelihood patterns are interwoven with their own socio-cultural ethos and values; and on the other hand, for being women they are taken as subordinate to their male members under the influence of non-tribal values. So, their role and status have been selected for the study at the economic aspect against the perspective of such marginalization. This situational backdrop, when the stakeholders are at the juncture of displacement and anti-dam agitations, and also when partial payment has been already made just to one village, makes this study more value added. Such assessment of socio-economic conditions at the pre-displacement stage would make serious contribution in giving useful insights into the related effects. This would, thereby, caution the planners and policy makers of the lacunae of the existing resettlement and rehabilitation policies and programmes, and hence, prompt the same to do the needful in accordance.

Four sample villages were purposively selected for the case study, looking at the availability of relevant data. Out of these, three villages, viz. Khagsabahal, Kutensilet and Khuntapali come under full submergence, whereas Barpita is to be partly submerged. Table 19.1 reflects the ethnic composition of these villages.

Table 18.1: Ethnic Composition of the Study Villages

	Full Sub-mergence	*Total HH*	*Gond HH*	*Saora HH*	*Other ST HH*
1.	Khagsabahal	170	136	—	—
2.	Khuntapali	450	29	—	—
3.	Kutensilet	140	3	73	4
	Partial Submergence				
1.	Barpita	225	10	35	5
Total		1015	178(17.53)	108(10.64)	9(0.88)

Source: Fieldwork, 2004; Status Report of L.S.I.P (Lower Suktel Irrigation Project), Balangir

Note : Figure in parenthesis indicates percentage.

Khagsabahal is a Gond dominated village that is strongly against the dam; Kutensilet, also with prominent tribal population, has accepted it as inevitable but expects fairer deal in the rehabilitation matter; Khuntapali is the only village to receive partial compensation in cash and it comprises very low percentage of tribal families.

Against the backdrop of these four different situations, this micro-level study was attempted. Research tools used for primary data collection were: observation, informal unstructured interview, focus group discussion (guided by a check list), public meetings and few case studies on selected typical households. Secondary data were collected from research and survey literatures, 'project reports, project officials, Government administrative officials and different experts. This study mainly focuses on the pre-project situation and envisions the obvious and the most predictable post-dam effects while, analyzing the study problem. It is noteworthy here that, the universe of study shows predominance of the Gond and the Saora, and a few other tribes like the Khond, the Binjhal and the Luhra are found in minor numbers. All these tribes exhibit quite a semblance regarding their economy with the regional economy. Therefore, an attempt has been made in this study to trace the most predictable overall changes in the role and status of these indigenous women under the impact of the proposed dam.

Brief Historical Background

Lower Suktel Irrigation project is a major irrigation project that is supposed to solve the extreme drought situation in the district of Balangir. The plan for this project was conceived in the sixties when the-then Chief Minister of Orissa, Rajendra Narayan Singh Deo invested his special interest in this project. However, it received government approval in 1999, and is currently under implementation with Central Loan Assistance from the Accelerated Irrigation Benefit Programme (AIBP) under Long Term Action Plan (LTAP) of undivided KBK (Koraput, Balangir, Kalahandi) region. The dam is proposed across the river Suktel, a major right tributary of the Mahanadi river; and would be constructed at a latitude of 20°46'26" north and longitude of 83°20'5" east. The map shows a profile of the location of this project. The construction includes a 1410 metre long, 36 metre high earthen dam with two canals. Total 26 villages would be affected of which, 16 villages would be fully and the rest 10 villages would be partly submerged. The command area encloses 177 villages of Balangir district and 12 villages of Sonepur district. Further, this project asserts to supply 17.89 MCM drinking water to Balangir town.

Present Situation of the Project and People's Reaction

While the project authority have currently received a strict instruction from the Collector to start the construction work by the year 2005, in the meantime, there is a strong wave of anti-dam protests and agitations for the last 3 to 4 years, from the stakeholders coming under the proposed *büdi anchanl* or reservoir area. This has created a difficult situation for the officials concerned to carry on their enumeration work.

Amidst all these agitations, Khuntapali have agreed to give in and have received a partial payment of compensation (as per the Resettlement and Rehabilitation Policy of 1994) excluding the Rehabilitation Assistance (RA) and the valuation for trees. It is interesting to note that the people of this village opt for upgrading the compensation amount, rather than opposing the dam issue.

With a prominent number of Saora, Gond and a few number of Binjhal, Kutensilet has accepted the project as inevitable, but has also raised a strong voice for suitable rehabilitation that would assure them of the well being of their post-displacement life situation. Especially, it is the nature of the livelihood and the earning scope they are most critical issues.

The Gond, who are in majority in Khagsabahal, are still stubborn with their anti-dam attitude. It is noteworthy here that, they have organized an anti-dam tribal group named *Adivasi Sangha* and have staged a strong protest meeting very recently by inviting all the *büdi anchalar adivasi* or "tribal people of the reservoir area". Even their womenfolk have attended this meeting. These women have been found to be equally sensitive and protesting, and their opinions are just not determined by that of the males. They have raised a clear voice of their own.

Barpita has been found to be in a precarious situation, as happens usually with the partial submergence case. It is facing the brunt of complicacies and uncertainties with the rehabilitation matter, although it is very much likely to get affected alike the villages enlisted for full submergence.

The nearby village of Hardatal alike the villages of non-submergence area, has been found to be not much reactive, though apparently happy with the prospect of getting better irrigation facilities from this project. Such villages are also looking forward to the prospect of getting more wage labours from the dam construction work. As Hardatal would directly lead to the approach road to the dam site and involve all communications to the project related works, so a few people from this village are also considering the prospect of opening small road side hotels.

It has been found that the payments made so far are on the basis of old valuation and only by considering the provision for the prescribed escalation every year as per official index (taking 1994 as the base year). The two subsequent amendments already made in 1998 and 2002, are not yet taken into consideration by the project authorities. Enumeration and estimation, on the basis of which Status Report has been prepared by this project, are mainly on the basis of the 1997 survey. And the result of the revised survey that was supposed to be made by November 2003 is not prepared and updated yet. Table 19.2 shows the result of this enumeration survey of the study villages:

Table 18.2: Enumeration Survey of the Study Villages by L.S.I.P

	Survey 1997		*Survey 2002*		*Property survey*	*Survey of trees*
Full Submergence	Total HH	ST HH	Total HH	ST HH		
1. Khagsabahal	151	115	170	136	Incomplete	Incomplete
2. Khuntapali	367	29	450	29	Complete	Complete
3. Kutensilet	77	62	140	80	Complete	Complete
Partial Submergence						
1. Barpita	167	50	255	50	Complete	Complete
Total	762	256	1015	295		

Source: Fieldwork, 2004; Status Report of L.S.I.P., Balangir.

Gender Dimension of Displacement and Economic Changes

Whether we consider the international perspective, the national, or that of the state level, gender disparity and discrimination against women remain as harsh reality even today. Though there is Constitutional Guarantee in India for gender equality in all spheres of life but women still today face the plights of lower literacy, greater poverty, manifold socio-economic marginalization and other hurdles (Ray, 1998). Hence, any social or economic development issue would lack complete assessment if gender dimension is not added to it. But while dealing with the dam and other development matters, it is a shocking surprise to find that gender issues have been hardly included as serious concern at any point relevant to development and displacement.

It is needless to mention that, most of the project-affected tribal people have been generally found to be falling below the poverty line. At the same time, it has been found that women produce 80 per cent of the food consumed in the poorest part of the world, as cited by worldwide network of different surveys (Khan, 2000). These altogether necessitates the relevance of the assessment of the economic role of the tribal womenfolk who actively participate in the sustainable livelihood.

The present study attempts to expose this dimension by especially focusing the economic perspective, from two broad viewpoints: analyzing the tribal women's economic role and status in the pre-project situation; and secondly, the most predictable changes that would obviously lead to socio-economic disarticulation under the impact of the project.

The Pre-Project Situation

Tribal economy is very much a different phenomenon, unlike the perception of general economy that is directly explained in terms of production, distribution and consumption. The economic aspect of tribal life goes much beyond this level of gross comprehension, which is inseparably interwoven with their socio-cultural milieu, beliefs and practices (Panigrahi, 2003). Irrespective of the ethnic differentiation, any tribal economy bears a multi-faceted alliance with nature and forest. In the study area, despite the fact of deforestation, this long term alliance has been observed to be existing in the form of long-term dependence on the common property resources (CPRs) for several generations, even though these people are primarily the settled agriculturist. The land holding status of tribal families in the study villages is reflected in Table 19.3.

Table 18.3: List of Landless Families of the Study Villages

	Total Families	*ST Families*
Full Submergence		
1. Khagsabahal	27	22
2. Khuntapali	63	25
3. Kutensilet	45	18
Partial Submergence		
1. Barpita	17	10
Total	152	75

Source: Fieldwork, 2004; Status Report of L.S.I.P., Balangir

Alike majority of the Indian tribal societies, which follow the patriarchal pattern for the rule of inheritance of property including lands, similar practice has been found among the study tribes. But still, their womenfolk are found to be enjoying a status rated higher than the caste women, in real practice (Vir and Manral, 1990). With this background in view, the economic role of the tribal women in the sample area has been studied.

Involvement in Agriculture and Seasonal Cultivation

Tribal women of this area play almost an equal role in making economic contributions to the family like their male counterparts, in terms of supplying the resource for the family's sustenance. They mostly have direct dependence on agriculture; even when they are landless; they work as agricultural labourers and earn wages. They partake in most of the agricultural operations like weeding, transplanting, harvesting, threshing, etc. - exclusively identified to be women's role.

As usual with the catchment area, the study villages show rich soil fertility and optimum ground water level, prospective of series of seasonal cultivations and engaging the women in such activities.

During summer, they grow non-paddy crops like ground nut, *rāhidi* pulse, *jhünga* or local beans. With the approaching of rain, they involve in preparation of the land, like weeding, manuring and sowing for raising different varieties of paddy. This keeps them engaged till winter appears.

When the paddy is almost ready for harvesting, they prepare bed for different pulses like *moong, biri, kuluth*; oil seeds like sunflower and groundnut; brinjals, cabbages and other vegetables.

Tribal women belonging to landless families are basically sustained by the agricultural labour for about 6 to 7 months in a year. They work for 6 to 8 hours a day and earn Rs.15 to 20 in cash or in kind.

Sustenance during Post-harvest and Lean Periods

Making of *bādan* or broom after collecting wild grass from the forest, is a vital source to supplement their family income (a thick bunch of brooms may be sold at Rs. 20 in the town area) during post-harvest phase of paddy cultivation. Once in a week they make such collection.

The toughest lean period comes to them during April-May; but as it is a harvest time for *mahül*[1] (*Bassia natifolia*) flowers, they manage to earn (Rs.4000 to 8000) by selling the flowers, and at the later phase collect the fruits (that fetch them 2 to 3 tins or 30 to 45 litre of oil which is sold at the rate of Rs. 18 to 20 per litre). Landless women often take annual lease of a *mahüla bürei or mahül* grove from a landholder. They also survive on other non-wood forest produce (NWFP) like *kendu*[2] leaves, tubers, roots, flowers, fruits, leaves, honey, etc. collected from the forest. *Ikera*[3] of kendu leaves fetch them about rupees 20 to25.

Stone quarry is also a significant source of earning for these women, especially during autumn and winter; they get engaged by the local traders who target the surrounding hillocks for this business.

These women generally do not go for non-agricultural and underpaid unskilled labour (they get unskilled job because of their low literacy status and insufficient exposure to the outside world) mostly available in the town and considered as of low status for women. When their male members go out in search of such jobs during slack phase, they mostly stay back in the village and utilize their time by collecting small timbers, bamboos, branches from the forest — for making furniture, agricultural implements, house repair, fencing, ropes, mats, leaf-plates and -bowls. With all these sorts of natural resources, they are able to manage their home and hearth with a low cost of living. In fact, this low cost management is vital for them as it is mainly the womenfolk who control the family economy (Fernandes, 2005).

Dependence on Nature for Ethno-Medicinal Practices

These tribal women have quite a sound knowledge of the medicinal properties of different kinds of herbs that grow abundantly in this region. Minor ailments like cuts, burns, indigestion and diarrhea are managed by this easily available natural resource. Varieties of such plants or parts of them are collected by them and are sold to the nearby ayurvedic colleges and ayurvedic centres by the male members.

Interdependence between the Land Holder and the Landless

A healthy power relationship exists in these villages between the *parjā* or landowner and the *sükhbāsi* or the landless. Women of the latter class work as wage labourers in the lands of these *parjā* and this gives them the job security year after years on the basis of this relationship of mutual trust.

This sort of mutual relation often helps these wage earners during urgent credit needs, often in the form of rice or paddy borrowed from the *parjā*, which could be conveniently adjusted with the service they render.

Tribal Women and Women Self-Help Groups

With new rural development measures on the scene, through the formation and functioning of Women Self-Help Groups (WSHGs) for the rural women's economic and social uplift, the married women at this grass roots level are being targeted. Many tribal women of the study area have been responding quite positively at this venture. They have already proved their organizational power and leadership skill through regular saving and income generation activities (a large part of these being dependent on land and CPRs). These have also been welcomed and supported by their menfolk at a great extent.

Such self-help performances, ever since initiated in Orissa under the programme of "Mission Shakti" in 2001, have certainly started improving their views and lives. This may be identified through several structural determinants of their present socio-economic status and role. Such as: improvement in their capacity building in economic activities, interaction with the outside world regarding financial transactions, self-dependence in deciding on financial matters without taking much help from the males, and the like. Especially, all these result into strengthening more decision-making power of the females in the family economy.

Socio-Economic Position within the Family

Apart from such significant role played by these tribal women in shaping their socio-economic outside their domestic boundary, they always have, in fact, a respectful position within their traditional family pattern. They actively participate in all sorts of decision-making and their men generally do not take any decision including those on financial matters, without consulting their wives or senior female members of the family.

The Prospects of Post-Displacement Phase, Most Predictable Effects and Socio-Economic Disarticulation

As have been already experienced through various dam-and-displacement issues of the past, it is now explicitly understandable that the government machineries settle the rehabilitation part much apathetically and fail to internalize the realistic costs of human displacement with due humane approach (Cernea, 1999). Today's social scientists through their academic research are repetitively raising questions on these failures of governance in development administration. This sort of failure pushes the project displaced families (PDFs) to get affected by what Michael Cernea[4] has depicted as "risk and impoverishment factors" identified on the basis of certain empirical evidences.[5] It is also well established that most of the dam induced displacements are actually forced displacements that result into "a spiral of impoverishment" (Cernea, 1991). In the study area, displacement has not taken place yet and it would take another 4 to 5 years for its occurrence. So, the post-displacement phase and its impact on the tribal women have been envisaged and analyzed here accordingly, from socio-economic viewpoint. These impacts have been viewed through both materialistic and non-materialistic perspectives:

Compensation Package and the Tribal Women

The direct materialistic issue comes up first with the compensation and rehabilitation package prescribed for the affected people. First of all, this project is not treating unmarried females above 18 yeas as individual units, whereas there is such provision for males (Agnihotri, 1998). The information about the recent amendments made in 2004 in the Rehabilitation and Resettlement Policy which has rectified this discrimination, has not reached these people yet.

As in practice, girls of these tribes are generally not differentiated from the boys within their social pattern and are valued equally, at least on the basis of their economic participation and contributions. So, such differential treatment quite obviously stands irrational within their socio-economic set-up. On the other hand, officially male members are considered on behalf of the family to deal with all the compensation related matters. This, slowly but surely is affecting the importance of these tribal women and forcing them to some extent towards subjugation under their male counterparts.

Since the resettlement sites are planned to be very close to the town, so there is every chance of accepting the non-tribal values and caste ideologies of woman's subjugation.

Compensation has been already paid partly to a village where mishandling of the money by spending it on liquor or by uncontrolled and unplanned expenditures has been observed. This has worried these women about the disruption in the family, which has been since long, a unit of independent production for them. Here, the economic contributions made by the males and the females are seen equally necessary. But the situation pacing towards such change, makes the women feel that they would lose their voice and the scope of their decision making power would get narrowed when the males would be handling the huge lump-sum amount without consulting the females, and would thus, disturb the family discipline.

Economic Disarticulation

The feeling of insecurity is also inevitably occurring at the prospect of being uprooted from their livelihood pattern that is totally based on lands, forests and natural resources, and in which women are the very active participants. In fact, they are more dependent on CPRs than the men do, as these natural resources form the foundation of their economic status.

Dislocation would obviously deteriorate their economy related status and position after they get alienated from these resources and their contributions to the family economy get reduced. This gets more substantiated by the fact that the resettlement areas selected so far by the authorities concerned, are not at par with the ecological set up they are acquainted with for generations. Rather, these relocation sites are very near to the town and do not at all resemble the rural perspective of the affected villages (although under the "Orissa Resettlement and Rehabilitation of Projects Affected Persons Policy, 1994", it is clearly stated that there should be special treatment for the tribes to maintain their customary rights on the forest and the forest produce and thereby, taking care of their relocation site accordingly).

With several natural resources quite easily available at hand, these women, till today are maintaining the family expenditure in an easy going manner. So, making their habitation away from these resources would naturally mean the loss of all such facilities in terms of paying for each and every item in their day-to-day life.

Shifting to a different geo-physical setting shows every possibility of these women losing the important environment related to their secondary occupations, for instance, collecting *kēndü* leaves and the quarry work—that are so vital sources of income during the lean periods.

Even all landless families are not happy with the apparently prospective side of the Rehabilitation Assistance (R.A.) that guarantees homestead land and agricultural land per male above 18 years. Particularly, when they very practically consider the occupational advantages and position they would lose and have to adjust and adapt themselves to a place alien to them from social, cultural, economic and many other angles. Mere rehabilitation packages can never make up for the strong community support and cultural security they are still enjoying at the pre-displacement stage. Tribal women who are basically wage earners, are not interested either to put their hands in business with the compensation money, as they are never acquainted and feel comfortable with such profession.

Discontinuity of Women Self Help Groups

Local development schemes like the programme of the "Mission Shakt" would undoubtedly be affected by the displacement process. Because the formation and sustenance of a self-help group primarily depends on the unity and integrity among the local members as well as the homogeneity amongst them (the president of a multi-ethnic SHG, a Saora woman has remarked, "How can we get the same acquaintance and attachment with the people of a different place?").

Post-displacement scattering would unfortunately disrupt the continuity of such a group which, till date, has been proved to be a viable alternative means for economic uplift in the rural areas, especially for the women wage earners in the tribal perspective. In the study villages the SHGs have been found to be supported by the Government which has no plan yet to formulate any concrete remedial measure for the groups that are likely to get affected in the displacement process.

Dislocation, Resettlement and Disarticulation in Social Network

The healthy power structure in the village, that symbolizes a symbiotic relationship and social solidarity between the *parjā* and the *sükhbāsi*, is very much likely to get affected when people of one village would scatter to different locations. Especially, for the wage earning tribal women, this would be an irreparable damage as such mutual understanding not only provides them the age-long job security as agricultural labourers within the village, but also provides the urgent but small and frequent credit needs from these landholders ("The *parjā* people are the patrons of our economic sustenance," said a Gond woman from Khagsabahal).

The idea of moving to another village with the same ecological surroundings does not seem to be much encouraging either, when they justify the problems they are expected to face from the host villagers. They are filled with much discomfort at the moment they think, how much embarrassing condition it would be for them to be treated like "unwanted" by the latter in every walk of life including whatever economic pursuit they attempt for in that new environment.

The solution does not lie only with the matter of resettling a whole village in one site and retaining the old social network among the people. At the same time, the neighbourhood network that is strongly built up through years amongst number of villages those are situated at the immediate vicinity is of more serious concern. The benefit they get by their collective economy related actions (like initiating the integrated watershed programme, one that has been found being run jointly by the tribal women of Kutensilet and Barpita), can never be revived practically at the post-displaced stage.

Economic Relevance to Marriage and Kinship Attachments

In these tribal societies, marriage proposals are accepted only after they are approved by the mother; even marriage expenses and other important aspects are also basically controlled by her. In this context, tribal women, especially those who belong to the landless families, have started getting worried over the prospect of their children's marriage during the post-displacement period when they would be detached from many of their kith and kin. The latter have always been considered a great source of help, as they usually shoulder the financial responsibilities jointly on such an occasion. Relocation also points towards the difficulties in searching for brides/grooms from the distant places.

They are also worried on the matter of expenses in observing their traditional clan/family rituals in the post-displaced situation, as the expenditures of these are till today collectively borne by all senior males of a joint family. Similarly, uncertainties have arisen with the village *jātrā* or festivals that are celebrated seasonally with great pomp by the whole village, irrespective of caste or creed, and are very much related with their seasonal cropping pattern (like the *Māhūl jātrā* observed in the month of *Phāgun* or February-March during the harvest of *mahūl* flowers).

"Their" Voice: Some Reflections from the Stakeholders' Angle

The issue of displacement for the sake of development was initiated during the days of British rule in this country (Mankodi, 1989),[6] and the Land Acquisition Act of 1894 has given unquestionable authority of displacing people for the said purpose, even without the consent of the people to be affected. This clearly indicates that there has been the lack of people's participation in such development programmes from the very beginning. However, Article 21 of the Constitution shows some ray of hope with its provision for "right to live with dignity" to withstand any deprivation of the livelihood sources. As has been already mentioned in this article, anti-dam agitations are still being organized in the study area. The tribal people are found to be more reactive than their non-tribal counterparts, because of the formers' greater community attachment and unity, as well as their greater adherence to their indigenous culture. However, history speaks of more failure than success of such protests as these indigenous people lack the exposure to the knowledge of the official formalities and also the technical approach to uphold and highlight their needs and demands strategically (Adams, 1993). In such hazardous situation women are more vulnerable than men (Indra, 1999), and if these women are indigenous, then their situation is more vulnerable. This study finally gives a mirror reflection of the overall situation of and the attitude on the problem through different opinions as voiced by these tribal women and narrated in the following:

- These women have been observed to be more realistic about the project, whether they find it inevitable or oppose it. Following the attitudes in the Khuntapali village, some men are seemingly satisfied with the paid money of sizable amount, but their women are seriously concerned over the impact of the long-term adversaries of the project and the disarticulation on their future economy. They are not much swayed by the large lump sum amount ("Can money really give an everlasting solution and compensate for every kind of loss?"— a question raised by most of these women).
- They, however, do not see any rationality in the idea of bringing about agricultural prosperity at the cost of disrupting the lives of so many families—specifically, when they feel that they are not going to get any direct benefit from this sort of water resource development.
- If the government assures the tribes on one hand, of their customary rights on abundant water resources (*jala*) and forest (*jangala*), then on the other hand how come these natural assets are snatched away from them?—a direct question they have raised with all their simplicity.
- Although the event of displacement has not taken place yet, but these women have started realizing the pangs of getting uprooted and all attachments severed from the lands of their ancestors.
- They also clearly suspect the real effectiveness of the government's rehabilitation programme in compensating their loss. It is not only that money is unable to solve or compensate each and every loss they would face in their uprooted lives, but also because the package does not seem to them at all compensatory, practically.
- Thus, they even do not find the rehabilitation process satisfactory, and also very much doubt the transparency of the compensation package and its implementation. Despite their repetitive request, the officials concerned, somehow, reportedly avoid providing them the details of the facilities they are entitled to.

- Apart from the numerous non-materialistic loss, whatever the government has decided for their materialistic compensation, even this they do not find much acceptable due to various obvious reasons. For instance, the compensation for the lands is practically not at all at par with the proper valuation of the lands they possess at present.
- They demand for good cultivable lands instead of those less fertile government lands (to be given in compensation) that would obviously enhance the cost of cultivation. They rationalize the act of giving them lands from within the command area, by which they too, can taste the benefit of this irrigation project.
- In addition, they have suggested a unique solution for the land problem. As the lands in the command area have been estimated to yield double cropping, so they justify the fact of giving them the half of the privately owned lands of that area, so that the resettlers and the old settlers both can enjoy the same extent of profit, instead of the former being pushed into the possibility of a very less or no cropping at all ("If the Government has the right to take away our lands for the people of that (command) area, then why can it not give us some land from that area?")
- Even those who have accepted the project as inevitable and have mentally prepared themselves for the displacement ("The inevitable facts of ringing of the death-knell in one's life and the order of the Government to give up our lands-are both very much unpredictable and unavoidable."), are also equally serious on the matter of suitable relocation sites and want to be assured by the responsible authorities that their present livelihood pattern be preserved, or at least there should be increased options for their survival.

Concluding Remarks

With already so much sacrifice made by the underprivileged section of this country in the name of large-scale water resource development that, the administration cannot any more avoid rethinking on the humane side of such projects. It is already high time to balance the maximum material benefit from the projects and simultaneously, handle seriously the impoverishments of the vulnerable level of the population, from the human rights point of view. At the same time, these dam-and-development projects cannot also be stopped as these provide large-scale economic output. So, the planners and the policy makers should be more pragmatic and democratic in their approach by involving the participation of the stakeholders. If these development projects are meant "for the people" and "of the people", then why not "by the people"? It would be the best measure if the affected people participate in making their own resettlement and rehabilitation strategies.

Moreover, as women constitute half of this country's population and are more vulnerable than men, their participation deserves more sincere attention. And for the tribal women, who are under more precarious and disadvantaged socio-economic condition at the grassroots level, the inclusion of their voice is a must. So, it becomes a noble responsibility of the social scientists, including the anthropologists, to delve into the deeper reality of gender as well as ethnic dimensions of the problems related to displacement. Besides, the study on the pre-displacement situation needs to be more encouraged as this can warn about the possible hazards of displacement in advance and hence, enable the authorities concerned to formulate the policies and programmes in accordance with the situation that is real and absolutely inevitable for the affected people.

Acknowledgements

Sincere gratitude is extended to Dr. A.B. Ota, Department of Anthropology, B.J.B. College, Bhubaneswar and Mr. David Sagar, Department of English, Patnagarh College, Balangir for providing us valuable information and critical suggestions while writing this paper.

NOTES

1. *Mahül* flowers are used for making a local liquor, viz. *mahüli* and also used as cattle fodder and for other purposes.
2. A kind of tree, the leaves of which are used for making *bidi* or the indigenous cigarette.
3. 1 *Kera* = 100 leaves.
4. A renowned anthropologist and also a well-known World Bank social scientist.
5. Cernea's Risk Impoverishment Model, developed in 1990, includes 8 risk factors: landlessness, homelessness, joblessness, loss of access to common property assets, food insecurity, marginalization, mortality and morbidity and social disarticulation.
6. <rronline.ignou.ac.in/guestentry/unit01/chapter1-10.asp-9k> is a useful internet source for further reference, as accessed on February 12, 2005.

REFERENCES

Adams,W.M. 1993. "Development's Deaf Ear: Downstream Users and Water Releases from the Bakolori Dam, Nigeria," *World Development,* 21 (9): 1405-1416.

Agnihotri, Anita.1998. "The Orissa Resettlement and Rehabilitation of Projects Affected Persons Policy, 1994: Some Critical Issues," (pp.85-90) in P. Mohapatra, A.B.Ota and R.N.Mohanty (eds.), *Development Induced Displacement and Rehabilitation.* New Delhi: Prachi Prakashan.

Baboo, Balgovind. 1997. "Big Dams and the Tribal: The Case of the Hirakud Dam Oustees of Orissa," (pp.92-104) in G. Pfeffer and D.K. Behera (eds.), *Contemporary Society: Tribal Studies (Development Issues, Transition and change).* Vol.2, New Delhi: Concept Publishing Co.

Barik, B.C. 1997. "Big Dams and Rehabilitation Issues: Who Shares the Sorrows of Oustees," *Journal of Social Sciences,* 1 (2): 103-111.

Behera, Deepak Kumar and Srikant Patel. 1997. "Trapped in the Development Wrap: The Case of the Project Affected Parjas in the Indravati River Valley in Orissa, India," *Journal of Social Sciences,* 1 (2): 113-123.

Cernea, Michael M. 1991. "Socio-Economic and Cultural Approaches to Involuntary Population Resettlement," *Guidelines on Lake Management,* Vol. II, World Bank Reprint Series, No.468. Washington D.C.: The World Bank.

_____. 1999. The Economics of Involuntary Resettlement: *Questions and Challenges.* Washington D.C.: World Bank.

Fernandes, Walter. 1997. "Displacement of Tribal: Struggles and Implications for Resettlement," (pp.78-89) in G. Pfeffer and D.K. Behera (eds.), *Contemporary Society: Tribal Studies (Development Issues, Transition and change).* Vol.2, New Delhi: Concept Publishing Co.

_____. 2005. "The Impact of Displacement on Tribal Women" (pp.70-85) in G. Pfeffer and D.K. Behera (eds.), *Contemporary Society: Tribal Studies (Tribal Situation in India).* Vol.6, New Delhi: Concept Publishing Co.

Indira, R. and Shanthi. 1997. "Gender Dynamics in the Context of a Tribal Society," (pp.169-179) in G. Pfeffer and D.K. Behera (eds.), *Contemporary Society: Tribal Studies (Structure and Process).* Vol.1, New Delhi: Concept Publishing Co.

Indra, D. 1999. *Engendering Forced Migration: Theory and Practice.* Oxford: Berghahn Books.

Khan, A.N. 2000 (May 13-19). "Human Issues Involved in Water Resource Development," *Employment News Weekly,* xxv (7): 1

Lower Suktel Irrigation Circle Office, Balangir.

Mankodi, Kashyap. 1989. "Displacement and Relocation Problems and Prospects," (pp.13-15) in Walter Fernandes and Enakshi Ganguly Thukral (eds.), *Development, Displacement and Rehabilitation.* New Delhi: Indian Social Institute.

Mohapatra, L.K. 1998. "Rehabilitation by the Government and by the People: A Case of Impoverishment of Salandi Major Irrigation Project Oustees," (pp.54-69) in P. Mohapatra, A.B. Ota and R.N.Mohanty (eds.), *Development Induced Displacement and Rehabilitation.* New Delhi: Prachi Prakashan.

(The) Orissa Resettlement and Rehabilitation of Projects Affected Persons Policy, 1994 (Dept. of Water Resources, Govt. of Orissa).

Ota, A.B. 1998. "Risk Factors and Their Negotiation Strategy in R & R Implementation: Case Studies from Four Irrigation Projects in Orissa," (pp.91-112) in P. Mohapatra, A.B. Ota and R.N. Mohanty (eds.), *Development Induced Displacement and Rehabilitation.* New Delhi: Prachi Prakashan.

Panigrahi, Nilakantha. 2003. "Displacement and Deprivation of Tribal in Orissa," (pp.118-143) in V.S. Sahay and Pradip Kr. Singh (eds.), *Researches in Indian Anthropology.* Vol.1, New Delhi: Serials Publications.

Radcliffe-Brown, A.R. 1971. *Structure and Function in Primitive Society.* London: Cohen & West Ltd.

Ray, Rita. 1998. "Gender Aspects on Dislocation," (pp.134-150) in P. Mohapatra, A.B. Ota and R.N. Mohanty (eds.), *Development Induced Displacement and Rehabilitation.* New Delhi: Prachi Prakashan.

Roy, Arundhati. 1999. *The Greater Common Good.* New Delhi: India Book Distributors (ISBN).

Status Report of Lower Suktel Irrigation Project (Department of Water Resources, Govt. of Orissa.). November-2002.

Vir, Dharam and Manju Manral. 1990. *Tribal Women:* Changing Spectrum in India. New Delhi: Classical Publishing Co.

NINETEEN

CHANGING OCCUPATIONAL ROLE OF SABARA TRIBAL WOMEN: An Empirical Study in the Resettled Village Krushna Nagar

ITISHREE PADHI and NIYATI P. LAL

The present paper discusses about the degeneration in the status of tribal women in terms of occupation as a result of displacement. The study has been conducted in Krushna Nagar, a resettled village adjacent to the urban centre of Bhubaneshwar, the capital city of Orissa. In an attempt to understand the aftermath of displacement of the tribal community, a field study was conducted, which reveals that displacement has caused more harm to the women folk in the tribal community as far as their occupational role is concerned.

Introduction

Inequality between men and women is one of the most crucial disparities in many societies (Dreze & Sen, 1997) and this is particularly so among the tribal communities. Although a large number of studies have been conducted on tribal by anthropologists, sociologists, economists and other social scientists, only a few are focused on tribal women. Thus the existing literature on tribal women is limited. Despite the protection given to the tribal population by the constitution of India (1950), it remains the most backward ethnic group in India, on the three most important indicators of development: health, education and income (Singh and Rajyalakshmi, 1993). The economic condition of tribal women remains even worse. Although significant changes have taken place in the status and the role of women in general in the process of development, little change has occurred to the low status of women in the tribal society. As in any other community, women in the tribal constitute almost half of their population. Hence, the welfare of the tribal community depends to a large extent on the status that the tribal women enjoy in this community. Although there is no dearth of literature on tribal study, only a few are focused on tribal women. Thus there is a need for generating studies which can fill the information gap about variations that exist and about the role and the status of tribal women from one region to another and one community to another (Singh, 1988).

Focus of Study

Traditionally, tribal women played significant roles in the economic, familial and cultural spheres of social life of the kinship based social groups. Changes in social structure and culture brought about by reasons, like displacement have adversely affected the role of women in their respective social context.

In a changed modern scenario, while women enjoy appropriate role in the society by participating in the development process, the tribal women on the other hand suffer silently because of their traditional role degeneration. This has become a matter of serious concern for the researchers. Hence, an attempt has been made in this paper, to make an in depth study on women focusing on their occupational role, in a displaced tribal community. The study presents the changing role of Sabara tribal women who have been displaced from their original forest based village, Dampada and resettled by the government of Orissa in a village named Krushna Nagar — adjacent to the urban centre of Bhubaneshwar. The thrust has been on their traditional occupational role which was found in the most vulnerable state and the other changes they face in the new social set up as a result of displacement. The findings of the study may help us to question our very approach to tribal community development in general and particularly in displaced areas.

Study Area Approach

Orissa is a land of tribes. It has a tribal population of 70,32,214 that constitutes 22.1 per cent of the total population. As many as 62 different tribal communities are located in different corners of the state. Sabara is one such tribe.

The village Krushna Nagar is a resettled colony where the displaced Sabara tribes of Banki Reserve Forest have been relocated. This village is

under Mauza Krushna Nagar (Darthunga Gram panchayat) under Chandka police station in Bhubaneshwar block of Khurda district. It is located at a distance of about 20 kms from Bhubaneshwar, the capital city of Orissa. The area is which these people live is a government land named as Krushna Nagar under Bhubaneshwar Tehsil. The displacement affected 47 families who were rehabilitated from Behenta Sahi, *Danpada* near Banki since July 1992. It is surrounded by Chudanga hills and the river Mahanadi flows at a distance of 5 kms from the village. For the present study data were collected from all the Sabara women in Krushna Nagar through questionnaire and observation. Two sets of questionnaire were prepared to collect data, one from the women folk who are our primary respondents (PR) and the second set from their male counterparts, our secondary respondents (SR). The questions were mainly concerned with the changes in the occupations and their nature — in terms of positive/negative evaluation.

The demographic profile indicates that the population of the village under study was 201 and women constituted around 46.27 per cent of the total population. Among the women, while 66.67 per cent were married, 17.23 per cent girls were below the age of 14 years. The following Table 20.1 gives the percentage distribution of tribal women on the basis of their marital status.

Table 19.1: Marital Status of Sabara Tribal Women.

Status	*Percentage*
Married	51.62
Widow	15.05
Unmarried	16.10
Children below 14 years of age	17.23
Total	100

In the Sabara tribe, both men and women were found mostly illiterate. During field study, it was found that only one primary school is located in the village premises. Although 56.25 per cent of the children showed interest in going for high school education, they could not do so, as one has to cover a distance of 10 Kms. to reach the high school in another village.

Traditional Family Role and Occupational Role

The fact that women play a significant role in the household activities since ancient times needs no further discussion and thus, the role of Sabara tribal women in this regard is no exception. The normal day for the woman of this community begins at around 4:00 am in the morning. After finishing their routine household activities, they collectively go to work in the field and return home by midday. At home, they again occupy themselves in activities, like fetching water, cooking, feeding young children, doing the dishes, running errands and serving food to the male members of the family etc. The Sabara tribal men never felt it necessary to help the women folk in the household activities.

Coming to the occupational role, it was found that agriculture was their primary occupation and a major source of income. Our data show that around 82 per cent women worked as agricultural labourers before relocation. While the men did more arduous and rigorous work, like preparing the field for cultivation, sowing seeds, application of fertilisers; women did other jobs like weeding and tilling, carrying and spreading organic manure and harvesting the crop etc. The work pressure on women increased many fold during peak season as apart from their regular job in the field, they engaged themselves in collecting leaves, litter and organic manure. Preparation and storing of fuel wood for the lean period was also done during this time. While the Sabara women worked for 14 — 15 hours per day in the peak season, in a normal day they worked for 10 to 12 hours to meet their basic economic necessities.

Change in Occupational Role after Displacement

Displacement and relocation of the Sabara tribe population from Dampada to Krushna Nagar has resulted in drastic changes in the traditional occupation of the women folk. In the traditional set-up, both men and women worked hand in hand on their own land to meet their basic needs. Displacement has caused them landless and forced them to work as agricultural labourers — a job that depends on the mercy of the land owner. Rehabilitation even after 10 years has failed to provide them with their own house as they were found living in half built thatched houses. Many (around 71% men) were found struggling to get ownership of the land given to them as *patta* (record of ownership right) is yet to be provided to them by the government.

A small percentage of Sabara men (around 13%) who possessed the land preferred share cropping (*bhaga chasa*) due to lack of irrigation facilities. The rest of the men cultivated land of other farmers bearing all expenses of cultivation and paying half of the produce to the land owner. Sabara women who once proudly worked on their own field are now reduced to the status of agricultural labourers. Unlike the men, the women folk of this tribe, on the other hand preferred to collect fuel wood and leaves from the forest rather than working as agricultural labourers. In course of discussion with our respondents, it was found that the Sabara women after collecting fuel from the forest, cut them into small pieces, make small bundles and carry them to the nearby market (Baranga is the nearest market) to sell. By sunset, they are back to their home with vegetables and other essential household items that they could buy with the money received from the sale of the fuel wood.

Our women respondents informed that apart from the agricultural season (when cropping and harvesting is done), the Sabara men mostly remained unemployed and hence during such period, the responsibility of running the households mainly fell on them. To overcome the financial burden, they need to go for different type of jobs which could supplement their income. 74.02 per cent of women reported that they go to the nearby construction sites to work on daily wage basis. Among them 76.19 per cent informed that they were underpaid and didn't receive their wage on time. Approximately 22.80 per cent women wage earners had to go through physical harassment including sexual exploitation.

The other job left for Sabara women to meet the family needs was to collect leaves from the forest, stitch them into plates and sell the plates in Baranga market. Few women in this village were found even rearing and selling goats, while some prepared and sold puffed rice.

The poor economic condition of the family sometimes forced even the girl children to work. Our study shows that out of 16 girls (below the age of 14), 11 were working in the Nandan Kanan zoo as daily wage earners. Thus, child labour was found to be a common practice among this displaced Sabara tribe. Recently, Self Help Groups (SHG's) have been formed for women with the help of *Anganwadi* workers. The purpose of SHG is to encourage women to save Rs. 10 per week in a nearby bank. This deposit could work as a security on the basis of which they can avail loans from the government to establish their own cottage industry. But due to the lack of surplus money in their hand, they were unable to deposit the minimum amount in the bank. Thus, the participation level of women was found to be extremely low in the SHG.

From the data collected during field study, it was observed that while the family roles of Sabara women remained unchanged in the pre and post eviction period, a significant change has taken place in their occupational role in the post relocation period. The work pressure on the women has increased tremendously resulting in deterioration in their health condition. The Sabara women were found struggling hard to cope with the changes in their post displaced life. The following table gives a detailed account of their familial and occupational role in the pre and post displaced period.

Occupational Role of Sabara Women Before Displacement

Primary	*Secondary*
Land preparation before sowing	Collection of fuel wood and leaves
Use and spreading of organic manure	Making leaf plates
Harvesting and threshing of crops	Keeping and selling goods
Horticulture of work	Preparing and selling puffed rice

Occupational Role of Sabara Women after Displacement

Primary	*Secondary*
Collection of fuel wood and leaves and selling them in the market	Keeping and selling goods
Working as labourers in others lands	Preparing and Selling puffed rice
Working as labourers in near by construction sites	Tailoring
Making and selling leaf plates	

Family Role of Sabara Women before and after Displacement

Before Displacement	*After Displacement*
Cooking	Cooking
Child rearing	Child rearing
Cleaning utensil and washing cloths	Cleaning utensil and washing cloths
Fetching water	Fetching water
Buying household needs (grocery and vegetables) from the market	Buying household needs (grocery and vegetables) from the market

The Need

The Sabara tribe women worked harder than men after displacement. They have been left homeless, landless, living an insecured life. They were found exploited socially and sexually. They were over worked yet were unable to meet both the ends squarely. Thus, the status of these women has been characterized by sub-human physical living condition which needs urgent and careful measures. The situation demands better employment opportunities for these people in the near vicinity of their habitat. Instead of isolating the tribal women specifically, or the tribals in general, necessary infrastructure facilities should be provided to bring them into the national mainstream through culture friendly, need based socio-economic development modules. Instead of making an effort to introduce them to the more sophisticated technology, efforts should be made to provide facilities to carry on their age-old occupation. In our society, the aim of welfare and development hinges around the schemes of socio-economic nature of development. These programmes are mainly in the field of health, nutrition and literacy. How far women are aware of these welfare programmes can be gauged from their involvement in these programmes and also from the change/impact that has come about on their status and socio-economic development. Studies (Brandon and Dixit, 1988, etc) reveal that proper implementation of development programmes can bring remarkable changes in the quality of life of the tribal women. However, the fact remains that, women are not aware of their rights and privileges officially granted to them under different programmes. Large scale ignorance in this regard by our respondent Sabara women can be taken as an evidence of a negative sign of development. In our study, it was found that 36.37 per cent of Sabara women have received vocational training like tailoring, knitting etc. Yet due to lack of finance they could not use their talent and make it a profession for livelihood.

The tribals whose life is mainly agro-based face survival difficulties in the absence of arable land and increasing trend of deforestation. Increased government control over the forest has adversely affected the life of these tribal women. This is evident from our study where we found that the work of Sabara women has become extremely difficult as the forest produce are now being collected by agents from outside. Collection of fuel wood has become more difficult because now it is more time consuming and less accessible. Thus, the Sabara women who were using fuel from the forest as a source of income now have to look for other sources. It was also found that lack of employment opportunities for the Sabara tribal men forced them to move towards urban areas in search of work and hence in their absence women had to bear the entire family responsibility. Due to poor economic condition, lack of nutritious food and the burden of work adversely affected their health. In our study, 89.61 per cent women were found suffering from malnutrition and anemia while 87.5 per cent children were reported underweight. The effort on the part of the government to address the health issue has not reached the Sabara tribe. Their ignorance about health and nutrition is very much evident from their physical appearance.

Some Suggestions and Conclusion

The displaced tribal women should not only be given frequent opportunities in the existing programmes (like, training in agriculture and horticulture, tailoring, making baskets and leaf plates etc.) but they should also be given initial financial aid in order to use their skill to make it their profession. These programmes must be flexible to cater to local needs.

More job oriented programmes, specifically for displaced tribal women should be introduced so that they will not feel alienated because of joblessness. This will enhance their self-confidence and raise their morale within the family as well as in the community.

The studies on tribal women should not remain only as a matter of academic interest. Measures should be taken both through developmental programmes as well as through policy decisions to bring them into the mainstream of civilization. The tribals possess little human capital and no physical capital that they could use for their benefit when there is a sudden dip in their income due to displacement. Thus, displacement if unavoidable should be followed by relocation with adequate financial compensation, especially for the women.

REFERENCES

Brandon, R.R. and B.N. Dixit 1988., "Sericulture for Tribal Women", in J.P. Singh, N.N. Vyas and R.S. Mann (Eds). *Tribal Women and Development, Udaipur:* M L V Tribal Research and Training Insitute, Tribal Area Development Dept., Rajasthan.

Dreze, Jean and A. Sen 1997., *India-Economic Development and Social Opportunity*, page no. 140, Oxford University Press.

Ghosh, S.R. 1984, *Women in Changing Society*, New Delhi, Ashis Publication.

Singh, Amar Kr. and C. Rajyalakshmi. 1993. Presented at the National Workshop on *Status of Tribal Women in India* organised by Council for Social Development, New Delhi and sponsored by National Commission for Women, New Delhi (22-23 Dec'93).

Singh, K.S. *Tribal women : Ananthropological perspective*, in J.P. Singh, N.N. Vyas & R.S. Mann (Eds.) *Tribal women and development* (1988).

SECTION IV

ECOLOGICAL, ECONOMIC AND SOCIAL VALUES

TWENTY

INDIGENOUS VISION FOR A SOUND ENVIRONMENTAL AND ECOLOGICAL FUTURE

BINAY KUMAR PATTNAIK

Today the environmental/ecological degradation of India needs no highlight and elaboration. The air, water, soil and spatial pollution is matched by rapid destruction of eco-systems in India. In addition to the lip services provided by the media, official paper works done by politicians and bureaucrats, contemplations, debates and discussions carried out by intellectuals, even grassroots level movements carried out by NGOs along with the people themselves, all to arrest the environmental/ecological crisis. From among the very many policies, legal and other corrective measures taken, alternative modes of development suggested, one policy and intellectual option which even could be complementary to the dominant mode of development, could be to learn from the indigenous environmental wisdoms as manifest in the Indian little traditions of folklores, cultures/world views of various tribal communities and traditional knowledge systems of various communities in order to shape our environmental research and policies. India's is an ancient civilization, much older than the west and hence has its own environmental wisdom, although embedded in the various cultural forms. Hence, in this context our role as part of the intelligentsia is to identify such embedded traditional wisdoms and direct the social action and policy making to imbibe such traditional wisdoms.

Such traditional environmental wisdoms can be found to be embedded in the cultural forms reflecting the indigenous vision. But this indigenous vision is never found to be in an integrated and unified one. Rather these have been discrete and community based, for, these communities have lived for ages in harmony with nature and have independently developed social practices, cultural forms and world views that contain serious ecological wisdom.

Defining Indigenous

In this context I mean indigenous are those visions that are rooted in the cultures/life styles and livelihoods tied up with the land in a system of mutual reinforcement. Reinforcement means a moral contract wherein human and non-human/ animate beings are basically attuned to the sensual rhythms of earth, the life maintaining capacity of the earth. Today it is necessary to keep these visions alive because these visions have been eroded and are in the verge of being lost on account of the invasion of modernity and ideas from the west. Truly these are endangered and hence need touches of intellectual sensitivity to be significantly related to the globalized world of today.

Methodologically speaking this is an ethnographic account of certain folk and tribal cultural elements, practices, world views and traditional knowledge systems of Indian communities. But more pertinent here is an epistemological issue that if the culturally embedded environmental wisdom that we are talking about is in consonance with "scientific environmentalism". Because it is suggested that such culturally embedded environmental wisdom ought to direct social action and provide for the basis of our environmental policy measures. It is imperative that these be in agreement with the principles of "scientific environmentalism". In the name of indigenous vision, we are not to promote those environmental wisdom (may be rooted in folk cultures and traditional knowledge systems) that do not satisfy/qualify the epistemological requirements of modern science, i.e. positivism. I must not give here the impression of being the votary of the so-called "ethno sciences" that epistemologically contravene modern science. Therefore, only such folk, tribal cultural elements and traditional knowledge systems must form the basis of our interpretation here that are in consonance with the principles of "scientific environmentalism". But such folk, tribal cultural elements and traditional knowledge systems that qualify the criteria of scientific environmentalism are in short supply. Never the less these can not be too rare to be located/identified for scholarly interpretations.

Hereafter it almost becomes an imperative, to note briefly as to how "scientific environmentalism" is conceived. In place of the human centered view of the world and a segmentalized/reductionist view of nature, a holistic view, a living and systemic view of nature (equipped with equilibrium maintaining capability, e.g. GAIA principle) governed by the laws of ecology, at least make the critical criteria of scientific environmentalism. Here it would suffice to merely epitomize the critical criteria:

Informal laws of Ecology

(a) everything is connected to everything else (indicating the interdependence and interrelatedness of the natural world),

(b) everything must go somewhere (indicative of the fact that by the systems of production and manufacturing human beings merely transform the matter in terms of shape and form (e.g. solid, liquid and gas) for consumption and generate colossal wastes that are environmentally hazardous),

(c) nature knows the best (suggestive of maintaining the organic link between man and nature, by which the nature continues to regenerate and supports life) and

(d) there is no such thing as free launch (implicit of the fact that resource intensive consumption and economic development experienced by human beings has an environmental/ecological cost).

Perception of Nature

(a) The nature centered view of the world makes the epistemological foundation of scientific environmentalism in place of the human centered view, wherein the functioning principles and the spirit of the nature are respected and rendered sacrosanct.

(b) Nature is a living system (Shiva, 1988: 14-37). Nature be perceived as a living organism, (not a body of inanimate objects/substances) empowered with the power of generation and regeneration. It is a system of interconnected things and functions holistically not segmentally as the reductionism understands it. It is an equilibrium maintaining system, as per the GAIA principle. Earth, to the GAIA principle (James, 1996: 351-359), is the largest living thing that maintains itself and supports life in it.

(c) Mentality of exploitation be replaced by the mentality of integration. As already said, since earth is the embodiment of eco-systems and not natural resources, human beings mentality of integrating itself to nature becomes the corner stone of environmentalism. In order to experience development nature be used in an interactive manner and not conquered and subdued for interrupting/arresting natural processes and rendered amenable to endless alterations.

Traces of such a view of environmentalism can well be located in the (1) Indian folk cultures, (2) Social practices, (3) Community world views and (4) Traditional knowledge bases. Such mediums of societal expression cannot be over emphasized but at the same time it cannot be undermined as these do mirror the inbuilt societal wisdom. Even social psychologist as eminent as David McClleland in his much celebrated thesis "need-achievement" had suggested studying the folklore and other cultural forms to measure societal "achievement motivation," for these are the true mirror of society. Let us take a few live examples of each of the above for examination:

Folk Cultural Forms

In eastern India forest (essentially an eco-system) has always been worshipped as Goddess (*Van Devi*) which is nothing but a feminine impersonification of nature. More importantly the Goddess (*Van Devi*) is guarded by tiger (*Van Raaj*) other wise known as her "*Vahan*". In the whole of eastern India tiger is revered and worshipped along with the Goddess (*Van Devi*). Particularly in the Sundar Ban region of West Bengal (as well as Bangladesh) such worshipping is wide spread. Even the festivals, songs, dances of this part of rural Bengal reflect such reverence. Tiger is being treated as a pantheon that protects the forests. The worship of both, forest in its feminine impersonification and the top predator for its awesome presence helps protect the fragile ecosystem of Sundar Ban's Mangrove forest. Even in the eastern districts of Orissa (like Balasore and Mayurbhanj) and the adjoining district of the Bengal (Medinapore) the folklore adores tiger as "Bagh Bahadur" the protector of the groves (in the form of folk dance).

A more lively and fitting example from the Oriya folklore reflecting the spirit of scientific environmentalism is an annual Hindu festival called *Raja*. It occurs during the 14th-16th June every year. Although a house hold festival but only celebrated by the unmarried women both young and old of the family who during these three days are to play swing (*Jhula*) and not to perform any household work. By this time the harvesting season is already over (in March along with *Dola Purnima*) and the farmer has been keeping the land open (exposing the soil to sunlight) and waiting for the first touch of monsoon.

But the symbolic meaning attached to the festival is environmentally revealing. The literal meaning of the Oriya word *Raja* refers to that aspect of the women's body chemistry which is usually tabooed. Because it refers to drops of menstrual secretions that is otherwise a sign of fertility. Orissa receives the first rainfall of the year during this period, for south-east monsoon arrives coastal and central Orissa in mid-June. And the mother earth gets ready for cultivation here after receiving the first rainfall of the season. Hence these three days of the *Raja* festival are symbolically equated to the menstrual period of earth (as it receives the first rainfall of the year) after which it gets ready for biological encounter (i.e. tilling of the soil by farmers) and subsequent conception for reproduction (i.e. agricultural output). Traditionally speaking, as love making is forbidden during the menstrual period, tilling of the earth by farmers for agriculture during these three days of the *Raja* festival is forbidden. Therefore, traditionally tilling of the fields in this region starts only after Raja festival. Thus, referring to the feminine principle of earth, Raja festival symbolizes virginity and reproductive power of earth (to produce crops). Hence, as a symbol of virginity and reproductive power, only unmarried women celebrate *Raja*. Interestingly during these three days of the festival unmarried women celebrating *Raja* are not to perform household works particularly cooking, because as part of the Hindu principle of "purity and pollution" during menstrual period women are debarred from house hold work particularly cooking.

Similarly the unmarried women of Singhbhoom region (of Jharkhand state) celebrate *Thusu* festival. The word *Thusu* is derived from the local word Tasu meaning dead crop. Hence, after the harvesting season, unmarried women of Singhbhoom region worship goddess *Thusu* an impersonification of the famine principle of earth to restore the lost fertility of earth during the last season and to give a bumper crop in the next season. (Mohapatra and Sahoo, 1997: 48-49).

This in other words is the invocation of the reproductive power of the earth in the *Thusu* songs to resurrect dead crops and come alive green again. Another example from the folklore of eastern India reflecting the respect for environmental principle of reproductive power of nature and restrained consumption is the celebration of the holy months of *Kartika* and *Margasira* in Oriya calendar (October and November in English Calendar). Notable that people in coastal and central Orissa are fish eaters. But during the holy months of *Kartika* (because of the holy dip in five sacred days known as Panchuka) and *Margasira* (because of the five sacred Thursdays known as the *Maanabasa Gurubar* during which Goddess Lakshmi is worshipped in Oriya households) fishing as well as fish eating are traditionally forbidden. During this period fishing and fish eating are considered as profane acts. However, implicit there is a serious environmental wisdom. October and November are the breeding months for fishes. During these two months fish eggs are laid out and hatched. Non-fishing during these months allows the fishes to multiply and grow. Fishes being the cleaners of the river/ water body eat away the unclean elements it had acquired during the monsoon and help keep the water clean. Thus the manifest function of the celebration may be giving continuity to the tradition but its latent function has been environmental.

Social Practices

The finest examples of social practices reflecting the environmental wisdom of conservation could be that of the Bishnois of Rajasthan. Founded by Guru Jambheswar-ji Maharaj, Bisnois' is a religious sect born out of environmental compulsions and convictions' of desert life. The basic philosophy of the Bishnois, enunciated in twenty-nine principles - is that all living entities (plants and animals) of different types have a right to survive and share in the available resources. Bishnois have been the worshippers of trees and protectors of trees (as well as wild life) in their areas of habitation. Such practices of conservation have been so strong among the Bishnois that in the history they have even fought the kings' soldiers to save the trees. Because of such strong social practices Bishnois have handsomely contributed to the social forestry/ afforestation programmes in Rajasthan. A brighter example of similar type of social practice displaying indigenous wisdom for environmentalism is the "sacred groves". Having survived for hundred of years, sacred groves, in India have been the finest instance of traditional conservation and common property resource management system. Sacred Groves are still wide-spread in India's west coast and western-ghats where groves are attached to temple deities as properties. In Kerala there are "wild-jungles dedicated to snakes" and are treated as sacred. It is this attached divinity that could save the forests from the so called scientific forestry introduced by the then British Government and from the hands of timber mafia. Hence in these groves survived many plant species which otherwise have faced extinction. Apart from the social and cultural (religions) significance to the locals, as pointed out by Roy Burman (1995: 246-251), practices of sacred groves have serious ecological values, for, these at places have prevented flooding, prevented soil run-off and most importantly have maintained ground water levels in their areas of location.

A still revealing social practice in conformity with sound environmentalism has been a type of shifting cultivation called as *jhum* (slash and burn cultivation). This is a type of cultivation typical to certain tribes in the north-eastern regions of India which is often described as a way of life for the practicing tribes as their social life and culture revolve around it. It is a wide spread misconception that shifting cultivation practiced by many tribes have been ecologically disastrous particularly, it is said that jhum cultivation has been greatly responsible for the loss of forest cover in the north east region.

On the contrary there are evidences to build up argument that *jhum* is a highly organized agro-system which is in harmony with the principle of re-generation by nature. The regeneration takes place adequately in the *jhum* cycle, provided the fallow period between two successive cropping is long enough. Because during this interim period the regeneration takes place and the soil fertility is restored. Earlier the fallow period use to be around 20 years which came down to ten years and of late it has further come down to 5 years (Ramakrishnan and Patnaik, 1992: 218). A standard feature of almost all the shifting cultivations is the practice of mixed cropping. Once considered as primitive by agronomists and soil scientists this practice is now a suggested means to increase world food production. Thus during the cropping phase the farmers raise 8 to 35 crop species on a small plot of 2 to 2.5 hectors with simultaneous sowing and sequential harvesting. This crop mixture provides a good crop cover against the loss of soil nutrients through run-off and leaching of water, helps in optimizing resource use on a patch of land by providing more space for the next crop that is ready to mature after the harvest of the earlier one. It facilitates recycling of biomass and soil nutrients through crop and weed residues and improve soil quality through surface mulching. Thus it is ecologically a very sound system of agriculture. A comparative study of yield patterns in various *jhum* cultivation cycles, showed that shorter the cycle lower is the yield and vice versa. But the optimum economic yield takes place in a cycle of 10 years (Ramakrishnan and Patnaik, 1992: 216). It may be an altogether different matter that today in north-east a jhum cycle of 10 years cannot be sustained because of the tremendous pressure on land brought in by the growing population.

World Views

The sustainable world view of the Warlis a tribe in the north of Bombay region confirms the parameters of sustainable environmentalism and eco- friendly lifestyle. The lifestyle of Warlis is based on their world view of a "living Nature" which is not exploitable. Warlis are the first green people to have impersonated green as *Hirva* and worshiped. To them *Hirva* is the source of all wealth. Natural resources are treated as the gifts of *Hirva* and hence all consumable wealth are the products of *Hirva* and not that of human labour and technology. The most revered deities of the Warlis are *Dhartari* (the earth Goddess), *Kansari* (the Goddess of grain) and *Palghat* (the goddess of tree and fertility). Accordingly their embedded customs and beliefs are directed towards the conservation of nature and trees in particular. Their songs, dances and paintings all reflect their respect and love for animals, plants and groves (Pereira, 1992: 182-191). Warlis consider themselves as the care-takers of nature rather than exploiters. They have restrained consumption practices by which they do not abuse/exploit nature and believe that nature will generously provide for continuously through its regenerative power. They have a detailed knowledge base on plant life, typology of plants and their several uses including those for medicines and pesticides. This knowledge system thrives in their oral tradition. With primitive mode of agriculture, Warlis lead a life which is completely embedded in nature. Thus in their world view as well as life style they maintain the organic link with nature. This non-modern world view of the Warlis is perfectly in agreement with the principles of "Deep Ecology"/"New Natural Philosophy", that advocates the "post industrial societies to go back to the state of nature" again. Notable that, deep ecology is perceived as the guiding philosophy of radical environmental movements of the world today (Devall, 1996: 125-135).

Traditional Knowledge Systems/Sciences

It would not be needless to remind our readers that as an ancient civilization India had once a system of science and technology of its own (indigenous) that has already faced extinction mostly because of the advent of modern science and technology from the west along with the British rule and of course because most of it were not systematized and documented (being hereditary). Here is one outstanding example of such an indigenous system of science and technology for water-harvesting and use which is ecologically sound. The cities of Jodhpur, Bikanir and Jaisalmar had thrived in the *Thar* desert of Rajasthan. Not surprisingly, these cities lived with sufficiency of water amidst the desert even before modern scientific system of water supply was introduced. This could be possible then because of the indigenous system of water-harvesting and use that made optimum use of the available water resources in the vicinity of desert cities. It has been unearthed and reported by the noted environmentalist late Anil Agarwal (1992) who himself was a civil engineer.

The massive rocky plateau at the edge of which is located the city of Jodhpur once made the main catchments area for water supply to the city. All along the catchments area ran big canals, carried huge volumes of rain water to be stored in the numerous tanks of the city. Notable was the tank of *Ranisar* built inside the ramparts of fort of Jodhpur in year 1500 to support the then royal nobilities and king's defense staff. The tank was located on a high hill and whenever overflowed the water used to be collected in a tank called *Padmasar* located in a lesser height. But both *Ranisar* and *Padmasar* were located at higher elevation to facilitate their seepage water to be collected through an extensive system of wells and step wells in the city. There were several other tanks in the city apart from the two mentioned which were fed by canals draining out water from the spread out upland areas surrounding the city of Jodhpur. So each locality in the city had a tank linked step well called as *bawdi*. These step wells were nicely carved and decorated and had steps going down three to four stories so that people could walk into and walk out. Thus, both the surface as well as ground water were fully utilized.

But of late the entire catchments area of uplands and the canal networks there have been seriously impaired by the advent of stone quarries in the area. Out of the total 14000 hectares of catchments area, nearly 11000 hectares have been taken over by 10,000 stone quarries (Agarwal and Narain, 1992: 223). The deep craters created by the quarries on the entire upland now trap rain water and prevent it from reaching the canals to flow down to the reservoirs. Even the canals are neglected, damaged and often chocked/ blocked with dumped rubbles of the quarries. Therefore, the connected tanks have either dried up or become cesspools with stagnant water. Thus modern system of water supply has taken the toll of an indigenous system of water management and use. This is a burning example of traditional sciences/ technologies that very well conforms the principles of scientific environmentalism.

It would suffice to depict another live example of a some what different nature, i.e. community based knowledge system which is least modern but reflects very high level of ecological wisdom. The local community centered knowledge bases that are unwritten, uncodified and unsystematic also form a part of the traditional knowledge base. These community based local knowledge bases are at times found to be store house of ecological wisdom particularly of the ecological services. These community based knowledge systems are developed locally, based on age old experiences of interaction with nature. In a recently published paper Sanjay Kumar (2004: 73-103) articulates such community based knowledge bases pertaining to "local ecological services" prevalent among the tribal villagers of Jarkhand the eastern India state. In his empirical study conducted in the three tribal villages of Jharkhand the author articulates the community centered knowledge bases about the ecological services embedded in the culture and livelihood of the Munda and Santal tribes.

Sanjay Kumar provides ample empirical evidences of the community based knowledge about the ecological services rendered by the local forests. The tribal villagers of the area studied have been found to be aware of trees as the controllers of pollution through their capacity to filter unclean air and trees as the regulators of air quality through their process of photo-synthesis. The people are very much appreciative of the fact that forest is crucial for clear air and in the absence of clean air people suffer from diseases like, tuberculosis, asthma, whooping cough, etc. and in support they point out the high incidents of such diseases in areas like Chakradharpur, Karaikela (near by towns) which have experienced massive deforestation in the last three decades. Therefore, the villagers appreciate trees with larger leaves, dense, shiny foliage like, *Sal* (*Shorea robusta*), Peepal (*Ficus religiosa*) etc. Further the tribal people are found to be aware of the fact that their forest plays a major role in shaping the water-regime of the region. Surprisingly they point out the forest to have affected the water resources in the catchments areas. These people believed that it is because of the forest in the neighbourhood that they receive more rainfall compared to their deforested neighbors in towns like Chakradharpur and Chainbasa. Elderly villagers readily recall that because of deforestation, the area is receiving less precipitation than before, which is causing the moisture in the ground to dry up even before January. Earlier, decades ago, the subsoil moisture used to persist until late March (Kumar, 2004: 81). This speaks of the falling productivity of rabi crop (winter crop) in recent years.

More amazingly, with regard to the Hydrologic cycle of the forest, Sanjay Kumar found that the tribal villagers are almost unanimous in their choice on the infiltration and water holding capacities of different plant species. The scale of water holding capacities of trees, constructed on the basis of household interviews is found to be not very different from the scale prepared by scientific forest managers of the department of forests. The tribal people also have observed the vicious cycle of soil moisture loss due to high run-off and forest degradation. So they cherish the month of August when a prolonged spell of low intensity rainfall facilitates slow run-off from forested hills and fills the low land paddy fields with right amount of water, loaded with soil nutrients. Further it retains the soil moisture for a longer period. Hence they observe that the flow of moisture from the forest to the low land paddy farms is longer if the forest is dense and had trees of high water infiltration capacity. For the same reason the tribal people dig-up *chuans* (small water holes) on the natural drainage line for drinking water in the dry season. Apart from fog, the formation of dew is observed to be higher in villages having better quality of forests in their vicinity. Dependent upon this knowledge is the "Lac" industry of Jharkhand. The villages that are away from forests or have been deforested only prefer to cultivate Lac, because dew kills "Lac" insects (2004:85). These tribal people display intimate knowledge of the subterranean water. But the *chuans* now-a-days dry up by the month of February only, while villagers recall that decades ago these chuans used to last till May-June. It is easily attributed to deforestation. Besides, the tribal villagers also could articulate the effects of forests on the quality of water in the area. It is popularly believed that water of streams passing through well stocked forest is *mota* (thick) but sweet, whereas stream water passing through open/non forested areas is *patla* (thin) but brackish. Therefore, it is said that, water of Ranchi city which is *Patla* consumes more time and fuel wood energy to cook rice. There fore the community knowledge is also prescriptive about choicest plant/tree species (like *jamun*) that enhance the water quality.

This knowledge is drawn from the long experiences of communities and cannot be discarded as unscientific as these too have evolved on the basis of systematic observations and certain conclusive observations are made on the basis of comparisons. It appears that comparisons are made between two points of time keeping the space intact, where the present phenomenon is compared with its community based reconstructed past in the same area. Similarly in other occasions comparisons are made between two places keeping the time intact, where the phenomenon in one village with forests is compared with the phenomenon in another village without forests.

The knowledge of the tribal people about the nature and extent of moisture and nutrients flow from the forests is very rich. The most productive farm lands in the sample villages are found to be those which fall within the direct line of moisture and nutrients flow from the forests. To corroborate this the author offers empirical evidence that the rich and the powerful in the tribal villages (i.e. Munda village chief, village priest and their kith and kin) posses a high proportion of farm lands nearer to the forests. These lands ensure not only high crop productivity but also lesser use of organic fertilizer in the farm, because of the flow of rich soil nutrients and moisture from the forest. It is also believed by the tribal farmers that frequent sighting of earthworms and oysters on the farm land is positively correlated to high productivity as these signify soil fertility. In addition to this, the villagers are also aware of soil erosion in the area caused by deforestation and run-off. In order to prevent farm-soil erosion the villagers traditionally make a *bund* between the forest and the adjacent farm land and even take other adaptive measures like plantation of species and shrubs known for soil binding capacities.

Sarhul is a major festival for the tribes of this region with serious ecological implications. In the eve of the festival in April-May the villagers harvest *Sal* (*Shorea robusta*) flowers from the forest. It is believed by the tribal people that collecting and consuming Sal flowers before the festival will invoke deadly snake bites. The latent meaning of the festival is to keep the flowers unharmed till pollination and seed setting is over. The tribal priest (*pahan*), during the *Sarhul* worship takes water filled pitcher to the groove/ forest and keeps it there overnight after prayer to bonga. In the next morning, if the water level in the pitcher is found reduced, the *pahan* forecasts inadequate monsoon and the farmers plan the agriculture accordingly. The vice versa is also true. The scientific reason behind this ritual is that the level of humidity in the atmosphere in the month of April that brings down or maintains the *pahan's* water level, is a rough indicator of cloud formation and rain (pre-monsoon) in the subsequent two months (2004: 98).

This knowledge could be an extremely useful tool not only in the joint forest management and local agricultural developmental programmes but also in ensuring sustainability of forest management in the area. Such informal knowledge of the community about the ecological-services is the missing link in plans/ strategies for empowerment of the poor and sustainable management of the forest resources.

Concluding Observations

Thus, based on examples of folk cultural forms, community based social practices, community based world views and traditional knowledge systems reflecting the environmental wisdom we could draw upon an indigenous vision to guide our thinking and collective action leading to policy-making. If we could be influenced by the reformist (sallow ecology) as well as radical (deep ecology) environmental movements of the west, why can not we be guided by our own indigenous vision based on traditional wisdoms. Such wisdoms are no less scientific and are more sustainable in the long run. Such indigenous vision may need more systematization and consolidation to serve as a source of relevant environmental ethics. This could be a source of inspiration for other non-western developing societies from East Asia and Africa facing environmental crisis. Lastly we may explicate the underlying assumptions on questions of pragmatic nature:

- Decision-making through highly centralized planning or authority system, particularly in large bureaucratic and political systems, do not find effectiveness in every part of the system. It lacks effectiveness and penetrative abilities in peripheries. Hence in peripheral areas, many problems related to governance have to be handled locally. Often local solutions or approaches are found to be sustainable.
- More effectiveness in larger political systems can be achieved by means of decentralization of power and micro-level planning coupled with empowerment of the people at grassroots level creating scope for popular participation.
- The suggestive idea in the paper provides seeds for future thinking in environmentalism. Because in the decades to come when a large political and bureaucratic systems like India's would be rendered beyond repair and central governance would be a problem of immense magnitude, local thinking and solutions are bound to take over.

REFERENCES

Agarwal, Anil and Sunita Narain. 1992. "Traditional Systems of Water Harvesting and Agro-forestry," (pp.221-232) in Geeti Sen (ed.), *Indigenous Vision*. New Delhi: Sage Publications and India International Centre.

Devall, Bill. 1996. "The Deep Ecology Movement," (pp.125-139) in Merchant Carolyn (ed.), *Key Concepts in Critical Theory Ecology*. Jaipur: Rawat Publications.

James, Lovelock. 1996. "GAIA," in *Merchant Carolyn* (ed.), op. cit.

Mahaptra, S. and N.K. Sahoo. (eds.). 1997. *Lok Sahitya Gabesana*. Cuttack: Friends Publishers. (published in Oriya Language).

Pereira, Winin. 1992. "The Sustainable life style of the Warlis," (pp.189-204) in Geeti Sen (ed.), *Indigenous Vision*. New Delhi: Sage Publications and India International Centre.

Ramakrishnan, P.S. and Suprava Patnaik. 1992. "Jhum: Slash and Burn Cultivation," (pp.215-220) in Geeti Sen (ed.), op. cit.

Roy Burman, J.J. 1995. "The Dynamics of Sacred Groves," Journal of Human Ecology, 6 (4): 245-254.

Shiva, Vandana. 1988. *Staying Alive*. New Delhi: Kali for Women.

Singer, Milton. 1955. "The Cultural Patterns of Indian Civilization," *Far Eastern Quarterly,* 15 : pp. 22-36.

Kumar, Sanjay. 2004. "Indigenous Communities' Knowledge of Local Ecological Services," (pp.73-103) in D. Nathan, G. Kelkar and P. Walter (eds), *Globalization and the Indigenous Peoples in Asia*. New Delhi: Sage Publications.

TWENTY-ONE

SOCIO-ECONOMIC DIMENSIONS OF WEEKLY MARKET IN TRIBAL AREAS: A Case Study among Kondh in Kandhamal District of Orissa

HARI CHARAN BEHERA

Market as a cultural construct, says Paul Alexander, suggests a new direction in economic-anthropology that is linked to areas more broadly researched by Stephen Gudeman (1986), namely "Cultural economics".[1] Market is the locus of exchange and the exchange of goods appears as a continuous social relation. While studying the Neur community, Evans-Pritchard said, one cannot treat Neur economic relationship by them, for they always form part of direct social relations of a general kind (Evans-Pritchard, 1940). The market institutions are defined as institutions comprising of supply crowd and demand crowd. This again is defined as the multiplicity, desirous to acquire or alternatively to dispose of goods in exchange (Polanyi, 1944). Almost all communities have reported to be direct link with market for the sale of their "produce" and the purchase of essential commodities. Every community in rural and tribal areas produces something for market like cereals, cash crops, and horticultural products (Singh, 1996).

The market, one of the economic factors, influences the cropping pattern and consumption habits of people. It has a significant role to play in improving the standards of living of even the most primitive people, living in remote tribal belts of India (Rao, I.M.K. 1988).

Tribal Scene

In tribal societies, the significance of marketing is not only noticed in the economic domain, but also embodied their socio-cultural activities. Tribal market is best represented by weekly market. It is the most vital organ of their marketing system. It seems to be more suited to the requirement of the vast majority of the country people. Weekly market may rightly be described as the nerve centre of the exchange system of the tribal region (Mehdi, 1987). They offer an ideal laboratory for observing the process of cultural change. They serve as the cultural point between tribal people, peasant groups and agents from government and from industrialized world. Indeed, the market centres in tribal economy are not only important for business but also centres of social gathering as they provide occasions for social get-together to discuss varied topics of mutual interests ranging from enquiries about crops, market trends, political issues and last, but not least are matrimonial affairs, which are usual at these places (Rao, I.M.K.1988). This place is important for exchange of information between individuals and also between communities. The availability of electronic media like radio, television leads the tribal to be exposed to the outside world. However, the exploitation by non-tribal in weekly market is very frequent and enormous. Tribal are very often exploited in the form of weighing, measuring, and evaluating the price of their products exchanged. Therefore, it needs to maintain fair marketing system in order to check such exploitation.

Several studies have been conducted on weekly market by anthropologists like S. Sinha's (1951) study on weekly market at Bamni, a south Manbhum village, D.P. Sinha (1968) on Banary weekly market, Punalekar (1980) in tribal areas of Surat-Valsad region of Gujurat, Carol Smith's (1974) economic studies of marketing system and I.M.K. Rao's (1988) marketing studies in tribal economy, etc. Most of the studies, regarding weekly market, deal with the nature and functioning, cultural association, business practices and social composition, etc. However, in addition to the discussion on nature and functions of business practices, the focus on the changing aspects of cultural tradition, globalization and its influences on weekly market participants and some existing issues that significantly contribute to the contemporary socio-economic discourses need to be discussed.

Methodology

For the study of weekly market, an extensive fieldwork was conducted in Kandhamal district in Orissa during February-April, 2003. For this purpose, four weekly markets in Phulbani and Phiringia blocks were taken into consideration through purposive sampling. This study was both qualitative and quantitative in nature. Techniques like observation, interviews (both structured and unstructured), case studies and schedules were used for data collection. The frequency of visits and variations of participation of the Kondh were studied. The socio-cultural and economic activities of all participants were deeply observed. A total of 46 respondents were interviewed for understanding weekly market. These respondents include males and females, adults and elderly people, sellers and buyers, and Kondh and non-Kondh. Case studies were taken from some tribal and non-tribal traders, who have been active participants over the years. For the purpose of using schedules, some participants were selected on the basis of random sampling. It was used for the purpose of deep understanding of the socio-economic status of the participants.

Profile of Kandhamal District

Kandhamal, the land of Kondh, was officially recognized as a separate district on 16 June 1994 from the undivided district of Phulbani in Orissa. Anthropologist, F.G. Baily, during 1960 came to this district as a researcher, and invited worldwide attention. Etymologically, Kandhamal signifies the mountainous nature of its landscapes as well as dominating presence of Kondh (Jena, 1999). The Kandhamal is an extension of the Eastern Ghats. It is situated between 1,500 and 1,700 feet above the sea level. This district is covered by seven districts like Boudh in the extreme north, Bolangir on the north-west, Kalahandi and Rayagada are on the west and south-west, Gajapati on the extreme south, Ganjam on the east and south-east and Nayagarh on the north-east directions. This district is girdled by precipitous mountains, which separate the area sharply from the plains around. The hills are covered around the district and most of the hills are covered by dense forests and a few of which are barren due to the over accessing of woodcutters and the jungle rackets. The most common trees are Sal (*shorea robusta*), mahua (*bassia latifolia*) and mango (*mangifera indica*). These trees are important in the economy of the people and are marketed by them to support their meager earnings.

The total population of the district is 9.8 lakhs of which 95 per cent lives in rural areas and southern hilly areas. Agriculture is the primary occupation of 82 per cent people of the total population. The district is inhabited by multi-religious, multi-castes, and tribal groups. The tribal are original Dravidian inhabitants of Kandhamal. They constitute 51.51 per cent of the total population, where schedule castes constitute 18.21 per cent (Census, 1991). Kondh are the original inhabitants of this district. Three sub-divisions of Kondh namely, Desia, Kutia and Dongria live in this district. However, the Desia Kondh who are commonly called as the Kondh are dominant inhabitants in this district.

Economy of Kondh

The Kondh are agriculturists. Their agriculture is based on plain-lands and hilly areas. The main production from agriculture is paddy. Besides paddy, they produce other millets like maize and jower; pulses like green-gram, black-gram, and red-gram; and turmeric, which is an important spice item in India. A few Kondh produce something for market. They sell their produce either in weekly market or in regular market in urban areas. Collection of minor forest produce is an additional economic support for the Kondh. Collection of minor forest produce (MFP) is basically the woman's work. MFPs like mahua, amla, sal seeds, sal leaves are common in Kandhamal district. Mahua is usually consumed by the Kondh in the form of cakes and liquors, and small quantities are sold in cooperative societies and in weekly market. Family is the unit of production and members of family work together for the economic production. In Kondh' society both men and women have equal role in economy. Other than family, their clan group co-operates each other for economic production. Recently, some Kondh have taken up vegetable cultivation and commercial plantation for their economic support. The Kondh produce vegetables like brinjal, potato, cauliflower and cabbage for their own consumption and for market as well.

Process of Marketing

Marketing is a process of transaction of goods and services between buyers and sellers or between givers and takers. Community members do not produce each and every item they need. Therefore, in order to fulfill such necessities, they depend on market, which may be formal or informal or both. In tribal society, the dependence on formal and informal sectors is common. The Kondh depend on both these sectors. They depend on the sources like moneylenders, community members, cooperatives, and weekly market etc. The Kondh depend both on the regular and weekly market for their marketing mechanism. However, the Kondh hardly visit any urban market centres for their day-today necessity items like salt, sugar, rice and tobacco etc. For such items, they either come to the regular market centres located in the towns and the adjacent towns or to the weekly market centres.

Minor forest produce (MFP) marketing in tribal areas is associated with weekly market. Even after the development of cooperatives or other possibilities, weekly market is an option for majority of the tribal. In recent years, the production of vegetables and other cash crops, apart from turmeric, is a new venture in Kandhamal district. Therefore, there is need of better marketing facility to sustain such practice. In this backdrop, it is essential to discuss how weekly market provides them the opportunities to meet their demands.

Weekly Market

Over the years, the Kondh of this district have been depending on haata as basic marketing mechanism. With a little knowledge of the outside world, Kondh depend on weekly market for transaction of goods and services. Kondh depend both on Kondh and non-Kondh for their marketing activities. Besides the transaction of goods and services, Kondh come to this place, which is a hub of cultural resources, where many forms of their social activities like negotiation of marriage, solution to disputes and exchange of information take place. *Haata* is a major place of marketing for the Kondh, who reside in hilly terrain. The Kondh of Patharakanali, Kanigiri, Nuagaon, Putudi, etc depend more on weekly market than the regular market centres because of lack of easy access of daily marketing. Their dependence on weekly market is very crucial. They collect the desired items from the *haata* in advance for a week. Besides the tribal in hilly terrains, the tribal from plain areas are also dependent on weekly market. They prefer weekly market centres to daily market centres. Both cultural and economic associations with weekly market encourage them to come to weekly market or *haata*.

Nature and Function of Weekly Market (*Haata*)

Haata is a periodical assemblage of purchasers and sellers on appointed days and time at some fixed place. *Haatas* are held weekly in different villages on different days e.g. Gumagada on Sunday, Phiringia on Tuesday, Phulbani on Monday and Minia on Saturday. People from different villages come to these *haatas* on the respective days to avail the marketing opportunity. The arrangement of weekly market is orderly, sections are earmarked and many traders have their fixed places. Some haatas occupy a space within the settlement and some outside the settlement. The sites are generally fixed and do not shift frequently. All these markets generally possess some specific characteristics. The sites of haata in Phiringia, Phulbani and Minia, are generally nearer to existing market and provide a common meeting ground in an open space and by the road joining the settlement with other settlements of neighbouring areas. These markets are followed by a weekly cycle and mobile behaviour of the merchants. The mobile shopkeepers carry out their business visiting several merchants on a regular basis. The merchant covers a long distance to come to the *haatas*. They buy items at a wholesale rate from the urban market centres like Phulbani, Berhampur and Paralakhemundi regions. The merchants travel village-to-village and respective *haatas* to sell their products. The business is of a very short duration in these *haatas*. The market starts right from the morning and continues till evening. The people start coming from morning and flock in a large number from 1.00 p.m. to 4.00 p.m. depending upon the climate. The peak hour of business is 3 p.m. in all these weekly markets, when a large number of participants gather in these markets. The entire site becomes full of buyers, sellers and common people.

Participants and Market Activities

People from various groups participate in the weekly market. Both the Kondh and non-Kondh come to these weekly markets for different purposes. Though different groups of people participate in the *haatas*, the participation of the Kondh is seen more than other communities. They constitute the most numerous and important section of people in these markets. The Kondh participate in both selling and buying. The tribal peasants, who produce a little for the market, bring with them rice or vegetables and sometimes Minor Forest Produce (MFP) collected by them. Similarly, both males and females from various communities participate with almost equal ratio for selling and buying. But the nature of selling varies between men and women. Women engage themselves in selling vegetable, dry-fish, MFP, cosmetics, etc. Tribal women generally sell MFP and vegetables and non-tribal women sell dry-fish and cosmetics. The male members sell vegetables, agricultural produce, cosmetics and grocery items. Sometimes, Kondh come with goats or fowls to sell them in weekly market. But there is no strict rule followed or any taboo associated in choosing the items for selling. The pattern of labour division shows the distribution or the allotment of works as per the easiness of the individuals. The Kondh generally participate in the *haatas* as the primary sellers and customer-consumers. They sell the items that are produced or collected by them directly from their agricultural field or from the surrounding forest. Agricultural items include vegetable products, spice items, cereals and pulses varieties. Among the forest produce tamarind, mahua, green leaves, amla, harida and bahada, etc. They purchase different varieties of consumer products such as clothes, tobacco, perched rice, gud, potteries, dry foods such as staple foods and objects of use, bamboo products, etc.

Both Kondh girls and boys come to tailors at weekly market for repairing their clothes. School-going children give their cloths to tailors for new wearing. Garments shops, which have a special position in weekly market, place themselves on both sides of the market place. Bargaining is common in these garment shops. For example, if a seller initially asks 100 rupees for a garment, Kondh start bargaining for it from thirty rupees, which is finally given at fifty or sixty rupees. Among Kondh participants, basically women come together to buy clothes. They buy an item if their fellow members choose it. Bargaining for other products is also common but comparatively less than garment business. Vegetable sellers sell their product with less than one or two rupees per kilogram of their "call-quotation" prices. Among dry fish sellers, it is also very common. Not only the Kondh go for bargaining, the non-Kondhs do it too. Middle traders collect the MFP and even agricultural produce at much less than market price through bargaining. The market price here is the average price of each item in the district. For example, if the market price of turmeric per kilogram is Rs. 28.00 in Phulbani, Kondhs can get only Rs 15.00 a kilogram and even less than this. The Kondh do not always get proper opportunity to sell their items at a reasonable price. Sometimes, Kondh would rather sell their items at cheaper price than returning with them.

Some non-tribal participate as whole-sellers, intermediaries and *mahajans*. They own most of the shops in weekly market. In Phiringia *haata*, the number of permanent shop is 34, where as at Gumagada, it is 13, and in Minia there are 2 permanent shops. The non-tribal traders at weekly market migrated from different places like Nayagarh, Ganjam, Boudh, and Kalahandi districts. The non-tribal have set-up shops selling groceries, tiffin centres, cloth stores and electrical shops in the region. Besides these small shops, a few commercial centres have been set-up by the non-tribal, who generally belong to Brahmin, and Shundi castes. The Kondh come to these commercial centres for selling and purchasing the items. The non-tribal traders usually do not adopt fair pricing practices. They try to deceive in weighing and measuring items and in the price mechanisms. The interaction between *Pana* (Scheduled-Caste) and Kondh is common in weekly market days. Baol, B.M. (1997) in her study among the Kondh has observed the historical connection of these *Pana* traders, who have been playing as the traders in weekly market and from village market. However, there is now a shift in trading practices among the *Pana* in Kandhamal district. The Pana people are now acting as the middlemen in the haata regions. They keep connections with both the primary sellers and the wholesalers. In similar fashion, people from Kumuti and Shundi castes too act as middlemen in *haata* areas. The middlemen station themselves around the paths leading into the market place. They solicit trade directly, which sometimes seem to be followed by the using of physical coercion. They grasp the tribal people basket of turmeric or any other produce and attempt to prevent the tribal going to other buyers. They collect the MFP in a cheaper rate from the Kondh and sell them in profit to the *mahajans*. The Kondh are also deceived by these middlemen while weighing and evaluating of the produce. The exploitation of Middlemen is similarly observed in other tribal belts of India. Gell (1982) from his study in Bastar district of Chhatishgarh had the similar observation. He noticed that the aggressive vociferous means the middlemen employ is deceptive to the extent that tribal are not genuinely coerced into selling forest products to a buyer not of their choice, and investigations did not turn up any significant differences in the prices being offered by different middlemen. The participation of non-tribal, basically plain-land Oriyas, is exploitative, who tries to get maximum profit out of the limited sources transacted in the weekly market. The participation of Scheduled Caste (SC) women in weekly market is often noticed. The damba women (from SC community) enjoin themselves in the haatas by selling and buying different items. Sometimes, they come with the bamboo crafts to the haata and sell them during the *haata* days.

The frequency and intensity of interaction between sellers and buyers through the process of transaction greatly differs from *haata* to *haata*. Similarly, the participation of people in one *haata* varies from the other *haatas*. The important factors, which determine the importance of a *haata*, are the geographical location and the price of commodity in the place. For example, Phulbani *haata* is held in Phulbani town. As it is located in the town, population of this *haata* is more in comparison to the other *haatas*. Due to the presence of district head offices, block office, many cooperative societies and Banks, and easy communication facilities, people's participation is quiet obvious in this place. However, the percentage of Kondh participation is comparatively less. They do not find it easy to participate in urban areas because of their language problem and adjustment with urban environment. The distance is also another problem for this non-participation. Though Phulbani town has good communication facilities, it is far away from many tribal villages, where the Kondh are unable to come by paying so much fare. But Phiringia *haata* is located in centre place surrounded by many villages and connected by the main road to Phulbani and Baliguda towns. People bring their products easily to the *haata* through various means like, buses and lorries or carrying by themselves on the specific day. Relatives from adjacent villages find it suitable to meet their fellow relatives on a specific day at this site. Besides, the production of vegetables is more in the adjacent localities of Phiringia *haata*. The Kondh come with heavy loads of vegetables and MFP from the nearby villages of Phiringia like Nuagaon, Sadingia, Kannada, Bisipara and Putudi. Therefore, a big number of participants assemble in Phiringia *haata* in comparison to other *haatas*. So the haatas in the Kondh economy can be classified into a definite hierarchical level depending upon their capacity to attract buyers, sellers and goods offered for sale. Taking the above into consideration, the Phiringia market ranks first followed by Phulbani *haata*, Gumagada haata and Minia *haata*.

Participants and Other Activities

In the *haata*, not all the participants are sellers or buyers. Some people come with others to participate as ordinary visitors. They come to *haata* to spend their leisure time with their respective groups and discuss about their socio-cultural activities, which include rituals, religious activities, marriages and sometimes for solving community disputes. Marital issues such as the elopement of couples, problem of bride price, etc are also discussed. These issues are resolved with the discussion among members of the respective communities. Now, some of the issues relating to Hinduization or Christianization have arisen in the Kondh areas. A Kondh adopting Christianity is not allowed to marry a Kondh adopting Hindu practices and *vice versa*. This is one of the important issues now. If such case happens, it is discussed among the members in the village or at haata regions. The Kondh discuss about their agriculture like crop production, vegetable cultivation and sericulture and issues and benefits relating to production and marketing etc. Sometimes, issues regarding credit and marketing are also discussed. The Kondh visit Block-office and Panchayat office, which are located near by *haatas*. They come to these offices to avail various schemes launched through these institutions. Elderly people also come to Block-office to enquire about their old-age-pension and widow-pension etc. Similarly, others come to these offices to enquire about loans and credit facilities given by blocks and Panchayats. People let Block Development Officer (BDO) and other officials know about their problems with regard to accession of schemes. They complain to BDO if any mismanagement is done in the form of enlisting Kondh under Below Poverty Line (BPL) category, and distribution of beneficiary schemes, etc. The presence of Large Sized Multipurpose Cooperative Society (LAMPS) in haata regions also helps the Kondh to avail the facilities given, such as distribution of kerosene, rice, and sugar. LAMPS, which extends the credit facilities are received by some Kondh people for agricultural improvement. They enquire and apply for agricultural loans here. In weekly market days, the Kondh come in large numbers to Panchayat and Block offices, and LAMPS, and also participate in haata. It becomes easy to the officials to pass the message or any information regarding disbursement and reimbursement of loans and launch of new schemes, notice to the defaulters, etc. the beneficiaries too avail the equal opportunities in accessing the above facilities.

The Kondh perform several ritual and religious activities like *Dharanipenu puja* (soil worshipping), *sarupenu puja* (mountain worshipping) and *Pitabali puja* (village deity worshipping). They celebrate both community festival such as *kedu* festival and Hindu festivals like, Danda Yatra, Sri Chaitanya Parva, and Dusserah, etc. Some Kondh, who have embraced Christianity, celebrate the new-year. In all these festivals, relatives are invited in weekly market regions. Sometimes, people greet each other during such special occasions. Information regarding the above are exchanged and passed easily through weekly markets

The socio-cultural activities are common in all the *haatas*. The Kondh discuss about their problems among relatives and try to solve them through proper interaction and cooperation among them. People eagerly participate in weekly market because it provides amusement and recreation. As the entire neighbourhood assembles at the market, it is the principal source of news as well as the clearing house-rumors. It is a place where the tribal get options to choose their desired items, to innovate their skills by exchanging ideas among participants. The Kondh sit at a different place for leisure time activities, which is a little far from the main market place. Sometimes, both Kondh and non-Kondh play cards in *haatas* at the specific sites. Adultery practices are also seen in weekly market regions. Fun making, joking and merry making are common in *haatas*. Both adult males and females tease each other and entertain themselves.

Weekly Market and the Sale of Commodities

An analysis of commodities, which are sold in weekly market, shows that they can be broadly classified into the following categories:

- Commodities produced or collected in the local and neighbouring region. They include agricultural produce, minor forest produce, pottery, etc. Agricultural produce like rice, blackgram, horsegram and vegetables are sold in the market according to the local price in the harvesting time of various crops.
- Commodities brought from outside the locality, which include imported goods such as, sweets, grocery items, milk-made products and readymade garments, brass makers, still utensils and other goods of similar nature. Similarly, some handmade products and small-scale industries' products are brought into the markets. These include necklaces made up of glass beads, wood beads, copper rings, bangles, cosmetics, etc.
- The third category includes products of national and multinational companies, such as cosmetics like soaps, face creams, and body talks etc. and cold drinks like Pepsi and Coca-Cola products.

It has been observed that people from many villages come to these haatas with commercial agricultural product like turmeric, MFPs like tamarind, mahua, and various kinds of vegetables and cereals. The Kondh sell vegetables and sometimes cereals directly to customers in weekly market. However, a Kondh hardly sells MFPs and turmeric directly to customers. They sell them either to middle traders or to the *mahajans* in weekly market. But the selling of these agricultural and minor forest produce depend upon their harvesting in respective seasons. The products are brought into the market based on their seasonal production. It is observed that during the end of December-January, the agricultural products start flowing into the weekly market and continues till March-April. The price of the product varies from season to season. For example, til and mustard are sold at Rs. 10.00 and Rs. 12.00 per kilogram during the harvesting season of Jan-February and it slowly increases till April and May and the price becomes Rs.18.00 to Rs.20.00. In rest of the seasons, the price is almost constant with slight variation. Recently, vegetable cultivation has been initiated in many Kondh villages like Karnada, Bisipara, Bhandarpadar, Nuagaon and Patharkanali etc. As a result, some Kondh households are able to bring vegetables into the *haatas*. Throughout the year, both tribal and non-tribal producers heap varieties of vegetables in the weekly markets.

Turmeric is the most important cash crop in the Kandhamal areas. During weekly market days, Kondh come with head loads of dry turmeric to sell in the haata. It is not sold directly to the consumers in *haatas*. They sell it either in the *Banijya Bhandar* (commercial centres) set up by the mahajans or to the middle traders located at the pathways of *haatas*. Dry turmeric is sold at the rate of 20 to 25 rupees per kilogram, while the raw is sold at a very cheaper price of 2 to 5 rupees per kilogram. The raw one is processed and dried up for selling.

For sometimes, the Kondh used to sell their MFP and agricultural produce at the existing co-operative societies like, Large Sized Multipurpose Co-operative Societies (LAMPS) and Marketing cooperative societies (MCS) in Phulbani and Phiringia Blocks. However, presently these cooperative societies have stopped purchasing such items from the tribal. Panchayats have been permitted to decide their procurement process of MFP after the enactment of Provision of Panchayat Extension to Scheduled Areas (PESA).[2] In the name of decentralization of power, the license for purchasing of MFP has been transferred to a few influential tribal persons in these areas. A few Sarpanchs have favoured their own people to be the license holders. Yet the village people are not able to select their own representatives even after the enactment of PESA. The decision power to Gram Sabhas in selecting the representatives has not been fruitful yet. Therefore, the present license-holders, who are selected by the Panchayat representatives, discriminate in the form of evaluation and weighing mechanisms. Very low prices are given on certain products like Sal seeds and leaves, Bhalia seeds, and hilly brooms, etc. This discrimination in the allocation of license to such influential persons has brought further critical problems in the marketing process. The rate of the products is often monopolized by the concerned dealers. After the closing down of MCS and diversion of LAMPS functioning, the Kondh prefer to sell their produce in non-institutional sectors. They sell their produce to middle traders and *mahajans* located at the weekly market centers. The middle traders and *mahajans* often cheat these tribal in the form of weighing and evaluating their products.

Turmeric, which is an important commercial product in the district, is being sold to non-tribal traders at a cheaper price. Allocation of credits with subsidies is now the major function of LAMPS for agricultural development. The government's objective to distribute funds to the poor tribal to enhance their agriculture development has not been achieved properly. Due to lack of security, poor Kondh are not allotted credit opportunities. Though some Kondh, having lands as security, are able to access credit facilities yet many number of households are not able to access it. The favouritism occurs in the supply of loan and credit facilities in the region. Influenced with the bribes many officials show biasness in releasing the loans for the real target groups.

Individuals who receive institutional credit are often not needy persons and they are misusing the loan amount by using it as capital for money-lending business.[3] Some Kondh use the money for buying sarees, ornaments, or for their daughters' marriages, etc. This case, particularly, happens in all sections of the borrowers of institutional credit. The defaulters' names are displayed on the board outside the society. People during *haata* days read them and discuss about the defaulters. In many cases, the innocent Kondh who are not able to repay due to crop loss or any personal problems are also blamed and criticized.

The Kondh also come to the *haata* for purchasing garments, cosmetics, bangles etc. Women in many numbers participate in haatas as buyers. They purchase such items from the *haata* and return to their villages in evening. The other types of commodities like products from outside localities and multinational companies' (MNCs) products are sold by the non-tribal. All cosmetic shops, garment shops, sweet stalls and existing big grocery shops belong to the non-tribal. Sometimes, both Kondh and non-Kondh in weekly markets, consume cool drinks of PEPSI and COCA-COLA products. Though these products were not seen earlier, however, after globalization, these products penetrated into all tribal market regions including the weekly markets.

With the advent of communication facilities and new technology, globalized products have entered into these weekly markets. Telephone booth, stationary shops, grocery shops are also located in weekly market regions. The non-tribal, who have migrated from Nayagarh, Ganjam and Boudh districts and the non-tribal of Kandhamal district permanently, settle these down in *haatas*.

Business Practices: Weights and Measures

A variety of weights and measures are used in the haatas. Apart from the traditional measuring system like the use of *tambi, ada, Buda,* and *Sula*, measuring is also done through approximation. In all the weekly markets these traditional methods of measuring are common. Exact quantity of products is not sold in the weekly market. While measuring, an extra amount is given or taken by the participant in these *haatas*. When the Kondh seller sells something to others, he adds a few extra quantities in his measuring. For example, when one *tambi* of horse-gram is sold to the *mahajans* and middle traders in the market, a handful of extra amount is given without any charge. These traditional methods of measuring are used in weekly market. This measuring is practiced not only in the Phiringia market but also in entire weekly markets. Measuring through approximation is common in all the *haatas*. Those poor Kondh sellers, who do not have proper weighing instruments, sell their produce to the purchasers through approximation. This process is commonly used in selling of vegetables. This system is used without proper measuring, which shows loss in their profit. Standard weights and measures like meter, liter and kilograms are also used in these weekly market centers.

Other than the use of traditional measuring mechanism, the use of modern measuring in the form of balance and electronic system is also seen. Some non-tribal traders in weekly market regions use electronic machines for weighing and measuring products. This is a form of measuring followed by the *mahajans* in tribal regions, where the tribal are misled. The private dealers, middlemen and wholesalers always want to get some extra benefits out of the weighing of items. In each time of weighing, they need some extra amount of produce to be given by the sellers.

Mode of Exchange

The economic scene in the tribal area has exhibited a significant change in the mode of exchange. Previously much of the trade in the tribal area was carried out through barter system. In recent times, the Kondh are using monetary mode of exchange. This observation is applied to all the commodities sold at the *haatas*. When a person goes to a *haata* with basket full of grains or vegetables, he brings back money or sometimes sweets or any other food items etc. If he wants to buy a piece of cloth he will do so only with money. Some of them come with money to buy their desired product directly while others come with some agricultural or minor forest products to sell them and buy their desired items. Barter exchange varies from season to season. In the month of harvesting, the barter exchange is more among the participants in weekly market. During the harvesting season, people come to weekly market with vegetables, food grains, and other agricultural products. So, the larger quantity of vegetables and food grains are brought to weekly market during this period. During this period the exchanges generally take place in this way, for example, one tambi of turmeric bartered with four tambis of rice, and one *tambi* of *biri* (blackgram) with two *tambis* of *koltha* (horsegram) etc. Many Kondh sell their vegetables and MFPs to middle traders and *mahajans* located in *haata* regions. A Kondh has to sell his product to mahajan because of their age-old relationship with each other. The Kondh respect the mahajans. According to the Kondh, *mahajans* are the rich men. They can help the former by giving money at the time of their needs.

Mahajans are the money-lenders in this locality. They give money to the Kondh in advance. And during harvesting season, Kondh repay their money in the form of agricultural or minor forest produce. Sometimes, Kondh-sellers are scared of selling their produce without the *mahajans'* knowldge. The Kondh, who sell their produce to the *mahajans*, do not get fair price of their products, which is even below their minimum support price. Poor Kondh never disobey the *Mahajans'* order. Some Kondh work often without any wages in the *mahajans'* houses during weekly market days.

Globalization and Weekly Market

As it has been discussed earlier, in *haata* regions, the uses of the new form of electronic measuring system, new form of consumer items are some of the examples of globalization. Here in this paragraph a little more attempt has been made for the understanding of globalization in weekly market. Normally globalization is understood as an economic idea. It is linked with liberalization. But, at the local level, when globalization comes to a tribal village, it changes a lot. Besides economic change, there is a cultural change (Jain, 2001).[4] Now-a-days, the Kondh in weekly market buy cosmetics with brand names such as Hindustan Livers Limited and Colgate-Palmolive Co., etc. They buy toothbrush and pastes of Pepsodent, Colgate; soaps like Lux, Rexona, and Denim etc; face creams like Fair & Lovely and Fair & Glow, etc. The use of herbal product in the Kondh villages like herbal stick for tooth brushing, turmeric as body cream and use of hand made soaps for washing are gradually being replaced by the above national and multinational products. The handicraft products like glass bead necklaces, *rudraksya* beads, clay toys are having less demand in the *haata* regions. This changing process has led to new consumerism.

In the trading process of local products some changes are observed. The liberalization in the marketing process enabled many agencies to come forward to collect the local products like turmeric, tamarind seeds, etc from the tribal and export them to the foreign agencies, e.g. Kasam and Samanwita some of the NGOs deal with the marketing processes of some of the spices items in the Kandhamal district. These products after processing are sent for packaging. Now these products are freely exported to foreign countries. These NGOs, of course, have tried to empower the tribal communities by giving them free training and involving these tribal in the developmental project. However, still inadequate steps have been taken up to preserve their local varieties and indigenous properties. The places, which were abundant resource of forest products and traditional agricultural products two decades ago become rare day by day. Yogendra Singh (1994) rightly observes that the new cultural changes that give rise to these phenomena are many. It may lead to the real as well as perceived threats to local knowledge and smaller cultural identities due to marketisation of culture.

Conclusion

Haatas not only perform economic function but also show a greater flexibility of social relationship between tribal and non-tribal. The institution of weekly market has become an essential part of organized life of the Kondh and non-Kondh. There is no barrier in caste, class, gender and religion in participation in weekly markets. It is one of the most important occasions for the tribal inhabitants to access their marketing opportunity. The channel to access different facilities such as access to information, buying and selling items, social interactions, etc. are some of the important activities in tribal weekly markets. The weekly market days provide opportunities to meet officials, enquire about the allotment of credits and launch of various schemes, etc. Weekly market has been a better place for transaction of goods and services for the tribal inhabitants in general and for the weaker sections, small-scale producers, MFP collectors in particular. However, the presence of moneylenders, the *mahajans* and middle-traders is an important issue in tribal market. These tribal have not been able to keep themselves away from the unscrupulous middle traders or mahajans. Another important issue, which has recently emerged, is the phenomena of globalization. Due to the advent of communication facilities and liberalization of trade policy, many global brand products have been pushed into weekly market regions. The weekly market is now influenced by globalization, which has linked the tribal to global culture. The status of weekly markets in tribal areas is in a transition where the mixture of both tradition and modernity continues. It is now essential to protect the tradition that is at risk in the era of globalization. Again, what is important here is to check out the exploitation in tribal areas, which is a persistent and critical problem. The interest of the marginal groups, small-scale producers, minor forest produce collectors need to be protected at this juncture.

Acknowledgements

The author is grateful to his guide, Prof. P. Venkata Rao, Department of Anthropology, University of Hyderabad, for giving necessary comments to prepare this article.

NOTES

1. Gudeman (1968) suggests that formal analysis drawing on western economic models only ever discover and reproduce in exotic materials their own assumptions. The centrality of culture must now be recognized in the analysis of economics. Culture does not stand opposed to economics, such that, say, cultural explanations are given to account for why their market practice does not coincide without market theory. Rather culture and economics are mutually constitutive. Trading practices in all markets and economics are culturally construed in terms of culturally specific common sensual knowledge and taken for granted understanding about how transactions ought to be conducted.
2. Provision of Panchayat Extension to Scheduled Areas (PESA) act envisages self-governance power to the *Gram-Sabhas* (Panchayats) in the tribal areas. After this act, Orissa Gram-Panchayat Act, 1997 was developed by which the Panchayats can make decision in the procurement process of MFP in their respective regions.
3. Raghav Rao (1973) and P.V. Rao (1988) from their study in Vishakhapatnam District, Andhra Pradesh had similar observations. The misuse of institutional credit is an important issue in many tribal areas in India and Kandhamal district is not get rid of it.
4. For more understanding on the Globalization in Tribal Areas, P.C. Jain's book *Globalisation and Tribal Economy* can be referred.

REFERENCES

Alexander, J. and Paul Alexander. 1991. "What's a Fair Price? Price-Setting and Trading Partnerships in Javanese Markets," *Man,* 26: 493-512.

Baily, F.G. 1957. *Caste and Economic Frontier: A Village of Highland Orissa.* Manchester: Manchester University Press.

Boal, B.M. (1997), *Human Sacrifice and Religious Change: The Kondhs.* New Delhi: Inter-India Publications.

Gell, A. 1982. "The Market Wheel: Symbolic Aspects of an India Tribal Market," *Man* (N.S.), 17: 470-91.

Gudeman, S. 1986. *Economics as Culture: Models and Metaphors of Livelihood.* London: Routledge and Kegan Paul.

Evans-Pritchard, E. 1940. *The Neur: A Description of the Models of Livelihood* and *the Political Institutions of a Nilotic People.* Oxford: Clavender press.

Jain, P.C. 2001. *Globalization and Tribal Economy.* Jaipur: Rawat Publication.

Jena, D. 1999. "A Critical Analysis of Tribal Uprising in Orissa: Case of Kandhamal," (pp.154-64) in D.K. Behera and G. Pfeffer (eds.), *Contemporary Society: Tribal Studies.* Vol. IV, New Delhi: Concept Publishing Company.

Mahalingam, S. (n.d.) *Courses on Planning and Management of Tribal Development Programme,* Hyderabad: NIRD.

Mehdi, Raja. 1987. "Structure and Function of Rural Market in Tribal Bihar," (pp.256-65) in M. Prasad (ed.), *Tribes, their Environment and Culture.* Delhi: Amar Prakashan.

Polyani, K. 1944. *The Great Transformation.* New York: Rinehart

Punalekar, S.P. 1980. *Weekly Market in Tribal Areas.* Surat: Centre for Social Studies

Rao, I.M.K. 1988. *Marketing in Tribal economy.* New Delhi: Inter India publication

Rao, P.V. 1988. *Institutional Framework for Tribal Development.* New Delhi: Inter-India Publication.

Rao, D.V. R. 1973. "Marketing of Produce and Indebtedness among Tribal," Waltair: Agro-Economic Research Centre (Mimeographed).

Singh, K.S. 1996. *Identity, Ecology, Social Organisation, Economy and Linkages and Development process.* New Delhi: Oxford publication.

Singh, Y. 1994. "The Significance of Culture in the Understanding of Social Change in Contemporary India," presidential Address, XXI, All India Sociological Conference, cited in P.C. Jena's *Globalisation and Tribal Economy.* Jaipur: Rawat Publication.

Sinha, S. 1951. "The Weekly Market at Bamni, a Village in South Manbhum," *Geographical Review of India,* XIII (4): 20-24.

Sinha, D.P. 1968. *Culture and Change in an Inter Tribal Market.* New Delhi: Asia Publishing House.

Smith Carol, A. 1974. "Economics of Weekly Marketing Systems: Models from Economic Geography," *Annual Review of Anthropology,* Vol. (3): 167-172.

TWENTY-TWO

KUTIA KONDH: Deconstructing the Gender Differences

DEBENDRA KUMAR BISWAL

Introduction

Does a tribal woman in India experience the same social status as a woman in the metropolitan city of Berlin in Germany, because the two are women? In this context, can we apply the same western concepts of "subordination", "oppression", "exploitation", "male dominance", "patriarchy" and so on in the context of women of both the countries? The ethnographic writings on Indian tribes were started by the European colonizers during the 19th century. These ethnographers represented the ethnographic data with the languages and concepts derived from their own religion, political structure and social institutions. Still these concepts are being used by the "indigenous Anthropologists" in their ethnographic presentations. The development of postmodern ethnography with the help of Deconstructionist approach/model gives us a space to think about the appropriateness of the use of European Philosophical discourse on problems of women, male dominance and female subordination.

Contemporary postmodern theory and deconstructionist approach (after 1990s) have strongly questioned the European discourse on gender ideologies and patriarchy. It replaced the word "gender" in place of "women". Thus, it had a profound influence on the study of women and focused the problem of translation (language) and of the dominance of western models and concepts and stressed the gender differences and diversities. The feminist anthropologists' assumptions of universal male dominance and female subordination (before 1990s) were questioned by the postmodern ethnography. The source of oppression rooted in major dichotomy of public/domestic, nature/culture and production/reproduction championed by feminist anthropologists were proved to be inappropriate in "other" culture. The ethnographic data concerning woman's position in the tribal society of India is mostly represented based on these assumptions leads us to question these assumptions.

This paper tries to explore the different traditional dimensions of patriarchy and to deconstruct these assumptions with the help of Deconstruction model among the Kutia Kondh, a primitive tribal community in Orissa. Firstly, it has examined the evolution and models of patriarchy. Secondly, how the modern methodology of postmodernism and deconstruction questions the European philosophical discourse on Gender and Gender ideology. Thirdly, the earlier ethnography of Kutia Kondh in relation to gender was deconstructed to bring out the appropriateness of the use of European philosophical discourse on dichotomies of female subordination, exploitation and oppression.

Models of Patriarchy

Patriarchy (literally, rule by fathers) means social organization based on men's control of power. Masculinism(ist) refers to an ideology justifying, promoting, or advocating male domination. Feminism as an ideology opposes male superiority and promotes women's interests and gender inequality. Patriarchy is generally viewed as a social construction that is inevitably oppressive and yet, contemporary western culture is still actively engaged in the reproduction of a patriarchal society. The analysis and questioning of the "process of patriarchy" is mostly found in the feminist theory[1] and Neo-Marxian theory of the last 30 years. The ethnographic data which analyses the male superiority and female subordination in the Indian primitive/simple societies are mostly based upon the theories which were derived from dichotomy of public/domestic (Rosaldo, 1974), nature/culture (Ortner, 1974) and production/reproduction (Edholm, 1977) developed by the feminist anthropologists of the 1970s. The above three dichotomy rejects the notion that the oppression of women is associated with something innate and biological about the human species. Sexual dimorphism in humans is a biological feature of the species but serves only to facilitate the possible oppression of women, not to mandate it or programme such behaviour into humans, located the source of women's oppression in culture and social structure, rather than in biology, and stressed that the idea that women's biology placed them closer to nature, outside production, or within the domestic sphere, was not a natural fact but a cultural elaboration on biological differences. "Patriarchy" then was universal, the normative construction within which people organized their lives. This was just a re-assessment of women's political rights through domestic sphere, sexuality and careers. It was to provide equal access for women in the public domain in the past and the present. The intent was to make visible and give voice to women validating claims of women as historical actors within a history previously written for and by men. Western centric values and norms were valuated in the light of patriarchy, linking the earliest societies to the present. In this way women were established within a historical context that progressed and merged seamlessly into contemporary western societies. Historically, patriarchy was located in the early societies of the near east and it was recorded how women were socially and legally segregated in the domestic sphere.

The feminist theory has progressed in three "waves"[2] from situating women in history (before 1970s),[3] to defining subjugation (1980s) and more recently to examine how sex and gender are culturally constructed (after 1990s). However, all the ethnographic representations on Indian tribal women are still dominated by the traditional ethnographic techniques of 1970s. We have hardly moved to the third wave, which interprets the women's situation on postmodern and deconstruction lines.

Gender in Postmodern Ethnography

Postmodernism is defined as an eclectic movement originated in aesthetics, architecture and philosophy. Postmodernism espouses a systematic skepticism of grounded theoretical perspective. Applied to anthropology, this skepticism has focused from observation of a particular society to the observation of the observer. It refers to the incipient or cultural dissolution of those social forms associated with modernity.

The postmodern critique presents four chief problems for the traditional ethnography: (1) attacking its representation of the field, (2) the value it places in "thick description", (3) the reliability and validity of its data, and (4) the construction of the ethnographic text (Bremer, 2000). They challenged the use of the words like oppression, patriarchy and sexuality as employed by white middleclass feminists [A postmodernist approach informed by post structuralism and deconstruction]. Thus, postmodernism deconstructs, de-centers and juxtaposes in short fragment, the coherence of pre-existing schemes. They were critical of authoritative knowledge, theory, time, history, language, use of men and women, dichotomies and structural theory.[4]

They claim that knowledge can be objective and truthful. Scientific knowledge is relative. Science is simply a language game. The deconstruction of both ideas into myths implies the disintegration of all the symbols of modern capitalist society and specifically in relation to truth. Postmodernism devices the existence of all universal truth statements, are replaced by variety, contingency, ambivalence and plurality in culture, tradition, ideology and knowledge. Postmodernist are suspicious of authoritative definitions and singular narratives of any trajectory of events. Postmodern attack of ethnography is based on the belief that there is no true objectivity. Scientific method is not possible. Since objectivity is an illusion, according to the ideological arguments, science results in subverting the causes of the oppressed groups, females, ethnics and third world people (Spiro, 1996). The leading figures of post-modernism are Jean Francois Lyotard, Jean Baudrillard, Jackques Derrida, Michael Foucault and Nancy Scheper-Hughes.[5,6,7]

The postmodern ethnographers were against the language being used by the early ethnographers. The skeptical post-modernists even considered the subject as a linguistic convention. The use of the word "man" is ambiguous, sometimes referring to "Homo Sapiens" as a whole, sometimes in reference to both simultaneously. Thus, the earlier ethnographers were limited to sexual distinctions which have only etic meaning. Sex is generally referred to the anatomical, biological (individual chromosomes, interior and exterior Sex organs and secondary sexual characteristics) and physiological characteristics of female and male bodies. People are said to be of the male sex or female sex, as determined by above three sets of characteristics. The word "sex" is also used to mean sexual intercourse. By contrast, the postmodern ethnographers widely used the word "gender" in place of sexual distinctions to describe the problem and oppression of women (the patriarchy). The concept of "gender" has not been well defined and understood. This is the emic definition of sexual distinctions. It refers to a set of qualities and behaviours expected from a female or male by the society. The other features of gender are—the ways in which male and female bodies are distinguished, the role each is seen in playing in reproduction, local understandings of the biological bodies of difference, cultural attributes assigned to the masculine and the feminine and the importance attached to these differences. Gender roles are learned and can be affected by factors such as education or economics. They vary widely within and among cultures. While an individual's sex does not change, gender roles are socially determined and can evolve over time. Gender roles and expectations are often identified as factors hindering the equal rights and status of women with adverse consequences that affect life, family, socio-economic status, and health. Because of cross-cultural differences in roles of males and females anthropologists generally use "gender" to denote the variable emic meanings associated with culturally defined sexual identities, and the phrase gender roles (instead of "sex roles") when referring to the expected patterns of thought and behavior that are associated with gender identities (Harris, 1993). Anthropological concern of gender revolves mainly around three aspects, cultural variability experiences, gender identity and subordination of females. However, the post-modernists have shifted towards more particularistic and historically grounded studies that place gender at the centre of analysis. Two trends have developed in elaborating power in relation to gender—(1) the first trend developed along a materialistic perspective. They focused on gender as it relates to class, the social relations of power, and changes in modes of production, (2) focused in the roles of motherhood, kinships and marriage.

The postmodern ethnographers have raised new and more complex issues of cross-cultural translations, universality, relationship between thought systems or system of classification and individual action, ideology and material conditions (Jordanova, 1980, Harris, 1980, Strathern, 1980, Barnes, 1973, Pinacabral, 1986).

The post-modern ethnographers rejected these "universal dichotomies" as these are the reflections of dominant western discourse, historically situated and socially and culturally specific. These dichotomies were criticized by the African anthropologists and members of other ethnic minorities. They felt white women as a creating force towards change, rather than a reason for understanding and separation. But failed to recognize that those differences expose all women to various forms and degrees of patriarchal oppression, some of which we share, some of which we do not—the oppression of women knows no ethnic or racial boundaries, true, but that does not mean it is identical within those boundaries (Minh-ha, 1989). They reject understanding of time because for them the modern understanding of time is oppressive in that it controls and measures individuals.

The postmodern ethnography rejects theory, because theories are abundant, and no theory is considered more correct than any other. They feel that theory conceals, distorts, and obfuscates, it is alienated, disparate, and dissonant, it means to exclude, order, and control rival powers. For this, they attack the structuralism model which is the basis of nature/culture dichotomy to justify universal subordination of women. The structuralism model argues that the structure of language itself products "reality"... That we can think only through language, and therefore our perceptions of reality are all framed by and determined by the structure of language. Secondly, that language speaks us; that the source of meaning is not an individual's experience or being but the set of oppositions and operations, the signs and grammars that govern language. Thirdly, rather than seeing the individual as the centre of meaning, structuralism places the structure at the centre… it's the structure that originates or produces meaning, not the individual self. By contrast, the deconstructionist's look at philosophy (western metaphysics) to see that any system necessarily posits a centre, a point from which everything comes, and to which everything refers or returns. Sometimes it's gód, sometimes it's the human self, the mind, and sometimes it's the unconscious, depending on what philosophical system (or set of beliefs) one is talking about.

For the feminists, Deconstruction is a useful method for the criticism of patriarchal thought and institutions. They have started using the deconstructive arguments to expose and criticize the suppression and marginalization of things associated with women and femininity. They are against the view that patriarchy was an unconquerable monolith. They are also against the view that "patriarchy's social construction had been so successful that women's very desires and identities were nothing more than the products of male power and privilege". Because social meanings are alterable, they are fluid and unstable, and always present possibilities of interpretive variance and play.

The Deconstructions look for unexpected relationships between different parts of a text does not show that all texts are meaningless; rather they are overflowing with multiple and often conflict meanings.

Kutia Kondh: Deconstructing the Gender Differences

Kutia Kondh is a Dravidian tribe and a Subdivision of Kondh tribe in Belghar, Guma, Lankagarh and Jhirni-pani Gram Panchayats of Tumudibandh block in Phulbani district of Orissa. This tribe is recognized as a Primitive Tribal Group by the Indian Constitution. They are inhabitants in 60 revenue villages and 13 hamlets, out of which two villages are inhabited. Very often the Kutia Kondh changes their settlements, even with new names. Their economy revolves around shifting cultivation and Minor Forest Products (MFPs).

The ethnographic writings on this tribal group were started by the British ethnographers such as John Campbel & McPherson in 1864 (Singh, 1994). Though, the present day writings on this tribe is little bit different from the earlier ethnographic writings, almost all the writings have the "British Legacy" or use of the European Philosophical discourse like "sacrifice", "exploitation", "oppression", and so on. The knowledge, truth, events, etc. are just being translated and given an outsider meaning (Jena, 1993; Nayak, 1976).

These ethnographic representations mention that the usual family system among the Kutia Kondhs is of nuclear and patriarchal. The father's decision ceases to function for married boy or married girls. Patrilocal residence is commonly practiced. Marriage is usually monogamous. After marriage, the bride goes to her in-law's house. The basic socialization starts in the dormitory. The divorce cases are decided by the village Majhi and the villagers. Women are always looked down upon by men, no head woman-ship, not allowed to act as political head, religious head, a *pujari* or a *kutaka*. They are not allowed to take part in a community meeting or a community decision. Even during the festivals, the women constitute different groups to dance. They are not allowed to *Madangbasa* or toddy drinking. The decision of a married woman is not taken into consideration and she is bound to abide by the customs and traditions, restricted to wear flowers on head and prohibited to take buffalo meat. Menstruating women stay in the *jaka kuda* and are prohibited to attend rituals and worships. A barren woman is looked down by all. A widow is seen differently in Kutia Kondh society. These are few findings by the traditional ethnographers, which have compelled them to interpret the Kutia Kondh society as patriarchal, women as oppressed, exploited and subordinated.

Now we will interpret the mythology and cosmology, historical and cultural construction of sexed bodies, local and self description of menstruation, rituals and power structure, tasks and economic activities assigned to different sex and status of women in relation to political institutions with the help of "deconstruction method" to bring out the appropriateness of the use of the different concepts associated with women. This study is based on a field work among the Kutia Kondhs on their health status. The methodology was of participant observation and deconstruction. It was kept in mind that postmodern interpretation is introspective and anti- objectivist. Which is a form of individualized understanding; it is more a vision than data observation. There are an endless number of interpretations. Foucault writes that "everything is interpretation", there is no final meaning for any particular sign, no notion of unitary sense of text, no interpretation can be regarded as superior to any other. Re-examination of the nature of ethnography leads to the questioning of ethnography itself as a mode of cultural analysis. Postmodernism insists that anthropologists must consider the role of their own culture in the explanation of cultures being studied. Postmodernist theory has led to a heightened sensitivity within anthropology to the collection of data.

The *kui Gaani* (the cosmological myth of origin/creation) and *Kapka Gaani* (one epic) describes the birth of the Kutia Kondh. It states that there are many people under the earth. *Narendali* (she has many other names) is the supreme lady who has given birth to other people under the earth. Population pressure is there under the earth and there is only darkness (*weda silae*). *Narendali* contemplates how to help her followers to come out. This is the beginning of time, beginning of thought. Through the process of thinking (*Edu itere, budhi etere. Inisatisi adine, Inisatisi Ranjine*) of Narendali, knowledge comes or consciousness arises which in turn solves the problem of how to do, what to do, how it will be alright and so on. Many a number of women took birth following *Narendali* to find out a passage for coming on to the earth. The gathering is termed as *atpa bicha* (seed). So each woman is like a seed, which will give birth to children of her own profession. *Narnedali* felt that the society looks handicapped without the presence of male folks. Certain works in the society can only be done by the male folks only. Without male beings, which would go for hunting, who would roam about the hills and hill slopes, who would worship; particularly who would organize the worship of *Dharni Penu* (earth goddess). She gave birth to male folk. None of the male folk so created occupied the dominant position of hero. Later on she created *Betamangera* (real lord). So Kutia women are the representations of *Narendali*—the mythical heroine. Many goddesses worshipped by Kutia Kondh are Dharmi Penu (in the middle of the village represented by three stones), *Satari Penu* (At the outskirt of the village, under a tree, represented in the form of wooden stumps) and *Wanga Penu* (village).this postmorden interpretation challenges the gender ideologies developed in the earlier ethnographic writings on Kutia Kondh. These earlier writings firmly believe that the males are spiritually superior to females and that females are dangerous and polluting, weak and untrustworthy. Secondly, it believes that Kutia Kondhs have a religion which is characterized by a pervasive functional inter connection between male dominated rituals and myths on the one hand and male political—religious supremacy on the other. This interpretation strongly claims that women have their own gender ideologies, which have not been properly recorded because earlier generations of ethnographers were primarily males and neglected or were unable to obtain the women's point of view. However, we can keep our discussion open on differences and inequality for biological referents. At least among the Kutia Kondhs, it can not be assumed that all cultures represent differences in the same ways or give sexual differences the same emphasis. The task and economic activities assigned to each sex varied enormously from culture to culture, but so too did the emotional and temperamental characteristics associated with females and males.

The Kutia Kondhs maintain their livelihood from agriculture and shifting cultivation. The agricultural produces are their subsistence economy and they cultivate a number of crops in shifting plots. They depend upon outsiders only for dry fish, salt and clothes. Most of the villages look deserted in the day time because all the villagers except few old men and women go inside the forest and hills for shifting cultivation. Maximum days of a year they stay outside the village. They depend on the manpower in the family for the cultivation of their own shifting plots and depend on the co-operative labour system during the slashing, burning and preparing the shifting plots. Use of co-operative labour is also marked during the harvesting of paddy and other cultivated crops in the plain lands. In the domestic sphere as well as in the agricultural sites male members do very negligible work in comparison to women. From the beginning of a day till late at night a woman would be found busy in various works. Carrying children in a cloth and hanging them from the shoulders, she keeps her hand busy at work.

Women are the chief input of labour in the agricultural practices. She goes for the collection of minor forest produces, food, spinach, tubers and so on. The domestic works of women include taking care of family members and livestock. In the shifting cultivation sites they do very hard jobs like cutting big trees by axe.

During the interview of around eighty households (both male and female members) it was observed that the products of women's labour are being highly used by the male members. However, the women themselves do not feel that they are being alienated by their male counterparts. Labour was not the basis of profit, as both types of labour viz. co-operative labour system and family labour are seen among the Kutia Kondh. The Kutia Kondhs have the subsistence economy, and also community based economy. So, they do not make the distinction between production and property, subject (family as well as community labour) and object of production. Thus, the interpretation of Marxist model of "suppression" and "exploitation" in the case of Kutia Kondh is inappropriate. Thus, it contradicts the idea of nature/culture dichotomy. The nature/culture dichotomy to explain female subordination is just one re-examination of the binary opposition between nature and culture propounded by Levi Strauss in his theory on structuralism. Ortner argued that cross-culturally women were represented as closer to nature because of their role in child bearing, lactation and socialization of children. This identification of women with nature and men with culture was not 'natural' but was culturally constructed, women to some extent mediated between nature and culture, by transforming the "raw" child into a "socialized" one.

According to the production/reproduction dichotomy, the subordination of women is regulated from their association with reproduction within the household, and their exclusion from relations of productions from public places. The Kutia Kondh women have more role than men in both production and reproduction. Even during pregnancies they go to the agricultural fields with the male members. They can not go for work only for 2-3 days before and 4-5 days after the day of child birth. The only evidence of inequality seen is the labour laid upon the women in different sexual sub-cultures.

Menstruating women (married or unmarried), are avoided by all. They are restricted to live in the house where her family members live. She is not supposed to use or touch others' dresses. She lives in the *Jaka Kuda* (a separate house made inside the village) or in the back side house for the menstruating period. She can not put her clothes at such places where there are chances of children touching it. Usually after 4 days, the menstruating women take a good bath, wash all their dresses and return to their house. Menstruating women are not allowed to attend rituals and worships (NCDS, 1998). But these are all put forward uncritically as the politically expedient patriarchal convictions about women. Women in pregnancy and child birth, women immediately after child birth, women in menstruation, are almost universally objects of "taboo", but these things, surely stem from the very nature of womanhood (like the nocturnal pollution among the males). The "taboos" are connected with the feelings within certain kinds of contact of the "unclean" nature, the polluting qualities of menstrual blood, etc., and the mysteries of their relation to fertility and creation. Kutia Kondh are concerned with the infectious consequences of menstruation. The "taboos", the "purifications", the beliefs and rituals, are rooted in the perception of the facts. They can not be held to have been invented by men to bring about the subordination of women. The women themselves say that they prefer to stay out of the house for the well being of their children.

Among Kutia Kondhs, the domains of public and domestic sphere is least differentiated. The men and women were likely to be egalitarian. The division of labour is not well marked. Almost all the works are done by both the men and women. There are a few specialists like *kutaka* (*pujara*, religious head), *jani* (political head) and *majhi*. They are ascribed with different duties with in the community. They perform rituals, dispute settlements, solve divorce cases, and so on. But these are very limited activities and all the members (both male and female) are allowed to attain. Thus, Kutia

Kondh culture does not articulate a radical opposition between the domestic and the public as such. The domestic units of Kutia Kondh are allied with one another through the enactment of rules that are logically at a higher level than the units themselves; this creates an emergent unit—society—that is logically at a higher level than the domestic units of which it is composed. The public/domestic dichotomy argues that the roots of female oppression cross culturally lay in the division between the public and domestic spheres, and the systematic undervaluing of the domestic, which was taken to be defined as those roles and activities revolving around women and children. Thus, the extent to which women were subordinate in a given society depends on the degree of division between the public and domestic spheres. The domestic sphere was subordinate to the public, and women, by their association with the domestic and their exclusion from the public were subordinate to men. Women's close association with the domestic context derives from certain structural conflicts between the family and society at large in any social system. The notion that the domestic limit - the biological family charged with reproducing and socializing new members of the society is opposed to the public entity—the super imposed network of alliances and relationship that exist in the society. Since women are associated with, and indeed are more or less confined to, the domestic context, they are identified with this lower order of social/cultural organization The distinction of public and domestic sphere according to the traditional patriarchal theory is hardly relevant in the context of Kutia Kondhs. This hypothesis is just an extension of metrosexual jargon, where the domestic sphere was subordinate to the public, so women by their association with the domestic were subordinate to men. But this model is proved to be inappropriate among the Kutia Kondh because of less differentiation of public and domestic domains. Thus, subordination of women because of public/domestic dichotomy is inappropriate.

Concluding Remarks

The traditional ethnographic writings on Kutia Kondh are male biased (andocentric) and Eurocentric. The present day ethnographic representations are also guided by the early writings. By which, it is always represented that women are subordinated, oppressed and exploited by the male members. These concepts are being brought from the industrial society by the colonial anthropologists and have been applied with the Indian tribal. Thus the ethnography is also Eurocentric and propagation of European ethnocentrism. These concepts are being used as intellectual weapons against the tribal groups on India. The deconstruction of women's status among the Kutia Kondh show that women are always kept on high in their society. The division of public and domestic spheres does not have much importance. The females themselves feel that they are not subordinated by their male counterparts. The re-examinations of sexual subcultures justify the distinctions on biological aspects, but nothing to add with power politics among the males and females. Thus, the different dichotomies which are supposed to be responsible for the subordination of women will have to be deconstructed with the help of postmodern ethnographic techniques to get the reality of women's status in tribal society in India.

NOTES

1. It developed against the notion that traditional anthropology was suffering from a double male bias; it was argued that professional anthropologists tended to be male or, whether male or female, to accept and work within male centered models of social organization and culture .secondly, anthropologists tended to rely on male informants during fieldworks, and therefore replicate the indigenous male view. The notion mostly used was men, women and children in the ethnographic writings. The prominent anthropologists of this period were Margaret Mead and Ruth Benedict.
2. There is overlap and intersection in many areas of feminist studies throughout these waves. The first wave feminist scholars emerged from the politics of 1960s (a continuation of suffragette movement) and concerned with finding women within the historical record. The second wave is identified as beginning in late 1970s and expands the question of women to encompass gender construction. The third wave takes hold in the mid–1980s, continuing to theorize sex and gender, all central in feminist thought a certain unity in maintained.
3. Mead's works contained an analysis of pervasive sexual asymmetry that fit with their reading of the ethnographic literature (Levinson & Ember, 1996: 488). Mead (1935) in "*Sex and Temperament in Three Primitive Societies*." New York: William Morrow, she explores the relationship between culture and human nature. Culture is dealt with as primary factor in determining masculine and feminine social characteristics and behaviour. Mead (1949) in *Male and Female: A study of the Sexes in a Changing World*. New York: Morrow Quill Paper backs, tries to brings out – (a) a greater awareness of the way in which the differences and similarities in the bodies of human beings are the basis on which all our learning about, our sex, and our relationship to the other sex are built. (b) The knowledge in all human societies to see what has been attempted in what situations, and what the results were (c) suggests ways in which our civilization may make full use of both a man's and a woman's special talents, Mead's analysis concerning the differences between males and females influenced many of the discussions that were to follow.

4. However, there are also contradictions in postmodernism. These are: (1) it is an Anti-theory which is essentially a theoretical stand, (2) Postmodernism stresses the irrational, instruments of reason are freely employed within perspective, (3) Postmodernists stress inter-texuality but often treat text in isolation, (4) postmodern prescription to focus on the marginal is an evaluative emphasis, (5) by rejecting modern criteria for assessing theory, Postmodernist can not argue that there are no valid criteria for judging, (6) postmodernists criticize the inconsistency norms themselves, and (7) postmodernists contradict themselves by relinquishing truth claims in their own writings.
5. Jean-Francois Lyotard opined that the postmodern would be that which in the modern invokes unrepresentable in presentation itself, that which refuses the consolation of correct forms, refuses the consensus of taste permitting a common experience of nostalgia for the impossible, and inquires into new presentations-not to take pleasure in them, but to better produce the feeling that there is something unrepresentable. In contrast to the ethnographies written by anthropologists in the first half of the 20th century, Lyotard is stating that an all encompassing account of a culture can not be done.
6. Baudrillard breaks down modernity and post modernity in an effort to explain the world as a set of models. He identifies early modernity as the period between the renaissance and the industrial revolution, modernity as the start of the Industrial revolution, and postmodernity as the period of mass media.
7. Derrida is identified as a poststructuralist and a skeptical postmodernist. In much of his writing he is concerned with the deconstruction of texts and the relationship of meaning between texts.

REFERENCES

Barnes, J. A. 1973. "Genetrix: Genitor: Nature: Culture?" (pp.61-73) in J. Goody & M. Fortes (ed.), *The Character of Kinship.* Cambridge: Cambridge University Press

Bremer, O. 2000. *Ethnography.* Buckingham: Open University Press.

Edholm, F., O. Harns & K. Young. 1977. "Conceptualizing Women," *Critique in Anthropology,* 3 (9 &10): 101-130.

Foucault, M. 1970. *The Order of Things: An Archaeology of the Human Sciences.* New York: Pantheon

Harris, M. 1993. *Culture, People, Nature.* New York: Harper and Collins College Publishers,

Hughes, N.S. 1995. "The Primacy of Ethical," *Current Anthropology,* 36 (3): 409-420

Jena, K.M. *et al.* 1993. "Ethnic Aspects of Indian Sago Palm: An Ethno-botanical Study among Kutia Kondhs," *Adibasi,* Vol. xxxiii (3): 29-33.

Jordanavo, L.J. 1980. "Natural Facts: A Historical Perspective on Science and Sexuality," (pp.42-69) in C.P. McCormack & M. Strathern (eds.), *Nature, Culture and Gender,* Cambridge: Cambridge university press

Levinson, D. and M. Ember. 1996. *Encyclopedia of Cultural Anthropology.* New York: Henry Holt and Co.

Lyotard, J.F. 1992. *The Postmodern Explained.* Sidney: Power Publications

Mead, M. 1935. *Sex and Temperament in Three Primitive Societies.* New York: William Morrow.

____. 1949. *Male and Female: A Study of the Sexes in a Changing World.* New York: Morrow Quill.

Minh-ha, T.T. 1989. *Women, Native, Other.* Bloomington: Indiana University Press.

Nayak, G. 1976. "A Study of Kutia Kondhs Foot," *Adibasi,* xvi (1): 41-49.

Ortner, S. 1974 "Is Female to Male as Nature is to Culture?" (pp.67-87) in M. Rosaldo and L. Lamphere (eds.), *Women, Culture & Society.* Stanford CA: Stanford University Press.

Parida, L. 1959. "Ama Kutia Bhai," *Adibasi,* iii (3&4): 3-11

Pinacabral, J. 1986. *Sons of Adam, Daughters of Eve.* Oxford: Clanendron Press.

Pine, F. 1996. "Gender," (pp.253-263) in A. Bernard, and J. Spencer (eds.), *Encyclopedia of Social and Cultural Anthropology.* New York: Routledge.

Rosaldo, M. Z. 1974. "Women, Culture and Society: A Theoretical Overview," (pp.17-42) in M. Z. Rosaldo & L. Lamphere (eds.), *Women, Culture and Society.* Stanford: Stanford University Press.

Singh, K.S. 1994. *Encyclopedia of Scheduled Tribes in India.* New Delhi: Oxford University Press.

Spiro, M.E. 1996. "Postmodernist Anthropology, Subjectivity and Science: A Modernist Critique," *Comparative Studies in Society and History,* 6: 759-780.

SECTION V

RITUALS IN TRIBAL INDIA

TWENTY-THREE

MUSIC, MUSICIANS AND NON-BRAHMIN PRIESTS IN WESTERN ORISSA

LIDIA GUZY

Introduction

This article presents some work in progress results from recent research on the music traditions of Western Orissa.[1] The project is a socio-anthropological analysis of the interrelationship between local music and dance traditions, prevailing social structures and the local value system. It is based on ethnographic studies in both urban and rural settings of Western Orissa and investigates the orchestral music of Harijan Ganda musicians in addition to the music of local non-Brahmin priests. Diverse features of music in Western Orissa represent diverse socio-cultural settings, which, in turn, interact with each other: (1) The ecstatic healing performances in the region integrate dance, music and ritual speech in order to heal, console and restore the continuity of the local value system; (2) The inter-village orchestra of Harijan Ganda musicians *(ganda baja)* brings together local communities and directs the flow of impurity and danger; (3) The music of the non-Brahmin priests appeases and commemorates the Dead and thus expresses and deals with the local concept of the inauspiciousness of death.

The article aims to decode the specific cultural language of sound in the Boro Sombar region of Western Orissa.[2] It concentrates on (1) the orchestral music of Harijan Ganda musicians (*ganda baja*) and (2) on the category of non-Brahmin priests and on the role of their music. I would like to present the ethnographic diversity of specific non-Brahmin categories in the Boro Sombar region in order to broaden the perspective on Indian religiosity. Often religious specialisation in India is associated only with Brahmin ritual specialists or ascetics. The example of Western Orissa illustrates the vitality and local predominance of ritual non-Brahmin specialisation in religious functions. Music in the Boro Sombor regions is the most important cultural memory. Often myths, explanations or complex ritual procedures can no longer be remembered, but through the still vibrant music traditions of non-Brahmin priests and the orchestral music tradition of *ganda baja* a unique cultural consciousness still exists. The music of the non-Brahmin priests transports and revitalises deeply engraved ideas of death and divinity.

Ganda Baja—The Orchestral Music of Western Orissa

Ganda Baja signifies the regional tradition of orchestral music in Western Orissa. In a traditional rural setting it is played exclusively by the Harijan communities of the Ganda/Pano. *Ganda baja* is an inter-village orchestra that carries with it indigenous concepts of rhythms, instruments, and goddesses, accompanying marriage alliances and religious ceremonies. The music sensually combines gods and humans and thus it is never absent during weddings or rituals for local gods and goddesses.

Traditionally in Western Orissa music and dance are embedded in the local belief system where instruments and rhythms represent the speech of local goddesses. In different rhythms the voices of various goddesses appear. In a rural context no socio-religious ceremony, such as marriage or *puja* for gods and goddesses, can be celebrated without baja. The musicians are invited though turmeric powder by different local communities such as the Binjal (ST), Gouro, Dhol Khond (ST), Mali, Kulta in order to perform in their villages. The music played by the Ganda musicians connects local communities, places and religious concepts. In its connecting and communicating function it can be considered as an inter-village orchestra, whose mediators are the Ganda musicians.[3]

The ensemble of the folk instruments is also called a *panchabadya*, which itself directly refers to the five instruments assembled in the inter-village orchestra, such as follows:

- *Dhol*
- *Nissan*
- *Tasa or Timkiri*
- *Mohuri*
- *Kastal/Jhang or Jumka*

Dhol

The *dhol*, which is the leading instrument, is a large membranophone. The big, lengthy drum (90 cm-1.5m length), is made from the trunk of a tree and is stringed with cow's leather *(gai chomora)* on two sides. The *dhol* also has stripes of cow's leather *(badi)* and annuli (or this one?) for the stripes *(kol kola)*. Ṭalli is the right-hand side skin, dhalya the left-hand side skin. Thalli are a bit smaller (37cm of calibre) then dhalya (38cm of calibre) and both sides are played by two rubber sticks *(chumta)* of around 40 cm length. The player of the dhol is called the *dholya*. Typically the *dolya* directs all changes of rhythms played by the *ganda baja* party. All rhythms are spontaneous but directed by the *dolya*. The rhythmic and melodic compositions are learned by the musicians by listening to various rhythms from early childhood on.

Nissan

The *nissan,* another membranophone, has a tapered half-melon-like form. It is often considered to be the most ancient instrument of the village orchestra. A *nissan* is made of wood and iron sheets. It is also played by two rubber sticks *(chimta)*. The leather *(chipra)* that creates the sound is made of cowhide or goatskin and is often decorated with colourful paintings.

The *nissan* is always played with maximum strength and has thus a deep and far-reaching sound. In the region of Sambalpur the *nissan* is decorated with deer antlers. Currently this decor is disappearing as hunting deer has been forbidden.

Tasa

The *tasa* (also called *timkri*), a small membranophone, is a drum made from clay *(matul)* and stringed with cow's leather *(gai chomra)* called *mola*. The tasa's shape is tapered with a base[4] and is played with two thin bamboo sticks. The sound of the tasa is high and thin.

Mohuri

The *mohuri* is an oboe-like instrument. Its sound, as the Ganda say, is a crucial element in the change of the character of the music. Usually it is associated with the seductive voice of a capricious woman, but it can also be related to the desperate voice of a mother who cries for a dead son.

Kastal

The *kastal/jhang* are iron cimbals; jumka, which may be used instead of the cimbals is basically a rattle.

All the instruments play together in both tune and rhythm. The most important criteria for a Ganda musician are to listen to the others playing and to learn to play together. Playing *baja* also implies a sophisticated culture of listening. The musical specificity of the *ganda baja* seems to lie in its orchestral character. With the beat of the right-hand talli side of the *dhol*, the *dhol* gives an orientation for the tasa, which then beats the doubled rhythm. The beat of the left-hand *dhalyia* of the dhol gives an orientation for the nissan which then strikes a counter rhythm to the *dhalya* beat. As the sound of the mohuri often has to resemble the flirting sound of a women's voice, it is played in an extremely alluring way.

All instruments of the inter-village orchestra are worshipped before being played. They themselves are used for the worship of gods and goddesses and they themselves require worship.

Ganda Baja and the Worship of the Goddess

The *dhol, nissan,* and *tasa* are directive for inducing trance. For instance the nissan represents the voice of the goddess Nissani and thus becomes identical with her. In a Nissani temple near Padampur in the Bargar district such identification between the drum and the Goddess can be observed: The altar of the temple assembles three nissan drums where Goddess Nissani is considered to be.

Ganda Baja and "Boil"—An Example of a Traditional Possession Cult

The relationship between *ganda baja* and the local worship of goddesses can be illustrated by looking at the local possession cult of "*boil*" in the Padampur/Borosombar region of Western Orissa.

The Ritual Scenery

Every Monday during the *dasara* month (October) when Goddess Durga is to be worshipped in the Boro Sombar region, the Goddess will appear in the body of her priest. At this time, *"boil"* comes upon the *pujari* (priest). Meanwhile *ganda baja* orchestrates the act of possession, which is embodied in the dance and the speech of the priest.

Definitions of Boil

Boil is a polysemic religious concept. It can be translated as either the "divine dance" or the "dance of gods and goddesses". This concept refers to the religious specialist and his or her ritual involvement. The priest *(pujari)* who becomes *"boil"* transforms into a sacred dancer of the Goddess Durga.

Boil can also be understood as an "opening" of the local priest *(pujari)* toward the entrance of a divine power and can accordingly be identified with "possession". *Boil* can also be simply translated as a divine power which comes upon the *pujari*. It is a procreative and creative power. "*Boil asile*"/ "*boil asi*" (boil came) "*boil asibe*" (boil will come) are terms which indicate the wild dance of the *pujari* who, while dancing, represents and becomes boil. On the one hand, boil is a condition, a state of trance. On the other hand it is the personified manifestation of the Goddess Durga. During *boil*, the *boil* may even completely loose his or her control and even fall down if not held or helped. Generally the *boil* of Goddess Durga is a man, but it is a man with feminine attributes. *Boil* have long open hair and wear a red sari during the time of the *boil* ritual.

"Boil charibe, jibe" (boil will leave) defines the end of the ecstatic dance and the end of the presence of the divine power. After the divine power withdraws, the boil is left numb and then returns to his or her original state—the daily priest.

Ganda Baja Rhythms and the Ritual Transformation

Ganda baja is of central importance in the ritual transformation of the human priest to the boil, the divine manifestation of the Goddess Durga or other goddesses and gods.

The concept of *bol/par*, the rhythm, plays a critical role in the ritual performance of *boil*-possession. The trance itself is expressed in rhythms which become representative of the goddesses. The *ganda baja*, which is essentially hetero-rhythmic, leads the possession performance particularly by playing the so called *borua par,* the holy 16 rhythms of boil possession.

Borua par/Sulo par

The *borua* par, the rhythms of the divinely possessed, have a structure of 16 rhythms, also called *sulo par. Sulo* par are the rhythms embodied in the *boil*, the possessed priest *(pujari)* of a goddess. Different goddesses will appear via different rhythms *(par)* in the body of the possessed. *Sulo par*, the 16 possession rhythms represent 16 different goddesses. The rhythms are named after the goddesses' names and are aurally recognised by the musicians.[5] Locally, the identifications of rhythms and goddesses can vary. Still, as a repetitive structure in possession and healing rituals, the sixteen rhythms can be considered as a sound liturgy of goddesses worship in Western Orissa.

Ganda baja, the inter-village orchestra orchestrates the ritual of possession and the worship of gods and goddesses. The music of the Harijan musicians represents in itself an "untouchable" entity of the sacred: it channels intangible local concepts of the divine as a wild uncontrolled power, expressed by the rhythms and the dance of the possessed priest. On one hand the baja transcends local communities in its function as a ritual inter-village orchestra. On the other hand, via its rhythmic expression of the transcendence, the baja enables the sensual experience of the local community and its communication with the holy sphere.

Ganda Baja as Expression of Local Identity

Ganda baja not only carries a form of religious expression, but it transmits to its listeners a strong emotional connection to local beliefs and identities.[6] To quote a Ganda musician: "*Listen to the baja. It touches your heart! It is the sound of the thunder storm. It is the sound of your heart beat.*" For all whose life has been accompanied by baja, this music represents a part of a local cultural totality and as such the music reinforces a feeling of cultural interconnectedness.

Non-Brahmin Priests of the Boro Sombar Region

In the Boro Sombar region in Western Orissa, it is rare that Brahmins any longer carry out religious tasks. Instead, many local non-Brahmin priests can be found performing multifaceted ritual specialisations. The non-Brahmin priests are always responsible for their own specific local community and have diverse names and functions depending on their specific religious tasks.

The Guilt and Expiation Priests

One very important ritual task of non-Brahmin priests is the handling of the period after the death of a person[7]. The priests I first refer to shall be labelled here "guilt and expiation priests". During mourning and remembrance rituals for a dead person they take the guilt *(dhan)* of a dead person and accept the expiation *(dhan)* of the living progeny. The distinction of the categories as guilt or expiation is based upon an attempt to translate the polysem category of *dhan,* which indicates on one side the post-mortem guilt of the deceased and on the other side the ritual handling of the death of the progeny. For both differentiations one and the same non-Brahmin priest is necessary. All local communities in the Boro Sombar region have their own guilt and expiation priests, who come on the 11th day of the death of a family member or sometime later in the year in order to take the guilt of the deceased and to accept the expiation of the progeny.[8] The specific categories of the guilt and expiation priests perform their religious tasks only for specific communities. The Gaoro and Soaro (ST) have their Gugia as guilt and expiation priest, the Harijan their Birthya, the Gond (ST) their Porgonia and the Mali and Kulta have their Dusi. The non-Brahmin priests transfer the taken death guilt further to another non-Brahmin priest category within their own communities or to a local goddess. In this way, the gift *(dan)* of guilt *(dhan)* is never kept but always given away.[9] The "death gift" is thus never totally accepted but only temporarily. Through the temporary acceptance of the death gift, given by the progeny of the dead person to the guilt and expiation priest, the inauspiciousness of the death is transformed. The ritual transformation from post-mortem pollution to purity is called *dhan cheka*. *Dhan cheka* ("the breaking of rice") means the "breaking" of impurity. It is the central death memorial ceremony and purification act. *Dhan cheka* means that the priest takes grains of rice, cooked food, new clothes from the progeny and that he receives utensils used by the deceased recently before his or her death. All guilt and expiation priests apply music for the entrance into the in between phase amid post-mortem inauspiciousness and purity, death and life, gods and humans. At night, at the 11th day of the death or at any other time during the year, the guilt and expiation priest sings songs and myths for the dead and for the ancestors. He sits at the threshold of the house of the deceased and he uses only a specific instrument in order to communicate with the dead and the ancestors. The Gugia of the Gaouro use the *balu boisi*, a long bamboo flute, called the "flute of a bear"; the Gugia of the Soara (ST) and of some other Gaouro categories use the *brahma beena* (a cither-like instrument), the Porgonia of the Gond use a *banna,* also a sort of a cither and the Brithya of Harijan communities use the *domburu,* a small drum in form of a sandglass.

In *dhan cheka* the cultural memory of the Dead is expressed through the specific language of music. The music played by the non-Brahmin priests carries the memory of the deceased and the ancestors. The ritual sound becomes the voice of the Dead and the Living. The texts sung by the priests tell about the death and its solitude which is contrasted to the collective ritual of remembrance and purification. Music of the non-Brahmin priests evokes the emotion of cultural continuity.

Local Theory of Guilt

From the polyvalent category of *dhan*, which means alms, guilt and expiation at once, a local theory of guilt can be disclosed. In the Boro Sombar region no death without guilt exists. This guilt refers either to the way of living and dying of the deceased as well as to the contribution of his or her progeny to the death. Death always indicates a social responsibility which has to be faced and ritually handled. Interestingly, ritual processes of the regeneration of purity as well as of the remembrance are always related to music. Obviously, the elusive sound of the music transports the memory of the deceased and accompanies the intangible transformation process of purification. Apparently, the medium of the sound captures best the inexpressible experiences of the death and of concepts of *post-mortem pollution*. The local concept of a transformation of guilt through the act of a "death gift" transmitted through music reveal a unique local concept of guilt and its absolution.

Ambivalence of Social Status

The guilt and expiation priests always have an ambivalent and contested social status. Somehow, they are considered to belong to the ritual client's community, somehow not. The priests regard themselves to be of a higher status then their ritual clients. On the other hand they are considered to be of a lower status by their ritual patrons. They are always the "other", sometimes higher sometimes lower in status. Somehow, they belong to one's own community, somehow not.[10] Indeed, the *dhan cheka* work is generally regarded as an *ashubba karjo,* which means an inauspicious work. Handling the death always indicates an unsure social status. This social ambivalence leads to the situation today that some families of non-Brahmin priests refuse to continue their ritual tasks and their music. They try to forget or to change their ritual occupation in order to get rid of their stigma of inauspiciousness *(ashubba)* and impurity *(ashudda)*. The local system of the non-Brahmin priests and their music in the Boro Sombar region is thus highly vulnerable to processes of modernisation.

Transformations of the Guilt and Expiation Categories

In order to avoid speaking of oneself as a Gugia, for example, (Gugia is the guilt and expiation priest of the Binjal, the Gouro and the Soara), some priests are beginning to speak of themselves as a Goswami, Gosain. They perform ritual worship for gods and goddesses as Soni, Trinath, Durga, Ganesh, Shiva or Saraswati. The Gosain`s instrument changes from a *brahma veena* to a one-stringed violin *sarangi* where the goddess Saraswati is considered to reside. The former Gugia starts to sing the myths and songs from the *Bhagavadgita.* As a wandering singer and priest he roams from village to village. No community calls him to perform his worship and he does not choose a specific community any more. He comes by himself in order to tell and to sing diverse religious stories. In return for his singing the Goswami receives lenses *(dal)* and uncooked rice *(dhan)* from the villagers.

This example shows how the guilt and expiation category Gugia transforms into the category Gosain which becomes synonymous with the idea of a wandering priest and singer.

Itinerary non-Brahmin Priests

Besides the guilt and expiation priests, wandering priests and singers belong to a variety of traditional itinerary non-Brahmin priests in the Boro Sombar region. They venerate local goddesses by playing specific instruments and usually act as local healers. Music in the context of the itinerary non-Brahmin priest has an especially healing quality.

Sarmangalia

The *Sarmangalia* is an itinerant non-Brahmin priest of the goddess Sarmangala/ Mangala whom he carries with all his care and love in a wooden portable altar. Some Sarmangalia also carry the goddess Thakurani with them. A Sarmangalia moves from village to village together with the goddess and his whole family. Sarmangalia's worship is heard from far away. "Ma Mangala likes the sound", he explains while playing the *sarmangalia dhol* drum. It is a small wooden drum made from lizard leather on the left side and from goat's leather on the right side. The Sarmangalia plays the drum with his left hand with a stick, with the right hand he scratches the skin. Deep, monotone and specific sounds are evoked and indicate the sound for the goddess Mangala. While playing the *sarmangalia dhol* drum and while singing the songs of and for the goddess, the Sarmangalia begs for food and for food offerings he can give to the goddess. The goddess is evoked and simultaneously identified by the sound. In the morning and in the evening the Sarmangalia completes his ritual worship *(puja)* by food offerings to the goddess and by playing thc drum. He mixes the sacrificial food *(bhog)* and distributes it among the villagers. Sarmangalia always purifies the village he visits with some flatted rice mixed with cow dung. It is believed that the Sarmangalia priest, who is also called *deheri,* local healer, cures the amendments of his donors. The sound of the *sarmangalia dhol* drum is assumed to evoke, appease and satisfy the goddess and to be at the same time her voice and religious advice. It is believed that this sound chases away bad dreams *(barna sapna),* protect from witchcraft *(tondei)*—especially when played on the crossroads-and to guard from bad spirits *(bhut pret)*. Both the puja and the sound are thought to prevent or heal illnesses such as small pox *(mata)*, chickenpox *(bosonto)*, fever *(jhoro)* and skin deceases *(khosa kujri)*. Besides these healing procedures, the Sarmangalia priest also sells self-made amulets *(dongria)* which contain aryuvedic medicine.

Bhairavi

Another common local category of wandering priests is the Bhairavi, also called as *Mali konti,* the talisman makers who make the talisman from the tulsi tree. The Bharavi also teach theatre *(nato kirtan siksan)* and carry out miraculous ear invocations *(kana mantra)*. They give secret spiritual advice to barren or ill patients which consider the secret whispering as a healing. Generally, they are regarded to be local healing specialists. For healing purposes the Bharavi make threads with a talisman which they sell by roaming from village to village. The music played by the Bhairavi is a *konjoni,* a tambourine from lizard leather, which bears a remarkable similarity to the Mahima Dharma ascetics in Orissa (Guzy, in press).

The Bhairava women tattoo *(juti)* women. The tattoos are made for the dead female body considering it to be the last covering of the carcass. In the tattoos, the local people believe, the forefathers *(pitru)* live. As one of the legends tells, the god of death, *Jom,* will ask each woman: "Do you have your tattoos *(juti)*?" If she does not, Jom will chase her away from the world where the deceased and the ancestors live. He will shout: "Go away! Your body is impure/not covered *(pinda suddhha nahi)*!" If thrown away from the kingdom of *Jom,* the dead women could become homeless ghosts *(pret)* and thus dangerous for the living.

Tattoos for women are considered to be a symbol of a safety for women. It is a sign that a woman is already wounded, marked by her blood. This impurity and imperfection gives her a guarantee not to die a bad death which would turn her into a *pret* and not to an ancestor *(pitru)*.

Conclusion

In this articlc I paid attention to two exceptional cultural and musical phenomena of the Boro Sombar region of Western Orissa: (1) to the orchestral music of Harijan musicians and (2) to the variety of local non-Brahmin priests and to their specific relation between music and death.

The inter-village orchestra of the Harijan Ganda musicians can be considered a crucial component of cultural identity of the Boro Sombar region in Western Orissa. As the *ganda baja* communicates with other cultural clusters-religious rituals and the local communities—it signifies a feeling of local and religious identity. The ritual musical performance expresses an abstraction of the experience of the local community.

It could be also shown that many categories of non-Brahmin priests are characterised by a handling of concepts of inauspiciousness of the death which create their ambivalent social status. Music is always applied to the processing of death, both socially and morally. Recreated on diverse instruments by the priests, music always plays a significant role in order to transport the elusive concepts of post-mortem pollution and to accompany the intangible processes of transformation and purification. The sensitive experience of the sound seems to entail the healing power of music so often applied in the local rituals in the Boro Sombar region. The sound of the music of non-Brahmin priests reveals moral and philosophical implications. It can hence be understood as the acoustic metaphor of a local theory of guilt and as an essential cultural memory.

Both music traditions—ganda baja and the music of the non-Brahmin priests-highlight an exceptional intangible cultural heritage and the strong cultural implications of sound in Western Orissa. The local music traditions can be understood as crucial characteristics of a unique cultural identity of the region.

NOTES

1. The research was conducted from Mai 2002 to April 2005 in Western Orissa. I thank the Deutsche Forschungsgemeinschaft (the German Research Council) for the generous grant without which the research could not have been undertaken. I thank Prof Dr. Deepak Kumar Behera for his permanent local help. I thank Surendra Kumar Sahu for his commitment and enthusiasm in his research work on music traditions of Western Orissa which guided and enriched my ethnographic encounter. For his assistance during my research I am deeply grateful to him.

2. It is the region around Padampur town, surrounded by highland and amid the holy places of Nursinghnath and Harishankar temples. According to the Sambalpur Gazetteer (Senapati and Mahanti, 1971) from 1971 the Borosombar Zamindari area is estimated at 2.178 square kilometers und 476 villages (p.516). The data are drawn from the Sambalpur and the Bargar district, here especially from the rural Padampur/Boro Sombar region.
3. For comparison on Pano in Koraput see Pfeffer, 1994: 14-20.
4. Tasa has also leather stripes.
5. As for instance: Durga Par ; Maha Kali Par ; Ma Magala Par ; Ma Tarani Par; Oila Devi Par; Subakesi Par; Tulsa Devi Par; Bontei Devi Par; Chandraseni Par; Ganga Devi Par; Parvati Par; Lakshmi Par; Boiravi Par; Buri Ma Par; Patmeshwari Par; Samleshwari Par.
6. On the emotional aspect of music see Feld (1982).
7. For comparison of how death is conceptualised in South Asia, see Schömbucher/Zoller (1999).
8. For comparison see the ethnographically rich work of Skoda (2005) who describes death rituals among the Aghria in Western Orissa. In his case two categories of Brahmin are needed in order to handle ritually the inauspiciousness of death. Up to the 11th day a low Brahmin is responsible for the handling with the inauspicious pret, the deceased but not yet ancestor; after the 12th day a high Brahmin handles the ritual communication with the auspicious ancestors (chapter 6).
9. For the ambivalence of the gift, see Mauss, 1954 (1950).
10. For this ambivalent aspect see the role of the Pordhan in: Chr.v. Fürer-Haimendorf/E. Fürer-Haimendorf (1979: 363-393).

REFERENCES

Feld, S. 1982. *Sound and Sentiment: Birds, Weepings, Poetics and Song in Kaluli Expressions*. Second Edition. Philadelphia: University of Philadelphia Press.

Fürer-Haimendorf, Chr.v. and E.v. Fürer-Haimendorf. 1979. *The Gonds of Andhra Pradesh: Tradition and Change in an Indian Tribe*. New Delhi: Vikas Publishing House.

Guzy, L. (in press). "From Non-Brahmin Priests of the Goddess to Ascetics of God Alekha—Some Reflections on Religious Transformation from Orissan Material," in H. Kulke, G. Pfeffer and H.V. Stietencron (eds.), *Studies in Orissan Society: Culture and History,* Delhi: Manohar.

Mauss, M. 1954. 1950. *The Gift, Forms and Functions of Exchange in Archaic Societies*. London: Cohen West.

Pfeffer, G. 1994. "Music in Context: Ethnography and Meaning," *Beiträge zur Musikethnologie,* 30: 14-20.

Senapati, N. and B. Mahanti. 1971. *Orissa District Gazetteers,* Sambalpur. Cuttack: Orissa Government Press.

Schömbucher, E. and C.P. Zoller (eds.). 1999. *Ways of Dying: Death and its Meaning in South Asia*. Delhi: Manohar.

Skoda, U. 2005. *The Aghria: A Peasant Cast on a tribal Frontier.* Delhi: Manohar.

TWENTY-FOUR

BAD MANGALBAR PUJA: A *Parab* for the Propitiation of the Deity 'Mangeri' Among the Kondh

NIBEDITA NATH

The Kondh

The Kondh are one of the sixty-two scheduled tribes of Orissa. Numbering close to one million they are the seventh largest tribe of the State (Ratha, 2005: 86; Sabat and Das, 1999). The tribe has its main concentration in the hilly districts of Kondhmal, Baudh, Rayagada and Koraput.[1] The tribe is known as Kandh, Kando, Khond, Khondho, Kondhv and Kondh (Pathy, 1995: 228; Mishra, 2005: 155). The term "Khond" and "Kondh" often appears in the Government documents. The tribe has a number of sub- tribes, viz. Kutia Kondh, Dongria Kondh, Kuvi Kondh, Desia Kondh, Languli Kondh, Penga Kondh, Jharia Kondh, etc. (Sachidananda and Prasad, 1998: 490; Sharma, 1979: 17 and Mohapatra, 1998: 301). The Kondh are well-known in the anthropological literature for their *meriah*[2] (human) sacrifice (Sabat and Das, 1999). In recent times, man as a sacrificial object has been replaced by buffalo.

Religion plays a vital role in the socio-cultural and economic life of the Kondh. They believe that the world is full of mysterious supernatural powers, which tremendously influence their lives. They, all along try to establish a good relationship with these unseen powers through various rites, rituals and festivals (Nath, 2004). Festivals and rituals are the important aspects of their religion. Of the different *parabs* (festivals), *Mangeri Sanpa* is considered to be a significant one in the Kondh community.

Objectives and Methodology

The major objective of the paper is to provide an account of religiousness of the Kondh community through the description of one of their famous *parabs—Mangeri Sanpa.* It also tries to throw light on the interrelations of invitation and propitiation of supernatural beings with welfare and illness. An attempt has also been made to find out the importance of the *parab* in the social structure of Kondh society through a detail discussion of the *parab* and its interpretation. The study[3] was conducted in the Kondh[4]—dominated village Robadi in Kolanara block of Rayagada[5] district, South Orissa. Data for the present paper were collected through observation, informal interview and focused group discussion.

The *Parab*

Mangeri Sanpa is performed by the Kondh of Robadi on the Tuesday just before *Kandul Parab*[6]. This day is considered as the most auspicious Tuesday in a calendar year. Therefore, the *puja* is popularly known as *Bad Mangalbar Puja*. It usually falls in the month of *Pus* (December-January). The village deity 'Mangeri' is worshipped in *Bad Mangalbar Puja*. The *puja* is performed by the *bejuni*.[7] I did not come across with any myth among the Kondh explaining the origin of this festival. The sole purpose of the *puja* is to propitiate village deity for the all round welfare of the Kondh in particular and the villagers in general. Replying to my question, (why is this *puja* performed?), Nage Himirika (a middle aged man) said:

> "By performing this *puja*, no evil incident occurs in the village. We try to please village deity to get her favour. If she is pleased all people in the village possess good health. Nobody will suffer from any major illness. By performing this *puja* all the villagers manage to overcome the crisis situations in that particular year".

The Day Before the *Puja*

The main *puja* is performed late in the morning on Tuesday. However, the deity is invited on the prior evening (Monday). The ritual of invitation of deity is usually performed in front of the *jani's*[8] house. The *janima*[9] makes all necessary arrangements (including required ingredients) for the ritual. The ingredients required for the invitation of the deity include: unboiled rice (collected for the deity from all the Kondh households, which is known as *padi*), *jhuna* (resin), *siali* leaves, low wooden stool, winnowing fan, half burnt charcoal, powder of *ragi* (Elesine Coracana), etc.

She invites the deity by moving the fingers of her right hand through the unboiled rice kept on the winnowing fan. She repeats the process of picking up a little rice from the winnowing fan to a height of about one feet and dropping those down again. Occasionally she throws a little rice to the front. She calls upon the deity reciting *mantras* indistinctively. Usually she pronounces hymn in the praise of the deity. Nath (2004) write "the words are intoned with such speed and repetition that it is difficult for any hearer to comprehend. It can be more or less understood by the Kondh community, except the occasional phrases". Hardenberg (2004) writes:

> "She recites ritual verses with a vibrating voice. These verses are made up of ritual speech using metaphors and parallelism. The meaning of these expressions is not intelligibly to everybody. Only specialists like the shaman or her assistants know the exact verses and can interpret its meaning...It is extremely difficult to understand for an outsider and without proper knowledge of the metaphors and the events referred to. One may easily mistake the spoken words for a kind of 'tribal poesy' concerned with the beauty of life and the greatness of the divine".

She drops powder of *mandia* (ragi) from a height again and again. When the deity comes the name of the deity is automatically got written on the ground. With the coming of the deity, the pitch of the *bejuni* increases and the musicians also enthusiastically beats the drums (*baja, badabja, damphu, tama*) for producing sound of high pitch. A wave of immense pleasure spreads over the audiences. The *bejuni* offers rice to the deity on the *siali* leaves.

The Very Day of *Puja*

On the day of *puja, bejuni* anoints her body with turmeric paste and takes holy bath washing hair early in the morning. She ties *ghunguru* (anklets/ ornament of ankle/small tinkling bells tied in a thread) on her feet. She also keeps her wet hair loose and puts on unboiled rice mixed with turmeric paste on her forehead in between the eyebrows. When I asked (later on) the *bejuni* reason of putting on the above mentioned mixture, she answered

> "If I put on unboiled rice mixing with turmeric paste on my forehead, the deity becomes pleased and she enters into my body".

As it is a community festival the *puja* is performed on the village road in front of the *jani's* house. The musicians prepare themselves for beating the musical instruments during the *puja*. The *janima* keeps all the ingredients, viz. *podi* (winnowing fan), unboiled rice, brass pot, half burnt charcoal, *sarju* (a special vehicle made up of bamboo and semel wood), bamboo basket, brass bowl and other required articles at the place where the *puja* is to be performed. The *janima* stands besides the *bejuni* to render her assistance. A picture of the *puja* ground is given below.

Picture of the *Puja* Ground

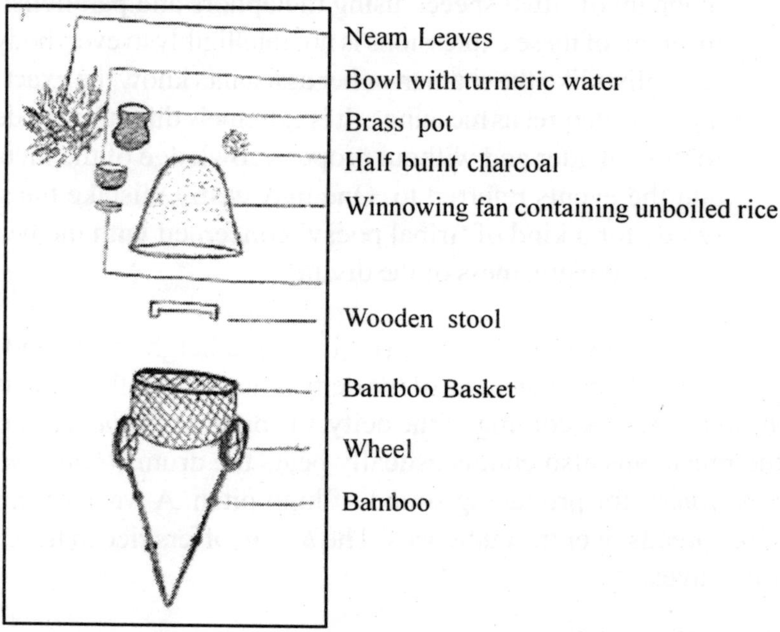

The *bejuni* initiates the *puja* by keeping the frontal side of the winnowing fan towards her. She moves the fingers of her right hand through the unboiled rice kept on the winnowing fan and calls upon the deity indistinctively in her own dialect. While doing so, she picks up a little rice from the winnowing fan to a height of about one foot and again drops those down on the fan. In between she throws some rice to her front. The process continues for quite some time after which she takes out handful of rice from the winnowing fan and stands up, turns around and scatters the rice in her back murmuring something in her own dialect. Then she starts singing and dancing in unison with the music of drums inviting other Gods/Goddess viz. *Nahu penu, Haru penu* (*dongor* deity) present at nearby places.

By the by she takes some rice from the winnowing fan and throws to the front. This process of taking rice from the winnowing fan and casting to the front is repeated again and again. Every time the scattering rice is followed by different kind of dance. This is because she calls different deities in different rhythms. The musicians also produce different sounds in conformity with dances. The musicians are expected to beat the drums with utmost perfection. Perfection in dance and music is an essential requirement of the *puja*. For this reason the *jani* and his son handle the drums. The *bejuni* too is supposed to ensure perfection. Hardenberg (2004) made more or less similar observations during *Bali Yatra* among the Dongria Kondh of the village Parsali near DKDA of Kalyansinghpur area. He writes:

> "The shaman rubs the rice of the winnowing fan with her hand in a circular motion. Then the shaman begins to dance, every time in a slightly different way. This alternation between dancing movements and phases of calmness when the shaman recites or rubs the rice can continue for an hour. Each time a new deity makes his or her appearance, indicated by the shaman calling its name, the drummers will change their rhythm, the correct rhythm often being a matter of dispute among the musicians".

While dancing at times she stands still keeping the right hand parallel to the ground and then the left in the same manner. Sometimes, she raises her left and right hands alternatively. It is observed that the change in music and dance is effected only after a brief pause. Being overwhelmed with devotional joy the *bejuni* remains completely engrossed in the music and dance. During the course of such dance, the deity "Mangeri" enters into the body of the *bejuni*. She finally gets possessed. With the entry of the deity into her body she starts showing abnormal behaviour. The *bejuni* goes on swinging her head making different postures of her body. The *janima* washes the *bejuni's* feet with turmeric water. She starts worshipping her with some lighted incense sticks. She puts some half burnt charcoal in front of the *bejuni*. She puts her palms on the head of few persons to bless them. Gradually she slows down her movements and starts getting cool.

The *bejuni* in trance makes forecasting about people's future and events. People (even the non-Kondh) take their chances to know more about their uncertain future and the causes of some ongoing problems. However, the *bejuni* in trance answers to people's questions as per her wish. While answering to my question, Sany Ulaka (an old Kondh man of the village) said:

> "The deity does not answer to the questions of those with whom she is displeased. Such people are the unfortunate ones. They are considered to be guilty in the eyes of deity because of some wrong deed/sin committed by them".

Holding a steel bowl containing turmeric water with *neem* leaves, the *bejuni* sprinkles a little of that holy water on the roof of each house. This sprinkling of holy water is done for the welfare of each house in particular and the whole village in general. The other *bejuni* collects straw from the roof of each house and keeps those in the bamboo basket kept on the *sarju*. I asked why the other *bejuni* is taking out straws from the roof each household. What does it imply? Shosi Huika said:

> "By taking out straw she is taking out all the inauspicious/evil/ misfortune and sins of each household. Those are kept in that *sarju*. The *sarju* is taken near the mango tree and this means taking out all the evils and misfortunes outside the village. Those are unloaded undere the mango tree for the purpose of adoration for the welfare of each house. Finally, those straws remain in that place after the *puja*".

At the end of *puja* the *bejuni* again starts dancing. While performing dance she occasionally takes unboiled rice from the winnowing fan and throws those to her front. She dances with pleasure and sings songs praising the deity. After a while, the *bejuni* stops dancing.

The small children between two and ten years of age are forcibly made to lie on the ground by their parents with their faces facing the ground. The *bejuni* holding the bowl containing the holy water passes by the children one after another, sprinkling turmeric water on each of them. The other *bejuni* follows her holding the winnowing fan on her head. The *jani* follows them holding a hollow frying stick with half burnt charcoal in it. The children are made to wake up one after another as soon as the two *bejuni* and the *jani* cross them. This is how the *bejuni* wards off the evil spirits from the children.

It is believed that those children will not have any health problem for major part of the year.

Soon after all the village functionaries start moving towards the mango tree (the ground under the mango tree is the founding place of the deity) located at one end of thc village. The *sarju* is rolled on and carried by a person to take it near the mango tree. The married females of the village follow the village functionaries carrying plates on their head with three leaf cups containing cooked rice to be offered to the deity. They are followed by other villagers irrespective of their age and sex.

While moving towards the mango tree, all people stop at a place. A small patch of land on the right side of the road is cleaned and smeared with turmeric water. Some half burnt charcoals are put on that place. Three to four leaf cups containing cooked rice are offered there to the deity.

People slowly gather around the mango tree for worshiping the deity once again. A small cottage of about 2 feet breadth and 1 feet height is made under the tree before hand. The winnowing fan containing unboiled rice, small hollow frying stick with half burnt charcoal and bowl with turmeric water are kept close to the cottage. The *bejuni* starts moving the fingers of her right hand through the unboiled rice on the winnowing fan and then invites the deity. She offers cooked rice to the deity. People present there eat the rice carried by their female folk to that sacred place. This is followed by the sacrifice of a hen (bought from the weekly market with a little money taken out from village fund) to satisfy the deity.

Holding the hen the *bejuni* makes it eat rice from the winnowing fan. Thereafter one male comes with a child and sits besides the *bejuni*. The *bejuni* gives the child some rice in its right hand and asks the child to feed the hen. Replying to my question why the hen is fed with rice? Marsa Kadraka says—

> "It is believed that if the deity is pleased, thc hen eats the rice quickly and delightfully, otherwise takes in delay and with hesitation. Therefore, the hen is fed with rice".

Then the *bejuni* passes on the hen to a person who cuts its neck. *Bejuni* pours the blood of the sacrificed hen in front of the cottage and thereby makes offering it to the deity.

This is followed by *bad bali* (cow sacrifice). Replying to my question, why do you sacrifice cow? Amna Bidika says:

"Cow is the most lovable sacrificial animal of the deity. She is pleased by cow sacrifice. We sacrifice cow once in a year only on this occasion. Goat, hen are sacrificed at different point of time in a year. For example, sacrifice is done with the fulfilment of the wish of any person. But *bad bali* is given only on this occasion. You do not know this is a grand *puja* of our *jati* (community)".

A strong *khunti* (bar) is posted. A cow (bought from the weekly market beforehand with the money collected from all Kondh households) is brought to the spot and fed with some straw. While the cow is eating, *jani* from the back gives a sturdy stroke on its head with an axe. Immediately, the cow falls down. The *jani* keeps on striking at a particular point of the cow's neck, with the butt end (non-working end) of the axe. Finally, the cow losses it's life. The *bejuni* squeezes the neck of the cow and collects the blood in a leaf cup. Then the collected blood is offered to the deity. Mean while an old man brings some dust from the ground and smears on the back of the sacrificer recalling the deity. This is done for expiation of the sin of the sacrificer. The sacrificed cow is taken to the other side of the road. The *bejuni* upsets the leaf cups with rice kept in front of the cottage. She sprinkles the water of the bowl on all the persons assembled there. The flesh of the sacrificed cow is distributed among the desirous persons of the Kondh community. The share never goes to a non-Kondh person. People then slowly start returning to their respective homes. Thus the ritual of sacrifice that is initiated on Monday comes to an end on Tuesday. This *Bada Mangalbar Puja* is performed only once at the end of a year where the *bad bali* (big sacrifice) is made.

Analysis and Interpretation

Bad Mangalbar Puja is a ritual of sacrifice centers round sacrifier, sacrificer and sacrificial animal and most significantly the Supreme Being for whom sacrifice is made. According to Dumont (1980: 358) "Sacrificer is he who puts the sacrificial animal to death and sacrifiers are the subjects to whom the benefits of the sacrifice accrue…who undergo its effect". The village deity 'Mangeri' is the center of the *parab* who is pleased and satisfied by the sacrifice. The whole villagers are the sacrifier; they are the subjects to whom the benefits of sacrifice accrue, who undergo its effects. *Jani* is the sacrificer who puts the sacrificial animal to death. Cow is the sacrificial animal.

The widespread sacrifices and offerings of living animals, food, vegetables, incense and even money are a way of approaching the supernatural by

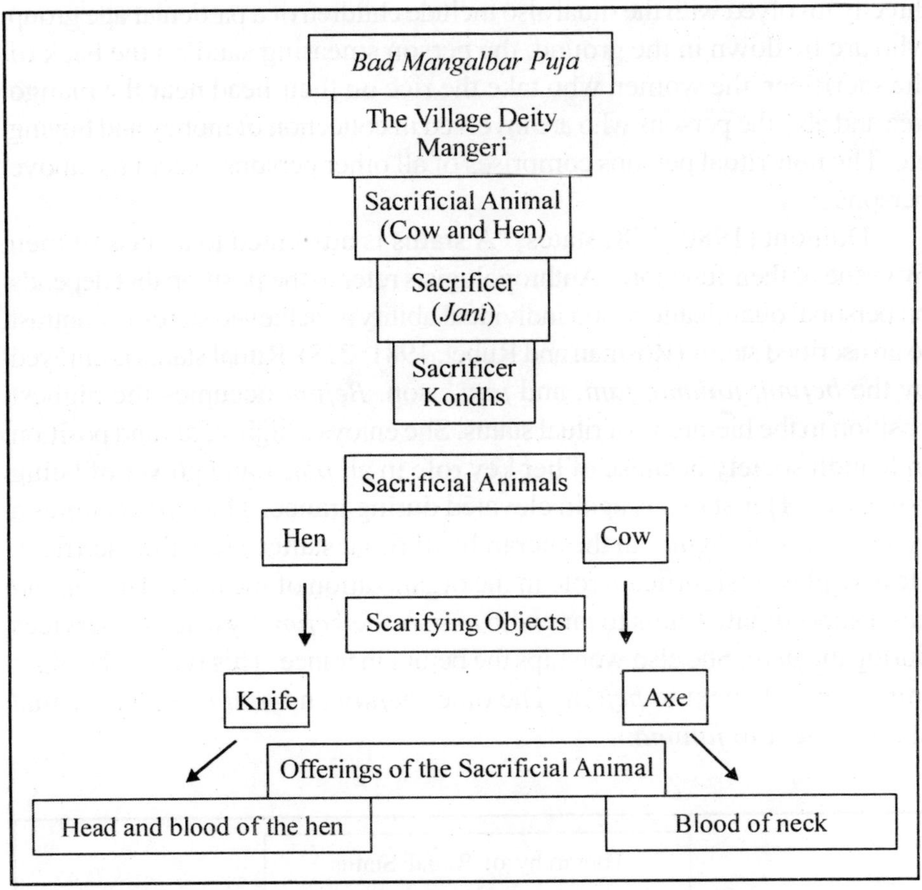

bearing gifts. Since the relationship between humans and the supernatural emphasizes the subordination of the humans, people can only hope for supernatural support in fighting wars, in warding off misfortune, sickness, and death and in providing fertility in exchange for their gift. The sacrifice of live animals is the sacrifice of life itself. The sacrifice consists of giving up something of value in an exchange with spirits (Rosman and Rubel, 1981: 271). The different types of beneficiaries of the *puja* are: The over all beneficiaries are all the households of the village i.e. all the villagers in general and people of the Kondh community in particular. The categorized beneficiaries are the children who are lie down and for whom the *bejuni* wards off evil eyes. The other beneficiaries are the persons whom the *bejuni* in trance tells or forecasts something, the persons who are answered by the bejuni and the persons on whom the *bejuni* keeps her hand.

Different categories of persons are involved in the ritual. The ritual persons include the *bejuni, janima, jani, jani's* son. The persons who are directly involved with the ritual also include children of a particular age group who are lie down in the ground, the person smearing sand on the back of the sacrificer, the women who take the rice on their head near the mango tree and also the persons who are involved in collection of money and buying etc. The non-ritual persons comprises of all other persons except the above persons.

Dumont (1980: 358) states, "A status is attributed to a class of men by virtue of their function". Anthropologists refer to the position that depends on personal qualifications and individual ability as achieved status in contrast to an ascribed status (Rosman and Rubel, 1981: 228). Ritual status is enjoyed by the *bejuni, janima, jani*, and *jani's* son. *Bejuni* occupies the highest position in the hierarchy of ritual status. She enjoys a high status and position in Kondh society because of her key role in all *pujas* and power of being possessed. Her status is again elevated during trance. The *jani* occupies a position next to *Bejuni* in the hierarchy of ritual status. He is the sacrificer. He also plays a significant role in the organization of the *puja*. The *janima* has a subordinate status to jani who assists the *bejuni* by offering services during the *puja*. She also worships the bejuni in trance. This is how she plays important role next to *bejuni*. The other *bejuni* and *jani's* son have ritual statuses next to *janima*.

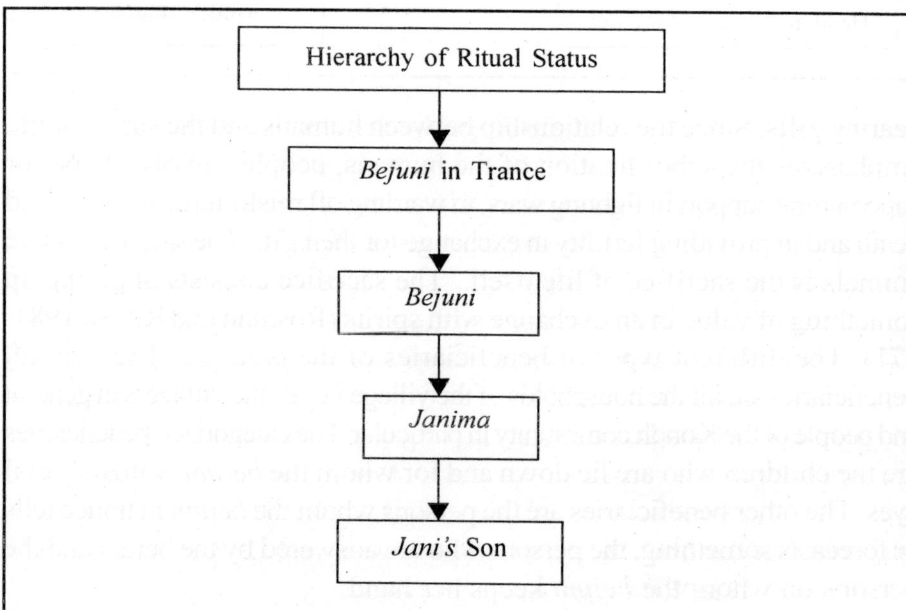

Inclusion and Exclusion

Inclusion	*Exclusion*
Within the Kondh community	Within the Kondh community
Straw is taken from the house during the pollution period	Rice is not taken from the houses that undergo pollution due to birth of a child
Outside the Kondh community	*Outside the Kondh community*
Straw is taken from the roof of the non-Kondh	Rice, money etc. are not taken from non-Kondh
Non-Kondh can ask questions to the deity i.e. bejuni in trance	The children of the non-Kondh are not made to lie on the ground during warding off of evil eyes
They can observe the puja both inside the village and outside the village	Non-Kondh they themselves do not go to observe the buffalo sacrifice
The *bejuni* sprinkles holy water on non-Kondh	The flesh of cow is not given to the non-Kondh

The ingredients which are used in the *puja* are the sacred objects. Those objects are unboiled rice, turmeric powder, *jhuna*, *ragi* powder, wooden stool, *siali* leave, neem leave. Of all the ingredients the core and most sacred ingredient is unboiled rice.

Space is a "practised place". No place can be neutral and places can become invested with meaning and trigger positive or negative emotions. Physical objects, human behaviour and use of space influence the nature of space. The ritual places of the *Bad Mangalbar Puja* are in front of *jani's* house, a place before the mango tree and the ground under the mango tree.

Concluding Remarks

Festivals and rituals are the important aspects of tribal religion and society. Anthropologists study the performative aspects of ritual and are interested in how participants "constitute through their actions" (Rosman and Rubel, 1981: 275). The local tradition of ritual varies. Externally it seems to be different. But the ideas and values behind the ritual may be the same, i.e. the propitiation of deity for welfare and happiness. The purpose of the *Bad Mangalbar Puja* is propitiation of deity and hence getting the blessings. Thus, there is a kind of inter relation of religious activity with social aspects of life. This type of interrelationship between the social and religious aspects of life exists in every society since time immemorial. Rituals play an important role in generating a kind of "we feeling" among the people. It brings in guests, enhances social solidarity, and provides opportunity for strengthening the social network. It is also a time for merry making and rejoicing (Nath and Behera, 2006). Ritual does not simply mirror society and culture, but helps to shape its defining features. The parab is thus a reflection of the social structure in the Kondh society.

Acknowledgements

I take this opportunity to place on record my thanks to my guide Prof. D.K. Behera (Chair person, IUAES Commission on Children, Youth and Childhood and H.O.D of Anthropology, Sambalpur University, Jyoti Vihar, Orrisa, India for his comments and corrections during drafting of the paper.

NOTES

1. During 1991-2001, 10 districts were bifurcated to create few new districts. The district of Phulabani was bifurcated and two new districts, viz. Baudh and Kandhamal were created. Similarly, the district of Koraput was carved out in to four new districts, viz. Koraput, Rayagada, Nabarangpur and Malkangiri.
2. Sharma (1979: 20) writes, "The *meriah* sacrifice is celebrated between March and May just before the hill clearings are sown with new crops. It is said that in earlier times Kondh used to indulge in human sacrifices on this occasion so as to propitiate the goddess of the earth". As reported by the colonial mercenaries, administrators and ethnographers, it may be briefly noted that *meriah* sacrifice was offered to the earth goddess and pieces of flesh were buried in the fields to ensure good crops, especially "the deep red colour of turmeric," and immunity from diseases and accidents (Frazer, 1890: 1-386). Mishra (2004: 156) noted that human beings used to be sacrificed to the Earth Goddess in return for fertility of the soil, plenty of harvest and for over all prosperity.
3. The present paper is a part of the ethnographic study made in 2000-2001 during the post-graduation period.
4. The Kondh of Robadi claim them as Dongria Kondh while some people (outsiders) tell them as Desia Kondh. The Kondh of Robadi are different from the Dongrias of Niyamgiri area. Further in depth and detail study in future by me or others on different types of Kondh would only provide us a clear picture.
5. As many as 42 tribal communities' inhabit in this district with a dominance of Kondh and Savara/Saura (Bulliyya, 2004).
6. *Kandul Parab* is an important festival of Kondh, which is observed in the month of *Pus* (December–January) for the ceremonial eating of the freshly plucked *kandul* (a local equivalent of red gram which is their staple food), just before its actual harvest.

7. *Bejuni* is the female priest and *beju* is the male priest. The *bejuni* performs all the *pujas* in the village. *Bejuni* is also the shaman who performs divinations through trance and recitation of incarnations so as to decipher the supernatural agencies responsible for the malady or disease or death or distress of some sort (Patnaik and Patnaik, 1982: 122). No *bejuni* learns the art of ritual performance on her own or from any other person. She/he learns the art through dream by the Deity. Deity enters her soul within that person and inculcates or instills the *pujapath* (skill of worship and propitiation of Deity) to the person whom she believes and loves. There can be more than one *bejuni* in a village. In the village Robadi, there are two *bejunis*. However, the head *bejuni* plays important role and rest assists her. Similar finding was also made by Patnaik and Patnaik (1982) who writes "In a village, there might be one or more *bejunis*".
8. *Jani* is the headman of the Kondh community. He is a secular as well as a religious specialist who occupies a very important position in a Kondh village (Patnaik and Patnaik, 1982:118). He assists the *bejuni* in the *puja*. He forecasts the future of the village and gives information to *disari, bejuni* and the villagers.
9. *Janima* is the wife of *jani*. She is held in high esteem.

REFERENCES

Bulliyya, G. 2004. "Anthropo-ecological Dimensions of the Eastern Ghat," *South Asian Anthropologists,* 4 (1): 73-88.

Census of India. 2001. *Provisional Population Totals (Orissa).* Series-22.

Dumont, Louis. 1980. *Homo Hierarchicus.* Chicago: The University of Chicago Press.

Hardenberg, Roland. 2004. "Bali Yatra of the Kond: A Ritual Performance and its Socio-historical Context," paper presented in the international conference on *Dialogues with the Gods* held at Sambalpur University during February, 20—22, 2004.

Mishra, Arima. 2005. "Kado Bikri: Informal Process of Land Transfer among the Kutia Kandhas", (pp.136-157) in D.K. Behera and Georg Pfeffer (eds.), *Contemporary Society: Tribal Studies.* Vol. VI. New Delhi: Concept Publishing Company.

Mohapatra, Sitakanta. 1998. "A Study on Socio-economic Condition of 'Kutia' Tribe of Orissa," (pp.301-318) in S.N. Tripathy (ed.), *Tribal in India.* New Delhi: Discovery Publishing House.

Nath, Nibedita. 2004. "Kandul Parab: A Festival of Harvest and Joy among the Kondh," paper presented in the international conference on *Dialogues with the Gods* held at Sambalpur University during February, 20-22, 2004.

Pathy, Jaganath, 1995. "Colonial Ethnography of the Kandha," *Economic and Political Weekly.* XXX (4): 220-228.

Patnaik, N., P. Patnaik and S. Das. 1982. The *Kondh of Orissa.* Bhubneswar: Tribal and Harijan Research-cum-Training Center.

Ratha, S.N. 2005. "Tribal Welfare Administration and Development in Orissa," (pp.86-97) in Deepak Kumar Behera and Georg Pfeffer (eds.), *Contemporary Society: Tribal Studies.* Vol. VI. New Delhi: Concept Publishing Company.

Rosman, Abraham and Paula G. Rubel. 1981. *The Tapestry of Culture.* New York: Mac Graw Hill Companies.

Sabat, Kalpana Rani and Nirmal Chandra Das. 1999. "Status of Kondh Women of Ganjam of Orissa," *Man and Life*, 25 (1&2).

Sachidanand and R.R. Prasad. 1998. "Kondh," in Krisna Sharma (ed.), *Encyclopedic Profile of Indian Tribes.* Vol. II. New Delhi: Discovery Publishing House.

Sharma, Krishna. 1979. *The Kondhs of Orissa.* New Delhi: Concept Publishing Company.

TWENTY-FIVE

RITUALS ASSOCIATED WITH THE NEW BORN AND ITS MOTHER IN A TRIBAL COMMUNITY OF SOUTHERN ORISSA

RASHMI PRAMANIK

The Constitution of India reserves certain privileges for some 84 million of the scheduled tribes as a bureaucratic category. This is 82 per cent of the Indian population. Orissa has the third largest tribal population in India. As many as 62 scheduled tribes live in Orissa. They approximately account for 25 per cent of total population of the State. Partly because of the isolation and partly because of their limited world-view characterized by lack of historical depth and an overall tradition orientation, they are integrated in terms of certain themes rooted in the past. These integrated themes and special cultural focus give them a separate cultural identity, and they often possess latent or manifest value-attitude and motivational systems which are remarkably different from those of the other people. The paraja are one of the tribal communities found mainly in the southern part of Orissa with maximum concentration in the district of Koraput.

Objectives

The paper seeks to analyze:

- Three different rituals, viz. *Nahihandisara, Sanahandisara* and *Ekosia* associated with the child birth, and
- The concept of purity and pollution relating to child birth.

Methodology

The study is conducted in the Pungar village of Kunduli Grampanchayat which falls under Similiguda block of Koraput district. It is a paraja dominated village. The study is conducted among the Boda paraja of pungar village. Data were collected by observation, case study and informal discussion with the paraja people of our sample village. Information was taken from only those families which had at least an infant.

The Tribe

According to the paraja legend, the rajas and parajas were once living like brothers later, the rajas slowly got used to a comfortable ways of living, leaving behind the parajas who continued to grill under conditions of abject poverty. The concept of purity and pollution and their cultural habits dichotomize the paraja tribe into two broad sub-divisions, namely, Boda paraja and Sana paraja.

Boda praja do not eat beef or buffalo meat and observe elaborate purificatory rituals even when a cow or buffalo dies in their house, whereas the sana parajas eat beef, buffalo meat and do not observe purificatory rituals like the Bada parajas. Generally it is found that the Bada parajas are relatively economically advanced than the sana parajas, hence they claim higher social position and ranking over the latter.

Major Findings

Rituals or ceremonies are the pivots round which some thoughts about supernatural rotate. Rituals are however nothing but the implementation of beliefs. Rituals are usually set apart as a body of custom specially associated with religious performances. A ritual many precisely be described as the way of performing religious act that is, of playing, singing, dancing for the gods making sacrifices or preparing offerings (Barua, 1999: 77). A ceremony on the other hand, involves a number of inter connected and related ritual performed at a given time. Hinduism has left its successful impression upon the paraja religious beliefs and practices. Some of the sanskritic rituals have been adopted by them without knowing their proper significance. Side by side, they retain their original tribal religion. They have their own way of worshipping their traditional tribal deities.

The birth of a child sends the signal of the arrival of the spirit of the deceased person of the house. They consider the coming of a child as the rebirth of one of their ancestors. Therefore, the new born is always given a warm welcome. In a paraja community, right from conception to the final purificatory rituals, a number of *taboos* (restrictions) are observed by the concerned women. A pregnant woman is subjected to many *taboos* (restrictions) with respect to her diet and daily activities for her well-being and safe delivery. A pregnant woman in a tribal community ordinarily works till the day of the child birth except certain restrictions are imposed on her diet and movements (Das, 1961: 121). However, paraja women remain engaged in their daily chores until a very advanced stage, even sometimes upto the moment when labour pain starts because of their cultural habits as well as for their economic necessity.

When a woman knows that she has conceived, she first informs her husband. An expectant mother has to observe a series of prenatal taboos. Few of them are listed below:

- She is not allowed to eat fish, meat and onions.
- She avoids seeing the lunar eclipse, as it is believed that it effects the growth of the child in the womb.
- She is not permitted to see or touch any dead body. She is not allowed to come out of her house during a storm, lightening and thunder.
- She is not expected to shout in alarm, otherwise the child will also have an inborn fear of the same.
- When wood is put on fire, the charcoal is not to be broken by her, or else the baby will have black spots all over the body.
- An expectant mother should not sit on a pillow or on the doorway, as it is believed that it leads to difficult delivery.
- After the fourth month of pregnancy her husband ceases to cohabit with her.

There are certain interesting beliefs regarding sex determination. They are as follows:

- When the fetus is on the right side, it is believed to be a male child. For a male child fears being burdened with the pitcher, which his mother carries it on her left hip.
- When the fetus is on the left side in the womb, it is believed that it is a girl child. For a female child is in a fear of being burdened with the spade and axe which is carried over the right shoulder.

At the time of child birth a women is confined to a room in a secluded enclosure where no male members are allowed inside. Only elderly and experienced women and traditional midwives attend the mother. The female priest (*Gurumain*) is called for conducting rituals for smooth delivery. A *Gurumain* not only performs rituals for smooth delivery, but she is a priest whose duty is to worship the village goddess on the occasion of rituals, festivals and for the recovery of ailing persons. In case the delivery becomes painful and complicated, the witch-doctor (Gunia) is called upon to prescribe appropriate herbal remedies.

If the child is born on the night of the new moon it is believed that she/he will be a notorious thief. If the umbilical cord is twisted round his/her neck, it portends the death of the father or the maternal uncle. This is warded off by the father or the maternal uncle by killing a fowl and wearing its entrails round his/her neck and subsequently burying them along with the umbilical cord.

In some tribal communities, after child birth the umbilical cord is deeply buried in the usual bedroom of the couple. After filling the earth heavy pressure is given by the foot. This act is always done by the husband. They never bury it outside, as it is believed that it may be affected by an evil spirit. Among the Tai Khamyans, the umbilical cord is buried within the compound and they never give any pressure on it. It is believed that if it is pressed heavily, the child many face difficulty in breathing. There is also a belief that the deeper the pit the larger the gap between the two issues (Barua, 1996: 162). More or less similar beliefs exist among the Sikligars. After parturition, the umbilical cord is buried underground, where care is taken in burying the umbilical cord deep. They believe that the deeper it is, the better will be the health of the mother and the child. It is buried with great caution and without any delay. Because according to their belief, if a barren woman happens to have it, she can trouble the baby a lot (Banarjee, 1987: 66).

In a paraja community, after the child birth the umbilical cord is cut by the mid-wife and the child is given a bath in luke warm water in the courtyard. The umbilical cord is buried in a hole in the backyard or in the place where the rain water falls from the roof. The mother and child remain polluted and secluded inside the house until the naval cord dries up.

The period of pollution indirectly helps the mother to take rest after delivery. The mother and the child are considered polluted for at least 16 days after the birth, though it actually depends on the falling of naval cord. The women are not expected to attend any household duties during that period as a result she gets rest for about 10 to 15 days. This period of pollution varies from place to place and from country to country. In Mayanmar, this period lasts for about five to eight days. In USA some years back women having children were expected to take rest in the bed for about six weeks, but now they observe four days rest (Mead, 1953: 172).

Purity of body and mind is a pre-condition for observance or rituals. Our mortal body comprising of sperm and blood is deemed to be impure. So to make it pure, several *samskaras* have been prescribed in the *sastras*. These *samskaras* or purificatory rites are to be observed throughout the different stages of a man beginning from conception right upto death. One of these *samskaras* is the *Jatakarma,* i.e. birth rites. The chief purpose of the *samskaras* is purification of the body of an individual. Excepting festivities and elaborate rituals, there are familial worships or rituals which are done as per vows. There is no specific date or place for performing the rituals associated with a particular spirit. Meticulous directions are received by the priest in dreams. As it is the prime duty of a physician in any society, amongst the Kukis also it is the responsibility of the priest to find out the causation (Herskovite, 1955: 221).

The present study discusses three important rituals associated with child birth. These rituals are observed within one month after the birth of a child. The rituals are namely: *Nahihandisara, Sanahandisara* and *Ekosia.*

Nahihandisara

This ritual is performed on the day when the naval cord falls, i.e. approximately within a week after the child birth. The mid-wife wraps the naval cord with palm leaves and throws it into the pit dug for this purpose in the backyard which is later on filled in with earth. A lamp is lit and incense sticks are lighted near the pit to ward off evil spirits. Then the mother and child take bath and change their cloths. On that day all clothes and utensils are washed and even the house is cleaned and plastered with cow dung. Turmeric and tulsi water is also sprinkled all over the house with the help of mango leaves. Family deities are worshipped for the well-being of the family as well as the new born. The pots, clothes and mat used in the delivery room are removed from the house. Then the mother washes the feet of the mid-wife with turmeric water and oil. The mid-wife is also given a new saree, some amount of rice, ragi, turmeric, oil and vegetables. This ritual is conducted to purify the mother and the family members from birth pollution. Here the mid wife helps the mother and the child from passing on from a stage of pollution to purity.

Sanahadisara

This ritual is observed soon after the stoppage of the menstrual flow of the mother. This flow stops within 12 to 15 days after the child birth. Before the performance of the ritual, *Sanahandisara,* the mother is not permitted to touch any family members in the house. She is even not allowed to fetch portable water from outside. She does not cook for any one in the house. The food is prepared by her husband, which only both of them can eat it. No other family members are allowed to partake the same food. The mother is considered to be ritually impure during that period. After the performance of *sanahandisara,* the mother is allowed to cook food for all the family members. On that day all the clothes used by the mother are washed by her. The house is also cleaned by sprinkling turmeric and tulsi water. The mother throws away all the old earthen pots which are replaced by the new ones. Then she takes a bath by washing her hair. On her return she worships the family deity, seeking blessings from the Almighty both for herself and for the child. Then she considers herself to be free from all sorts of pollution. She resumes all her normal activities soon after this stage. It is significant to note that unlike the previous ritual, here the mother herself performs all the required rituals for overcoming the stage of pollution.

Ekosia

It is a ritual that is performed on the 21st day of the child birth which also includes the first hair cutting and name giving ceremony. However, due to conditions of abject poverty sometimes this day usually gets postponed to a subsequent date and time as per the convenience of the concerned family. In this ceremony the maternal uncle and grand parents play an important role. On the day of *Ekosia* they bring along with them a dress for the child, a saree for the mother and a *dhoti* for the father. Apart from that they also bring one towel and six numbers of brass plates and cups. The mother applies milk on the head of the child. The traditional astrologer *(Disari)* cuts the hair of the child. Then the hair are collected in a leaf cup and taken by the mother to a stream where those are thrown to the river wishing long life to the child. After that the mother and the child take bath and wear new clothes. A *Disari* acts as the village astrologer who determines auspicious dates for ceremonies and rituals. He knows the names of the constellations and of the planets. He makes calculations and foretells evil or good.

On that particular day another ritual is performed to select the name of the child. Here it is important to know the mason (ancestor) from which the child is born. By keeping the child on the lap and holding a brass plate, the maternal uncle is made to sit on the courtyard. Here all the family members gather together. The *Disari* takes turmeric water in a leaf cup. Then he takes seven grains of rice and drops it into the turmeric water by uttering the name of their ancestors one after another. In the grains of rice start floating while uttering a particular name, it is believed that the child has come from that ancestor. Then the members present there wash the feet of the child with milk and give money on the brass plate held by the maternal uncle. At last a feast is given to all the members in that village, which is cooked in a new hearth.

Concluding Remarks

The study reveals that the mid-wife plays a key role in performing the ritual, *Nahihandisara*. She throws the naval cord after it drops. In *Sanahandisara*, the mother herself occupies the key position in doing the purificatory rites. She washes her clothes, cleans the house and replaces the old pots with new ones. *Disari* is an important person in performing the ritual *Ekosia*. He does the first hair cutting ceremony and decides a name for the new born child. So far, the parajas have retained their own way of life which distinguishes them from other tribal and non-tirbal communities. In a paraja community the birth of a child is believed as the gift of the ancestors. It argues that the observance of the aforesaid rituals is a kind of reflection of social realities. Individuals are sources of social disorder. One reason is that their psychic lives are complicated and constantly changing, driven this way and that by desire, self-interest and who knows what else. Social order requires that observers understand people to make clear commitments in occupying certain roles or carrying out certain acts, yet such clear commitments cannot be solidly anchored in the shifting sands of individual psychic life, which might lead a person to want to be ally one day but not really feel upto it the next. This is where ritual comes in. By publicly obligating people and conveying information about the obligation indexically, ritual protects social process from psychic "noise" (Robbins, 1999: 103) and gives the social order a well-delineated quality.

REFERENCES

Banarjee, B.G. 1987. *Child Development and Socialization.* New Delhi: Deep and Deep Publication.

Barua, I. 1996. "Socio-cultural and Environmental Factors of Health and Economy: A Case Study among the Taikhamyangs," Paper presented in the seminar "Human Factors Resource Management and Development," held in New Delhi, October 3-5, 1996.

Barua, B. 1999. "Buddhist Festivals and Rituals in Bangladesh," *Man in India*, 79 (1& 2): 77-87.

Das, J.K. 1961. *The Tribes of Orissa.* Vol-XII. Census of India Publication.

Herskovites, M. 1955. *Cultural Anthropology.* New York: Free Press.

Mead, M. 1953. *Cultural Patterns and Technical Change.* Paris: UNESCO.

Robbins, J. 1999. "God is Nothing but Talk: Modernity, Language and Prayer in a Papua New Guniea Society," *American Anthropologist,* 15 (3): 101-113.

TWENTY-SIX

NATURE-MAN-SPIRIT COMPLEX OF THE SAURIA PAHARIA OF SANTHAL PARGANA: Changes due to Intervention

A.K. HALDAR

Nature-Man-Spirit complex is a frame for analyzing the culture of a community. L.P. Vidyarthi used the concept for of looking into the Maler style of life as early as 1963 (Vidyarthi, 1963). As mentioned in his writings that the common name of the tribe is "Pahariya". The term "Saoria" or "Sauria" has been accepted by the earlier scholars (Bainbridge, 1907). The local people also call them as Sauria. The meaning of the term Maler in *malto* language is "man" (Vidyarthi and Rai, 1976). The Paharia community after their bifurcation from the Oraon from the Rohtasgarh, migrated towards Santhal Pargana and settled in the hills of that area long ago. In course of time the Paharia community got divided into three groups, namely, Sauria Paharia, Malpaharia and Kumarbhag Paharia. Politically Sauria Paharia have been put under the Primitive Tribal Group (PTG) by the government keeping in view their lower level of literacy and pre-agricultural economy.

Distribution

The Sauria Paharia are distributed in the Rajmahal hill range of Santhal Pargana. They are mostly concentrated in the present Sahebganj district. They live in the Sadar Subdivision and are spread over five blocks, namely, Sahibganj, Borio, Barhait, Taljhari and Pathna. Their number is negligible in the other two blocks - Rajmahal and Barharwa.

Considering their local ecological variations, inaccessibility, exposure to the regional culture and the people of the area, the Sauria are divided into three district cultural groups. These are the *Pobia*, the *Bare* and the *Chete*. The *Pobia* are distributed in the eastern side and are an exposed group. They are in contact with outside population as well as regional culture. Their extreme opposite or the traditional group with lesser exposure is the *Chete* group. The Bare group comes in between the two extreme opposite groups generally living in parts of the Borio block. These groups follow different customs, dress pattern and style of living. But inter-marriage is practiced among these groups (Haldar and Roy, 1998). These intra-Sauria groupings have not been discussed by any of the earlier scholars who studied the tribe.

The Village

The Sauria Paharia represented by their bare group was selected for intensive study. Binderi Bandarkola village was selected for conducting a total study. The Bandarkola hill is one of the highest hills of the area. In spite of its proximity to the Boreo Block township (4 5 km) the hill top- Bandarkola is more than 1.5 km from its Patharghatta base on the hill tract. The village is divided into seven *tolas* (hamlets). They are Barkatola and Shyamtola on hill top, Indian Niwas Resettlement Colony, Patharghatta, Simratola, Gonda and Hathikuta on plains or some smaller heights. The distance of the different tolas from Barkatola (hill top) varies from 2-4 km in different directions. The paths are mostly inaccessible. The village was selected because of its inaccessibility, utter negligence by the development officials to reach the village and the multifarious problems that the community is facing today in spite of best efforts of the government to develop these people.

Myth: Adamṣumari

Once there was a custom of taking census in the village. The village chief at one point of time developed this peculiar custom of taking census of the village inmates and their families. The myth about the counting of the heads goes as follows: They call it *Adamsumari*. A day was fixed by the chief for this Adamsumari. On that day all the villagers had to gather at a place and they were counted. Any person failed to be present at that place during the time of counting would be killed in order to maintain the exact number which came out at the time of counting.

Once while *Adamsumari* was on, it so happened that Rama Paharia, a co-villager did not turn up as he went to the deep forest for cutting fire wood. His wife (name unknown), son-Bhima and daughter-Chandi were present during counting. The number which came out was 240 persons. According to the rules of the village, Rama was killed. At that time his children were too young to understand anything. But when they were grown up, they started asking their mother about their father. Initially the mother used to give different causes for the absence of their father. At a later stage she had to narrate the truth to her children. Both the children were taken aback and with profound grief they also decided to give up their life. Before that they cursed the villagers that the number of families of the village would never increase above 60 and the number of member would never exceed 240 and that it would go on decreasing. If it exceeds, the villager would have to face natural calamity. After that Bhima was lost inside a tree and Chandi in a basket made up of bamboo. The villagers believe that after this incident, their population is fast decreasing. The incidence of natural calamity was narrated by Sunjap when there was an incidence of increase in the number of families over 60.

Settlement Pattern

The individual families built their houses in different hamlets of the village. The number of houses vary from 4 to 25 in each hamlet. The homesteads are known as *adda*, which are mostly arranged in rows parallel to each other. The houses are constructed in rectangular type. They are erected in north-south direction. The single room houses serve the purpose of bed-room, store room, guest room and kitchen. It is mostly with two doors. The houses do not have any window. The materials used in the house construction are bamboo, sal, arhar stem, thatching grass, *sabai* rope and mud. They collect these materials from their environment. The main items and portions of the house is represented by the specific *gossaiyans,* e.g. *addogossaiyans* or the home God is represented by the *bali* (door) of the hut, the main pillar inside the hut which keeps the hut erect is representative of *gomogossaiyan* and the main item inside the hut, the hearth, is situated just by the side of the door which is supposed to be the representative of the *attoigossaiyan.* The household and agricultural materials of the Sauria consist of only those articles which are needed in their day-to-day life.

Cultural Frame

Now it will not be out of place here to give a brief description of the Sauria Paharia culture in the frame of the Nature-Man-Spirit inter-dependence.

Nature

These people live in the hills of Sahebganj district of Jharkhand. Their villages are situated at some heights ranging from 100 to 1000 ft from the surface level. The village under study is grouped under the category of high hilly village and the height of its main tola comes to about 1000 ft from the surface. The natural ecology of the village consists of the hill, the forest, the spring and the small rivulet. The water resources for the village consist of a few wells dug here and there in addition to the spring. The flat land on the hill provides them the settlement area and some amount of paddy land recently developed. The huts are constructed from the materials of the forest. The sloppy undulating areas of the village have a number of fruit trees, wild trees, shrubs, creepers, bamboos, etc. Some area of the hill is also covered with wild grass which is used as roofing materials. The village used to be covered with three concentric rings of forest. The forest has mostly faded out due to indiscriminate cutting.

The economy of these people revolves round forest and shifting cultivation. They practice slash and burn type of rotational cultivation popularly known as "*kurwa*". The forest not only provides them the main economic base for food collection and shifting cultivation but also provides them with the land for "*bari*" and "*dhani*" cultivation. For the indigenous communities of this area forest supplements their economic activities whatever it may be. It also serves various other needs of the people.

Man to Man

The Sauria Paharia myth tells that *beru gossaiyan* after creating the universe created the first man (Maler) and sent him to the hills to live. He also asked the Maler to utilize the hills and forests for his livelihood. Since then they have been living on the hills practicising shifting cultivation. Their society is divided into two groups (i) *manjea toka* and (ii) *rayat toka malem*. The *manjia toka* is again divided into two groups, i.e. *manji toka malem* (belonging to the same *gotia*) and *manji toka maler* la (non-*gotia*). The *rayat toka malem* is also divided into two groups - *emki maler* (*Nadeno Doki*, *Rayat Tokano Doki*) or the *gotia* group and the *em toka hala* (non-*gotia* of Manjhi). The concept of clan is absent. Marriage within the gotia is strictly prohibited. *Manjia gotia* in Rayat is called *naber* and *manjhi's gotia* in *manjhi toka* is called *bach nakpore*. The lineage can be traceable only up to three or four generations. In the absence of clan they follow specific rules for selecting bride or grooms for their sons or daughters.

Birth is an important event in the Sauria family. The placenta is put on the highest branch of a tree by the father to save the child from evil forces on the one hand and to space the next child at a longer gap. They put the dried naval chord in the hole of a tree on a small earthen cup along with some miniature implements and grains, etc. with the hope that the male child will be a good hunter and protect the society from outside forces while the female child will be a good housewife. Here again they put oil on the naval chord with the belief that the next issue will come after a long gap. They take special care of the child during its infancy and early childhood days. During the later part of the late childhood the boy or the girl is sent to the *kodadda*. There is no separate house for *kodadda*. The young boys and girls cannot sleep with their parents in the single-room huts. All the young boys sleep together on the closed verandah of a hut while the young girls in another verandah under the care of the housewife of that hut. They get training here through their elder inmates. The other functionaries of *kodadda* have ceased to exist now-a-days.

As soon as the child attains puberty arrangement for his or her marriage starts. He or she has to enter the stage of adulthood with a brief adolescence phase and had to face the realities of hard life. Marriage at a very young age leads to frequent divorce. It seems that they are giving a trial of living together. Around the age of 25 years the matter settles down and the actual married life starts at this age. In spite of the fact that a boy is to pay a high amount of bride price the woman is bound to labour hard for the family and she has to maintain several restrictions. Drinking outside the settlement area is strictly prohibited for the wife. Violating such restrictions she has to face severe beating and scolding. This and such other practices observed during fieldwork lead us to conclude that the position of women is very low in the Sauria society even though the female child is not unwanted or neglected. But they equate the lazy wife with that of lazy bullock and treat them in the similar fashion.

Old persons are asset to every society. But in the Sauria society none of the aged persons want to be burden on their children. Even a man can marry an aged woman at his age of 65 or more years. Regular form of marriage can take place and a separate living is accepted. The aged woman even if she does not marry can stay with her son of any husband. In that case also she is an asset for the family as well as for the society as she takes care of the younger girls and trains them in a proper way.

Political Organization

Both traditional and modern political systems are working side by side. By tradition *manjhia* is appointed the *pradhan* (headman) of the village. The forefathers of the present *pradhan* happened to be the sardar of 180 villages and now the *sardar* system has been abolished. The *pradhan* is the aristocrat custodian of the tradition. The people have faith on him. But the *mukhia* hails from another village and has earned money through unfair means and so most of the people do not possess good opinion about him.

They have rich tradition of folkloric materials. The *malto* language has greater impact of Urdu than Sanskrit. They have various types of myths about the creation of the universe, the Paharias, their ecology, development, village, different places, etc. But their songs and dances are mostly related to the marriage and festivals.

Spirit World

The hilly and forested habitat of the Sauria Paharia have made them dependent upon supernatural and the spirit world. A closer look into every aspects of their culture including ecology, economy, social relationships and personality formation is influenced by the spirit world. Every item in their house is devoted to some of their *gossaiyans.* They have different types of gossaiyans who are propitiated at the village level by different specialists. The *manjhia* is the religious head of the village. He is assisted by the *guraits.* The post of *manjhia* is hereditary but the religious *guraits* are selected considering their experiences. The religious functionaries are guided by the *gossaiyans* themselves. In addition there are the gurus who are the specialists of the natural and supernatural world. With their expertise and experience they help the people to avoid maladies and suggest remedies relating to the health and happiness. There are a few demons who communicate the dissatisfaction of the deceased person (spirit) to the family members. Again it may be said that most of the family heads have a tutelage spirit who guides him on various matters.

The Problems

The analysis of the Sauria culture in the frame of nature-man-spirit complex encourages us to look to their problems in the same frame. It is generally assumed that the root of the problems lies in the culture. Culture also helps the people to overcome these problems. So here an attempt is made to find out the problems of Sauria in the frame of Nature Man-Spirit Complex.

Nature

Sauria ecology consists of hills and forests. Rich ecological condition is being disturbed by indiscriminate cutting of forests by the contractors either by taking lease or even without it. The Sauria tried to resist but failed. Now the hill from the roadside looks plain. Again the *mahajans* (money lenders) are cutting the hill from the Simratola side. The stones are being sold out. The plan was then to construct a dam on this side by the Government which failed after the cutting of the hills. The plan was then abandoned. The *mahajan* has taken the advantage of cutting the hill and selling stone without paying any attention to the poor Sauria who possess those lands. Very few animals are found in the forest except a few wild cock, peacock fox, snakes, etc.

Economy of the people revolves around collection of food and other necessary materials from the forest, shifting cultivation, wage earning, wood selling etc. They have also taken up paddy cultivation. Government is giving all help to the Sauria Paharia for their economic development. But the things do not reach the people at the time of their necessity for lack of proper co-ordination. It has helped the *mahajans* to tighten up their grips. The *mahajans* without investing anything sucking the blood of these simple people. For the whole year most of the people have to starve as the *mahajans* snatch away all the food materials at half of the market price when they return from the *kurwa* with their grains. This cannot be checked as the Sauria believe that the other officer will not stand behind if he files a case against the *mahajan*. Economic development can come only with initiative of the people themselves. Motivating some Sauria youths to look after the welfare of their fellow Sauria may be helpful.

Man to Man

A closer look into the simple demographic variables of the village under study reflects that the Sauria Paharia of the village are faced with the problem of decreasing trend in birth-rate coupled with increasing death-rate resulting in the lowering of the annual growth rate of the population. Though not a negative growth, it is an alarming situation to record that annual growth rate has decreased from 3.83 to 0.76 during last five years. It is high time to control the death rate of the population by making available all the modern medical facilities right at the village. Proper care must be taken by the modern experts so that the people do not feel that they are in the hands of alien people and system.

The age group distribution of the people shows that there are very few infants (4.28%) and aged people (4.94%) of the age above 50 years. The number of adults is maximum (47.53%). The adolescents are also very few in number (9.5%). The sex ratio of the village show excess of female. A look into the marital status shows that the marriageable age is from 16 onwards though a few persons in the age group of 11 to 15 years are also married.

The lower age at marriage poses various problems ranging from hard labour for the female and ill-treatment by the male resulting in divorce, maternal mortality, infant mortality and neglect of the infants. The higher number of female divorce possesses problems of adjustment, moral laxity, etc. The higher proportion of females may also pose a threat to the growth of population of the village community by their out-migration through marriage. Squeezing of the adolescence population has also posed a threat which may take a different form in the near future.

Rehabilitation

Professor Vidyarthi rightly commented that the Sauria do not want to come down and settle in the rehabilitation colonies. They can only come down and settle in the rehabilitation colonies when the colony is built in their own land and their *gossaiyan* permits them to come down. The story of rehabilitation colony of Banderkola is very interesting. The *gotias* of Surya Paharia have come down as it is situated in their own land. Surya first came down during the construction phase and was living in a hut which was blown away by a storm. Then the *jhanda gossaiyan* asked him to stay in the Pucca hut constructed at the Indira Niwas Colony. Having established Jhanda gossaiyan he has been staying there for a long time. After some time his son and other persons came down. Some of them have dual settlements.

Spirit World

These people were fully dependent on their natural resources for their livelihood and on their spirit world for maintaining good health and curing diseases. Ecological degradation has posed problem of dependence on nature and spirit world. They are not aware of the vices that have entered into their society which needs to be cured through their supernatural world. Impacts of Hinduism and Christianity deteriorated their traditional position and they are looked down as untouchable. The problems have cropped up due to interaction between the greater culture and the Sauria culture. The systems in the greater culture are alien to them. Several examples may be cited here which needs cultural interpretation.

On the whole it may be said that the Sauria culture which earlier revolved round the forest is now facing crisis due to ecological degradation. Tribe-caste marriage has also posed some social problems. They are also being constantly exploited in their own land. Programmes for economic development can only be implemented with a deeper insight into their cultural framework. The educated youths should be motivated to take up the lead.

REFERENCES

Bainbridge, R.B. 1907. "Saorias of Rajmahal Hills, Calcutta", *Memoirs of Asiatic Society of Bengal,* II (4).

Haldar, A.K. and K. Roy. 1998. *The Sauria Paharia: A Study of Ethno-Medical System, Bidisa.* Midnapur: Rarh Sanskriti Sangrahalaya.

Vidyarthi, L.P. 1963. The Maler: *A Study in Nature-Man-Spirit Complex of a Hill Tribe in Bihar.* Calcutta: Book Land Private Limited.

Vidyarthi, L.P. and B.K. Rai. 1976. Tribal Culture of India. New Delhi: Concept Publishing Company.

NOTES ON CONTRIBUTORS

Ali, Md. Basar did his M.Sc. in Social Anthropology from Vidyasagar University of Paschim Medinipur district of West Bengal in the year 1996. The main interest of his study is Livelihood and poverty eradication. He served the 'State Council of Educational Research and Training', Government of West Bengal in the capacity of Research Assistant in a research project. He worked in an NGO, 'West Bengal Council for Child Welfare' as a Research Investigator. He was engaged during 1999 to 2000 as a Research Assistant in an Economic and Social Council, U.K. funded project, which was conducted by the University of Cambridge and the University of Keel of United Kingdom. He worked during 2000 to 2001 as a Research Assistant in a project under department of Anthropology, Vidyasagar University, West Bengal, India. He was engaged as a Junior Research Officer in a Department For International Development (DFID), funded project, under Center For Development Studies (CDS) of the University of Wales Swansea, United Kingdom, through its Indian Partner Institute—The Institute for Socio-Economic Development (ISED), Bhubaneswar, India. Presently he is doing his PhD. on rural development issue in the Department of Anthropology, Vidyasagar University, West Bengal, India.

Mailing Address: Md. Basar Ali
Department of Anthropology
Vidyasagar University
Medinipur-721 102
W.B, India
Email: <basar_ali@yahoo.com>

Banerjee, B.G. did his M.Sc. in Anthropology from the University of Delhi and Ph.D. from the Panjab University, Chandigarh. He was awarded UGC National Fellowship for doing Ph.D. research work and later was awarded UGC Career Award for conducting independent research work among the immigrant Tibetans settled in India. He is a full-time Professor of Anthropology at Panjab University, Chandigarh since 1998. His interest in Medical Anthropology and Social Demography is well- known in academic circles. He also specializes in Socialization and Gender Studies and Tribal Anthropology. He is the author of four books and edited two volumes. He has contributed several research articles in edited volumes and learned and professional journals.

Mailing Address: Prof. B.G. Banerjee
Department of Anthropology
Panjab University
Chandigarh-160 014, India
Email: <bgbanerjee@yahoo.co.in>

Behera, Deepak Kumar is professor and the head of the department of Anthropology, Sambalpur University, India. He obtained his Master's degree (Gold Medalist) and Ph.D. from Sambalpur University, where he has been teaching anthropology since 1985. He has more than 70 research publications in reputed journals and edited volumes. Most of his publications are in the fields of tribal studies and children and childhood. Professor Behera has authored/edited sixteen volumes. Of those, six published volumes of *Contemporary Society: Tribal Studies* (Concept Publishing Company, New Delhi) are jointly with Professor Georg Pfeffer of Institute of Ethnology of Free University of Berlin, Germany. Some of the books published by Professor Behera in the field of children and childhood are: *Contemporary Society: Childhood and Complex Order* (Manak Publication, New Delhi, 1996), *Children and Childhood in Contemporary Societies* (Kamla-Raj Enterprise, New Delhi, 1998), *Public Images of Children* (Guest Editor, Special Issue of *Journal of Social Sciences,* New Delhi, 1999) and *Children and Youth in the Metropolitan Cultures* (Guest Editor, Special Issue of the *International Journal of Anthropology,* Florence, June 2001), *Childhoods in South Asia* (Pearson Education, New Delhi, 2006). He has successfully completed more than a dozen research projects funded by UGC, ICSSR, Ministry of Welfare, National Literacy Mission Authorities, Winrock International, Shastri Foundation, WHO, etc. Professor Behera has participated in 19 different international conferences held in Mexico, Germany, Belgium, Sweden, Israel, Denmark, USA, South Africa, China, Japan, Italy, Norway, France, UK, Bangladesh, Brazil, France, Singapore, etc. He has delivered several invited lecturers in different overseas universities and research institutes. Professor Behera was a Fulbright Vsiting Professor at California State University, Long Beach during the Fall semester 2007. He was also a Visiting Professor in the Dept. of Anthropology, University of Free State, Bloemfontein, South Africa (2001, 2003), Dept. of Anthropology, University of Durban-Westville, Durban, South Africa (2001), Institute of Psychology, Federal University of Rio de Janeiro, Brazil (2004) and Maison des Sciences de L'Homme, Paris, CNRS-EHESS, Toulouse (2006). He was the editor of the *Journal of Social Sciences* during 1997-2002. Professor Behera is a member of the Executive Board of International Union of Anthropological and Ethnological Sciences (IUAES) for the period 1998-2008. He is the Chairperson of the IUAES Commission on Children, Youth and Childhood. As the Chairperson of the international commission, he has organized more than half a dozen panels and sessions relating to children and youth in different international conferences and symposia. Professor Behera was the Coordinator of the Symposium titled "Everyday Experiences of Children in Asia-Pacific' of the international conference *Asia-Pacific Childhoods* to be held at National University of Singapore during July 17-20, 2006. He is also the Officer-at-Large of the International Sociological Association Research Committee-53 - Sociology of Childhood for the session 1998-2006. He is a member of the International Advisory Board of the Journal—*Sociological Analysis* (North Carolina, USA), *Boyhood Studies* (New York, USA), *Practicing Anthropology* (USA). Professor Behera is also a member of Advisory Board of the Greenwood Encyclopedia of Children's Issues Worldwide (Greenwood Publishing House, USA) and Global Gutter Press (Cambridge, UK). He is the Director of the Institute of Evaluation, Research, Documentation and Training. Nine scholars have already received their Ph.D. degree working under the supervision of Professor Behera. His current interests in research are: tribal studies, children and youth.

Mailing Address: Dr. Deepak Kumar Behera
Professor and Head of the Department
Department of Anthropology, Sambalpur University
Sambalpur - 768 019, Orissa, India
Email: <deepakbehera@hotmail.com>

Behera, Hari Charan is a Research Scholar in Anthropology at University of Hyderabad. He completed M.Sc. and M.Phil in the same subject with all first class. He has successfully worked in some developmental projects funded by DFID and IFPRI in different states like Orissa and Uttar Pradesh. He has attended and presented papers in several National and International conferences on tribal issues and development. Apart from that, he has attended several workshops carried out by CSD, NIRD, etc. on various aspects of social research.

Mailing Address: Hari Charana Behera
Department of Anthropology
Hyderabad Central University
Hyderabad
A.P, India
Email: <haricb21@yahoo.com>

Bhowmick, Pradip Kumar (*b.* 1955) did his M. A. in Rural Development from S. V. University, Tirupati. In the year 1988, he was awarded Ph.D. from Indian Institute of Technology, Kharagpur. The D. Litt has also been credited to his career from Ranchi University in the year 1998. At present he is an Associate Professor in the Rural Development Centre, Indian Institute of Technology, Kharagpur - 721 302, West Bengal.

Dr. Bhowmick published different articles on various issues related to Tribal and Rural Development in reputed journals. He has authored some of the books namely, *Dynamics of Tribal Development* (1993), *Rural and Tribal Development Practices in India* (1994), *Level of Tribal Literacy in the state of West Bengal* (2000), *Ecology, Tribals and Rural Development: The Case from West Bengal* (2001), *Land Reforms Programmes and Rural Development in the State of West Bengal* (2001), *Delivery Services among the Tribal Communities of Bengal and Orissa* (2002), *Tribal and Sustainable Development* (2005), *Women Empowerment* (2005). He is also co-author of the books namely, *Tribal Movement* (1994), *Land and Forest: Twin Tribal Problems* (1998), *Some Aspects of Indian Society and Culture* (2005), *Social Justice for the Tribals* (2005). Dr. Bhowmick, author of several research papers is keenly interested in teaching, training and conducting researches among the rural and tribal communities. In addition to the above he is the Managing Editor of the journal—*Man and Life.*

Mailing Address: Prof. Pradip K. Bhowmick
Rural Development Centre
Indian Institute of Technology
Kharagpur-721 302
West Bengal, Inida
Email: <pradipb@hijli.iitkgp.ernet.in>

Biswal, Debendra Kumar got his Master's degree in Anthropology from Sambalpur University in 1995. He then enrolled himself in the M.Phil. programme of the Center for Social Medicine and Community Health, Jawaharlal University. He completed his Pre-Ph.D with a JRF funded by University Grants Commission, India. He has to his credit a good number of publications on themes like international relations, globalization and tribal livelihood, medical anthropology, reproductive health, etc. Presently he is a SRF in the Department of Anthropology, Delhi University and associated with ISS, New Delhi. His areas of interest are: Gender, Critical and Clinical Medical Anthropology, Development of Third World Countries, Ecology and Health and Impacts of Globalization.

Mailing Address: Dr. Debendra Biswal
Department of Anthropology
University of Delhi
Delhi-7, India
Email: <dkbiswal@rediffmail.com>

Carrin, Marine anthropologist, is director of research with the CNRS at the Centre d'Anthropologie, Toulouse. She has worked among the Santals for many years and is the author of *La Fleur et l'Os: symbolisme et rituel chez les Santal* (EHESS, Paris 1986) and *Enfants de la Déesse: prêtrise et dévotion féminine au Bengal* (CNRS éditions and MSH, Paris 1997) as well as a large number of articles. She, has edited *Managing Distress: therapeutic cults in South Asia* (Manohar, Delhi 1999) *Resistance et Autonomie:Tribus et basses castes en Inde* with Ch. Jaffrelot (EHESS, Paris 2002)and with Harald Tambs-lyche—*People of the Jangal: Reformulating identities and adaptations in crisis* (*NIAS*, Copenhagen, in press). She has also written with Harald Tambs-Lyche: *A Peripheral Encounter, Santals, Missionaries and their Changing Worlds 1867-1900* (Manohar, Delhi, in press). A book on Santal ritual discourse is in preparation.

She has recently published several articles on the Bhuta cults and related themes in South Canara, India.

Mailing Address: Dr. Marine Carrin
182 rue Lemerchier
80000 Amiens
France
Email: <tambslyche@hotmail.com>

Das, Ashis Kumar (*b.* 1976) passed B.Sc. with Honours in Anthropology in 1998, M.Sc in Social-Cultural Anthropology from Visva-Bharati University in 2000. He received Merit Scholarship for securing the First Class Second position in M.Sc. He did a Research work on "Role and Function of Magioco-religious Specialists among the Mundas: Continuity and Change" from Anthropological Survey of India (Eastern Regional Center, Kolkata) as Junior Research Fellow for three years. He has published a number of papers in national and international journals on shamanism and other social issues. A write up and photograph awarded from Context Based Research Group, Baltimore and published in Margaret's Walking Stick *(A International Internet Journal)* in July 2003 issue. Beside all these anthropological research work, he is an author of a book on the selection of Essays of Rabindranath Tagore in Bengali named Chirobondhu Chironirbhara. Now he is a Research Scholar in the Department of Anthropology, Vidyasagar University. As a Programme Associate he is now attached with Research and Training Unit of CINI ASHA (Child in Need Institute), a non-governmental organization in Kolkata.

Mailing Address: Ashis Kumar Das
Ph.D. Scholar, Vidyasagar University
35 /2/1, Bhattacharyya Para Lane, Howrah-711 104
West Bengal, India
Email: <ashiskechai@yahoo.com>

Das, Reetuparna obtained her Master's degree (first class) and M.Phil. degree (first class, topper) in Anthropology from Sagar University and Sambalpur University respectively. At present, she is an ICSSR doctoral fellow (institutional) under N.K.C. Centre for Development Studies, Bhubaneswar (Orissa). She is presently working under the joint supervision of Dr. P.K. Acharya and Prof. D.K. Behera. The theme of her doctoral research is women empowerment. Apart from doctoral research, she has also worked as Research Associate in research projects. She has qualified UGC-NET for Lectureship in Anthropology. Ms. Das has presented papers at the State level and national level seminars and international conferences including IUAES Inter-Congress, 2004 held in Kolkata. Her multiple areas of research interest encompass gender issues, tribal studies, children and childhood matters and social issues related to religion, humane values, morality and ethics.

Mailing Address: Reetuparna Das
N.K.C. Centre for Development Studies
ICSSR Regional Institute, Chandrasekharpur
Bhubaneswar-751 013
Orissa, India
Email: <reetuasitanth@yahoo.co.uk>

Erasmus, Piet A. is Professor and Head of the Department of Anthropology, University of Free State, South Africa. He is a member of various scientific organizations and also serves as consulting editor for different scientific journals. He has published various research articles and reports, as well as a number of books and chapters in books. He has presented a number of papers at national and international conferences. He has done fieldwork and research among different ethnic groups in rural and urban areas. His current research interest is land reform, indigenous communities and ethnic identities.

Mailing Address: Prof. Piet A. Erasmus
Department of Anthropology
University of Free State
P.O. Box 339, Bloemfontein 9300
South Africa
E-mail: <erasmusp.hum@mail.uovs.ac.za>

Guha, Abhijit (*b.* 1956) took his Masters' in Anthropology from Calcutta University in 1983 and M.Phil. in Environmental Science from CU in 1984. Worked at the Centre for Studies in Social Sciences, Calcutta as ICSSR Doctoral Fellow during 1984-85 on Bengali Kinship under the supervision of Prof. Surajit Sinha. Teaching at the Anthropology Department of Vidyasagar University for the last 18 years and took his Ph.D. in Anthropology from VU in 2002. Dr. Guha did his Ph.D. on Land Acquisition and Displacement of Peasants in West Bengal under the Left Front Government which is the first of its kind in this field. He has published at about 50 articles, comments and book reviews in various International and National level peer-reviewed journals, newspapers and edited volumes which include *Current Anthropology, Population and Development Review, Journal of the Indian Anthropological Society, Journal of Human Ecology and The Statesman* since 1985 and presented papers in many seminars and conferences in India and abroad.

Mailing Address: Abhijit Guha
Department of Anthropology
Vidyasagar University
Medinipur-721 102
West Bengal, India
Email: < abhijitguhavu@rediffmail.com>

Guzy, Lidia is a research scholar of Institute of Ethnology, Free University of Berlin, Germany. She did her doctoral research on anthropology of religion in the context of Orissa. She recently completed her post-doctoral research on dance and music traditions of western Orissa. She has a good number of publications in reputed journals and edited volumes. She has made many presentations in national and international conferences. She plans to continue her research in South Asia.

Mailing Address: Lidia Guzy
Institute of Ethnology
Free University of Berlin
Drosselweg 1-3
14195 Berlin
Germany
Email: <lidiaguzy@gmx.net>

Haldar, A.K obtained his M.Sc degree in Anthropology form Ranchi University in the year 1967. He was a recipient of B.N. Sahay's Gold Medal. He received his Ph.D. from Ranchi University in 1978. He retired as a Professor of Anthropology from Ranchi University. He conducted intensive fieldwork in various pockets of Chotanagpur belt and published many scientific articles on the tribes of that region. He was the co-editor of the book (jointly with Prof. L.P. Vidarthy) *Research Methodology in Social Science in India* (Today and Tomorrow's Publication, New Delhi, 1985). Dr.Haldar was also the co-author of the book *Techno-Cultural Implication of Industrialization on the Tribes of Middle India* (Concept Publishing Company, New Delhi, 1988). He has completed a number of research projects financed by national level funding agencies. He had the privilege of working as a Research Officer in the Indo-Japanese Project "Life of the Bharia Tribe of Pathankot (MP)". His current interest in research is tribal studies.

Mailing Address: Prof. A.K. Haldar
Qr. No. 25/9 University Colony
Bariyatu, Ranchi
Jharkhanda, India
Email: <satadru_haldar@yahoo.com>

Jana, Shyamal Kumar (*b.* 1967). He obtained his M. Sc degree in Anthropology with specialization in Physical Anthropology from Vidyasagar University, West Bengal. Taught Anthropology at Seva Bharati Mahavidyala, P.O. Kapgari in Paschim Medinipur district in West Bengal as Guest Lecturer (1993—1995). He has submitted his Ph. D thesis on "Health and health-related Problems among the Tribes of Midnapore, West Bengal" to the University of Ranchi, Ranchi - 834 008 (2005). He has conducted extensive fieldwork among the different tribal communities of West Bengal, Jharkhand and Orissa. He has over ten years of research experience and has to his credit ten published papers in Indian journals and chapters in books. His research interest includes Sustainable Health Development, Reproductive and Child Health, Food & Nutrition, Sanitation and Ethnicity. He actively participated and presented papers in a number of national and international seminars, conferences. He is a member of various professional bodies and also Associate Editor of the journal — *Man and Life*, published from Kolkata.

Prior to joining to Rural Development Centre, Indian Institute of Technology, Kharagpur-721 302, West Bengal he worked as Research Assistant and Research Officer in different NGOs and development agencies of repute. He has extensive experiences in the areas of rural and tribal development; NGO and socio-cultural development; project planning, implementation, monitoring and evaluation; gender empowerment, small enterprise development. Currently he is attached to Rural Development Centre, Indian Institute of Technology, Kharagpur - 721 302, West Bengal in a DST sponsored research project on 'Medicinal and Aromatic Plants' as Senior Project Assistant'.

Mailing Address: Mr. Shyamal Kumar Jana
Rural Development Centre
Indian Institute of Technology
Kharagpur-721 302
West Bengal, India
Email: <shyamaljana@hotmail.com>

Lal, Niyati is currently engaged in teaching in the University Institute of Engineering and Technology, C.S.J.M. University, Kanpur, India. She has a Ph.D. in Economics from the Centre for Economic Studies and Planning, Jawaharlal Lal Nehru University. Apart from her teaching work, she is actively involved in various Socio-economic developmental activities. Her studies mostly encompass issues that relate to urban poverty, unemployment, gender inequality and environmental problems. In the above areas, she has done extensive field work in Delhi and Orissa. She also has a deep understanding of slum related problems. During one of her field studies, the author got interested in tribal studies as well. Her association with different developmental projects from time to time has resulted in a great deal of research work on the tribal of Orissa.

Mailing Address: Dr. Niyati P. Lal
Department of Humanities
IET Kanpur, Kanpur University
Kalyanpur-208 016
UP, Inida
Email: <niyati1@hotmail.com>

Mannan, Manzurul is a social anthropologist and a teacher at the Independent University, Bangladesh (IUB). He coordinates Master's programme in development studies and also offer courses in the ethnographic history of South Asia and Bangladesh at IUB. Prior to joining the university, he worked as Researcher, Development Manager and Trainer in NGOs and development agencies. He has extensive experiences in the areas of teaching and training, development and partnership management; NGO and socio-cultural development; project design and planning; organization development; gender, human rights, small enterprise development and micro-credit. He was one of the key architects in developing an international academic program Global Partnership for NGO Leaders and Managers with its three centres at Bangladesh, Zimbabwe and USA. In addition, Mannan had developed research and training programmes; and monitored and evaluated projects for the European Commission, Save the Children (Australia), BRAC, ITDG, NORAD, etc. He had been responsible for writing research and administrative reports on projects' progress, prepared and monitored budgets.

As a social anthropologist, Mannan has a thorough and deep understanding on cultural, political, economic and social issues of Bangladesh and South Asia. Mannan has published 14 articles in international journals and chapters in books. He has written over 30 research and evaluation reports on development, technology, competencies of NGO managers, fundamentalism, gender, environment, partnership, etc. Currently, he is working to complete two books on Kinship, Class and the State in Bangladesh; and NGO and Poverty with Business.

Mailing Address: Prof. Manzurul Mannan
School of Liberal Arts and Science
Independent University, Bangladesh
58 Park Road, Baridhara
Dhaka-1212
Bangladesh
Email: <monzurul@bangla.net>

Mishra, Jharana is a social researcher involved in the development sector since a long time. She has done her Doctorate on the Juang women of Orissa India. Her areas of interest are tribal studies, sociology of women and sociology of health. She has got her own documentation centre-cum-children's library that has been procuring lot of books, journals, periodicals and newspapers. Basing on these, several information sheets are being compiled on thirty selected themes. The information centre caters to the needs of several social scientists. She is Secretary, Alumni Association, P.G. Department of Anthropology, Sambalpur University.

Mailing Address: Dr. Jharana Mishra
Qrs. No.: A-48, HAL Township
Sunabeda-763 002
Koraput, Orissa
Email: <mishra_jharana@yahoo.co.in>

Nath, Nibedita is a guest faculty in the Department of Anthropology, and MSW, Sambalpur University. She worked on slum children for her doctoral degree getting centrally administered doctoral fellowship from ICSSR, New

Delhi. She was a part-time lecturer in the Department of Anthropology, Sambalpur University. Dr. Nath has qualified UGC NET. She has obtained her B.A, M.A. and M. Phil degrees in anthropology under Sambalpur University, Orissa. She topped the merit lists by securing first class first position at B.A., M.A. and M. Phil levels. She was the recipient of OSANY AWARD for being the best graduate of humanities under Sambalpur University for the year 1999. She has worked in projects funded by Win rock International and WHO. She has presented some papers in international conferences including the inter congress of IUAES held within India. Dr. Nath had gone to Norway in 2005 to present paper in international conference at Oslo. She has to her credit published more than a dozen of papers in both national and international journals including edited volumes. She was the associate editor of the sixth volume of Contemporary Society: Tribal Studies jointly edited by D.K. Behera and Georg Pfeffer and published by Concept Publishing Company. She has own several prizes in Chancellor's Cup Debate and Governor's Cup Debate and Essay Competitions. She has delivered several popular lectures in All India Radio. Her current areas of interest are children and childhood, gender studies and tribal studies.

Mailing Address: Dr. Nibedita Nath
Department of Anthropology
Sambalpur University
Sambalpur-768 019
Orissa, India
Email: <nibedita_nath@rediffmail.com>
<drnibeditanath@rediffmail.com>

Padhee, Itishree (*b*. 1965) is currently working as a reader in the Department of Anthropology, BJB Autonomous College, Bhubaneswar, Orissa, India. She obtained her Masters degree (gold medalist) in 1987 from Berhampur University and M.Phil (1989) and Ph.D. (1993) Degrees from Sambalpur University. She has presented a number of research papers in many national and international seminars which have been published in different books and journals of international repute. Dr. Padhi joined as a lecturer in 1989 and since then she has been in teaching profession. Her book on problems of working mothers has come out in the year 1999.At present she is working with her postdoctoral project on "Higher education among Tribal girls". Her research interests include gender issues and problems associated with children.

Mailing Address: Dr. Itishree Padhee
Department of Anthropology
BJB College
Bhubaneshwar-14
Orissa, India
Email: <pkacharya1@yahoo.co.in>

Pattnaik, Binay Kumar is a sociologist and teaches sociology at India's premier academic institution, Indian Institute of Technology Kanpur. His principal areas of research and teaching have been Social Studies in Science and Technology. His main contribution to this area of study has been defining scientific productivity in academic science and application of scientometric technique to this area. Besides, Environmental Sociology, Sociology of Development and Sociology of Voluntary Sector have been his areas of interest too. While being at IIT Bombay in the 1990s he was instrumental to the introduction of a PG programme in Planning and Development and was the Programme Coordinator for several years. Now at IIT Kanpur he is actively engaged in research, guidance and consultancy services. He has been in the advisory board of the Sociological Bulletin the premier journal of Indian Sociological Society, Board member of the International Sociological Association RC23 and its session organizer too. He has written and edited more than three books and authored more than 20 research papers that have been published in international journals of repute and edited books. Pattnaik's forth coming books pertain to Scientific Productivity and Unique Competencies of the INGO. Having already published two special research articles on the Joint Forest Management Practices in Orissa and in West Bengal and their environmental implications in the well known journal like *The Economic and Political Weekly* (April 1996 and December 1997) currently he is working on the 'Ecological Foundation of Hinduism and its Contributions to environmental ethics' (being published by the Ethnographic and Folk Culture Society).

Mailing Address: Prof. Binay Kumar Pattnaik
Professor of Sociology
Department of Humanities and Social Sciences
Indian Institute of Technology
Kanpur-208016, India
Email: <binay@iitk.ac.in>

Pfeffer, Georg is professor of social anthropology in the Institute of Ethnology at the Free University of Berlin since 1985. He studied ethnology, sociology and history of religions at Freiburg University, Germany, where he obtained his doctoral degree in 1970 with a thesis on *Paria groups of the Panjab*. His postdoctoral thesis of Habilitation at the University of Heidelberg bore the title: *Puri's Sasana Villages: Basis of a Regional Elite*. In 1971 he was appointed Assistant Professor at the South Asia Institute of University of Heidelberg where he was promoted to the position of an Associate Professor in 1979. He has conducted fieldwork for several years in various parts of India and Pakistan. Since 1980 Prof. Pfeffer has undertaken numerous extended excursions to the middle India tribes. In addition to his teaching and research obligations in Berlin, he is an active member of several national and international academic societies and on the editorial board of the German *Zeitschrift Fur Ethnologie*. Prof. Pfeffer has published a number of articles in reputed international journals. He has brought out six edited volumes on tribal studies jointly with Prof. D.K. Behera of Sambalpur University, India. Religious cults and kinship structures of the Scheduled Tribes in the Koraput and Phulbani districts of Orissa (India) are Prof. Pfeffer's key areas of interest.

Mailing Address: Prof. Georg Pfeffer
Institute of Ethnology
Free University of Berlin
Drosselweg 1-3
14195 Berlin
Germany
Email: <gpfeffer@gmx.net>

Pramanik, Rashmi is a social anthropologist, working presently as a part-time Lecturer in the Department of Anthropology, Sambalpur University, India. She obtained her Master's (Gold Medalist) and M.Phil degrees from Sambalpur University in 1998 and 1999 respectively. She got her doctoral degree on "Overburdened School-going Children" in the year 2004. Dr. Pramanik has also done a Post-graduate diploma in Rural Development under the Indira Gandhi National Open University in the year 2005. She had been to Singapore in 2006 to present paper in a conference. She has participated and presented papers in many national and international conferences. Dr. Pramanik has to her credit half a dozen research articles published in reputed journals and edited volumes. Her area of research interest includes children's everyday experiences, tribal studies and gender issues.

Mailing Address: Dr. Rashmi Pramanik
Department of Anthropology
Sambalpur University, Jyoti-vihar
Sambalpur-768019
Orissa, India
Email: <rashmipramanik@yahoo.co.in>

Pujari, Saswat Chandra is working as Head of the Department of Sociology, Aeronautics College, Sunabeda since 1997. He has completed his Doctoral work on Juang children of Orissa, India. His areas of interest are sociology of aging, sociology of childhood, tribal studies and informal sector. He has to his credit a few publications. Dr. Pujari has attended several national and international seminars and workshops. Besides his academic interest his involvement with Development Sector particularly with organizations like UNICEF, VHAI, DANLEP, ISI & N.L.M. He is president, Alumni Association, P.G. Department of Sociology, Sambalpur University.

Mailing Address: Dr. Saswat Chandra Pujari
Head, Department of Sociology
Aeronautics College
Sunabeda, Koraput
Orissa, India
Email: <pujari_saswat@yahoo.co.in>

Sarkar, Jayanta (*b.* 1943), M.Sc. (Gold Medal), Ph.D. (Ranchi) in Anthropology. Served the Anthropological Survey of India in different capacities for 33 years. Retired as the Director-in-Charge of the Survey. More than 37 years of research experience in the field of cultural anthropology with special reference to social change among the tribal and non-tribal populations living in the industrial, urban and rural settings. Conducted intensive field investigations among the Artisan Communities of Mysore City, tribes of Arunachal Pradesh, Meghalaya, Madhya Pradesh, Chhattisgarh and Chotanagpur. Besides such research works in the mainland of India, studied the most isolated hunter and food gatherer tribes like the Jarawas, Onges, Great Andamanese and the Sentinelese in the islands of Andaman and Nicobar. The research results have been published in various journals and books. Have written popular books and articles in Bengali in order to disseminate anthropological information among the Bengali speaking general population. Authored eight books jointly edited 10 volumes and published more than 60 anthropological articles in various anthropological journals and edited volumes. Life member of the Indian Anthropological Society and Indian National Confederation and Academy of Anthropologists.

Mailing Address: Dr. Jayanta Sarkar
Former Director-in-Charge, Anthropological Survey of India
'Aparajita', 3
Ferryfan Road
H.B.Town, Sodepur, 24
Parganas (N)-700 110
WB, India
Email: <sarkar_jayanta@yahoo.com>

Serekoane, Motsaathebe is a junior lecturer at the Department of Anthropology, University of the Free State in South Africa. He started his career as a therapist and later joined cultural studies with the aim to reconcile the contrast that exists between "science" and "culture" in the treatment of "pathology". He is actively involved in helping South Africans create a country of cultural acceptance and tolerance, through trainings in understanding diversity.

Mailing Address: Dr. Motsaathebe Serekoane
Department of Anthropology
University of Free State
P.O. Box 339, Bloemfontein 9300
South Africa
Email: <serekomj.hum@mail.uovs.ac.za>

Sinha, A.K. received both his Master's and Ph.D. degrees from Ranchi University, Ranchi. He started his career as a Research Investigator at the Centre for Advanced Study in Anthropology, Ranchi University, Ranchi. Then he joined as Research Associate in same department. Presently Dr. Sinha is Reader in Social Anthropology in Panjab University, Chandigarh. Prior to this Dr. Sinha was Lecturer (Senior Scale) in the Department of Social Anthropology and Tribal Development, G.G. University, Bilaspur, M.P.

He has published around 45 research papers in reputed national journals. Besides, he has also authored four books. His areas of specialization are social anthropology and tribal studies.

Mailing Address: Dr. A.K. Sinha
Department of Anthropology
Panjab University
Chandigarh-160 014, India
Email: <anilksinha58@rediffmail.com>

Strümpell, Christian is a social anthropologist from Berlin, Germany. He did his M.A. in Munster (Germany) under Prof. Jos Platenkamp writing on anthropological models of kinship in Northern India. After that he joined a research project sponsored by the DFG (German Research Council) in 2000 and remained within it until its end in April 2005. As a member of this "Orissa Research Project" he worked on two sub-projects investigating on local processes of industrialization. He did field research in a small industrial settlement in South Orissa and the huge steel city Rourkela in the North-West under the guidance of Prof. Georg Pfeffer from Free University Berlin. He wrote his Ph.D thesis on social relationships in Orissa's industrial milieu and is working currently on its publication. As a member of the DFG-project he attended several international conferences talking on a wide range of topics related to his research and published a handful of articles in international journals and chapters in books. He is about to continue his field research on industrialization in Orissa soon and will shift his focus from the narratives of migrant labourers to those of the local Scheduled Tribes.

Mailing Address: Dr. Christian Strümpell
Institute of Ethnology
Free University of Berlin
Drosselweg 1-3
14195 Berlin
Germany
Email: < rwe55@rediffmail.com >

Tanner, R.E.S. obtained B.Sc in Social Anthropology from Oxford University and Ph.D. in Criminology form Stockholm University. He joined the Tanzanian Administrative Service in 1948 and continued to serve there till 1960. He was the chairperson of East African Institute of Social Research from 1964 to 1967. He served the University of London as Lecturer in Comparative Religion from 1968 to 1980. He has been actively engaged in research for last 18 years. He has authored a number of books like *Homicide in Uganda, Transition in African Belief, An East African Problem, The Social Ecology of Religion and The Biology of Religion.* He has contributed a large number of articles on translation problem in religion, religious hysteria, ancestor worship, witchcraft, Tanzanian agriculture, cattle theft, gossip, ecumensia, etc.

Mailing Address: Dr. R.E.S. Tanner
The Footprint
Pudworth Common
Readings
RG 74 QG
United Kingdom
Email: <restanner@kutkai.fsnet.co.uk>

Tripathy, P.K. (*b.* 1955) is the Professor of Economics in Sambalpur University, India. His major fields of specialization are quantitative economics and political economy. He has published more than 35 papers in different national and international journals. He has also participated in many seminars and conferences at the state and national levels. He has handled one major UGC research project entitled, "Land Reforms in Tribal Areas in the State of Orissa". He is a member of the consultancy team constituted by Govt. of Orissa to submit a memorandum to Ninth and Tenth Finance Commission. He is also a member of the State Commission to enquire in to "Regional Imbalances in the State of Orissa". He was also a consultant to VISWAS on the Food for Work Programme. He was served as consultant to AGRAGAMEE in a study on Upper Indravati Hydroelectric Project. He has already produced four Ph.D. scholars.

Mailing Address: Prof. P.K. Tripathy
Department of Economics
Sambalpur University
Sambalpur-768 019
Orissa, India
Email: <pktripathy55@yahoo.co.in>

Van Horn, Lawrence F. received his Ph.D. in 1977 in anthropology from The Graduate Center of The City University of New York. He is a cultural resource specialist in the Planning Division of the Denver Service Center of the National Park Service, United States Department of the Interior, 12795 West Alameda Parkway, Denver, Colorado 80225-0287 USA. He may also be reached at lary_van_horn@nps.gov by e-mail and by telephone at 303-969-2255. The views expressed here are solely his own and do not represent those of the National Park Service.

Mailing Address: Dr. Lawrence F. Van Horn
Planning and Design Services
Denver Service Centre
National Park Service
12795 West Alameda Parkway
Devner, CO 80225-0287
USA
Email: <julavaho1@mindspring.com>

Venkateswar, Sita has been a lecturer in social anthropology at Massey University since 1997 and has been involved in research on child labour in Nepal since 1999. She has been conducting field research in Nepal since August 2000. Dr. Venkateswar's earlier dissertation research was conducted in the Andaman Islands over an 18-month period between 1989 and 1992 and was funded by a dissertation improvement grant from the National Science Foundation. She obtained her Ph.D. from Rutgers University in 1997.

Mailing Address: Prof. Sita Venkateswar
Social Anthropology Programme
School of Global Studies
Massey University
New Zealand
Email: <S.Venkateswar@massey.ac.nz>

INDEX